# SPARTAK MOSCOW

## A History of
## the People's Team
## in the Workers' State

ROBERT EDELMAN

Cornell University Press  Ithaca & London

*Frontispiece: Spartak Moskva: Offitsial'naia istoriia.*

Copyright © 2009 by Cornell University

First published 2009 by Cornell University Press

Printed in the United States of America

*Library of Congress Cataloging-in-Publication Data*

Edelman, Robert, 1945–
   Spartak Moscow : a history of the people's team in the workers' state / Robert Edelman.
        p. cm.
   Includes bibliographical references and index.
   ISBN 978-0-8014-4742-6 (cloth : alk. paper)
   1. Spartak (Soccer team)—History.   2. Soccer—Soviet Union—History.
3. Soccer—Social aspects—Soviet Union.   I. Title.
   GV943.6.S64E34  2009
   796.33409473'1—dc22

2009019268

Cornell University Press strives to use environmentally responsible suppliers and materials to the fullest extent possible in the publishing of its books. Such materials include vegetable-based, low-VOC inks and acid-free papers that are recycled, totally chlorine-free, or partly composed of nonwood fibers. For further information, visit our website at www.cornellpress.cornell.edu.

Cloth printing    10 9 8 7 6 5 4 3 2 1

*For Louis, Nicholas,*
*and Elizabeth Edelman*

# Contents

# Preface

Sitting here more than forty years after the fact, I have come to realize I have been studying Spartak since 1965. That summer, I went to the USSR for the first time to learn Russian at Moscow State University. The Vietnam War was just heating up, and like many undergraduates of that era, I was less than enamored of the United States and its imperialist ways. As many had done before me, I had come to Moscow to see how the "future" worked. Though I had studied Russian history for the previous three years and knew the USSR had its problems, I had hoped to find something positive about the place. After about a month, our group was taken to nearby Lenin Stadium to see that year's cup final between Spartak and Dinamo Minsk. I cannot say my initial exposure to Spartak was a case of love at first sight. The entire experience turned out to be chaotic and frightening, with overzealous police beating drunk and disorderly fans. A halftime visit to the restroom is best left undescribed. By the time the night was over, I was well convinced the Bolshevik Revolution had been a big mistake. Soviet soccer fans were not a good advertisement for what many of us later came to call "presently existing socialism."

I returned in 1970 as a graduate student to spend the academic year at Moscow State while researching my dissertation on prerevolutionary gentry politics. Living and working in the Soviet Union was far from an easy experience. Eventually I came to understand that I might hang on to a bit of sanity by engaging in the same kinds of activities—in this case sport—that had helped me deal with stress in America. I made friends with male Soviet students who were glad to take me to football matches. After about ten such games, I began to wonder why one of the teams we went to see was always Spartak. I also wondered why the only sport they cared about was soccer. "Couldn't we just once take in some gymnastics?" They sat me down and explained. Football was the "people's game," and Spartak was "the people's team." "No one cares about all that Olympic stuff." They also informed me that everyone hated the secret police, who funded Dinamo Moscow. Spartak had stood up to them. What's more, they said, Spartak's leaders had been sent to the gulag "by Stalin." The Spartak-Dinamo rivalry was the greatest in all of Soviet sport. On a global stage, it seemed to be as rich in political implication as the clash of the Spanish giants Real Madrid and Barcelona, the Glasgow "Old Firm" of Celtic and Rangers, and the Buenos Aires derbies of Boca Juniors and River Plate. For me, a sports-loving leftist critic of the Soviet regime, this seemed too good to be true. I could root for Spartak and live my politics. As I later found out, this was too good to be entirely true. Accordingly, my subtitle should be read ironically; not heroically.

Over the years, as I researched other aspects of Imperial Russian history, I never failed to go see Spartak play. I was always able to engage with Muscovites sitting in the stands, and I always got some version of my friends' story. Similar conversations in scores of Soviet kitchens confirmed this view of Spartak as a site of judicious resistance. This did not mean that my fellow "soccerati" were about to break bread or share toasts with Sakharov and Solzhenytsin. These were not dissidents. Although they were not entirely satisfied with their world, they did not seek the overthrow of Communism. Rather, Spartak gave them a safe way to express a complicated and often contradictory set of attitudes.

While in Moscow, I began to do the things sports fans do the world over. Every day I tried to read the USSR's most popular newspaper, *Sovetskii sport*. In 1975, I bought a small television at a hard-currency shop and sneaked it into my dorm room at Moscow State. I watched every game I could, improving my Russian in the process. After a while, I could converse with any Moscow cab driver on the finer points of the game. I had an instant topic of mutual interest to discuss with most Soviet men. In an authoritarian system, winning the trust of strangers was difficult, but football created a bond that could lead to deeper friendships. It provided an entrée into parts of Soviet society that were not readily available to most visiting scholars, whose contacts with Soviet citizens were largely limited to fellow intellectuals. With a few notable exceptions, the famed Russian intelligentsia was indifferent to such matters of popular culture as sport. Thoroughly enmeshed in the life of the mind, for the most part these were not people with much interest in matters of the body.

For decades, Western academics took their cues from their Soviet colleagues. Sport never made it onto the scholarly screen. In this respect I was no different from anyone else. It never occurred to me that I could do anything with all my "research" on Soviet sports; writing a book on such a topic was a shortcut to academic marginality. In 1986, however, Stanford University decided to put its imprimatur on sport by organizing an international conference. I was invited to give a paper simply because I was a student of Russia who had also worked as a stringer for the Associated Press covering the National Basketball Association. At the time, there was no one else in the United States working on the topic. This was during early perestroika, and I decided to write on what was then the contemporary spectator sports scene, using *Sovetskii sport* and newly available television transmissions that I obtained at Columbia University and the RAND Institute in Santa Monica. After giving the paper, I continued collecting material, largely because doing so was fun. I could pop in a tape, open a beer, lie back and "work." A couple of years later, I gave a lecture at the University of Michigan, where several colleagues convinced me I had the makings of a book. After some contemplation, I decided to proceed, but not until coming to the conclusion that such a work should be a history rather than a commentary on current events.

I completed the research in 1990 after working in the library of *Sovetskii sport*. There was still a Soviet Union at the time, and it was not possible to use the relevant archives. Equally problematic was the fact that not everyone I met was willing to speak openly. Published in 1993, the book covered the full range of sporting experiences. Although I continued to keep up with the subject, I never intended to write another book on sports. By 1999, however, a great deal had changed. Sports history, especially the history of soccer, was now a booming field. The study of Soviet history had exploded with the opening of the archives after 1991. New questions were being asked, but in many cases the evidence needed to answer them proved hard to find. It became clear to many that we needed to look for new kinds of sources, new analytical realms and topics.

The peculiarities of the Soviet case made sport an especially rich source of fresh information and understanding. In the ten years previous to my starting this project, a number of authors, most of them British but not all of them academics, had produced studies of European soccer teams, including Glasgow Rangers, Barcelona, Real Madrid, West Ham United, Hansa Rostock, and many others. These works provided prisms through which it was possible to comprehend both the larger societies in which those clubs operated and the ways those societies influenced the clubs' operations. Spartak, I thought, could do much the same for our understanding of Soviet history.

––––––––––

As I write this, the twenty-ninth Olympic Games are taking place in Beijing. The intensity of the sporting competition mirrors the sharp-elbow competition of the new China. Yet it was not always so. In 1963, Premier Zhou Enlai reminded the nation's table tennis team, "Friendship is more important than the competition." These words became the mantra of Chinese sport, through the tragedies of the Cultural Revolution until the economic reforms of the 1980s. It is fair to say that Mao Zedong's closest political partner was a man not without fault, but one can find in the words of this tough-minded revolutionary a kernel of humanity.

I have had the great fortune to be part of two cohorts of historians who have always put friendship first. Students of Russian history and students of sport are particularly humane groups. Over the years, I have received generous aid, support, and criticism from colleagues in both fields. They have enriched my work and provided examples of engaged scholarship. According to the hoary sports cliché, they have been role models. Ron Suny and David Nasaw have been along for the entire journey, and when times have been tough, their wisdom and warmth have helped pull me through. Both have heard more than they have ever wanted to hear about Soviet football, and both have helped me make the necessary connections between a personal obsession and the concerns of the profession. The same can be said of Harry Scheiber, whose lingering attachment to the memory of the Polo Grounds can be forgiven. Upon my arrival in California, the late and much-missed Reggie Zelnik, yet another Giants fan, took me in and became a surrogate mentor. That keen student of sport Steve Cohen has been a champion of this project, and his support proved crucial to the work's completion. John Hoberman and Bruce Kidd guided the early steps of my job retraining as a historian of sport. More recently, Christopher Young has provided many of us a place to develop our subfield into an accepted part of the discipline. He practices the very best sort of academic entrepreneurship. My colleagues in the history department at UC San Diego have provided a warmly human and intellectually enriching environment. At one time or another, Pamela Radcliffe, Stefan Tanaka, Paul Pickowicz, Daniel Widener, Frank Biess, John Marino, Deborah Hertz, and Hasan Kayali have shared thoughts that have sharpened my focus. Along with Hasan, Eric Van Young, David Goodblatt, and Michael Bernstein have read all or parts of the manuscript. Susanne Hillman helped translate materials from the German made available by Manfred Zeller.

Anne Gorsuch, Tony Mason, Louise McReynolds, Lewis Siegelbaum, Bob Moeller, Geoffrey Hosking, and Ethan Pollock read various parts of various drafts with real rigor and no fear of insulting me. This is true friendship. Barbara Keys, Tim Paynich, Dan Brennan, and Orlando Figes were good enough to share some of the fruits of their labors. Larry Zeman was generous enough to share part of his immense collection of Soviet newspapers. Gale Stokes, Silke Steets, and Dan Orlovsky provided early opportunities to test out an ill-formed idea. More recently, John Efron and Niko Katzer have provided forums for a more finished product. Arch Getty, Toshi Hasegawa, Adrienne Edgar, and Kiril Tomoff, my colleagues in our Southern California intercampus Soviet seminar, have taught me much and forced me to sharpen my thinking. As always, the masterful Wayne Wilson has provided wisdom and sources. Edward Derse helped fill in the immense gaps of my soccer knowledge. My longtime friend, colleague, and fellow veteran of "Zona V," John Ackerman, has been a wonderful editor. Most important, funding for this book was provided by the research committee of the UC San Diego Academic Senate and the John S. Guggenheim Foundation.

My debts in Russia are equally, if not more, enormous. Twenty years ago at an Olympic training center in Abkhazia I met Vladimir Titorenko. For years I had been reading his work in *Sovetskii sport*. He was the paper's leading basketball writer. Today he is editor in chief of the national sports daily *Sport-express*. Over the years he has provided a home away from home, transport, fine food, and entrée to the world of Soviet and now Russian sport. He is a true friend. I also owe a huge debt to the greatest of all historians of Soviet football. Aksel′ Vartanian is a historical journalist who writes for *Sportexpress.* Since 1987, he has immersed himself in the archives, combed the press at all its levels, and spoken with hundreds of practitioners of the USSR's most popular sport. He has unselfishly shared his vast knowledge and passion with me. I owe much of the originality of this study to him. Over many years, Igor Rabiner, Elena Vaitsekovskaia, Vladimir Geskin, Pavel Aleshin, Leonid Trakhtenberg, and Vladimir Kuchmi have all helped me make sense of Soviet sport. Fyodr Uspensky generously helped me navigate the riches of the Sportexpress Photo Agency. Leonid Weintraub has been my guide through the mysteries of Russian archives and Moscow restaurants. Irina Bykhovskaia, head of cultural studies at the Russian State University of Sport, Physical Culture and Tourism, has been a wonderful colleague who helped open the riches of her institution's vast library. Its directors, Tataiana Medziankovskaia and Irina Zhilina, have helped me obtain many of the library's holdings. Recently, Gennadi Bordiugov has provided an opportunity for me to share my work with the Russian audience.

In the introduction to her recent book, my colleague Deborah Hertz wrote that she needed to apologize to her book for the time she spent with her family. No doubt this volume would have seen the light of day much sooner had I not driven so many kids to so many soccer practices. I cannot say I regret any of that, and so this book is dedicated to Elizabeth, Louis, and Nicholas Edelman, who, as the old saying goes, have enriched my life and given it purpose. May they make a better world than the one that has been left to them. Perhaps now they have a better chance to do just that.

Victoria Yablonsky has tolerated far too many complaints about the inability of Spartak forwards to capitalize on good approach work. She has made me a better person and a better scholar. When we met, I was alienated from the profession, and she showed me the path to reembracing my work. Aside from their annoying habit of sticking their noses under my elbow and sending the computer mouse flying, our dogs have helped as well. They have pawed over the manuscript and left their mark.

Finally, I owe a special debt to Yuri Slezkine, lifetime Spartak fan, great historian, and pal. He was one of the few in the profession to understand the point of a book such as this from the outset. At times I thought I had shot myself in the foot by choosing what seemed like a marginal subject, but Yuri's enthusiasm kept me going. He has read the manuscript thoroughly and generously. Neither he nor the humans and animals mentioned above are responsible for any mistakes. All errors are mine, but so too has been the pleasure of the journey.

# Some Words on Usage

In the interest of avoiding repetition and serving as many audiences as possible, I have adopted a transatlantic vocabulary that employs both American and British terms. The sport described herein is called both "soccer" and "football." "Games" are also "matches." "Fields" are also "pitches," etc.

I have also sought to simplify some of the bureaucratic language that evolved over the course of Soviet history. The institution that controlled sport changed its nature and name repeatedly. Few of those changes assumed any real historical importance. For the purpose of clarity I will almost always refer to this body as "the state sports committee." Additionally, the names of the various divisions of Soviet soccer changed numerous times. I will be calling the highest level of the game either "the first division" or "the top flight." Below that, I will be describing "second" and "third" divisions.

The system of transliteration is Library of Congress II.

# SPARTAK MOSCOW

# Introduction

On September 30, 1939, the members of the Soviet Union's most popular soccer team, Spartak Moscow, prepared to take the field at Dinamo Stadium, where they were to play the semifinal of that year's national cup competition. Currently in first place in the USSR's domestic league, they faced their closest rival, Dinamo Tblisi, the pride of the Georgian Republic and favorite team of Lavrenti Beria, the powerful and notorious head of the secret police. As the two teams walked out to begin the match, the scene seemed no different from thousands of others. Yet this confrontation was unlike any that had ever occurred or would ever occur in the history of the world's most popular sport. Spartak had already defeated Dinamo Tblisi 1–0 on September 8 in the semifinal. The goal had been disputed. Dinamo Tblisi filed a protest that was quickly denied by the State Council of Physical Culture. Four days later Spartak took the cup. Its captain, Vladimir Stepanov, received the trophy and took it on the traditional lap of honor. The regular season then resumed. Spartak had played two matches when the Central Committee of the Communist Party overruled the state's sports officials, annulling the result of the semifinal and ordering that the game be replayed. Spartak's leaders protested to their own powerful friends in high places but to no avail. For the first and surely the last time a semifinal was to take place *after* the final had been played and the competition completed. It appeared Beria would have his way after all.

As was true of so much else in Soviet life, sport and politics were joined at the hip. Following that logic, this book uses a small piece of history to answer a big question. The small piece of history concerns Spartak. The big question is this: What did ordinary Soviet people think of the system under which they lived? The answers have proved elusive. Indeed, for decades, Western scholars, journalists, and other observers made little attempt to discover popular attitudes. In their defense, finding out was no easy task. In democratic systems, public opinion is revealed by election results, social surveys, and a free press. Needless to say, sources of this kind were not available to students of the USSR. When the Soviet state set out to survey the mood of its citizens, it relied on the reports of the secret police. Foreign scholars, of course, could not access these sources until after the collapse of the USSR. Moreover, even when they were available, just how reliable were such sources? After all, if no enemies existed, the police were out of work. To make themselves useful, the guardians of order needed to find, and perhaps invent, disorder.

Communism did not give the citizens of the Soviet Union much freedom of choice, but sport was one of the few areas of life in which ordinary folk did have options. As I learned while researching an earlier book, the peoples of the Soviet Union were free to support their favorite teams and free to worship their own heroes. It was never possible for the authorities to dictate fan loyalty, especially when it came to the country's most popular game, football. There were teams supported by factories, trade unions, student groups, the police, and the army. In picking a favorite, members of the largely male sporting public were making subjective statements with objective implications about who they were and what they thought about the world around them. These were matters of identity, and their preferences had political meaning.

Those choices, which created group solidarities, were expressed publicly at and around the stadium and in semipublic discourses (on streets and in courtyards), but the decision to support one or another club was at the same time private (in the apartment and family kitchen, in front of the radio and later the television). Picking a club was one of many small steps through which each individual in all these ways created a self.[1] As was true in much of the world, the loyalties of Soviet fans rarely changed. From the midthirties on, Spartak and its supporters used sport to manifest attitudes toward a variety of institutions and groups, including the party-state. In the early nineties, soon after the breakup of the USSR, a Soviet anthropologist explained the implications of these choices to a visiting British journalist: "In a Communist country . . . the football team you supported was a community to which you, yourself chose to belong. . . . It might be your only chance to choose a community, and, also, in that community you could express yourself as you wished. To be a fan . . . is to be gathered among others and to be free."[2]

During the ascendancy of Stalin and Khrushchev, Spartak, more than any other Soviet team, came to embody the sentiments of its fans. It was, if not always the best, certainly the most popular of all Soviet clubs. More than any of the other civilian sides in the Soviet league, Spartak gave its fans a way to distance themselves from the hated "structures of force" (the police and army) who had their own teams. In the words of one anonymous Soviet scholar, Spartak provided its supporters a "small way of saying 'no'" to all that was going on around them.[3] Rooting for Spartak became one way of demonstrating dissatisfaction with the authorities. It cannot be said, however, that this dissatisfaction ever rose to the level of massive support for what we now call regime change, nor was politics the only reason to support Spartak. The short answer to the big question turns out to be maddeningly ambiguous. If the "people," whatever that amorphous term may mean, were never so discontented as to take up the cudgels of a politically coherent opposition, this did not mean they were entirely satisfied with their lot either. Conversely, there were many different kinds of people in the USSR, and more than a few of them surely were content.

The dream of Communist leaders may have been to dominate *all* areas of human life, but football was one field of human activity in which a purportedly powerful Soviet state exercised limited control. The game proved to be what the British journalist Simon Kuper has called a "slippery tool" in the hands of dictators. Of course, to make such a claim is not to apologize in any way for the Soviet version of Communism. In expressing a wide range of grievances, many citizens of the USSR could resort to violence, but more often, as the history of Spartak shows, they resisted the power of the regime in ways that were indirect, surprising, and unexpected.[4] Something similar happened under other authoritarian regimes. In Franco's Spain, the Catalan club Barcelona became a symbol of regional autonomy, as did Atletic Bilbao in the Basque country. In Argentina under the generals, critics of the regime were more likely to support Boca Juniors than River Plate.

## Situating Spartak

The four Starostin brothers (Nikolai, Aleksandr, Andrei, and Petr) formally founded the Spartak Sport Society in 1935, but the club's history actually spans the entire twentieth century. Throughout the many twisting and wrenching changes of Soviet history, the Starostins' team took on new forms, both reflecting and influencing the swiftly evolving society of which it was so visible a part. Spartak traces its roots to a particular working-class neighborhood of prerevolutionary Moscow, the Presnia, where the Starostins led their young pals in games of street football. During the 1920s they took advantage of the semicapitalist New Economic Plan (NEP) to create local teams that became successful business enterprises. With Stalin's accession to power, the Starostins adapted to new circumstances and organized Spartak. Through energetic and sometimes inspired networking, the brothers found political and financial support for their club. Such was their great sporting success and massive popularity that they ran afoul of the secret police, whose own team had previously dominated Soviet soccer.

The Starostins were arrested during the war and sent to the gulag. With its leaders away, Spartak's fortunes suffered. In 1954 the brothers returned from exile to their careers with the first wave of returnees. During the years of cultural relaxation and optimism under Khrushchev, Nikolai took back the helm of the team, found new sponsors, and again led Spartak to the top of the Soviet league; the period known as the "Thaw" proved to be Spartak's Golden Age. In February 1956 Khrushchev gave his famous "Secret Speech," denouncing Stalin's crimes. By the end of that tumultuous year, Spartak had won the league, and the Soviet national team, composed primarily of Spartak players, took the Olympic gold medal. During the Brezhnev era, Nikolai Starostin was forced to adapt to increased competition from newly powerful provincial sides. Once again, he changed his approach in ways that violated many of the old principles that had guided his work. When finally perestroika arrived with its emphasis on profitability, he was well prepared to revive the business methods of the NEP and turn many a ruble.

Unlike so much else in Soviet history imposed from above, Spartak emerged from the society below. The club's roots in the Presnia gave it an independence that many deemed attractive but others thought dangerous. Throughout its history, much of the drama that surrounded the team centered on the Starostins and their fate. They had risen from a modest background to reach the pinnacle of wealth and fame, only to become victims of the purges. Instead of dying in the gulag, they were rescued by football, coaching in the camps and returning after the death of the tyrant to lead their team back to the top. As an image, this tale of triumph, tragedy, and subsequent victory has been hard to resist, and for most fans that image has always been more important than the truth. In paraphrasing Clifford Geertz's famous line about the "deep play" of the Balinese cockfight, one British sociologist wrote, "The game is the place we tell ourselves stories about ourselves."[5] The Starostins' epic tale has been far too good for the club's supporters to let go.

Throughout the entire course of its existence, Spartak was the chosen favorite of Moscow and later Soviet fans. It maintained this status despite ups and downs on the playing field. Spartak was not always good, but, according to team legend, its fans were always loyal. It became an article of faith (but not fact) that when the team finished next to last in 1976 and was relegated to the second division, the stadium was still filled the following season. This situation, if not unique, was at least highly uncommon in the annals of world sport. Juventus, Manchester United, Bayern Munich, Boca Juniors, and others have all enjoyed great runs at the top of their respective leagues, but when their success waned, so did support outside their home cities. Spartak, by contrast, was for decades the single most popular club among the USSR's lovers of football.

Team support as a social, cultural, political, or even personal marker has long been a characteristic of large European and Latin American cities with numerous teams. It was not always so in the United States, where sport became a profit-making enterprise earlier than it did in Europe. Starting in the last quarter of the nineteenth century, major league baseball teams were granted territorial franchises. No club could have a competitor within seventy-five miles of its home field unless an indemnity was paid. A single U.S. city had one, maybe two teams that were the property of owners who were free to move them. The mobility of these businesses reflected the mobility of the larger population. Outside North America, the territorial franchise was not guaranteed, and scores of teams were required to fight continually for local preeminence. Soccer teams did not move. If things went badly for long enough, they simply ceased to exist. Initially, the clubs were not enterprises. Instead, they emerged from various settings, including churches, factories, pubs, block associations, or, as with Spartak, groups of neighborhood friends. Teams were deeply embedded in their communities, and decisions to root for a particular club said much about the ways supporters saw themselves. Individuals and groups made these choices freely—even in the USSR.[6]

The triumphs of Soviet Olympic teams created the widely accepted and lasting belief that the state's administration of sport was proof of the system's overall competence. On more than one occasion, the regime used the image of athletic invincibility to advance its goals, both domestic and international. As we now know, however, rather than reflecting the system's strength, its Olympic machine was one of the more effective masks of its fatal weaknesses. Football, however, was another story.

Over the course of the twentieth century, soccer in the Russian Empire and then the USSR was a thoroughly male world, often violent, highly corrupt, spontaneous, and unpredictable. It was a place for drinking and humor, what the British scholar Eric Dunning has called "an enclave of autonomy in a world of surveillance." Football fit badly into the heroic and moralistic Olympic model. Yet the game was by far the most popular sport in the USSR, a fact that did not always please the guardians of order and discipline. A 1959 article, written by a physician in *Sovetskii Sport,* suggested there was a need to distinguish real athleticism from the male soccer culture of "nicotine, alcohol, rough play and raw strength." The author called for a higher, more cultured Soviet masculinity to counter the crudeness on display at football games. The ancient Greek sports ideals could still be found among weight lifters, gymnasts, and discus throwers but not among soccer players.[7] While it would be stretching the evidence to call football in the USSR a consistent form of organized political opposition, it was clearly what we now call "contested terrain." If the state's representatives could not control what came to be called "sporting society," neither could the players, coaches, journalists, and fans consistently impose their will on the state's organizers of sporting spectacles.

## Structure

This book covers four broad areas. The first is a chronological survey of Russian football from the beginning of the last century up to the Spartak Society's founding in 1935 (chapters 1 and 2). The second slices the history of the team into smaller time periods, starting with the founding of professional soccer in 1936 and continuing up to 1948, a time of eclipse for Spartak. Chapters 3 and 4 are largely a history of Spartak and the working-class men who comprised the overwhelming majority of the football audience in the USSR before the Second World War. Chapter 5 examines the impact of the war. I look at the transition to a new social structure and with it a new soccer audience. Both the larger society and the part of it that watched soccer had become far more complicated over the course of the war. Skilled professionals, regardless of political hue, were needed during the conflict to perform all sorts of complex tasks. After victory, these groups continued to grow along with the economy, and the coming of the cold war forced an expansion of defense industries. All of these trends pushed millions into swiftly growing cities, the sites of virtually all Soviet sporting activity. The football public evolved, and with it so did Spartak. While Spartak maintained its popularity, its fan base changed. Industrial workers did not abandon the club, but now they were joined by intellectuals along with specialists and other professionals who also used the team to create a political breathing space.

The third area examined in the book is Spartak's return to the top of the Soviet game. This process began in 1949, precisely when the regime had regrouped and reconstruction was completed. It appeared that repression and conformity had returned. In chapter 6 (as well as 5) I suggest that soccer did not fit this dark and schematic picture, nor was it exceptional. Indeed, we now know there was a great deal of nonconformist activity and profound questioning both inside the regime and among the Soviet public. Much of the explosion of thought and public expression that emerged after Stalin's death was rehearsed in the immediate postwar years.

Chapters 7 and 8 cover the Khrushchev period. After the death of Stalin all of Soviet soccer achieved a greater measure of distance from the crudest forms of political interference. With its tradition of independence, Spartak provided a place for its new fan base to join the old working-class supporters in saying no to the less fearsome but still meddlesome authorities. From the midfifties to the midsixties, a multisided struggle took place to free the nation from the Stalinist legacy. Intellectuals and students spoke out in favor of change; others resisted. The battle lines in the fight for what was variously called de-Stalinization, liberalization, or reform were never clear. Instead, much of the struggle was played out within the minds of Soviet citizens rather than between precisely defined groups and factions. When the Starostins came back to Moscow, it seemed logical that as returnees, they would be sympathetic to the need for change. Before the brothers' arrests in 1942, Andrei Starostin had been befriended by writers, actors, and musicians, and he resumed his contacts with figures who hoped that the future might include a more democratic, less repressive version of Communism. From these connections and the excitement of these years, Spartak became, despite itself, a small symbol of the possibilities of the era when it appeared a civil society had begun to emerge within the old authoritarian structure. It also turned out that this period corresponded to the club's greatest success on the field. Spartak's Golden Age and the Thaw were both parts of this time of hope.

In the last section of the book I return to the chronological focus of the earlier chapters. Chapter 9 covers the entire post-Khrushchev period and ends with the collapse of the USSR in 1991. After 1964, the political position and cultural role of Spartak changed dramatically. Until the late fifties, Soviet soccer had been dominated by the big Moscow clubs. The Spartak-Dinamo rivalry, with its intense political implications, had been the league's centerpiece. That domination ended in 1961 as the game expanded its reach throughout the entire Soviet Union. For the Soviets, football, the quintessential game of the twentieth century, was about modernity. As development continued, scores of provincial cities, many in national republics, were able to build stadia, field teams, and contest for prestige and profits.

Aided by the growth of television, Spartak developed a national following under Khrushchev. Yet after 1964 it ceased to be the only favorite of Soviet fans, who now had local suitors for their affections. Instead, Spartak became, as has been globally true for Brazil, everyone's second-favorite team and the biggest single gate attraction when it played on the road. The state, which had intervened directly in the game for decades, could no longer micromanage the sport. There were now too many constituencies to please. Broad supervision replaced doomed attempts at control. After Khrushchev, Spartak was no longer a political prism through which one could easily understand the central issues of Soviet history. It became instead one team of many, and often it was not very good. The juxtaposition of sporting rivalries in the capital and high Kremlin politics no longer provided a way to make sense of popular attitudes toward the regime. The model of overtly politicized sport that explains much before 1964 cannot be sustained for the latter decades of Soviet power. Instead, Spartak's evolution during these years can better be read as a marker of broad social trends that did not directly reveal popular attitudes toward the state.

## Methods

My approach to the history of Spartak grows out of my interest in the interactions, in whatever time and place, of the political and the social. Particularly in the book's first half, I am indebted to the traditions of labor history long practiced by British and American historians and the work of German scholars on everyday life. However, I move beyond these fruitful approaches to explore two different aspects of the political: the politics of what has been termed "body culture" and the relationship between popular culture and politics. The political and social differences between the two great sporting organizations of Spartak and Dinamo were amplified by a variety of ways of viewing, training, disciplining, and organizing the fundamental unit of athletic activity, the human body. As Pierre Bourdieu has noted, "Sport is with dance one of the areas in which the problem of relationships between . . . language and the body arises in a most acute form. . . . There are a great many things we understand only with our bodies."[8]

Throughout the Soviet era, the political, social, and cultural differences between the two great sporting organizations were amplified by the very different body cultures they practiced. Dinamo sought to project a public image of discipline and rectitude, treating sport didactically. Spartak, on the other hand, was much more relaxed. For its players, especially for the Starostins, sports were about entertainment. Dinamo sought to control the bodies its organizations presented; Spartak proved more comfortable with the body's spontaneous movements.[9] Since "the body is inescapable in the construction of masculinity," the contradictions between Dinamo and Spartak were deepened by the differing versions of manhood practiced by the teams' fans.[10] To paraphrase the British historian Richard Holt, the history of Soviet soccer is a history of men, and over the course of Soviet history male citizens were offered a wide variety of conceptions of manhood. Spartak's older, nineteenth-century proletarian tradition of fan behavior was often violent and little concerned with the Victorian concept of fair play. Dinamo athletes, on the other hand, were supposed to project the respectability and sportsmanship derived from middle-class ideas about what was called "rational recreation."

In either its proletarian or middle-class variants, sport was seen as a dynamic, modern activity offering urban Soviet men of all classes models of strength, responsibility, and vigor, but conceptions of masculinity were in constant flux during the twentieth century. Before and shortly after the revolution, rural migrants to the cities had to abandon peasant definitions of manhood and forge a new urban approach. Soccer gave these new workers an arena for the display of manly strength and power away from the fields of Russia's villages. After World War II, even newer men, who did not work with their hands at all, sought an acceptable concept of manhood without the sweat of daily labor on an assembly line. Football, a sweaty activity played and watched largely in the company of other men, literally provided a field on which competing masculinities, like those of Spartak and Dinamo, could work out and elaborate their differences.[11]

The competing body cultures and conceptions of manhood were in turn tied to the two different models of sport the Bolsheviks inherited from the West: professionalism and the amateurism embraced by the Olympic movement. The new Soviet leadership had problems with both approaches. It was critical of the exclusion of workers and women in the early Olympics and refused to take part until 1952. At the same time, the Bolsheviks publicly opposed the commodifying of bodies and games that came with making sport an enterprise. Football was not only the most popular sport but also the most professionalized game practiced in the USSR, and Spartak, from its earliest days, was the most professional of clubs. For it, soccer was meant to be entertaining and exciting in order to attract ticket-buying customers. By contrast, the army and police contributed many more Olympic champions than Spartak in sports like shooting, fencing, and rowing with limited domestic audiences.[12]

Ultimately, Spartak and Dinamo took different approaches to the production of cultural events. Soviet popular culture was always torn between the twin goals of education (Dinamo) and entertainment (Spartak). Mass culture was supposed to teach, but it could not do so if no one listened. For cultural products to be effective as teaching tools, they also had to be pleasurable for the public to consume. The state may have controlled the menu of attractions, but it was constantly changing the content and forms of mass culture in order to make them popular. There was never any single approach that could be called "official culture." In this struggle, the power of boredom may have been one of the Soviet public's few weapons, but it turned out to be quite effective.[13]

As capitalist advertisers have learned, you cannot convince people if they are not watching. In this sense, there was a market, if an unusual one, for popular culture in the Soviet Union. This was especially true when it came to sport. It turns out soccer was not an unchallenged weapon of state domination and power. To be sure, the regime's intervention in the game over the course of Soviet history was a constant, but soccer could also be, to use James Scott's now famous phrase, a "weapon of the weak."[14] If football did not support outright opposition, it did help Soviet citizens resist the regime's incursions into the privacy of friendships and family, preserving in the process some small piece of their souls.

# 1

## Spartak's Roots

*Futbol* in the 'Hood, 1900–1917

Recollecting his tour of duty in prerevolutionary Moscow, the British diplomat Robert Bruce Lockhart mused about the relationship between football and the upheaval he had so recently witnessed. Had Russian workers played and watched soccer as avidly as their British comrades, he wrote, the Bolshevik Revolution might never have occurred at all.[1] It seemed as if Lockhart had read the writings of prewar socialists on what they thought to be the pernicious influence of the game. Certainly he agreed with his political opponents that there was a connection between sport and politics, but Lockhart's conclusions were precisely opposite those of the revolutionaries. For leftist intellectuals, the "people's game" was a hated diversion from the class struggle, but for a conservative British politician, it was a godsend.[2]

Could it then be that Lockhart, in his naive sporting romanticism, was actually right? Did the absence of a professional football league make a workers' revolution more likely in the Russian Empire? The opposite argument, after all, had been made more than once about Britain. If, as many then claimed, the secular religion of sport was the glue that kept an often fractious Victorian society together, could its relative absence in Russia explain the fall of the Romanovs?[3] Needless to say, a dose of caution is in order before embracing the notion that, after decades of exemplary, archivally based scholarship on the causes of the Russian Revolution, football, overlooked by most historians, should turn out to have been the central contradiction. Tempting as it would be to make such a claim, I will refrain from offering what is, admittedly, the kind of counterfactual argument historians are ill equipped to evaluate.

The actual number of working people in Russia touched by soccer before 1917 was quite small. On the eve of the war, there were some eight thousand formally registered players in the entire empire, and those on official lists were scarcely likely to have been artisans or factory hands.[4] It is best instead to turn Lockhart's formulation around and look not at football's impact on society but at society's impact on the practices of football. If soccer in Russia was insufficiently important as a cultural activity to attract the attention of all the empire's toilers, we can still usefully examine the sporting practices of those males, nearly all youthful, who were part of the soccer subculture. How did their participation in this modern, urban activity affect their political, cultural, national, and gendered identities, and how did those evolving and multiple identities reflect the rapid social changes of the prerevolutionary period?

My focus in this chapter will be on that relatively small group of boys from a single Moscow neighborhood who went on to play and root for the succession of teams that in 1935 became Spartak. In doing this, I have two purposes: first, to examine football as an element of the links between popular culture and the politics of working people in the empire's second city, and second, to foreshadow Spartak's postrevolutionary development. As we shall see, those connections were attenuated. The direct involvement of the future *Spartakovtsy* in prerevolutionary party politics was minimal. Their names do not appear in either the Western or Soviet-era literature on labor before and during the revolution, nor were they an immense fraction of the working population in prerevolutionary Moscow. Beyond this, their formal contributions to Russian football before 1917 were not immense. Only after the 1917 revolution, and especially after the formation of the Spartak Sport Society in 1935, did this cohort of young males become historically important. Yet their earliest sporting experiences very much influenced the ways they came to run, on the one hand, and support, on the other, what began as a local club.

With its larger community of foreigners, St. Petersburg was usually ahead of Moscow in adopting most forms of Western popular culture. Football was no exception. In 1912, Boris Chesnokov (1891–1979), a player, organizer, and chronicler of working-class football, wrote that the game was Moscow's most popular sport, but he also took pains to mention that only a thousand men, most of them from propertied families, actually played soccer on an organized basis. Before 1917, lower-class groups also played and watched, but it is not likely they did so in similar numbers. Football was not yet a form of mass culture, given that the masses did not yet play it. Nevertheless, the prehistory of Spartak affords an opportunity to deal with a number of important matters that go beyond the empirically limited connections between proletarians and sport.[5]

For Russian males of all social stations, sport was a way of accepting modernity. Athletic activities demanded much the same discipline, organization, and structure as the industrial capitalism then growing so rapidly in Russia's cities. The constant striving for improvement characteristic of sport, along with its related bodily pleasures, expressed the dynamism and joys, as well as the dangers and risks, of the new age. Both subordinate and dominant social groups shared these particular values, but the ways sporting activity came to be practiced in Russia divided rather than united men along what can properly be called class lines. While games provided the working- and middle-class males who practiced them with a variety of new ways of seeing themselves, those new identities were not universal. Bourgeois and proletarian men differed not only from their forebears but also from each other in the way they used their bodies. Consequently, these two groups generated different versions of manhood, which further reinforced the polarizations developing between classes in late Imperial Russia.

Without always realizing it, the boys who went on to found Spartak were at the leading edge of these changes. While they lived in one of the city's largest factory districts, not all of them could strictly be called working-class, nor did they all exhibit something that traditional Marxists would have called "class consciousness." All, however, were members of subordinate social groups who, as Richard Holt has noted about British workers, were using sport as a way of establishing new urban identities, developing local pride, and enjoying male camaraderie.[6] At times, these boys literally had their noses pressed against the glass of department store windows as they watched new forms of popular culture emerging before their eyes. At the same time, these "children of the city" helped create many of those same novel cultural forms. Aside from playing football, they shopped in stores as well as open markets, read detective novels, and went to amusement parks, music halls, and occasionally movies. While we have extremely limited information on their social backgrounds, most of them were born in Moscow, and a sizable portion were sons of workers. Nearly all had grown up in the city and were comfortable on its streets.

This last point is crucial. While the peoples of the Russian Empire had created rich, largely rural folk cultures over the course of centuries, much of the new urban, commercial entertainment was seen as foreign, specifically Western. This was particularly true in the case of sport. Russian peasants played games in their moments away from the burdens of agriculture.[7] The best-known pastimes, along with skiing, skating, and hunting, were the ball-and-stick game *lapta* and the bowlinglike *gorodki,* not to mention the semiorganized form of fistfighting, known as the *stenka.* Throughout the world, organized sport with its federations, schedules, rules, referees, leagues, and record-keeping was not part of rural life.[8] The same was true in Russia, where sport was decidedly urban and modern. There were no myths of the pastoral, so much a part of British and American sporting ideologies. Those who practiced sports in Russia were instead staking their claims to life in the empire's rapidly expanding cities. They did not dream of the good old days of "village football," nor did they harbor fantasies of carving baseball diamonds out of cornfields.

The question of the "peasant-ness" of urban life in the Russian Empire has been central to the study of the historical role of the laboring classes, understood in the broadest possible sense of the term. At one time, the receptivity of Russian workers to revolutionary appeals was explained by their ties to the countryside. The brutalities of rural life had perpetuated, it was said, an irrational tendency toward violent behavior.[9] This was especially important in a city like Moscow, which was the epicenter of massive and continuous in-migration from the villages.[10] In response, a later generation of both Western and Russian scholars with access to archival materials came to associate political militancy and revolutionary activity with extended residence in the city.[11] While most lower-class soccer players in Moscow either were born in the city or had moved there at an early age, this fact by itself did not make them revolutionaries. It is, however, important to remember that those working people, nearly all male, who had come to take part in sports, especially football, were far more likely to have cut their ties to the countryside. If they were not all radical militants, they were at least drawn from the same milieu that produced those militants.

## Desirable Imports

While we have several excellent accounts of early Russian football, the story requires retelling, if only in part. Soccer came to Russia late in the nineteenth century. While cricket was the game the soldiers and bureaucrats of the British Empire so graciously gave to the native peoples of their far- flung colonies, football was the sport of the informal commercial empire.[12] Where the crown was not supreme, British influence was spread in indirect ways. However, when it was exported to foreign shores, football, the great pastime of the domestic working class, became at first a middle-class activity. With deflated balls and rule books stuffed into their luggage, thousands of merchants, engineers, managers, technicians, diplomats, entrepreneurs, and students proselytized a new secular religion wherever their work took them. This process played out in such disparate places as Spain, Argentina, Germany, Brazil, South Africa, and France. The introduction and absorption of the sport followed nearly universal patterns, to which Russia provided no exception.

The growth of soccer in Russia was one of many signs of the profound changes sweeping through the empire at the end of the nineteenth century. The first football activity appeared a decade after the 1861 abolition of serfdom. The standard Soviet-era histories of the game make mention of sailors visiting the ports of St. Petersburg and Odessa during the 1870s. They occupied their time on shore by kicking around the proverbial pig bladder wherever they could find an open space. English employees of two large St. Petersburg factories organized teams in 1879.[13] Much the same thing at much the same time was going on in France, where Britons, especially Scots, formed a club in the port of Le Havre.[14] In Russia, however, these episodes do not appear to have made an impression on the local populations. It took some time for capitalist activity in urban Russia to gather pace after the peasant emancipation. As a result, football, in any of its forms, did not catch on immediately. By the late 1880s and 1890s, however, the cityscape of the empire began to change under the impact of the proindustrialization policies of the minister of finance, Count Sergei Witte. Sports and other new urban cultural practices began to appear along with growing middle and working classes who were receptive to them.

Foreigners, attracted by the acceleration of capitalist activity in Russia, brought their new pastimes with them. Following the organizational practices developed at home, they formed a variety of socially exclusive clubs, primarily in the capital. Many of these were single-sport groups, composed entirely of expatriates. The first multisport organization was the St. Petersburg Yacht Club. Founded in 1860, the group included the most elevated of Russian aristocrats along with foreign diplomats. Following the Victorian example, the club specifically excluded anyone who had ever engaged in manual labor. Even before the creation of this body, the royal sport of horse racing had long been hugely popular among Russian elites, along with fencing and swimming.[15]

The organization of sports changed in the 1880s to encompass activities popular with the increasingly powerful and numerically expanding middle classes. Between 1880 and the turn of the century, clubs were formed for cycling (soon to become the most popular spectator sport), weight lifting, track and field, boxing, ice hockey, and, finally, football. Much of this activity was organized and propagandized by commercial promoters, working with businessmen, especially industrialists, who sought to provide healthy activities for their employees while gaining a measure of social prestige. St. Petersburg was the center of this activity. Moscow trailed behind despite the presence of a vibrant merchant and entrepreneurial community that would eventually embrace sports wholeheartedly. In the second city, a yacht club did appear in 1867, and a gymnastics society was formed the next year. Only much later, in 1898, did a weight-lifting and body-building club appear.[16]

In the United States and Europe, this period witnessed the bureaucratization of sporting activity with the creation of numerous national and international federations in such sports as gymnastics, swimming, figure skating, track, and dozens of others. While they attracted the participation of politically powerful elites wherever they appeared, these new institutions were formally independent from governments. The founding of international federations led to the emergence of new types of sports officials who came to generate the ideas and practices that eventually gave rise to the modern Olympic movement.[17] In the Russian Empire, similar organizations began to emerge alongside the older clubs and circles. Foreigners played leading roles in this process, but the fig leaf of independence from the state, so central an element of British practice, was impossible in the Russian Empire. No group, however innocuous, could exist without official government sanction. All organizations had to pass muster with the authorities, who felt it necessary to observe, if not control, any activity that brought significant numbers of people together.

Soccer was a relative latecomer to the world of Russian sport and entertainment. Foreigners had been playing among themselves for some time, but the first organized group devoted solely to the game was the Victoria Club, formed in St. Petersburg in 1894 and composed of English and German employees from local factories. The impetus for the creation of this new group had come a year before when an exhibition match was staged during the interval between bike races at the Semyonov Hippodrome in St. Petersburg.[18] At the time, cycling was hugely popular, along with horse racing and wrestling. Accounts of this first game, played in a driving rain, describe a crowd as large as ten thousand who laughed at the spectacle of mud-covered men kicking wildly while sliding around in the muck.

The process of organizing soccer in Russia began apace. In 1896, Georges Duperont (1877–1934), a Russian-born Frenchman from a merchant family, organized a team at the St. Petersburg Circle of Amateur Sportsmen, where track and field had previously been the dominant activity. Duperont would become a hugely important figure in the growth of the sport. He translated the rules into Russian, and on October 24, 1897 (OS) led a team from his club against a side from the Vasilostrovskii Football Society on a field belonging to the First Cadet Corps.[19] While teams had been playing for several years in a number of Russian cities, this 1897 game is usually cited as the birth date of organized football in Russia. Whatever the case, Duperont, along with leaders of the British expatriate community, took the lead in organizing a St. Petersburg league in 1901. In the next five years, dozens of new teams were organized, composed of Russians as well as Britons and other foreigners. The Aspden Cup was created for the city champion. Duperont continued his leadership role thereafter. In 1912, he spearheaded the organization of the first national soccer organization, the All-Russian Football Union. This body, which eventually conducted an annual national championship among city select teams, was formed after the Russian soccer team's disastrous performance at the 1912 Olympic Games in Stockholm.[20]

British men dominated the affairs of the new league, which conducted its meetings in English, effectively excluding most Russians from power. This situation was replicated throughout the world at the turn of the century as local groups came to resent foreign tutelage and control of playing opportunities. Tensions between British and Russian teams were not limited to meeting rooms, however, and confrontations on the field were often violent, stirring spectators to take matters into their own hands from time to time. Following the Victorian model, these clubs were formally amateur with high membership dues to keep out the poor. At one club, the entry fee was ten rubles, and the annual dues were twenty rubles, slightly more than the average monthly wage for a typical laborer. Other clubs were less expensive but similarly elite in social composition.[21] Regular league games were played on fenced-off grounds with several hundred to a few thousand ticket-buying spectators drawn from the same privileged social milieu.

Before 1907, football was far from the form of mass culture it had become in the United Kingdom. Quite simply, the Russian masses were not involved, nor did the sport's organizers wish to attract them. Additionally, the leisure time and disposable income that West European and American workers had won after years of hard political and trade union struggle were still only limited parts of working-class life in Russia's cities. Even after the 1905 revolution, in which the eight-hour day was a central demand, twelve hours were still typical in most industries and trades. Workers still sent extra income back to families in the countryside, but on the eve of World War I, things had begun to change.[22] Increasingly, ties with the countryside were attenuated. More and more young working-class males were born in cities. As kids, they were attracted to football before entering the workforce. Some of them, whose parents had hopes for social mobility, played in schools, commercial academies, and *gymnaziia*. Hundreds would descend on the vast parade ground at Khodynka for weekend pickup games. The official leagues, which publicized matches on posters and in the press, caught the attention of these young city folk who now wanted to watch and play the game wherever and in whatever manner they could.

When young men from working-class neighborhoods could not get to open fields, they played where they were. Moscow was no exception to the worldwide phenomenon in which street football was played in apartment courtyards, vacant lots, cemeteries, meadows, fields, and parks. Kids played in boots and barefoot. Games could be struck up anywhere. With no referees, fights were common. Training was similarly primitive. Andrei Starostin's memoir account of his first practice ground could have been written by a poor young man almost anywhere in the world:

> I began my daily training sessions shooting at a crudely painted goal in my "courtyard pitch." Seventy years have passed and I can still distinctly hear the sound of the smack of the homemade ball hitting the fence and seeing pieces of newspaper come flying out of the stocking that held them together.[23]

Starostin's experience seems thoroughly generic, differing little from that of British legend Stanley Matthews, born eleven years later in Stoke-on-Trent: "When I wasn't playing football on the waste ground with my pals, I'd play by myself at home. I had a small rubber ball that I spent hours kicking against the backyard wall. . . . I used to place kitchen chairs in the backyard and practice dribbling the small ball in and out of them."[24] The activities of these teenagers eventually gave rise to the creation of spontaneously formed teams, known in Russian as *dikii,* which literally means "wild" but is best translated here as "outlaw."

The outsider status of these nonelite teams was confirmed first by the existing clubs, who shunned their presence, and second by the police, who feared a gathering of footballers could be used to mask revolutionary activity. Outlaw soccer would prove crucial in the prehistory of Spartak. Accordingly, I will be giving this most interesting sporting practice considerable attention. I mention it at this point, however, to highlight the ways in which football, along with many other sports, divided social classes and exacerbated the growing polarizations then undermining the stability of prerevolutionary urban Russia. If football had diverted the workers of much of the world from the joys of class struggle, it served instead in Russia to alienate many laboring men and boys from the educated and propertied elements who played and socialized in the empire's sports clubs.

While St. Petersburg was the center of soccer activity in the empire, the sport had also spread to a growing number of cities, including Kiev, Odessa, Kharkov, and—most important for soccer's further development—Moscow. While the working population of the second city maintained stronger links with the countryside than their counterparts in the capital, the geography of Moscow, with its unclear boundaries and many open spaces, actually made finding a place to play less problematic than in St. Petersburg with its more spatially circumscribed and homogenous proletarian regions. Nevertheless, the sport established its first beachhead outside the city limits at the Morozov textile mill in the village of Orekho-Zuevo on the border between Moscow and Vladimir provinces. In 1894, the British engineer Harry Charnock (1875–1948), along with his brothers and a host of other "specialists" imported for their soccer abilities, taught the game to local workers. Morozov had hired the Charnocks to provide a healthy leisure activity for his employees, but inevitably, the foreign managers and technicians formed their own elite team, which came to dominate football in the Moscow region right up to the eve of the war.

The presence of British specialists was nothing new in Orekhovo. They had been coming there since 1840, but members of Old Believer sects, who occupied important positions in the textile business, had frowned on the playing of such games. Nor can it be said that the workers' increased sporting activity created social peace at the Morozov factories, which witnessed violent strikes in 1885 and again in the late 1890s.[25] It was not until 1905–1906 that much of this resistance to the Charnocks' work was broken down.[26] Finally, in 1910, the company constructed an excellent field with comfortable locker rooms and viewing areas for as many as ten thousand.

Other factories had followed Morozov's example, but initially the new sport's biggest impact was on those well-off residents of the city, including many foreigners, who spent summers at their *dachas* (vacation homes) and had the time and means to play. Following the example of their privileged neighbors, less wealthy employees and the so-called minor intelligentsia who also summered in these regions took up the game, creating a social link with urban lower-middle-class groups. Having seen soccer at Orekho-Zuevo, the *dachniki* spread the sport to neighboring locales. What had started as a casual game became organized. Leagues sprang up along the many railroad lines that emanated in all directions from the city. These organizations had to have official charters signed by the provincial governor. It was in just such a league that Lockhart, then a vice consul in Moscow, came to experience Russian football firsthand. Later, he would actually play for the Morozov team in Moscow league competition.[27]

At the turn of the century, most of what passed for soccer in Moscow was played in the city's suburbs at the height of the summer. Soon, however, a number of groups began to organize in the city itself. The spring and fall were

**1.1** Dacha football. *Futbol skvoz' gody.*

also times when it was possible to play the sport. During 1895, the Gopper factory built a field in the heavily industrial Zamoskvorech'e district, across the Moscow River just south of the Kremlin. Initially, this "stadium" was used exclusively by members of the city's British colony.[28] The first group of Russians to organize formed a club and constructed a field in the northeastern part of the city on Shiriaevo Pol'e in the giant Sokol'niki Park.[29] This effort was led by the jewelry magnate Roman Fyodrovich Ful'd (1870–1946?), later

**1.2** Soccer in Sokol'niki Park. *Sto let Rossiiskomu futbolu.*

the first head of the Moscow league and president of the Moscow Olympic Committee. Ful'd continued to play a leading role as an organizer right up to the revolution.[30]

The pace of this activity was considerably slower in Moscow than in Petersburg, and only after 1905 did new clubs begin to form in significant numbers. That year, Ful'd helped organize the new Sokol'nicheskii Klub Sporta (SKS), building a new field, this time with stands for spectators. The growth of soccer activity by September 1907 created a sufficient number of players in Moscow for one of the crucial steps in Russian sports history to take place. Select teams from St. Petersburg and Moscow (most from the Sokol'niki clubs) were formed to play against each other in what became an annual series dominated by the capital. Throughout the world, the initiation of intercity matches was a crucial moment in the development of sport. By allowing teams to play outside their hometowns, this new level of competition fostered the process of national coherence and connectedness while simultaneously intensifying city pride. The improvement of rail transport in Russia quickened journeys to other towns, while new urban tram networks, which appeared in Moscow just before the 1905 revolution, helped develop connections between suburban and urban groups.[31] More dacha clubs were established in the following years. The historically important Obshchetsvo liubitelei lyzhnogo sporta (OLLS) (Society for the Lovers of Skiing) was formed in 1901 but later turned considerable attention to football. Union, in the north of the city, emerged in 1908 with the construction of a field on Samarskii Lane. It was soon joined by the Moscow Skiing Club and the Zamoskvoretskii Klub Sporta (ZKS). New teams appeared in Petrovskii Park to the northwest and just to the park's south in the Presnia region.[32]

These clubs practiced more than soccer. However, competitions among their

**1.3** The ZKS Stadium in industrial Moscow. *Sto let Rossiiskomu futbolu.*

football teams soon provided occasions and reasons for the members of these organizations to foster group solidarities beyond the walls of their individual clubhouses. Supported by wealthy merchants and industrialists, the clubs provided recreation and social interaction for those well-off urbanites who could afford to join. Other businessmen provided fields for teams at their factories. Foreign managers and technicians, usually British, dominated the first teams of these clubs. Russian employees and workers, hopefully diverted from the twin demons of vodka and revolution, comprised the second to fifth teams. The patrons (*metsenaty*) of these organizations did not see this sporting activity as a source of profit. Rather, it was a way for them to enhance their social prestige and political influence. As Louise McReynolds has asked, "What better way to gain a sense of self than through association with like-minded individuals?"[33]

It is difficult to know what sort of football these elite, formally amateur players engaged in. There is no available film record, and photographs tend to be highly generic. It is possible to see that some fields had good sod, with well-constructed goals and clear markings. In pictures of official league games, players appear well shod and clothed, using normal-looking balls. Yet given the dismal record of Russian teams once foreign sides came to tour the empire after 1910 (seven wins, twenty-one defeats, and seven ties), it is fair to say the quality of play was fairly low. Existing accounts by veterans of this era tend to be uniformly generous about the players' abilities. Even subsequent histories, including encyclopedias of the game, list only the positive qualities of the pioneers of Russian soccer. Players were credited with high work rates. Some were said to dribble well and possess good feints. Others were said to be good passers or shooters. Almost none played well in the air, a Russian weakness that persisted through the entire Soviet period and is still a problem. Russian teams followed the classic formation of early soccer with five forwards, three midfielders, and two defenders. Positions were rigidly adhered to with little switching. Players were spread out all over the field, making the game, in Andrei Starostin's words, "panoramic." Trapping and other technical skills seem to have been poorly developed, making for fairly scrappy play. If one believes the few available accounts, shooting was a strength, and the less than knowledgeable crowds cheered mighty blasts, no matter how far off target. Moscow teams were said to favor a vigorous long-passing, hard-running game, close to the British style. Short passing and possession were more likely to be seen on the fields of St. Petersburg.[34]

The rush of new Moscow clubs created after 1905 established the momentum for the organization of a city league in December of 1909. On June 2, 1910, a kickoff dinner was held at the fashionable Hermitage restaurant, but the first official league game took place only on August 15. Four clubs took part in the first season, including the SKS, Union, Klub Sporta Orekhovo (the Morozov factory) and the British Sports Club (BKS). The national balance was thus divided between two Russian and two British clubs who competed for a cup donated by Roman Ful'd. In later years they were joined by the Zamoskvoretskii Klub Sporta and the OLLS, which had taken up soccer. There soon were the new Kruzhok Futbolistov Sokol'niki (KFS) and the Moskovskii Klub Lyzhnikov (MKL), which played at the Khodynka parade ground. Dozens of other teams appeared, as membership in the Moscow league expanded exponentially. Matches took place on the same sorts of fenced-off fields as in St. Petersburg. Many of these "stadia" were carved out of highly urbanized districts. Pictures of the Zamoskvoretskii club's field on Kaluzhskaia Street, the finest inside the city limits, show factories and apartments in the near background.[35]

Tickets were made available to the wider public but rarely in advance. Relatively high prices limited the audiences to the same social elites from which the players were drawn. Accordingly, gates were usually a few hundred to a few thousand. Principal matches between leading teams could attract several thousand, however. Intercity games drew similar numbers of spectators. There were also matches against foreign opponents, who began to arrive regularly after 1910 when the Prague superclub Slavia (traveling under the name of Corinthians) played in Moscow and Petersburg. These games attracted huge audiences by the day's standards. While expensive tickets were supposed to keep out manual workers, their children found it possible to sneak in or save enough to enter the ground legally. Many of the boys who went on to play for Spartak and its predecessors first experienced organized football this way.[36]

Along with the game, the associated commercial practices associated with football also grew in Moscow. Matches were advertised with posters on kiosks, walls, and trams. Balls, shoes, and uniforms were on sale in the city's better department stores, such as Muir and Merrylees on the Petrovka, and in specialty shops like Bitkov's Vse dlia sporta (Everything for Sport) on Bol'shaia Nikitskaia Street.[37] Periodicals devoted to sports, like K sportu (Let the Games Begin) and its St. Petersburg counterpart, Russkii sport, reported on matches and related developments. The daily press, elite and penny, also offered game

**1.4** Advertisement for football gear from Muir and Merrilees department store. *Sto let Rossiiskomu futbolu.*

accounts. Top players like the (football) left-winger Vasiliy Zhitarev (1891–1961) of ZKS became celebrities, worshipped not only by young middle-class men but by others from lesser social groups who were exposed to soccer in the still limited organs of prerevolutionary Russia's sporting media. As a result, more men were drawn to the game and more clubs and leagues were created.

In Moscow, this shift in sporting activity came relatively late in the imperial period. Only after 1912 could commentators credibly claim soccer had become the city's most popular sport. Even the outbreak of war did not stop the growth of the game. Despite the drafting of millions of young men, the tsarist government encouraged the expansion of football and other forms of entertainment during the conflict. Many more teams were formed at factories, as well as at other enterprises, including even Muir and Merrylees itself. Theaters, cabarets, and cinemas were also well attended, along with the circus and racetrack.[38] In fact, soccer expanded so quickly during the war that the Moscow league could no longer limit its schedule to Sundays. For nonelite groups, this was a step backward. Matches now took place on weekdays, further limiting the participation of those players from working families who might have gained a measure of social acceptance with their successes on the field.[39]

Members of the lower-middle classes in Moscow proved especially responsive to the sport's attractions. Many had sent their sons, who had finished the required four years of primary school, to commercial academies, where they played soccer on school teams. A number of future Spartakovtsy were first exposed to the sport in this way. The connections between the elite clubs of the Moscow league and the lower-middle class in turn made it possible for the children of working-class families to learn the game. Unlike neighborhoods in St. Petersburg, those in Moscow were far from homogeneous. Even in the most industrialized regions, factory workers lived side by side with artisans, clerks, salespeople, and others in transportation and construction. Even employers and downwardly mobile nobles lived in districts outside the city center. Groups of football-playing friends could come from diverse backgrounds.[40] If social and economic barriers, as well as exclusionary rhetoric, had been erected to keep working-class youth from membership in organized soccer, this was not true for all elements of the city's lower orders.

Men and women of a wide variety of professions and backgrounds came together in the city's neighborhoods. According to Victoria Bonnell, "There was no such thing as *the* factory workers at the turn of the century. Instead, St. Petersburg and Moscow harbored a great diversity of factory groups, facing different kinds of work situations and internally differentiated along such lines as skill and gender."[41] If anything, that diversity was greater in Moscow than in the capital. More than the factory floor, the shared experiences of living, shopping, drinking, and playing together produced the later solidarity shown by Muscovites in the revolutionary moments of 1905, 1912–1914, and finally 1917.

The children of this heterogeneous brew played together on the streets. Football had become one of the favorite new activities of both local teenage boys and young workers throughout the city. Played with primitive equipment, without uniforms, referees, or coaches, on whatever empty space might be available, this spontaneous street play, reminiscent of urban youth the world over, provided the roots for the phenomenon of dikii football, mentioned above.[42] However, the pickup games of kids must be distinguished from the organized but unofficial "outlaw" activity of teams and clubs drawn from a variety of nonelite social groups. Dikii football, therefore, was not synonymous with worker football, just as the Moscow working class was not synonymous with the factory. The sport attracted not only workers but students, petty bureaucrats, clerks, and white-collar employees (*sluzhashchie*). At the time, Chesnokov estimated there were some thirty-five teams operating in Moscow outside the league structure.[43]

If not a pure reflection of the factory proletariat of Lockhart's imagination, the social composition of outlaw soccer was very much typical of the broadly defined Moscow working class described by Bonnell. Because the history of the outlaws would seem to impinge most closely on the interesting question of politics and sport, it is especially frustrating that we know so little about them. Of all the periodicals covering sport, only *K sportu* paid them any sustained attention. Their outsider status and relatively small numbers resulted in virtually no archival record of their games. Even Soviet-era information guides and histories note this lack of information. We are left instead with a few memoirs from the postwar period and several journalistic accounts based on interviews given largely in the 1960s. It is difficult to verify these accounts, but they are worth describing precisely because they show the genesis of what would later become local "football lore." A land in which rumormongering was a national pastime, Russia had its full share of sports myths and legends that generated interest in the game and fertilized the arguments and conversations it provoked.

Chesnokov was the central figure in Moscow's world of dikii football. Born in Pavlovskii Posad in Moscow Province, he was the son of a white-collar railway employee who moved from place to place with each new assignment, eventually locating to Moscow.[44] In 1905, while a student at Gymnasium Number 4, Chesnokov took up the game at the urging of a teacher. An all-around athlete, he also skated at the nearby Chistye Prudy (Pure Ponds). Small of stature, he nevertheless subsequently became a successful wrestler. The city's circuses were often the sites of major competitions in what had long been one of Russia's most popular sports. Chesnokov's early experiences brought him into contact with professional wrestlers employed by circuses and inspired in him a lifetime love not only of wrestling but of circus life.[45] For Chesnokov, as for many of his young companions, sport was but one of several items on the ever-expanding popular culture menu of post-1905 Moscow. While the evidence is minimal and in no way systematic, it appears that most young soccer players were not so obsessed by their sport as to ignore the many other new urban attractions and entertainments of the day.

Soon after taking up the game, Chesnokov and his three brothers began a campaign to get their noncomprehending but sufficiently well-paid father to buy them a ball. After they succeeded, they began to play each other in the courtyard of their apartment house, a practice followed by urban boys well into the Soviet period. Throughout the world, such courtyards and alleyways have been the first playing field for millions of city kids. At some point the more gifted and driven realize the necessity of finding larger and safer playing fields. The Chesnokovs found such a spot near the Kalitinskii Cemetery on Aleksandrovskii Street, near the Guzhon factory in the Rogozhkskii region of the city on its southeast border. According to one version of the story offered by Soviet journalist Lev Gorianov, their activities attracted the attention of workers at Guzhon, who joined pickup games on weekends.[46] Word spread throughout the region. More and more players appeared. Soon what had been a fairly spontaneous scene became more organized as entire teams from other parts of the city showed up for action.

Although Gorianov does not take us through the details of Chesnokov's organizational work, he does describe a process by which at least some of the teams gathering at Kalitinskii considered the possibility of joining the Moscow league at its lowest level. Their path into organized football was, however, blocked. High annual membership dues at the clubs ruled out the possibility of joining an existing team for most of Chesnokov's comrades, nor could they afford to enter the league as a group. During 1910, the police, fearing the gathering of so many members of the lower orders (or perhaps fearing raising the dead), evicted the weekend warriors from their cemetery idyll.[47]

Chesnokov soon took up a collection among the teams and was able to rent a field near the Annengorfskii Grove. A nearby barn served as a locker room. The resulting Rogozhskii Sport Circle (Rogozhskii kruzhok sporta) has been called the first workers' sports club, but as Chesnokov would write at the time, the social composition of the group was a good deal more varied. Students, some from comfortable backgrounds like Chesnokov's, joined with workers and the sons of the lower-middle class to create a space for plebeian male bonding and physical expression that afforded them self-confidence and pride. No available account of this process describes the hatching of revolutionary plots under cover of football, and there appears to have been little overlap between the soccer world and radical worker subcultures. Still, both groups were engaging in behaviors that made them modern men of the new Russian cities, cutting ties to no longer meaningful peasant versions of manhood. If the still numerically limited football crowd was not busying itself with the reading of Marx and Lenin, it is fair to say they were nevertheless transforming themselves into the kinds of experienced urbanites who would listen to, if not always act upon, the appeals of the Left during the 1912–1914 labor disorders and again in 1917. Certainly their treatment by both football's elite organizers and the forces of law and order did not desensitize them to the intensifying antagonisms of prewar Russia. If there were not yet enough of them to defend a decent-sized barricade, their presence in the city and the nature of their activities made them markers of significant social change.

After the formation of the Rogozhskii club, Chesnokov sought out as many other outlaw teams as he could find in the hope of organizing a league of their own. In the process, he invited several talented young men to join, and quite quickly Rogozhskii lost its regional character. Additionally, Chesnokov joined the staff of K sportu early in 1912 and used his position to push for further recognition of the outlaw teams. That year he was able to organize a league, as well as a cup competition, which was won three years in a row by Rogozhskii. This activity attracted the attention and antipathy of the official Moscow league. In response, they raised their membership dues and refused to let league referees work outlaw games. Finally, in 1915, the police appeared at the Annengorfskii field and broke up several ongoing games. The next day, Chesnokov and his teammates took their rental agreement to the local police station, but they were not allowed inside.

Faced with this level of interference, the Rogozhskii club ceased operations, but Chesnokov continued to seek opportunities. He had maintained cordial relations with the official league club, Novogireevo, also based in the southeast of the city. At first, Novogireevo offered to accept a few of Rogozhskii's stars, but Chesnokov insisted on a complete union. The impact on Novogireevo was immediate. They won the city championship, defeating the mighty Morozov team, which had dominated the league since its inception.[48] This result established the legitimacy of outlaw soccer. Additionally, it was the first such championship won by a team composed entirely of Russian players. Even before then, a number of outlaw teams had been able to get their charters signed by government officials, and talented players had been scouted and recruited from their ranks onto league teams. By the outbreak of the war, success had bred a measure of acceptance, mitigating, but hardly obliterating, the class tensions characteristic of football in Russia.

Crowds of several thousand from various social groups became common at both international matches and important games of the Moscow league. Soccer was a still nascent form of popular culture that mirrored the dynamism of Russian urban life before the revolution. Nevertheless, football's acceptance in the Russian Empire paled before similar developments in the West, where sports of several varieties, organized by commercial agents, came to attract tens of thousands on a weekly rather than occasional basis. Even if soccer could have performed the "political work" Lockhart thought it could, there was simply not enough of it in Russia at this moment in history to have had a decisive impact.

## Local Lads

My concern up to this point has been to trace the history of the game both in Moscow and in the rest of the empire. My purpose has been to suggest possible, if tenuous, links between sport and political developments. In this section, I want to focus on one specific neighborhood in which a group of young boys found football and through it each other. Their shared experience created the basis for what would eventually evolve into Spartak Moscow, the Soviet Union's most popular sports team. At this point, however, they were less concerned with sporting destiny and more interested in having a good time. As Andrei Starostin would later write, "Spartak had many sources but just one birthplace—the Presnia," renamed Krasnaia (Red) Presnia after the Bolshevik victory for the special militance shown by its residents at the most crucial revolutionary moments.[49]

The district had been the last to give in to the government during the rising of December 1905, and barricades went up all over its streets in October 1917. Despite this history, one cannot meaningfully correlate political militancy with football activity. Although many of the Presnia's young men and boys actively kicked whatever objects they could find around the district's dusty streets, courtyards, alleyways, vacant lots, cemeteries, and parks, this highly industrialized neighborhood was no more or less a hotbed of the sport than many other regions. Nevertheless, it is worth examining the character of the Presnia district in the larger context of Moscow's dizzyingly rapid economic development during the late nineteenth and early twentieth centuries.

The tenth-most-populous city in the world, Moscow had expanded at what contemporaries called "an American pace," growing "not by the day but by the hour." The fast, if slightly belated, development of soccer was but one of many results of that growth.[50] Other consequences of this expansion, however, were not so positive. If the process of Moscow football's development shared much with other urban experiences in other places, the larger context in which it emerged was quite different, raising yet again a question historians of Russia have always confronted. Did the city's involvement with the sport resemble that of such centers of the metropolis as Manchester, Marseilles, and Munich, or were its patterns more typical of the colonial experiences of Buenos Aires, Sao Paulo, and Lima? In Russia, the tensions between British expatriates and locals more closely resembled the Latin American experience. At the same time elite soccer in the empire was similar in infrastructure and playing style to the game as it had evolved in continental

Europe. Here football seems to represent yet another case of the uneven development so characteristic of the Russian Empire on the eve of revolution.

Moscow's booming industries, especially textiles, attracted tens of thousands of migrants from the countryside each year.[51] The peasant presence in Moscow was overwhelming, leading many to describe the city as a "big village." Three-fourths of the population had been born elsewhere; two-thirds were officially members of the peasant estate.[52] The new residents worked in suburbs with low wooden buildings on dusty streets, paved intermittently with huge cobblestones. Many families had gardens, and quite a few maintained some livestock as well. Huge factories existed side by side with the most rural of practices, as the city literally blended into the surrounding countryside.

Moscow's rapid growth brought with it staggering poverty, dreadful housing, crime, disorder, and disease. While many well-intentioned local authorities were unable to remedy these conditions, in far too many cases, the national government, fearing any independent action, proved unwilling to even let them try. As Blair Ruble has noted, Moscow was Europe's most poorly housed city and, after St. Petersburg, its least healthy:

> Nowhere on the continent was poverty more destructive than in Russia's great industrial towns and cities. Deplorable housing conditions were marked both by limited space and by poor sanitary standards. Harshly cold winters exacerbated matters, as did heavy reliance on wooden as opposed to brick and stone construction. The failure of the Russian authorities at all levels to alleviate such horrible conditions fed social unrest every bit as much as did employer parsimony, greed, and denigrating paternalism and imperial arrogance and obtuseness.[53]

Because Moscow was spread over a considerable territory and could expand into its suburban hinterlands, the density of its growing population was a good bit less than that of other European capitals, but the number of residents per housing unit was the highest on the continent. In 1910, wages in Moscow were lower and rents higher than in any other European city.[54] In 1912, there were 8.2 residents per housing unit, compared with 3.9 in Berlin, 4.2 in Vienna, and 4.5 in London.[55] It was rare for the members of a single family to share a single apartment or house. Tens of thousands lived in company barracks. Many lived in basements, while thousands of workers rented cots under staircases or in the corners of others' houses.

Conditions of this sort were most likely to be found on Moscow's outskirts. Two ring roads, both with islands of grass and trees on their medians, formed concentric circles around the wealthier, more modernized districts in the downtown part of the city near the Kremlin and Red Square. There, in the Tverskaia, Miasnitskaia, and Arbatskaia regions, one could find Moscow's social elites, along with its leading cultural institutions, including libraries, theaters, and the university.[56] Most factories, by contrast, had been built on the periphery beyond the outer ring road, where two-thirds of the city's population came to live by the turn of the century. The placement of industries in these regions did not lead to the creation of clearly demarcated working-class neighborhoods as had emerged in St. Petersburg. According to one American scholar of Russian labor:

> Historically, Moscow had never developed distinctly industrial districts like Vyborg and Narva in St. Petersburg. Instead, its largest textile factories and metalworking plants were distributed around the city, interspersed among thousands of artisan shops and small manufactories. The one major exception was the Presnia district, a Moscow working class community and factory district that became famous for its role in the December, 1905 uprising.[57]

This may slightly overstate the region's exceptional character, but it is correct to note the extent to which the Presnia was a coherent community. Social heterogeneity, so much a mark of most of the city's regions, was less pronounced in the Presnia, where there were very few homes of the well-to-do.[58] Even today, after waves of urban renewal, a walk through Krasnaia Presnia with its small parks and tree-lined streets full of residential units and commercial spaces still gives the observer a feeling of neighborhood.

Deriving its name from the Presnia River, long since covered over by urban sprawl, this district, with its loosely defined borders, was located to the west of the city center, just outside the ring road. An area of industrial activity as early as the eighteenth century, by 1900 the Presnia had approximately 135,000 residents and some seventy factories, including, among others, Danilovskii Sugar, Dukat Tobacco, Shmidt Furniture, Til'mans Candy, and the Aleksandrovskii rail yards. The neighborhood's northern edge ran along Tverskaia Street, the city's main thoroughfare, between Triumfal'naia Place on the eastern edge and the Belorusskii Train Station to the west. The Vagan'skoe Cemetery, site of many a spontaneous game and later the fitting final resting place of the Starostins, marked the region's amorphously defined western edge. In the southeastern corner of the district, along the Moscow River, was the giant Prokhorov textile mill, founded in 1799.[59] As Joseph Bradley has described it, this immense, paternalistically run factory had a profound impact on the Presnia:

> By 1890 it was Russia's nineteenth largest factory with a value of production of five million rubles and a work force of 1,230. By 1900 the work force had quadrupled, and by 1914, 8,000 workers operated 45,000 spindles, 1,500 looms, and forty cotton printing machines. . . . At the beginning of the twentieth century, Prokhorov operated four day schools, a Sunday school, dormitories for single and married workers, and a clinic with twenty-two beds and an attending physician. As the manufacturers themselves frequently pointed out, the largest factories were better able to adopt safety measures, as well as to provide medical and cultural services, than the smaller factories or domestic industries.[60]

The relatively unskilled nature of textile labor made the Prokhorov a magnet for incoming peasants, especially those from western provinces who arrived by nearby rail and river transport.

Roughly 70 percent of the Presnia's residents were immigrants from the countryside, most employed in the various textile trades. This peasant presence was typical of Moscow. Many in the semirural Presnia had gardens and kept livestock. About four thousand of the more recent arrivals lived in the Prokhorov company barracks.[61] Others, because of the long working day and the high cost of public transportation, found shelter near the plant, putting a huge strain on a largely wooden, one-story housing stock. Nearly two-fifths of households in the Presnia had needed to take in boarders to make ends meet.[62] Cramped housing was exacerbated by an erratic, poorly organized labor market that created frequent periods of unemployment and massive, ongoing personal insecurity even for those who had long lived in the city. The Presnia was something less than the happiest place on earth:

> This quarter represented the classic pattern of working class misery: ramshackle wooden houses, crammed along mud streets, in which workers rented cots or corners in rooms that were unsanitary, vermin ridden and overcrowded. Presnia's western periphery was a center of hooliganism, petty thievery and cheap prostitution, an area so dangerous even to its lower-class inhabitants that police permitted workers at the Mamontov varnish factory near the Presnia Gates, to carry guns for self-protection.[63]

With such permission, it should not be altogether surprising that Presnia workers had little difficulty arming themselves during the decisive and bloody street battles of December 1905. The Presnia had seven factory-based armed fighting squads at that decisive moment, more than any other region. While specific party affiliations appear to have played only a limited role in workers' lives in late 1904, a stronger tradition of localism contributed to the intensity of their resistance by the end of the 1905 revolution.[64] The enlightened owner of the Prokhorov plant gave his employees food and allowed meetings to be held in the factory, making it easier for his workers to come out in support of others throughout the city during the October general strike.[65]

If the residents of the Presnia did not shrink from violence in 1905, it may well be that this had something to do with the ongoing violence of everyday life. This noisy, dirty, and crowded district was always rife with crime. Although not so concentrated a den of iniquity as the notorious Khitrov market east of the city center, the Presnia was not safe.[66] For young boys out on its streets, this was a place of both danger and temptation. Football, even if it took place away from the centers of neighborhood criminality, could not always protect all the young from such perils, but it did offer a way to avoid a world of drinking, gambling, easy sex, drug taking, and more than occasional murder.[67] In the memoirs of Moscow's footballers, there are depictions of several neighborhoods before 1917. Only in the accounts of "Presnia lads" do we get a sense of a powerfully criminal surrounding environment.

It is, of course, more than likely that this impression is partly the result of the subsequent fame and literary skills of the Starostins, especially Andrei, who came to associate with many of the USSR's most famous writers. More than others, their accounts pay attention to the Presnia's often colorful criminal underworld, but all those who played a role in the district's soccer life were touched by this dangerous environment. Running through the Presnia from north to south were the roughly parallel streets—Malaia (small) and Bol'shaia (big) Gruzinskaia (Georgian). Filled with all manner of shops and living units, the "Georgians" presented the young men of the neighborhood with a full catalog of hooligan and otherwise illegal activities. Both streets flowed into Bol'shaia Tishinskaia Place, site of the notorious Goriuchka, a vacant lot, home to a mélange of criminal activity led by the notorious Shirokovka gang. Gambling, fencing of stolen merchandise, mass vodka consumption, fights, and killings gave this place a terrifying reputation.[68] Several attempts were made to force the criminals out by constructing buildings on the lot, but all were met with arson—hence the name Goriuchka, from the Russian verb *goret'* (to burn). To much of the local Presnia youth, the denizens of this place were not villains but heroes, and many boys fell under their influence. Even Andrei Starostin, rather than wrapping himself in the pious mantle of the abstemious future sportsman, later recalled that the only reason he kept away from the Goriuchka's pleasures was fear of getting caught by the police and punished by his severe parents.[69]

Many others who shared the joys of spontaneous football fell to the district's baser temptations and did not make the journey to elite sport. Here the Starostin brothers were different from their less-well-off neighbors. Their father, Petr, and uncle Dmitri, both successful hunting guides, had brought the family from their home village of Pogost in Pskov Province to Moscow, where their employer, the Imperial Hunting Society, set up both families in a comfortable house at number 46 Presenskii Kammer-Kollezhskii Val, two blocks from the Goriuchka.[70] Each family, Dmitri with his one son and wife and Peter with his six children and wife, lived in a separate wing of this structure, while the kitchen and bathroom were shared, in the traditional peasant manner. All the Starostin children, with the exception of the eldest, Nikolai, had been born in Moscow. As hunters, the elder Starostins were completely surrounded by dogs. Attached to their house was a kennel housing twenty-five purebreds, belonging to various wealthy clients who did not want to keep the beasts in their fine houses or apartments. The presence of so many of man's best friends may have given the family a somewhat greater sense of security than their Presnia neighbors enjoyed. If the dogs did not do this, the large number of hunting rifles in the house may have done the trick.

The Starostins' somewhat elevated circumstances made them liminal figures—that is, they were able to move easily between the streets of their neighborhood and the nearby institutions of elite organized sport.[71] This was particularly true of Nikolai (1898–1996), who, after completing the required four years of primary school, was enrolled at the Mansfield Commercial Academy, where he was introduced to the game at the age of nine. As a further indication of the Starostin family's hopes for their children's social advancement, all the sons and daughters followed Nikolai into commercial academies. The entire family had a variety of pleasant experiences with the world of entrepreneurship, and this positive attitude toward business may have derived from their Old Believer merchant traditions. Although their father had married an Orthodox woman, remnants of the Starostins' religious practices did survive the transition to the city.[72]

With their father often away on hunting trips, the Starostin boys and girls had plenty of time to play in the streets. At night, the brothers engaged in games of two-on-two soccer in their bedroom. What the English peasantry had fashioned out of an inflated pig's bladder, the Starostin boys made with newspapers and Mom's old stockings. In the process, they destroyed no small amount of furniture while enraging their uncomprehending parents. Eventually, their home became headquarters for the Presnia's young footballers, whose street games were a threat to the local carters who filled the district's crowded thoroughfares.[73] Flying balls, usually of the self-made variety, could scare horses, causing the carters to take the boys' creations away. As the young *futbolisty* dissolved into tears, their opponents for street turf would laugh in contempt.

Football was not the only Western creation to have an impact on the cultural lives of the Presnia's young men. They regularly read detective fiction, most prominently Sherlock Holmes, Nick Carter, and Nat Pinkerton. Trams, usually hopped without paying a fare, could take them all over Moscow. They came to know the city's new emporia, and a few were able to scrape together enough money to take in a movie.[74] Beyond the world of the city, their father's work as a hunter provided the younger Starostins an acquaintance with the world of the new commercial culture of Moscow's rich and powerful. Summers were spent in their home village in Pskov Province. A constant parade of merchants and industrialists drove up from Moscow to partake in hunting parties. Their beautiful cars would be filled with treats from the famed Eliseev Gastronom on Tverskaia. After the hunt it was common for the father and uncle to share a large dinner and much other conviviality with their clients. The children were part of these jovial scenes, which took place in the Starostins' comfortable summer *izba* (house or hut). The men of wealth were fond of teasing and playing with the children. Aleksandr Nazarovich Gribov, head of the Gribov Brothers manufacturing firm, was especially attached to Andrei, and "Gribov" became Andrei's family nickname. These experiences familiarized the boys with the rich and enhanced their own self-esteem. Thereafter, they were not intimidated by such folk. Throughout the Soviet period and even after, Nikolai had no trouble approaching powerful men when they had something he wanted. Andrei, in particular, appears to have developed a firm sense of entitlement that he, too, was worthy of the privileges and comforts available to members of the Soviet elite. After 1917, the brothers felt themselves to be important people, and they expected important people to be interested in them.[75]

The Starostins were scarcely the only football-playing brothers who pioneered the game in their community. Aleksandr Ivanovich Kanunnikov, who worked at the Lakokraska dye works, was a longtime resident of the Presnia who discovered football as a mature adult. "Alas," he would say, "I was born too early" to play, but this did not prevent him from becoming a passionate fan. Each Sunday, his wife would pack pirozhki in his knapsack, and Aleksandr Ivanovich would set off to take in as many games as he could find. Ads on buses, trams, and kiosks or in the press became common in Moscow only after 1910. Telephones were a rarity outside the center of Moscow. Instead, there was a "wireless fan telegraph." By each Friday, the word would have spread among the knowledgeable. According to Leonid Gorianov, Kanunnikov "would sit down and with a bookkeeper's accuracy write out his schedule of games on Saturday nights. He would decide where to go and what route to take, a difficult matter for those times, with only a few trams running on weekends."[76]

Our fan had four sons, Aleksandr, Pavel (1898–1974), Anatoly, and Nikolai, all born in Moscow. As soon as each was old enough, he was taken along on their father's Sunday excursions, acquiring a love of the game in the classic male pattern. All four boys became involved with sports. Pavel became the Krasnaia Presnia team's greatest star and an early Soviet celebrity who played in many international matches for the earliest versions of the national team.[77] Like the Starostins, Pavel Kanunnikov first played organized football at a commercial academy. Also like the Starostins, Kanunnikov's parents had charted a path for him of upward social mobility into the lower-middle class. Trade and commerce were to keep him out of the factories.

Soccer games went on constantly in the academy's large courtyard, and at the end of the day students spread out throughout the neighborhood, looking for any kind of pickup game. In 1913, at the age of fifteen, Pavel made his school team as an attacker. Possessed of a thin, boyish upper body on top of massive thighs, he had an exceptionally powerful shot and quick burst of speed that attracted the attention of Boris Chesnokov, who was always on the lookout for young talent. Chesnokov invited Pavel to join the Rogozhskii Sports Club, where he quickly starred at inside left. When the police broke up the team in 1915, Kanunnikov followed Chesnokov to Novogireevo of the official league.[78] In the process, Kanunnikov became the idol of local youth, including one Andrei Starostin.[79]

Ivan (1895–1968), Sergei (1909–1953), and Petr (1901–1983) Artem'ev were three of five brothers who comprised the other great clan of Presnia football royalty. Their father, Timofei Artem'evich, had brought the family from the village of Lobkovo in Ryazan Province shortly before the 1905 revolution. Unable to survive on the land, Timofei did somewhat better in the city with his skills as a boot maker, bringing Ivan into the business at the age of ten. In the

**1.5** Young footballers from the Presnia, Pavel Kanunnikov standing left. *Futbol skvoz' gody.*

immediate wake of the failure of the 1905 revolution, it was difficult to organize so much as a pickup game of street football in the Presnia and elsewhere in Moscow. The police broke up any gathering of lower-class youth, but by 1908 the repression had eased. The Artem'ev boys discovered the game at this time, much to the horror and mystification of their uncomprehending father. Nor was their mother any too pleased to see them arrive home with bruises, scratches, and torn clothes. They agreed to let their sons play this alien game only after neighbors assured them that the boys were quite good at it. Ivan soon formed a close friendship with Pavel Kanunnikov, and the two practiced continually, even in the dead of winter.[80]

In 1912, Pavel and Ivan were invited to play for the Presnia Society of Physical Education (Obshchestvo fizicheskogo vospitania—OFV). Their coach was Boris Efimovich Evdokimov, a Bolshevik underground organizer, who used the society as cover for influencing local youth. While Pavel appears to have been, by and large, apolitical, Evdokimov did have an influence on Ivan's subsequent direction. In 1914, Ivan moved to Novogireevo at the behest of Chesnokov, later to be joined by Pavel. After one season, Ivan was drafted into the imperial army, served two years at the front, and returned to the Presnia in February 1917 a committed Bolshevik. Immediately arrested by the Provisional Government, he was freed during the October Revolution. The most politically engaged among the future Spartakovsty, Artem'ev later played the leading role in the founding of the Krasnaia Presnia team and the construction of its first stadium. Like Kanunnikov, Ivan had a following in the Presnia neighborhood, especially among workers at the Prokhorov factory, for whom he had made boots and shoes.[81]

Other groups of brothers, including the Moshkarovs, Gudovs, Golubievs, Vinogradovs, Vorobievs, and Sheliagins, were also part of this first generation of Presnia footballers, but the Starostins, who went on to have the most distinguished sports careers, have left the richest accounts of the district's street life. In recounting the long trek to his first organized match, Andrei Starostin, something less than a stickler for accurate chronology, recapitulated stories found in literally hundreds of athletes' autobiographies. He did, however, seek to put a special Russian spin on his trip. Earlier in 1916, Nikolai had gone to far away Sokol'niki Park to see a Moscow league game at the home ground of the OLLS.[82] At the time, there had not been enough money to bring along little brother Andrei, who then determined to make the journey on his own. Nikolai, in classic big-brother fashion, thought his ten-year-old sibling too young for such an excursion and had not been forthcoming with directions. Andrei was then forced to figure out the long and time-consuming tram ride across the entire city through parts of town highly intimidating to a young boy traveling alone. This was, he thought, a rite of manhood, something "real men" (*muzhestvennye liudi*) embarked on to build their "toughness of character."[83]

In order to simplify his trip to "the end of the world," Andrei opted for a slower but simpler route along the outer Ring Road on tram "B" with a single change for the "6" at the chaotic, notorious, and immense Sukharevka open market, a place that rivaled the Khitrov and dwarfed the Goriuchka. The Sukharevka was not Covent Garden in London or Les Halles in Paris, both of which, it should be noted, were eventually covered. This was more a scene from Hogarth than a place of orderly commerce. Barely regulated and policed, the Sukharevka was thoroughly emblematic of the disorderly ways Moscow changed as it embraced capitalism. Similarly, riding trams did not involve queuing in an orderly manner and paying the fare. Instead, Starostin, in the best international tradition of the street kid, did his traveling clinging to the back of the wagon. That Sunday, he brought along a single *grivenik* (ten-kopeck piece) to pay for his game ticket. Hopping off from time to time, he spent half an hour gazing into the window of the Bitkov sporting goods store, admiring a collection of the sort of soccer shoes that were still a rarity on the fields of the Presnia. Nikolai and Aleksandr had saved up their school breakfast money and acquired gear, but Andrei could only dream of such luxury.[84]

Resuming his journey, Andrei fell into a pleasant reverie that soon turned to terror when his tram began to crawl through an "ocean of people," many of them desperate and more than a few disposed to the criminal. This was the Sukharevka. Neither warnings nor lurid descriptions had prepared Andrei for the subsequent shock. While changing for the number 6 tram at a stop inside the market, a drunk boy, barely twelve, stumbled out of a tavern, accosted him, and demanded money. After freeing himself, Andrei decided the safest place for his precious grivenik was inside his mouth in the tradition of the old Russian merchantry. After almost an hour, arriving at his destination in a calmer state, he began to move his tongue, searching for the coin. It was not, to his horror, to be found inside his personal "safe." A check of pockets yielded no result either. In a detail that may well have been suggested by his friend, the famed writer Iurii Olesha, Andrei recalled coming to the conclusion that he had swallowed the money. The delicacies of Brezhnev-era discourse being what they were, Starostin could not have included graphic proof of his assertion. A bump may well have jarred Starostin's coin loose, but, clearly, swallowing it made for a better story. It should be noted that the grivenik does not make an appearance in his three other accounts of the trip, but only a curmudgeon (or historian) could cast doubt on such a lovely legend.[85]

Luckily, the stadium used by OLLS consisted of an eight-foot-high fence surrounded on three sides by the birch forest of Sokol'niki. It proved no problem to climb a nearby tree for a view of the field. Several others had done the same. Spread out below him was the sort of transforming sight experienced before and since by millions of athletes and fans:

> Before me was a fantastic panorama. A huge green carpet crossed by white lines, players in blue shirts and white shorts. All of them were wearing boots!! Four flags on the corners of the field, goals with massive rectangular posts, painted white with iron nets that made a ringing musical sound when the ball hit them. . . . From the height of a birch tree's branch, it all seemed like a wonderful dream.[86]

He would return safely, again through the Sukharevka but this time without incident. If he came back not yet a man, he was surely no longer a boy, having crossed the divide between the street football of his neighborhood and the contemporary elite version of the Russian game. Thousands of others would take this same step, transforming themselves into true devotees and, in many cases, professional athletes.

For the boys of the Presnia, watching an organized match did not solve the problem of finding a "civilized" place to play near home. This job fell to Nikolai, who, with his many contacts at all levels of local society, was already showing signs of becoming the deal maker he would turn out to be later in life. One of his buddies had suggested the seemingly bizarre idea of using the dreaded Goriuchka as a playing field. While Nikolai was intrigued by the proposal, others—most notably the conservative Uncle Dmitri—were appalled and threatened to call the *gradonachal'nik* (district governor).[87] Nikolai, however, enlisted the aid of an immense, usually drunk and always toothless local tough guy with criminal ties. This denizen of the Presnia's meaner streets was named Ivan Zakharych, known to his pals as "Fan" (the toothless pronunciation of Ivan). A bully when he had to be, Zakharych happily played the role of protector for the younger boys he came to know through their participation in the "wall-to-wall" fistfights of which Zakharych was the star figure.

These fights, some attracting crowds of up to ten thousand to the banks of the Moscow River in winter, were a centuries-old practice that provided lower-class rural and later urban dwellers with a form of male bonding and entertainment, surrounded by elaborate codes, rituals, and betting. In the villages, the fights had become a way of dealing with violations of male practices of sociability.[88] Daniel Brower saw in their danger and violence the cultural roots of later revolutionary working-class disorder.[89] In his final memoir, Nikolai Starostin painted a rosier picture of a highly conscious, preplanned, rule-bound contest between geographically defined groups that toughened young urban boys and provided a school for manhood that could be hard to find in the city.[90] Additionally, Starostin assured his readers that this custom disappeared soon after the revolution. Needless to say, it did not.

In winter, the Starostins and their friends skated on Patriarshie prudy (Patriarch's Pond), located just inside the outer ring road, across from the northeast corner of the Presnia. Carved out of an entire city block, the pond was surrounded by comfortable modern apartment houses. It was but a fifteen-minute walk from the chaos and crime of the Presnia to the peace and tranquility of this upper-middle-class neighborhood into which the Starostins would settle during the 1930s. The proximity of two such different regions facilitated Nikolai Starostin's evolution into a liminal figure who could navigate easily among the very poor and very rich. His cousin Ivan (the son of Uncle Dmitri) was a speed skater who had been recruited by the Russian Gymnastic Society (RGO), which had offices nearby. Among those who came to know and help out the neighborhood's young athletes was one Nikolai Giubiev (1868–1942), a buyer from Muir and Merrylees. Giubiev's job required extensive journeys to the capitals of Europe. In some accounts, he was said to be in charge of sporting goods; in others he was supposed to have "traveled in" ladies clothing.[91] A fanatic sportsman, the childless Giubiev would invite local kids over to his apartment, where his wife provided them with tea and jam. He was also vice president, later president, of the ZKS.

It was in this capacity that the younger Andrei had earlier become aware of Giubiev. Andrei had been sent out one day to buy meat for the hunting dogs in their father's care. On the way he had seen a sports magazine in the window of a kiosk. Using his change to purchase this periodical for the first time, Andrei came across a picture of the ZKS soccer team with the elegantly dressed and mustachioed Giubiev by their side. The impression was so strong that Andrei became a fan of ZKS and an admirer of their leader. After 1910, sports magazines, like the St. Petersburg-based *Russkii sport,* became a part of the family's life. Father Peter and Uncle Dmitri, as hunters and lovers of animals, were also great fans of horse racing, covered extensively in this weekly. Football, in much smaller measure, was part of the journal's menu, and the boys gained much of their early knowledge of the game through this modern medium.[92]

Giubiev introduced Nikolai to colleagues at the RGO, which soon recruited Nikolai as a speed skater. Like the ZKS, the RGO had a soccer team in the Moscow league, but, unlike ZKS, it had no home field. Starostin proposed to the society's secretary, Nikolai Mikheev, a member of the Russian Olympic Committee, that a deal be struck with the Shirokovka gang to use the Gori-uchka. At first, the RGO's chief patron, V. N Shustov, owner of the Kolokol cognac factory, was uncertain about how such associations would affect his reputation, but he was ultimately persuaded, perhaps by the fact that many of the Shirokovtsy were surely consumers of his product. With Fan Zakharych serving as a go-between, Nikolai led a well-dressed but petrified delegation of gentlemen-sportsmen into the Presnia's center of sin. Starostin proposed that the RGO would clean up the grounds, build locker rooms, and use the field one day a week. The rest of the time the "turf" could return to its "normal" activities. For a sizable rent the leaders of the Shirokovka agreed to the deal. "You'll play cards, and we'll play football, like good neighbors," said team captain Mikhail Petukhov. The harmonious feeling of the moment was soon undermined when Mikheev, upon leaving the Goriuchka, noted that his wallet had been stolen. An angry and embarrassed Fan Zakharych was forced to intervene and retrieve the item, to Starostin's considerable relief.[93]

The work was soon done, and the day arrived with much excitement. Nikolai was to make his organized football debut in the yellow and black of the RGO. The night before, in another male rite of passage, the brothers had laid out Nikolai's uniform on his bed. They had gone about their task with what Andrei described as "the kind of tenderness and love reserved only for a wedding dress. The next morning on a beautiful summer day, we led our groom to the altar. The church was the Goriuchka. The bride was the game."[94] Unfortunately, on that beautiful summer day, the altar was occupied by a dead horse belonging to Fan Zakharych. The deceased beast was removed from the field of play and buried. Once play started, the day did not go well for the RGO, which lost, or for Nikolai, who could not keep up with the speed of his older opponents. The entire spectacle became bizarre when the dead horse's corpse began to expand under the summer heat, causing the burial mound to rise. At later games, the Shirokovtsy began to show up in order to root for their "co-tenants." They did, however, have the disconcerting tendency of beating up visitors who had the temerity to win, requiring RGO players to intervene for the protection of their opponents. Once they were told this sort of behavior was frowned upon in official league circles and could sever what had become a profitable relationship, the local gangsters were good enough to desist.[95]

There is some uncertainty about just when this incident actually occurred. Determining whether this bit of local color took place just before or just after the revolution is important, as it speaks to the likely veracity of the brothers' separate accounts. Nikolai claimed it occurred after the revolution in 1918, a time when the RGO still existed and league play continued, albeit at a reduced level with the outbreak of civil war. Andrei, who also paid little attention to matters of chronology, offered several more detailed accounts that, most likely, could not have taken place after the Bolshevik victory. There would have been no *gradonachalnik* for Uncle Dmitri to complain to in 1918, and the owner of a cognac factory, had he not emigrated, would have had a lot more important things to worry about than his reputation. In the deprived conditions of the civil war, even its first summer, it is difficult to imagine resources being made available for the construction of so unnecessary a facility as a football field, especially one paid for with money from a private source. Additionally, the gangster activity of the Goriuchka would have been less lively and conspicuous during 1918, and well-dressed gentlemen would have more likely tried to procure many other things from criminals than the use of a vacant lot.

The richer context of Andrei's version makes it considerably more convincing than Nikolai's brief account. In 1983, the chronologically challenged Soviet journalist Leonid Gorianov did go so far as to note that Nikolai's first game had preceded the revolution, but he offered no precise date. Andrei obliquely dated these events as 1918 in his final memoir, published posthumously, but quite likely he was not in Moscow in the summer of 1918, since younger members of the family were evacuated to their village with the outbreak of civil war. Given the detail with which he described these events, it is likely he was actually present at Nikolai's debut.[96] Additionally, Andrei mentioned that Nikolai was fourteen at the time of his football debut, which, given the commonly cited but incorrect date of Nikolai's birth (1902) would set the event in 1916.

This, however, raises another set of problems. It is difficult to imagine Nikolai playing his first game of elite soccer at such a young age. Even a future star would have found it tough going, as he did, against the grown men with whom he played. They were not stiffs. A few of the players that day, most notably Konstantin Kvashnin (1899–1982), went on to have distinguished sporting careers. Perhaps, then, Nikolai was not so young at this moment. There was always a mystery swirling around the birth date of the "great football patriarch"—confusion the eldest Starostin brother did little to clear up. Previously uncited archival sources from army and police files as well as materials from the Soviet state sports committee give 1898 as Nikolai's date of birth. If this version is correct, it means his organized sports debut occurred when he was eighteen, a much more plausible age.[97]

The Starostins' stories became part of what can be called "Spartak lore." I have discussed the logical gaps and factual errors in their accounts not to discredit them but rather to introduce the necessary caution that must be used in reading any memoir. Memories fade. People tell stories about themselves so often they come to believe them. In this sense, the Starostins' failings are normal and human. Consciously or unconsciously, they were creating an image of Spartak as a team that came from the mean streets of Moscow. In the process, millions of ordinary workingmen came to identify with them, regardless of the precise veracity of their accounts. By stressing the spontaneous and genuine character of their team's origins, they were emphasizing their own independence to later audiences.

## The Presnia and the Revolution

When the tsar was overthrown and the Provisional Government installed in 1917, the worlds of both elite and street football did not come to a sudden halt. Even the Bolshevik victory in October did not stop the game. None of the Starostins' multiple accounts gives a great deal of attention to what many thought were earth-shaking events. Gorianov's works simply describe such young men as the Kanunnikovs, Artem'evs, Starostins, and their friends as welcoming the new government. Only Ivan Artemev, an actual Bolshevik, appears to have taken part in the events, along with his brother, Petr. Nikolai Starostin does mention that his "liberal" father had welcomed both revolutions and had gone to the center of Moscow to observe the demonstrations during October. The names of these future soccer stars, however, do not appear in the memoir accounts of those who defended the barricades in the Presnia, nor are they mentioned in the rich Western and Russian literature on the revolution in this highly active district.[98]

The Prokhorov plant had been a center of militancy throughout the year. To the extent its workers supported any political party, they preferred the populist Socialist Revolutionaries (SRs) to either the Mensheviks or the Bolsheviks. In the June elections to the local soviets, the SRs had outpolled combined support for the Mensheviks and Bolsheviks by almost five to one. As documented by Diane Koenker, the political situation in the Presnia as well as the rest of the empire changed dramatically in September after the failure of the counterrevolutionary coup led by the former tsarist general Kornilov. In the September soviet elections, the Bolsheviks were now the leading vote getters in the Presnia. They appear to have been popular with more than just factory laborers, indicating that much of the heterogeneous population of this region chose to support them at this particular moment.[99] Those workers, artisans, clerks, professionals, and others who did not wish to take part in the October days tended to leave the city for the quiet of their home villages. Our young futbolisty stayed at home, however, safely off the streets until the shooting had stopped.

Before the revolution, the vibrant Moscow merchantry along with the rest of the second city's middle-class citizens had created a specifically Russian but thoroughly modern commercial culture with a vast array of new entertainments. If football in Moscow did not become a mass culture industry with tens of thousands of lower-class fans filling stadiums on a weekly basis, it did become a healthy participant activity for many members of the new Russian elites. Their example had the positive consequence of causing exercise to trickle down to a variety of subordinate social groups, who took up the game despite the many obstacles. Members of both groups were cementing their place in the city, creating new urban identities by engaging in what was a modern urban pastime.

At a time of dizzying social and cultural change, young soccer players were also developing new versions of masculinity by playing this tough, man's game. For Mikhail Romm (1891–1967), an educated Moscow Jew who at one time captained Russia's national team, football was a "hard, manly sporting struggle" (*muzhestvennaia, zhestkaia sportivnaia bor'ba*).[100] Andrei Starostin would later describe soccer as a "manly sport." Peasants looked down upon city dwellers as somehow soft, detached from the land and sexually ambiguous because they were less likely to be married than rural cultivators. Workers who had forsaken the countryside for the city now had to elaborate new urban forms of masculinity. In writing on St. Petersburg proletarians, Steven A. Smith has noted the complexities of this transition and the role sport could play in it:

> The tens of thousands of young males who migrated to St. Petersburg brought with them an essentially "traditional" understanding of masculine identity: male status derived from marriage, work on the land and a form of "embodiment" that emphasized *physical strength and stamina*. In the city, this continued to be a dominant idiom, but it was freed from patriarchal authority. . . . In the urban-industrial environment, by contrast, work, family, and leisure became differentiated sites upon which men constructed their understanding of what it meant to be a man.[101]

Football gave both propertied and unpropertied Muscovites a different way to prove their manhood in a new public space where they could demonstrate physical strength and stamina. These practices did not mean professional men and proletarians found mutual understanding on the playing fields of Moscow. Bourgeois and working-class masculinities were by no means identical. While workers were seeking to break free from peasant masculinities, middle-class men were evolving elite versions of manhood that differentiated them from an aristocracy with historic roots in military service.

If football in prerevolutionary Moscow could sometimes be the shared social pleasure of Lockhart's fantasies, it more often served to remind subordinate groups of their place in a fluid but still very real social hierarchy. It is by no means clear that if a great many more plebeians had played and watched football, they would have been diverted from the class struggle. Even at the Morozov textile plants, those great temples of the early Moscow game, thousands of workers engaged in strikes and violence. Football in late Imperial Russia was neither entirely conservative nor necessarily revolutionary. Like so much else, it was contested terrain. The decisive factors determining victory or defeat, activity or passivity, militancy or indifference were located away from the field of play.

Early Russian football followed the universal patterns of the game's development. The Russian context, however, was decidedly different. Elsewhere this game, invented or imported by the middle classes, was eventually taken over by members of subordinate social groups. In the Russian Empire that process was blocked by a combination of police control and elite resistance to young workingmen (and their younger brothers) who wished to take up a game already played by millions of ordinary people around the globe. On the eve of revolution, there were signs that the kind of sporting evolution that had occurred elsewhere was beginning to take place in Russia. The events of October 1917 simultaneously stopped this process and opened the floodgates for vastly many more Russians to take up the game.

# 2

# Before There Was Spartak, 1917–1935

Between the revolution of October 1917 and the outbreak of civil war in April 1918, the Bolsheviks moved cautiously to implement the promises on which they had based their political victory: land, peace, and bread. The Decree on Land, issued on the second day of Soviet power, addressed the peasants' demands. The Treaty of Brest-Litovsk with Germany, signed in the spring, seemed to deal with the matter of peace. Bread turned out to be another matter. Even further down the list of things to do upon seizing power was a revolutionary policy for football. If there were only a few Bolsheviks among Russia's prerevolutionary futbolisty, there were even fewer players in the party's ranks, especially at the top. When Russia left the world war and was invaded by multiple armies, there were matters far more pressing than soccer.

The assumption of power had been a relatively bloodless process, but the struggle to maintain that power was an altogether different matter. Hopes for a decentralized, democratic socialist order had to be put aside as the Bolsheviks moved quickly to consolidate their control. The increasing authoritarianism that ensued led to a militarization of both society and economy. Some in the party called for a set of militias to defend the revolution, but Leon Trotsky, the new commissar of war, instead demanded the creation of a professional army. Despite some reservations, Trotsky's proposal was accepted, and the new Red Army rapidly took shape.

Like so many other parts of life, sport and physical culture were adapted to meet the needs of the moment. The harsh conditions of the world war had eroded the health and conditioning of the peasants and workers who were drafted into the tsarist army. Now the commanders of the new revolutionary fighting force confronted the same problem. In May 1918, a system of courses and schools of physical education was created to improve the fitness of recruits under a new institution known as Vseobshchee voennoe obuchenie, or Vsevobuch for short.[1] Such important figures in Spartak's subsequent history as the Artem'ev brothers, Konstantin Kvashnin, and Mikhail Kozlov (1895–1964) became instructors in this new organization, which paid little if any attention to soccer.[2]

The operation of Vsevobuch was based on the conviction that physical fitness was essential to success on the battlefield. It is noteworthy that the leadership of the early Olympic movement was studded with generals and admirals who held the same view of the relationship of sport to war, but in the quest for fitter soldiers, not all sports were created equal. Both Vsevobuch and the first Olympians favored events like track and field, swimming, wrestling, fencing, and equestrian sports—all of which had direct military applications. These activities were deemed to be rational and respectable forms of recreation. Soccer, with its unpredictability and occasional violence, appeared ill suited to the training and disciplining of soldiers. The game was something military men, mainly the enlisted, played to let off steam away from those other physical activities that inculcated discipline and respect for authority. Thus, while the sport was eventually included as part of Vsevobuch's training regimen, it played a marginal role in early Soviet official sports practice.

The civil war was accompanied by massive hunger, disease, disorder, and urban depopulation. The ludic pleasures of so spontaneous a game as football, with its unruly, entertainment-seeking fans and often loutish players, fit poorly into the needs of a new regime in peril. This particular war was truly serious business, and fun could be had only at its margins. With time and resources taken up by more pressing matters, principally acquiring food and fighting the White armies, little time remained for play. In cities near the front, primarily Petrograd, there were now even fewer places to play football. To feed the city's starving population, scores of fields were planted with vegetables. Farther away from the battle lines in Moscow the situation was less dire, if far from comfortable. Faced with the trials of fending off hunger, much of the Starostin family, but not Nikolai and Aleksandr, returned to their home village. The need for food forced their father to sell off many of his prized hunting rifles. Soon thereafter, in 1920, Petr Starostin died of typhus, leaving Nikolai the eldest male. The year before, the Artem'evs had lost their father in a fire in Ryazan Province, to which the family, but not Ivan and Petr, had returned to find nourishment.[3] In such difficult conditions, sport in the city seemed an afterthought. If the young men and boys of the Presnia still wanted to play football in such difficult conditions, they, along with their counterparts in other Moscow neighborhoods, had to do so on their own.

The previously existing institutions that had supported Moscow football were left alone. So were their infrastructure, property, and equipment. While some fields were used for military drill, others were still available for games. The old Moscow league continued to operate. Even the traditional Petersburg-Moscow matches went on throughout the civil war. The alphabet soup of clubs—ZKS, KFS, RGO, OLLS, etc.—remained in place. A number of stars of the pre-1917 era stayed on. Still, the biggest change was human. While massive numbers of the propertied men who had played for and run the empire's sports clubs had left, such leaders as Robert Duperont remained, along with Nikolai Mikheev, who stayed on at RGO, and Nikolai Giubiev, who assumed the presidency of ZKS.[4] The foreign colony, however, evaporated, cutting Russia's ties to the motherland of football, Great Britain. New, less privileged social groups, who had been excluded before the revolution, now found the entrances to the playing fields open.

Of course, not all citizens of the new state could take advantage of these limited leisure opportunities. Many of those who had supported the revolution were busy serving in the Red Army. Others could not lace up their boots for fear of arrest, execution, or troops overrunning their playing fields.[5] In depopulated Moscow, shortages of electricity meant tram service did not operate on weekends, when most games were scheduled. Instead, the city's streets saw a multidirectional, pedestrian migration not only of futbolisty but of fans. With some journeys taking several hours, Andrei Starostin recalled the singing of quickly composed "soccer ditties" (*futbol'nye chastushki*) and the telling of all manner of stories, coarse and refined, to combat the boredom of these treks.[6]

Along with everything else, the quality of football deteriorated under the new circumstances. Hundreds of skilled players, referees, and organizers had left. While a significant number of prerevolutionary stars did stay on, not all of the new soccer practitioners had played the game in structured settings. International isolation meant no easily purchased equipment at Muir and Merrylees. Lack of food and fuel must have had an impact on the athletes' energy levels. Free time was also in short supply, but despite the obstacles, the Moscow league was able to maintain a reasonably well-observed schedule, along with a small number of intercity matches. Members of subordinate social groups, who had not been able to afford tickets before the revolution, came out to watch at a time of few entertainment alternatives.

These first, relatively low-key seasons of Moscow soccer were dominated by the prewar power ZKS, still run by Giubiev. Pavel Kanunnikov stayed on at Novogireevo, only to have his team broken up, forcing a transfer to Kruzhok Futbolistov Sokol'niki, far from his Presnia home. He was joined there by his buddy Ivan Artem'ev. ZKS featured several future stars of Krasnaia Presnia, including center half Konstantin Blinkov (1896–1947) and the brilliant eighteen-year-old center forward Petr Isakov (1900–1957), known as "the Professor" for his precise passing and overall vision of the game.[7] With Petrograd under siege in 1918, the traditional intercity match was hastily arranged and held in Moscow. Unable to send its best players, Petrograd uncharacteristically lost to its old rivals 9–1. During the next three years the players from what was now the old capital avenged their defeat. The revolution also produced a significant shift in the ranks of the Moscow selects. The 1918 Moscow side included only four holdovers from 1917, most notably Isakov and Pavel Kanunnikov. They were joined in 1920 by Petr Artem'ev.[8]

**2.1** Petr Isakov. *Spartak Moskva: Of-fitsial'naia istoriia.*

There was also a necessary reordering of the Moscow league. Only nineteen teams were able to contest the championship in 1918, but the number grew significantly by 1921 as the civil war wound down. Pavel Kanunnikov and Ivan Artem'ev had settled in at KFS. Others, like Nikolai Starostin and Konstantin Kvashnin, continued to play for the RGO, but the Goriuchka, with its fences burned for firewood, was gone.[9] The footballing residents of what was now called Krasnaia Presnia could play organized soccer only far from home. While the Zamoskvoretskii region was fairly close to the Presnia, Sokol'niki was a particularly trying journey under civil war conditions. Weekday practices meant long tram rides after work, but the lack of transportation in the city on weekends forced the *Presentsy* to stay overnight with teammates when there were matches on those days.

Finally, late in 1921, with the civil war over, Ivan Artem'ev, the most ardent Bolshevik of the Presnia sports crowd, took the lead in calling for a facility back home in the old neighborhood. Krasnaia Presnia, he reminded the district Komsomol, had been an especially militant place during 1917. He argued that a new organization with its own fields and infrastructure should be created for the gallant, sports-loving workers of revolutionary Krasnaia Presnia.[10] Although Artem'ev surely did not realize it at the time, his demands began a process that led, some fourteen years later, to the creation of the most popular sports team in Soviet history.

## Endeavor, Enterprise, and Entertainment

With the end of the civil war, soccer was no longer a marginal activity, ill suited to the needs of the moment. Instead, the game adapted well to the dramatically changed conditions. After the trials of world war, revolution, and civil war, the new regime faced the enormous challenges of recovery and reconstruction. In some party circles, the exigencies of the civil war had fanned a not always rational ideological exuberance about the imminent achievement of Communism. Always tactically light afoot, Lenin instead realized that with the war winding down, the time had come to shift away from the policies of the war years. With armed conflict no longer dictating state policy, the debate about the future course of the revolution was fully joined.

At the pivotal Tenth Party Congress in March 1921 Lenin announced the new course, the so-called New Economic Policy, or NEP. It embarked on a "strategic retreat" from state control of the economy in favor of a limited restoration of the market. In effect, the young state accepted the limits of its power and asked less of the population.[11] The choice had been made for a slower "transition to socialism," but just how slow was the question that sparked much anxiety and debate for the next seven years. For some, the NEP became a long-term strategy for achieving the regime's goals. Others, impatient for a redirection toward a Communist future, could not wait for it to end. The NEP did succeed in bringing back a considerable measure of prosperity, especially in Moscow, but "the values and behaviors that accompanied this prosperity (dancing, fancy dress, expensive restaurants) were at odds with how Bolshevik moralists imagined communism."[12]

If the NEP was a time of uncertainty and discomfort, it was also an era of great possibility. In the absence of clear blueprints for most of the details of a postrevolutionary society, debates raged across a wide range of human activities. A considerable variety of groups openly debated the proper role of revolutionary culture in a society where a revolution had been made in the name of the masses. Who should be in charge? How innovative should the new forms be? What should be preserved of the old? What would be the role of the consumers, as opposed to the producers, of that culture? Physical culture and sport were part of these arguments, entwined in what turned out to be a multidirectional tussle for the support of the state and the favor of the new Soviet audiences.[13]

Neither the avant-garde intellectuals who sought entirely new forms of expression nor the members of the competing plebeian Proletarian Culture movement had much use for the two predominant models of sport practiced under capitalism. The elitist world of amateur sport and the Olympic movement had excluded workers and women. On the other hand, the practices of professional sport had commodified games and the bodies of those who played them. Of the two models, early Soviet experimentalists were likely to see the many forms of amateur sport as more potentially redeemable than football, which had, it was thought, led the working class away from revolution-

ary politics. As Anatoly Lunacharsky, head of the Commissariat of Enlight-
enment, and a host of others contemplated what to do with sport, football was
something of an afterthought.[14] Nevertheless, the sport fit well with the newly
liberated worlds of popular culture, proletarian and otherwise, that burst forth
in a society where vast numbers of ordinary Soviet women and men could
make their own choices about entertainment, leisure, and recreation.

The change was quick and dramatic. While the state retained control of
what were called the "commanding heights" of the economy, the retail trades,
services, entertainments, and a wide variety of consumer industries were allowed to return to previous or new ownership. Thousands of companies and
stores were created by private businesspeople. The change was quick and dramatic. All sorts of commodities, both luxurious and staple, quickly returned
to newly opened stores and fashion-conscious boutiques.[15] Revived foreign
trade and international tourism brought the USSR back into contact with the
dynamic global cultural flows of the early twenties, and Moscow became the
center of NEP consumerism.[16] The members of this new class of wealthy entrepreneurs came to be called NEPmen (not all were men), and by 1926 there
were as many as one hundred thousand people in Moscow alone who fit this
description.[17]

Not knowing how long the "retreat" would last, this overnight bourgeoisie
spent its gains lavishly and ostentatiously, creating a decadent world of fancy
restaurants, night clubs, casinos, and cafes, which were the scenes of drinking, gambling, dancing, drug taking, and widely varietal sex.[18] Rented Lincoln touring cars prowled the streets. Private cabs, painted with the universal
yellow and black checkerboard pattern, were everywhere. The postwar Jazz
Age with its flappers and fast times found an Eastern outpost in Soviet cities.
Hundreds of private sheet music companies and dance studios opened up.[19]
Soon, the music and dances of the West were being enjoyed in far wider circles than simply those of NEPmen and NEPwomen. Young male and female
proletarians, even party members, joined the action, tangoing and foxtrotting
well into the night at workers' clubs and private parties. The prewar movie industry revived. Alongside the new politically didactic and formally radical
films favored by both the avant-garde and international audiences, another
group of Soviet directors sought to make movies that were comprehensible to
ordinary folk. Nevertheless, high ticket prices and a lack of theaters limited
the expansion of this form of popular culture, on which the state would later
place such high hopes.

Like sports, the movies were a particularly modern form of leisure especially attractive to the young.[20] Both had ties to discredited prerevolutionary
entertainment and business practices; they were also central and visible parts
of the newly global world of highly commercial and increasingly massive popular culture. The international stars created by both forms of entertainment,
such as the actress Mary Pickford and the boxer Jack Dempsey, became famous throughout the world. More important, Soviet audiences could now see
themselves as participants in this new era of global culture.

The NEP turned out to be an environment in which the Starostins, stars in their own right, felt quite comfortable. Andrei, who was fifteen at the outset of this period, recalled this time with special vividness: "The youth of my generation passed in complete contact with the life and morals of this era. Moscow had not long ago been hungry. Now it was full of everything. The number of delicatessens, dairy stores, and vegetable shops grew not by the day but by the hour. The tempo of life sped up, We went to sleep late and got up early." New fashions challenged old ones. Chic clothes could be found at Kuprianov's, fancy shoes at Jimmy's.[21] The restaurants and cafes along Tverskaia became the brothers' haunts. The enormous Praga on the Arbat was revived.[22] The Starostins and their fellow players were regulars at the restaurant of the posh Hotel National. They also frequented the Bear on the corner of Briussovskii Street, the Café Fillipov on Kozitskaia, and the KuKu with its gypsy choruses on Sadovo-Triumfal'aia at the northern edge of the Krasnaia Presnia region. Football players were always welcome at the Skala, where many a "discussion of tactics" was lubricated by a few beers (or stronger stuff).[23] The Skala's owner also loved poetry, and it was there that Andrei Starostin first heard Sergei Esenin and Vladimir Mayakovsky read their work publicly. Outside the restaurants, well-dressed prostitutes patrolled Tverskaia from the KuKu down to Trumfal'naia Place. "Restaurants with closed booths," Andrei Starostin duly noted, "worked day and night."[24]

Horse racing, another raffish pastime, was revived in 1922 under the control of the Ministry of Agriculture, and the brothers, who shared their father's passion for horses, were regular bettors at the track. The Hippodrome on Begovaia Street in the northwest part of the Krasnaia Presnia regularly welcomed a host of celebrities from the stage and literary worlds, most notably that great lover of cavalry horses, writer Isaak Babel', and the orchestra leader and showman Leonid Utesov.[25] Football stars were welcome among such company, and talk would often turn to sport. Although absolutely no evidence exists to confirm any illegal practices, it is not unreasonable to ask whether the betting was limited to horses.

The dubious sporting practice of professional wrestling also revived during the NEP, and Andrei took in as many shows as he could. He went most often to the Nikitin Circus, just north of Tverskaia on Sadovo-Triumfal'naia. Wrestling shows took place in these venues largely because they were the only sizable indoor arenas in Moscow. The sport, in both its legitimate and theatricalized versions, had grown up in the environment of the circus and carnival, surrounded by all the shadiness and drama of those worlds. In time, Andrei became close friends with a host of wrestlers, both foreign and domestic, including the greatest of all Soviet champions, Ivan Poddubnyi. Additionally, as Andrei made clear in his various memoirs, he was no stranger to the insides of casinos and pool halls, especially the luxurious billiard parlor at the Hotel Metropol', where he played against Mayakovsky, Iuri Olesha, Aleksandr Fadeev, Mikhail Bulgakov, and a host of other literary celebrities— all of whom were always eager to talk football with him.[26]

This cornucopia of pleasures—some brought back from tsarist days, others imported from the vibrant postwar West—were expensive and readily available only to the elite elements of NEP society, including businessmen, top party leaders, stage performers, crooks, and high-performance professional athletes. Workers returning to the cities after the travails of the civil war found a variety of profit-oriented businesses operating according to the dictates of what was still a limited labor market.[27] The very proletarians who had supported and fought for the revolution could not take part in the new "good life." Moscow now had fine restaurants, cinemas, and theaters, but it was also a place of unemployment, crowded housing, and strike activity.

Nevertheless, the fluidity of the NEP created a broad range of options for young men, workers included. Identities, too, were fluid during the 1920s, and young people could therefore make their own cultural choices, often to the dismay of their elders. Sport, by its very nature, was just such an activity of the young, and football was the game most attractive to the audience of laboring boys and young men. Others, especially white-collar workers, might have joined in, but the core of the game's public was proletarian. As Konstantin Beskov, Spartak's coach from 1977 to 1988 and earlier a star for Dinamo, described NEP soccer fans, "The public was the simplest possible—working people. They were dressed very simply and pretty much the same, wearing Russian-style shirts and jackets with their pants stuffed into the top of their boots."[28]

While football had become a healthy activity for those youths who played it, it also provided an affordable entertainment for the few women and many men who came to watch games in ever-growing numbers and who were increasingly willing to pay for the privilege. This trend proved highly significant in the semi-capitalist context of the times. Government support for sports clubs and their teams was still minimal, even for those groups founded by the state itself. If this situation created problems, it also gave rise to opportunities, and it turned out that the young men of Krasnaia Presnia, particularly the commercially trained Starostins, were well suited to operating in the NEP's relatively uncontrolled market for entertainments.[29]

Elite soccer in the early Soviet Union came to create stars whose exploits attracted the attention and money of their fellow citizens. The football audience, which had been created before the revolution and maintained during the civil war, now began a steady and dramatic expansion in numbers. Ivan and Petr Artem'ev, along with Nikolai and Aleksandr Starostin, found new room to maneuver in pursuit of their own ends as power relations within the still-evolving state edifice began to shift. The seemingly monolithic structures of the Stalin years were yet to appear. Instead, as Lewis Siegelbaum has written, "The Soviet state evolved after 1917 . . . as a constellation of four functionally distinct subsystems or networks—a military and police state, a civilian state based on the Soviets, an economic state revolving around the commissariats and the trade unions and a political state residing within the . . . Communist Party."[30]

In attempting to form a new sporting institution in Krasnaia Presnia during 1921 and 1922, the young men of the neighborhood would eschew the kind of support from the police and military that would have made sense during the civil war. Instead, their most powerful supporters were elements of the civilian state described by Siegelbaum. The impetus for the creation of the team that eventually became Spartak came not from above but from the streets of Krasnaia Presnia, propelled by a group of young men from the neighborhood. Nikolai Starostin recalled the team as "a small club, uniting people thirsting for football."[31] The spontaneity and even entrepreneurship demonstrated in the team's creation fed a tradition of relative independence, even autonomy, that later became an important part of what can properly be called "Spartak ideology." It is likely that the legend of the club's founding has been embellished with each passing player memoir, and it is entirely possible that some less than legal measures may have slipped from the historical record. Nevertheless, the creation story of what was initially called the Moscow Sport Circle (Moskovskii Kruzhok Sporta, or MKS) became an essential part of Spartak lore.

While the existing accounts are based largely on personal recollections, all confirm that Ivan Artem'ev took the lead in organizing the first sports club in postrevolutionary Krasnaia Presnia. Soccer was to be just one of the activities at this new institution, created with the largely moral support of the executive committee of the Krasnaia Presnia district Komsomol, which included Petr Artem'ev among its members. The initiative, in Andrei Starostin's words, "came from the football players living in the region." Created by neighborhood friends, the future Spartak was like so many of the "Rovers," "Wanderers," and "Rangers" of early British football who traveled from place to place in search of a game. With a chance to play in their old haunts and avoid the rigors of Moscow transportation, local stars who had been playing elsewhere were quick to return home. The Artem'evs and Kanunnikovs, along with Stanislav Mizger and Pavel Tikston, came back from Sokol'niki. Konstanin Kvashnin and Vladimir Khaidin, along with Nikolai and Aleksandr Starostin, switched over from the old RGO, while Viktor Prokof'ev left the Strekozy of Zamoskovorech'e and crossed over the Krymskii Bridge back to the Presnia.[32] This group of experienced and talented players became the core of the new team and its associated club. They took on the tasks of organizing and executing the construction of what became Krasnaia Presnia Stadium.

The site of the future Moscow Sport Circle was a small empty space that had become a potato field and pasture during the civil war. Located near the Lakokraska dye factory in the extreme southeast of the district near the Presnia Gate, this bit of land had belonged to the prerevolutionary Society for Physical Education and was called the "Fizichka."[33] Just to the west was the giant Prokhorov plant, which had been nationalized in 1918 and renamed the Trekhgornaia Manufaktura. Its factory school served as a temporary office for the MKS.[34] The local Komsomol had given permission to build on the Fizichka and allowed the club to move the sizable house of an exiled merchant to the site for offices and locker rooms. Money was another matter. None was forthcoming, and none could be promised in the future. In the face of this dilemma, Artem'ev decided to organize a series of fund-raising concerts in the Prokhorov cafeteria. Many of the futbolisty who where neighborhood celebrities performed songs and dances. Kanunnikov, the Artem'evs, and a newcomer, Stanislav Leuta (1903–1980), all performed, as did Kvashnin, who played the balalaika.[35] As pleasant as the evenings were, it became clear that amateur talent could not draw enough fans to pay for the stadium. To make the shows more attractive, professional actors and other artists were invited to perform. Posters were put up at the major intersections of the district and at factory gates. Pavel Kanunnikov, the group's treasurer, took on the task of selling the tickets personally. A local hero, Kanunnikov used his fame to attract buyers who simply wanted to meet him.

Not all the performances were particularly edifying. For one show, Ivan Artem'ev took a horse and led a bear borrowed from the Nikitin Circus through the district's wintry streets in order to advertise a wrestling match between the bear and all comers, in the finest tradition of village carnivals.[36] After a few such spectacles, however, the Komsomol regional committee began to insist that any evening's entertainment be preceded by "reports" from the party on current affairs and related matters. At times, these political education sessions lasted so long that the planned event could not begin until midnight. Actors who had been engaged for the performance had long gone home, and funds were less plentiful than earlier. The venue was then shifted to the smaller Lakokraska factory, and the fund-raising continued throughout the winter. Finally, according to team legend, Ivan Artem'ev raised the last bit of needed revenue by returning to his native village in Ryazan and selling a cow.

Work began on the sports club's new facility in March 1922. The first step was to move the merchant's mansion, but the logs covering its exterior had been stripped away by thieves and hidden, no doubt to be used for fuel. Artem'ev had learned the hiding place from neighborhood cronies, but soldiers refused to assist in returning the timber. Instead, he and Leuta, borrowing old uniforms and bayonets and armed with their order from the Komsomol, surprised the looters and, at gunpoint, demanded the logs be returned immediately. Still worse, our young sportsmen imposed a "fine" on the terrified thieves, who later had the temerity to complain to the police about Artem'ev and Leuta's act of impersonation. The two were briefly detained but quickly released, their impetuousness forgiven by the authorities. Work went on at a feverish clip. Volunteers in the thousands, led by the players and including many Trekhgornaia workers, were able to move the mansion, erect three rows of seats holding 1,500, and fence in the property. The entire ground could accommodate a few thousand more standees. Facilities for a host of other sports, including gymnastics, track, and weight lifting, were also part of the new complex.[37]

**2.2** Krasnopresenkii Stadium, 1924. *Sto let Rossiiskomu futbolu.*

### Football in the Early NEP

On April 18, 1922, the competitive debut of MKS's soccer team was marked by a "comradely" (*tovarishcheskii*), or "friendly," match against the six-time Moscow champions, Zamoskvoretskii Klub Sporta. In an upset, MKS triumphed 3–2. A 5–1 win over the same opponent five days later made them the talk of sporting Moscow. Placed in class B of the Moscow city championship, the new team, staffed by a host of veterans from class "A," easily won the five-game spring competition. MKS, already known by its fans as "Krasnaia Presnia," also won the fall class B championship, which ended on August 19.[38] In those days, club soccer went no further than the intracity level. What passed for a national championship was contested among city select squads. As proof of MKS's strength, Nikolai Starostin, Pavel Kanunnikov, and Viktor Prokof′ev, despite playing in class B, were named to the Moscow city team, which, in the absence of Petrograd, went on to win the first championship of the Russian Soviet Federated Socialist Republic (RSFSR).[39] Both the city and national championships had a decidedly ad hoc character. No one at any level of authority had a clear idea how best to organize these competitions, and each year different structures were tried. While the city leagues were an annual event, the national championship was held only occasionally.

MKS's auspicious start was all well and good, but the next year brought the first fundamental change to the young Soviet football scene. In the calmer context of the early NEP the state finally sought to put in place a structure for all of Soviet sport. In the process new kinds of sponsoring arrangements had to be developed. The old city leagues were broken up, and the clubs that had been formed before 1917 were disbanded. New entities were created, taking over the previously existing infrastructure. The changes were part of a larger process that witnessed the creation of a Supreme Council for Physical Culture (Vyshii Sovet Fizicheskoi Kul′tury, or VSFK), under the All-Union Central Executive Committee (VtsIK), the most powerful state institution. The council was part of the Ministry of Health headed by N. A. Semashko. Clubs were to be organized on what was called a "territorial-production" basis. To limit the professionalism that had already emerged, teams were not allowed to draw members from all over the city. Instead, all the players on a team were to come from a single district or factory. Sport in the capital came under the control of the Moscow City Soviet of Physical Culture (Moskovskii Gorodskoi Sovet Fizicheskoi Kul'tury, or MGSFK).[40]

The party held that sport was an entertainment that should not be a business with tickets selling for sizable amounts, nor, despite the market mechanisms allowed under the NEP, did the leadership wish to see athletes bought and sold. Yet so appealing an entertainment was football that it eventually became part of the world of commercialized spectacles during the 1920s. In the 1923 season, the structure of the official Moscow city championship changed, with new opponents replacing the disbanded clubs. OLLS, for example, became OPPV (Opytno-Pokazatel'naia Ploshchadka Vseovobucha). SKZ, located close to the Moscow River, was renamed Raikomvod Yakht-Klub. A host of others followed suit. The spring and fall seasons were contested on completely contrasting bases, with Krasnaia Presnia winning an Olympic-style knockout tournament in the spring and finishing last in a regular league setup that fall when its best players were summoned to the national team for a tour of Scandinavia.[41]

In all, the club played only nine official Moscow league matches, but this did not mean the players remained idle. Between the twenty-ninth of April and the twenty-first of October, Krasnaia Presnia's first team took part in a total of fourteen "friendlies." On May 20, they played a 2–2 draw in Orekho-Zuevo against what was now called the Tsentral'nyi Orekho-Zuevskii Proletarskii Futbol'nyi Klub (TsOZPFK). Ten thousand fans were in attendance. While figures for the other thirteen games are not available, the purpose of these events was clearly the making of money. Neither the state nor many factories were yet in the business of lavishly sponsoring sports teams. As Nikolai Starostin made clear in his 1986 and 1989 memoirs, written during glasnost, ticket sales were the sole source of his team's income, a fact omitted from his earlier works. The price of a ticket was still fairly low (forty-five kopecks for standing room), and the crowds were usually smaller than the gathering at the beautiful ground near the old Morozov factory. Krasnaia Presnia played five matches outside the city, allowing the Moscow club to fill its coffers while giving provincial fans a chance to see what then passed for big-time football in the USSR.[42]

Eventually tours became an important revenue stream for the best teams. Later in the decade, games were organized as far away as central Asia and the Caucasus.[43] In the process, players, who all still held jobs, were often away from work for several months, requiring that they be compensated, if only to make up for lost wages. Such payments, called "broken time" in Britain, had been one of the classic fiddles of so-called amateur sport all over the world.[44] While they had formally rejected the professional-entertainment model, Soviet sports authorities were not able to avoid the market dynamics surrounding human activities that attracted sizable audiences. Each year, official games were consistently outnumbered by exhibitions. Interestingly enough, even when the NEP ended and the market for entertainments changed, the practice of money-making comradely matches continued until the very end of Soviet power.

Systematic information on friendlies is available only for Spartak and its predecessors, and that material has been gathered only recently. Complaints often appeared in the press about profit-making trips conducted by several other teams. Dinamo toured the northern and southern Caucasus in 1928, but it is impossible to determine whether Krasnaia Presnia was more active than others in this arena.[45] While more exhibition games were played than official contests, scarcely any mention was ever made of the extent of the practice in Soviet-era accounts of the game's history. Episodically, authors have mentioned an exhibition held here or there. Certainly, when big-time teams came to provincial centers, the local press made no attempt to hide these events—quite the contrary—but until now we have not known just how widespread the practice was and how much time and energy it consumed.

Initially, the goal of the teams was surely simply survival, but once significant crowds began to show up, the possibilities were not lost on the parties in question. When finally a full-time professional league was organized in 1936, the diet of regularly scheduled matches increased significantly, and provincial teams were eventually guaranteed regularly scheduled visits by the giants of the Soviet game. Until then, it would seem, the demand for soccer—like that for most desirable consumer goods—far outstripped the official supply. The practice of numerous friendlies followed patterns that had appeared throughout the world, with haphazardly organized matches the rule rather than the exception until the establishment of officially sanctioned and organized leagues.

Still, NEP football was never fully professionalized. The majority of players held jobs. In the early twenties, Andrei and Nikolai repaired tractors. Kanunnikov sold sporting goods. At the same time, Soviet soccer was not purely amateur either. Mikhail Sushkov, a star for Raikomvod Yacht-Club and Trekhgorka, described the character of soccer during the twenties:

> Football [was] an abundant soil for all kinds of machinations. . . . You can construct an underground *totalizator* . . . for betting on horses and teams. . . . It is business and the excitement around the game is much like what happened in the West. You could finance a team, free its players from work, put them on the field and have a big advantage over your opponents. This was against the wishes of the authorities. [It was] an underground football black market.[46]

Given the need to generate funds on their own, teams understood that they had to play well, and in order to play well, they needed to attract good players. Stars had been part of the prerevolutionary soccer scene, and the twenties were no different. Rules concerning player transfers were vague, and clubs competed for the services of the talented. In one celebrated case during 1922, Petr Isakov sought to leave his old club, ZKS, which, unusually, objected to the transfer. The Professor was forced to sit out the initial season of the new Moscow league and postpone until 1923 his move to Krasnaia Presnia.[47] While neither of the two memoir-writing Starostins went into detail about Krasnaia Presnia's business methods, it soon become clear that Nikolai's deal-making abilities were crucial to the club's success in signing stars. In 1923, at the age of twenty-five, he was named captain.

In those days, the captaincy also involved the roles of coach and general manager. While Mikhail Romm, one of the early Soviet Union's few trained soccer coaches, described Nikolai as a "born organizer," Starostin himself simply remarked that his "organizational abilities had been noted." On another occasion, he attributed his talents to his father's early death in 1920. As the eldest son, he had become the head of a large family with six children, inculcating a strong sense of responsibility.[48] Once Nikolai was picked for the Moscow selects and later the national team, he was named captain of those sides as well. These positions brought him into contact with both soccer-loving NEPmen and important political figures, contacts that came to benefit his club as well.

Krasnaia Presnia was, of course, not the only significant team in Moscow soccer. Rivalries have always been crucial to the success of any spectator sport, and during the 1923 season, Krasnaia Presnia was confronted with a new foe that eventually became its most hated and feared opponent, on and off the field. The Dinamo Sport Society was founded on April 18, 1923. Ignoring the so-called territorial-production principle of organization, the new organization was neither a neighborhood club nor a factory team. Founded and supported by both the regular and secret police and responsible to Feliks Dzierzhinskii, head of the Cheka, Dinamo was called a voluntary sport society (*dobrovol'noe sportivnoe obshchestvo*, or DSO). Maintaining the close relationship between state power and sport first pursued by Vsevobuch, Dinamo also inherited much of Vsevobuch's infrastructure and personnel. Unlike Krasnaia Presnia, Dinamo was to be a national organization, designed to raise the physical fitness of the nation's guardians of order. Initially, anyone who shared the organization's goals could join, but after a few years, membership was restricted to employees of the Ministry of Internal Affairs.[49]

Soon after Dinamo's founding meeting in the capital, branches were opened in several provincial cities, including Penza, Ryazan, Petrograd, Rostov, Nizhni Novgorod, and Astrakhan. Sections were formed in a number of sports, with particular attention given, not surprisingly, to rifle and pistol shooting. Dinamo's emphasis on sports with military and police applications did not mean the new nation's most popular game was ignored. One of the new group's first steps was the formation of a *pokazatel'naia* (demonstration) soccer team in Moscow.[50] By the end of the decade, Dinamo became the Soviet Union's best-endowed sports club, and support from the state budget was more substantial than that received by any other sports group. The construction of the USSR's first modern stadium in 1928, undertaken by and named for Dinamo, was emblematic of its status.

Initially, however, the young government had few resources to devote to physical culture and related practices. To fund its activities and provide equipment for its thousands of athletes, the Dinamo Society, in the spirit of the NEP, opened a network of sporting goods stores throughout the country. Other commercial activities, including friendlies for Dinamo soccer teams, helped support the new group's work. As in the case of Krasnaia Presnia, ticket sales were an important source of money. By 1925, all this buying and selling had come to embarrass and repel the society's antimarket leadership. Profit making was reined in.[51] Later, important operating differences would emerge between Dinamo and Spartak's predecessors, but in the early 1920s both organizations faced similar problems and found similar ways to stay afloat.

In soccer, Dinamo sought to compete successfully with Krasnaia Presnia from the outset. Fiodr Chulkov, a veteran goalie, was asked to assume the task of putting together a team. Chulkov chose experience:

> I gave some thought to what kind of a team we should form. . . . It was possible to assemble a young, frisky team from the Komsomol section of the GPU. But with that kind of a team you wouldn't achieve much. You could not overcome mastery with the will to win, no matter how great it was. It was difficult to invite players from other teams. Our collective had just been formed and had no reputation. We decided to invite declining but still well-known players to our first team.[52]

Despite the seeming modesty of Chulkov's designs on other teams' players, the most curious episode in Dinamo's first year of existence came after the end of the 1923 season when Ivan Artem'ev was lured away from the Krasnaia Presnia club he had done so much to found.[53] While the elder Artem'ev's Bolshevik political sympathies may have played a role in his transfer, this is far from clear. Curiously, though Ivan was joined at Dinamo by Krasnaia Presnia's all-star attacker, Dmitri Maslov, Artem'ev's equally militant—not to mention talented—younger brother, Petr, stayed at Krasnaia Presnia. The few existing accounts of this episode are confusing. Just how active Chulkov was in effecting the move is unclear; after all, Ivan's name did not appear on a list of those who first received invitations from the new "bully on the block." In his final memoir, Nikolai Starostin suggested that becoming captain in 1923, he had inadvertently insulted Ivan by not naming him to the starting eleven for an important but unspecified match.[54] More likely, Artem'ev was recruited by Dinamo during the RSFSR selects' successful autumn tour of Scandinavia.[55] Indeed, Nikolai's 1969 and 1986 memoirs contradict his 1989 account, noting that he became captain of Krasnaia Presnia only after Artem'ev had left.[56] More probably, a true political believer like Artem'ev, while attracted to the goals of Dinamo, was especially interested in the drama of starting yet another new club.[57]

As for why Ivan's equally Bolshevik younger brother, Petr, stayed with Krasnaia Presnia, it is perhaps best to remember that during the twenties the rivalry between Dinamo and the future Spartak was not as intense as it would
later become. Indeed, in 1927, Ivan, then thirty-two, returned to join his old
mates for a season but played little and left the next year.[58] It may appear at
first glance that a powerful national organization created by the state from the
top down had been able to poach the star of a local neighborhood team, built
from the bottom up. Was this a sign of what Moshe Lewin has called the "state
swelling up"?[59] If this was the case, those in the neighborhoods would not
prove entirely defenseless. Nikolai Starostin may have lost this early battle,
but he was not without resources in the struggle for soccer supremacy and
fan favor.

Dinamo was not the only early Soviet sports organization that sought to
play on a national level. A year before the formation of the police club, a far-
reaching and ambitious sports organization emerged in Petrograd, led by local
Komsomol members. This group's name was, of all things, "Spartak." This
first Soviet Spartak took over most of the prerevolutionary clubs in the old
capital and soon had branches in other towns as well. Its work in soccer was
supplemented by a wide range of commercial activities, including stores and
publications. All these enterprises filled the group's coffers and permitted it
to attract top athletes in a wide range of sports. In the words of Aksel' Vartanian, Russia's leading historian of the game, "sport throughout the Soviet
Union was under the threat of complete Spartakification."[60] The challenge
roused those in the trade union movement to contest Spartak's growth.
Moscow's Komsomoltsy also resisted Spartak's attempts to spread its influence to the capital. They found supporters at the highest levels of the party,
who cracked down on Spartak's business activities. The first Spartak, very
much a child of the NEP, had challenged the wrong interest groups and died
a slow but certain death. Its entrepreneurship had been too blatant, its board-
inghouse reach too long.

The growth of soccer and the kind of money and privilege it could generate made the sport one form of a popular culture that discomfited members of
the government, particularly in the ministries of education, health, defense,
and interior. Many intellectuals in the party, following Lenin, had historically
mistrusted the spontaneity of the uneducated masses even as they wished to
serve them. For these figures, football, when watched rather than played,
seemed dangerous. It brought together several thousand members of less than
fully cultured social groups in an irrational and uncontrollable spectacle that
aroused emotions and often ended in violence.[61] For the guardians of order,
there seemed to be no shortage of pathology in the soccer world. Players, especially stars, were in a position to seek greater privileges, higher compensation, and better traveling conditions. City selects and even the newly formed
national team were not above making such demands just before taking the
field. Krasnaia Presnia stayed in the luxurious Hotel Evropeiskaia when the
team played in Leningrad. Player movement became common, and money-

making exhibitions proliferated. In 1925, Krasnaia Presnia's first team played twenty-three friendly matches, while two September matches at an expanded Krasnaia Presnia Stadium each drew ten thousand fans.[62]

At this early stage of Soviet soccer, the discipline of serious conditioning had not yet become a priority, and now that they were decently compensated, players were freer to sample the NEP's good life.[63] The young players of Krasnaia Presnia, it turned out, adapted perhaps too well to this set of circumstances. In their recollections, all shared an enormous sense of excitement that after the restrictions and deprivations of the prerevolutionary years, they were now playing organized football with good equipment on nice fields before large and appreciative crowds of spectators. Their names appeared in newspapers and magazines. Their faces were known to strangers.

It is fair to attribute a good measure of Krasnaia Presnia's success to the multiple talents of Nikolai Starostin. On the field he had emerged as a dangerous and speedy attacker out on the right flank, becoming an unofficial Soviet all-star by 1924. After Pavel Kanunnikov refused the captaincy when Artem'ev left, Nikolai was invited to lead the team. Starostin quickly proved adept at acquiring new players while navigating the various worlds of NEP politics to find influential sponsors and supporters. Never particularly savvy in the technical aspects of the game, he was able to find able future coaches, like Konstantin Kvashnin, and well-established advisers, including Mikhail Romm and Mikhail Kozlov.[64] The significant numbers of comradely matches could not have gone on without his direction as the team's leader, and it is fair to assume these games provided revenue that made the acquisition of talent a good deal easier.[65] As he had already demonstrated before the revolution, Starostin was a highly capable and energetic networker who could bring together the various elements needed for sports success.

Early on, Nikolai had formed an alliance with Nikolai Pashintsev, head of the Krasnaia Presnia regional party executive committee. Pashintsev served as the team's political protector through several incarnations and affiliations until the early 1930s. The constant changes in the official as well as unofficial organization of sport created a minefield that Pashintsev helped the team navigate. At the same time, the Starostins' education at commercial academies surely enhanced their ability to create the kinds of sporting spectacles that attracted ticket-buying crowds. The fact that all of Krasnaia Presnia's players had come from the district had initially been a source of pride, but the pressures of competition soon forced Starostin to cast his net wider for talent despite the restrictions of the moment. On June 27, 1925, the team played the Odessa city selects in Moscow, winning 2–1. So impressed were they by Valentin Prokof'ev (1905–1939), Odessa's speedy left wing, that they recruited him immediately. Despite the prohibitions against midseason transfers, Prokof'ev somehow appeared for Krasnaia Presnia in a regular season Moscow league game on August 9.[66]

Their new left-winger only added to Krasnaia Presnia's reputation as an attacking side. Anchored in the back by Aleksandr Starostin's defense, with

Konstantin Kvashnin and Petr Artem'ev at halfback, Nikolai was free to roam the right flank feeding Isakov, Kanunnikov, Prokof'ev, and Konstantin Blinkov, who had joined the team in 1924 from PKMGSFK (Pokazatel'naia Komanda Moskovskogo Gorodskogo Soveta Fizicheskoi Kul'tury).[67] In an era when the point of football was to score more goals than one's opponent, Krasnaia Presnia scored goals. It was an offensive side that understood the need to entertain an audience. Still, the accounts of this period and the few minutes of available film footage provide no basis for a more precise description of their approach to the game.

The creation of stars proved to be another important part of marketing a team. Young boys admired their manly footballing heroes as they constructed their identities as urban working-class youths in a time of fluidity and uncertainty. Local kids and their dads were willing to pay for the privilege of watching these stars, and Krasnaia Presnia provided its fair share of idols. Anatoly Akimov (1915–1984), who would become Spartak's starting goalie in the 1930s, grew up in Krasnaia Presnia. Starting with the 1923 season, Akimov's father regularly took him to games. The young Anatoly's hero was Pavel Kanunnikov, who was often seen in the neighborhood. He and his pals harbored the belief that Kanunnikov had a tattoo on his left leg inscribed with the words "I shoot but do not answer for it." According to Andrei Starostin, the tattoo read, "I shoot. I kill." Of course, no such tattoo ever existed, but so powerful was Kanunnikov's shot and so great his stature that the legend persisted well after his career ended. At one game, which did not involve Krasnaia Presnia, Akimov, then ten, was about to be thrown out by an usher who thought he had stolen his ticket. A crowd had gathered around the crying boy when suddenly Kanunnikov appeared from nowhere, ascertained the situation, and told the usher that he had in fact given Akimov the ticket in question, although as Akimov made clear in his memoir, the two had never met until that moment.[68]

Such stories were part of the mythologies that swirled around sports heroes. Similarly, placing players on the Moscow selects and the national team was a sign of an athlete's aura and his club's success. Kanunnikov, Petr Isakov, Dmitri Maslov, and the Artem'ev brothers all took part in the hugely successful tour through Scandinavia, Germany, and the Baltic taken by the RSFSR selects in 1923.[69] Along with massive defeats of worker sports clubs, this excursion included a victory over the Swedish national team, which was officially amateur but was composed of representatives of what were called "bourgeois" clubs. Trips of this sort took precedence over local city championships, which went on even if a team's best players were out of the country.[70]

Requiring teams to play regular league matches without their best players was but one part of the chaotic nature of the Moscow city championship. Each year the competition was rearranged, creating enormous confusion. In the early twenties, Krasnaia Presnia was the strongest team in the Moscow league, although it did not dominate its rivals, who also won titles from time to time. Dinamo, during this period, was still struggling to establish itself, usually finishing in the middle of the standings. Ironically enough, its fortunes would

**2.3** Krasnaia Presnia takes the field against Norwegian workers' team, 1922. *Spartak Moskva: Offitsial'naia istoriia.*

begin to change after 1927, when Ivan Artem'ev left the team and went back to his old comrades. Artem'ev was replaced by the tall and mobile Fyodr Selin, a Soviet international. One of the few players of his era (or any Soviet era) who played well with his head, Selin was known as the "king of the air."[71]

International competitions were limited during the 1920s by the new state's diplomatic isolation. The Soviets were not members of soccer's international federation, known by its French acronym as FIFA (Fédération Internationale de Football Association). Games against foreign teams, especially at the level of national sides, could not take place without FIFA's sanction, which was never forthcoming. The Soviet-supported Communist Red Sport International, which competed intensely with a similar group organized by Social Democrats based in Lausanne, could provide competition only against workers' sports clubs, just a few of which could give Russian sides a game. Competition with other national teams was restricted to the less isolated Turks, who did have the advantage of being members of FIFA. The first of several interwar meetings between the two postrevolutionary nations took place on a frigid November day in Moscow with fifteen thousand fans packing the old ZKS ground to see a 3–0 Soviet victory over the shivering, underdressed Turks. Petr Isakov was Krasnaia Presnia's only representative on this first version of the USSR national team. A year later, when the Soviets returned the visit, he was joined by Kanunnikov and Petr Artem'ev.[72]

International matches in Moscow, along with significant intercity games, drew large crowds, providing publicity for players who could then attract fans to regular league games and friendlies. Accounts of this period describe the highly politicized process of choosing such squads. Here the early Soviet experience was not much different from that of any other nation. In trying to have their players named to national teams, the institutions supporting clubs sought to enhance their prestige and extend their visibility and attractiveness to the football audience. Even at this early stage of Soviet history, the creation of heroes was part of the game, and the state was not alone in this process. Already adept at navigating in the highest councils of the sport, Nikolai Starostin proved capable of using his position to protect his club's interests at this level as well. Players on various select teams became celebrities, enjoying the fruits of their fame, and the chance for fans to see such international stars in turn enhanced the attractiveness and popularity of their clubs.

If young men looked up to soccer players and sought to emulate them and older men wished to be their friends, what about the other part of the audience? The dashing Starostin brothers may well have attracted many female as well as male fans, but the subjects of sex and women simply never appear in the Soviet-era sources. The numerous anecdotal and impressionistic accounts of the soccer audience do make it appear overwhelmingly male. Nevertheless, as Andrei noted, he and many of the other top players could well afford to appear in public stylishly dressed, and they moved comfortably in the fast crowd of the NEP years. Yet the only discussions of what went on in those fashionable restaurants on Tverskaia (especially those with closed booths) concern exclusively male conversations. Nikolai, who had a reputation as a straight arrow, constantly warned his younger brothers about the temptations of hanging out with "bohemians," and Andrei did describe playing games in a hungover state after nights of foxtrotting and tangoing.[73] One must assume he did not dance alone.

Still, women appear in the soccer literature only as wives or girlfriends. Pictures of them in players' memoirs make it clear that the almost universal practice of male sports stars' marrying physically attractive women held true in the Soviet Union as well. What may have occurred while teams were on the road, the great temptation of all sportsmen (and later women), was never mentioned in the available sources. What can be stated clearly, however, is that the Krasnaia Presnia football team had become a highly visible part of the Moscow scene, and the Starostins and their teammates were happy to accept the rewards of the station they had attained through their efforts.

### Changing the Rules; Changing the Game

By 1925, the NEP had created a new stability. Agriculture had been restored to prewar levels relatively quickly. Eventually both producer and consumer industries caught up as well. A rough balance had been achieved, but it was highly tenuous, both economically and politically. With the difficult task of recovery more or less accomplished, it now became necessary to ask what came next. In the light of the failure of several attempts at world revolution, was the

NEP still a viable road map for the ultimate goal of a Communist society and economy, or should it be abandoned? Was Stalin's compromise slogan of "socialism in one country" a realizable project or a mere word game?

These questions were debated by a party leadership that was sharply divided along both personal and political lines. The bulk of the party rank and file had coalesced around Stalin and Nikolai Bukharin in favor of a continuation of the NEP. For the ideologically sophisticated Bukharin, the commitment to a set of policies, particularly those favoring the peasantry, was no doubt sincere. For Stalin, it may have been more important that his great political opponent, Leon Trotsky, along with the Left Opposition, be defeated. The Left had wished to see the NEP ended and the construction of socialism begun, but by 1927, this wing of the party had been defeated and Trotsky expelled. The intersection of the debates over the pace of industrialization and the succession struggle bought more time for the NEP's experiment in semicapitalism. Nevertheless, both the party and society as a whole remained anxious about the future. Sensitive to these concerns, elements within the Soviet leadership began to scrutinize the economic and cultural practices that had come to characterize the NEP. Attempts to rein in certain excesses did not immediately stem the flood of popular culture. There were even more films, soccer games, jazz concerts, casinos, fine fashions, posh restaurants, and general jollity in the second half of the decade. The period was not called "high NEP" for nothing.

By late 1927, however, the surface calm of high NEP began to unravel. The peasantry, allowed to respond to the opportunities of the market, had prospered to the point that many urban dwellers viewed them as the moral and political equivalent of NEPmen. When grain procurement did not meet expected levels, food, once so abundant, became harder to find in the cities. There was a steady erosion of living standards which led to further calls for an end to the NEP.[74] Ironically, with Trotsky removed from the political scene, his views and those of the Left were no longer forbidden topics of discussion. The balance that had characterized the years of recovery was now threatened, and the peasantry received much of the blame. The NEP no longer seemed so convincing a road map to the socialist future. Its fragility had also been exposed when the rupture of diplomatic relations with Britain produced a war scare. If the internationally isolated USSR was to defend itself, it would have to improve its military capacity. This in turn demanded the rapid growth of heavy industry, which necessitated the reallocation of both human and material resources. The enemies of the NEP became more aggressive. The future became more uncertain.

Increased anxiety did not, for the moment, dampen the ebullient spirit of NEP culture. Andrei Starostin, born in 1906, reached maturity in the latter part of the 1920s. His celebrity, along with that of his brothers, provided an entrée to a world of entertainers and creative intellectuals. These figures not only influenced Andrei's personal evolution but expanded the team's base of support outside the imprecise borders of the largely working-class Krasnaia

Presnia district.[75] With highly articulate supporters, the team that would become Spartak acquired a group of talented propagandists who were able to help the Starostins and their colleagues craft an image that expanded the club's popularity. When accused of offering a debased entertainment or engaging in sleazy business practices, the Starostins were able to deflect their critics by invoking an aura of "culture," which in Russian conveyed a sense not only of learning but of respectability.

In 1926, Andrei began a lifelong friendship with Mikhail Ianshin, a star of the Moscow Art Theater. Starostin had been a fan of Ianshin's wife, the gypsy singer Lyalya Chernaia, who sang at the Arbatskii Podval, one of Andrei's favorite hangouts. One summer evening they ran into each other on Tverskaia, and Chernaia introduced Andrei to Mikhail. The two quickly became buddies, with Ianshin taking Andrei under his wing and introducing him to the world of the Moscow intelligentsia, or at least one particularly colorful segment of it. This coterie of friends met almost nightly in the basement of an apartment house at Staropimenovskii Lane. In his 1978 memoir, Andrei recalled "wonderful evenings in the midst of these artists showing their talents to each other. . . . For many years I walked down this small wooden staircase into that large subterranean apartment which became an evening university, an education in aesthetics, ethics and culture in general for a young football player."[76] He soon became a regular at the theater, while Ianshin came to attend important matches and spend time with his pal at the Hippodrome. It would later be said that those wishing to be certain Ianshin was appearing on a given night at the Moscow Art Theater were well advised to check the soccer schedule.

Not everyone, however, was comfortable with the state of elite Soviet soccer. In April 1926, the Moscow City Soviet of Physical Culture sought to reorganize soccer with the aim of controlling the manifestations of professionalism that had already emerged in the sport. Regional sports groupings were now to be broken up and replaced by clubs supported by a trade union or factory. Only the teams of the police and army, Dinamo and OPPV, respectively, were exempt from the new order. Krasnaia Presnia managed to work its way through this new problem thanks to the efforts of its chief patron, Pashintsev, who was then leaving his position with the district party committee to become head of the Food Workers Union (Pishchevik). He was soon followed there by all of Krasnaia Presnia's players, who formed a team appropriately called Pishchevik.[77]

There were pluses and minuses to the new situation. On the positive side, the Food Workers Union had acquired a plot near Petrovsky Park on the far northern edge of the district. In 1923, the Krasnaia Presnia Komsomol had been given control of the parcel, but the lot remained unimproved until Pashintsev arranged its transfer to the union, which promised to build a multisport complex and construct what would then be the Soviet Union's largest stadium. The prospect of more seats meant more tickets and more rubles. On the other hand, some team members feared the move would cause them to

**2.4** Tomskii Stadium. *Spartak Moskva: Offitsal'naia istoriia.*

lose contact with the old neighborhood, even though the new arena was no more than an hour's walk from the old ground near the Presnia Gates.

As things turned out, their fears proved largely groundless. The new stadium, named for M. I. Tomskii, the head of the trade unions, was built as promised. Initially there were places for thirteen thousand spectators. Eight thousand more seats were added a few years later. The team began play there on May 3, 1927, losing a friendly 0–2 against the new team of the Trekhgornaia Manufaktura, which had been given the old Krasnaia Presnia stadium, a short stroll from the factory gates. They were also able to assemble a very strong team that included such stars as Mikhail Sushkov (1899–1983) and Evgenii Eliseev (1908–??).[78] Pishchevik's competition with Trekhgorka was intense. Each team won its share of titles in the brief period the two coexisted (1926–1931), but theirs was a friendly rivalry, unlike Pishchevik's with Dinamo. The latter had improved its play by 1928, when it won the Moscow championship, beating Pishchevik on June 17 for the first time ever, by a 3–1 score before twelve thousand fans at Tomskii. Pishchevik, Trekhgorka, OPPV, and Dinamo were the leaders of football in the capital. The success of one or another of these teams depended as much on the vagaries of the constantly changing structure of the Moscow league as it did on the clubs' actual play on the field. Players could be called away for international play at a moment's notice. The result was a maddening inconsistency. Pishchevik was particularly

**2.5** Nikolai Starostin (white jersey) at Tomskii. Fotoagentstvo Sportekspress.

vulnerable to this sporting disease, beating an archrival in one game but falling to some outsider in the next. The club came to be known as a "team of moods" (*komanda nastroienia*), a flaw it carried throughout the rest of its history.

Meetings of the best teams attracted ever bigger crowds, making the game an even larger part of the world of high NEP popular culture. As things turned out, the lads from the old neighborhood had little trouble making the journey to Tomskii on game days. Pishchevik came to feature three of the four Starostin brothers, along with Petr Artem'ev, Kanunnikov, and Isakov. As a result, the club attracted new fans from all over the city. Important matches among the capital's "Big Four," both regular and friendly, routinely attracted ten thousand spectators who paid sixty kopecks to sit or forty-five to stand. This was cheaper than the cinema or theater. Games involving either the Moscow selects or the Soviet national team cost a ruble or seventy-five kopecks and attracted even larger crowds. Tomskii Stadium kept 40 percent of the gate receipts, with each team taking home 30 percent.[79]

In 1926 and 1927, it had appeared that the antiprofessionalism reforms were having some bite, for the number of exhibition games fell off dramatically. By the end of the decade, however, Pishchevik was back to playing twenty or more exhibitions, in some cases traveling far afield. By 1928 the sport had become a much bigger business than ever. If the number of money-making exhibition games is any indication, it appears the top teams' sports entrepreneurship actually outlived the market conditions of the NEP, which was formally abandoned in 1929.[80] The construction of Dinamo Stadium greatly expanded soccer's possibilities. Built for the first Soviet Olympic-style sport festival, the 1928 Spartakiad, the new arena had thirty-five thousand seats and room for another twenty thousand standees. The semifinals and final of the soccer competition at the Spartakiad filled what the press called "a giant concrete bowl" as the Moscow selects, featuring Aleksandr and Nikolai Starostin, won the title.[81] Another quarter of a million ticketless fans milled around outside in Petrovsky Park. The final was the first sports event broadcast across the USSR. During the course of the Spartakiad, no other sport came close to filling Dinamo.[82]

The construction of Dinamo Stadium put the USSR, despite its isolation, at the forefront of a worldwide expansion of spectator sport in the twenties. In 1923 Yankee Stadium, with sixty-three thousand seats, began business in New York, while the hundred thousand–seat Coliseum opened in Los Angeles. That same year London's Wembley Stadium was built. It has been estimated that a quarter of a million people overflowed its one hundred thousand–seat capacity the first time its gates were opened. In Paris the sixty thousand–seat Parc des Princes was often filled as well. Dinamo became the national stadium, the chief site for any match of importance. Over time, as many as ninety thousand would cram into every one of its nooks and crannies. It still stands today. Ten years ago, its wooden benches were replaced by modern plastic seats, but, shockingly, only thirty-six thousand of those seats could fit into the giant concrete bowl.

The 1926 attempt to rein in football's excesses had clearly failed. More or less on its own, a spectator sport industry had emerged that undermined the ways the state sought to make use of sport. In 1925, the party had embraced elite competitive sport, but in doing so it sought not to create thousands of fans who merely watched high-performance athletes but instead to inspire their audiences to exercise, becoming fitter soldiers and better workers. The structure of elite sport during the NEP did not, however, further this process. In 1927 the national sports newspaper, *Krasnyi sport,* a publication of the All-Union Council of Physical Culture, complained about a hypothetical worker named Ivan Spiridonovich:

> What could be Ivan Spiridonovich's relationship to sport? Does he run the hundred meters or pole vault? No, he is a soccer player, and not the kind of player who runs on the field in shorts. Quite the opposite, he is part of the public. . . . By his profession Ivan Spiridonovich is a metalworker, but in his true essence, he is a food worker [*pishchevik*]. "The food workers, there's a football team," he says. And sure enough the food workers do have a team.[83]

In the context of Spartak's history it is particularly significant that the author of the hypothetical piece in which the author could have named any team chose Pishchevik. To have named either Dinamo or the army team as Spiridonovich's favorite would only have confused the message. Rather, in attacking harmful practices in sport, the author made his point by picking on a civilian team, sponsored by a trade union, which had succeeded in attracting large numbers of ticket-buying supporters. Nor can it have been an accident that of all the civilian teams the newspaper should single out Pishchevik, run by the commercially trained Nikolai Starostin. Football apparently had the capacity to induce the dreaded "false consciousness" in the minds of the working class. Spiridonovich was supposed to be a metalworker, considered by the party the most militant and politically reliable segment of the proletariat. Yet the soccer virus had so addled poor Ivan's brain that he instead thought he was a food worker, in official eyes a much less respectable trade.

This attack was not the only criticism of big-time soccer to appear in the press in 1927. Two official histories of Spartak refer to an article published that year entitled "Do We Need Professional Football?" The author complained that the 1926 reform had failed to remedy the problem of professionalism. While it was true that civilian teams now had to be supported by a factory or trade union, there was no requirement that the players actually work in those industries. Of Pishchevik's leading players only Petr Isakov, who was listed as a worker at the Dukat tobacco factory in the Krasnaia Presnia district, could be said to fit this criterion. Andrei and Nikolai Starostin worked at a tractor repair station, Aleksandr was listed as a worker at Tomskii Stadium, while Kanunnikov sold sporting goods at a department store. None of the other players came close to the more politically respectable occupations of assembly line workers. Somehow the fiction that futbolisty were not being paid seemed easier to preserve if the players were thought to be actual workers in the factories that sponsored their teams. Eventually, this more stringent rule would become a requirement, with a decidedly negative impact on trade union soccer.

On the eve of the 1928 season, the opponents of professionalism were once again disturbed when the Moscow City Council for Physical Culture announced that unrestricted free transfers from one team to another would now be allowed. The concept of athletes selling themselves to the highest bidder, fully in tune with the ethos of the NEP, discomfited those who wished to keep sport under tighter control. When 175 players signed up in response to the opportunity to switch teams, the proponents of greater control were aghast.[84] Pishchevik lost Valentin Prokof'ev to Dinamo. Ivan Artem'ev had left Dinamo the season before to return to Pishchevik. At the age of thirty-two, he had played little during 1927 and now switched to Trekhgorka. The carousel seemed to be spinning out of control. If sport was supposed to teach young people loyalty to teammates and club, football was failing miserably.

The game's problems seemed to reflect the weaknesses that had begun to appear in the entire NEP system. The political forces that led to the abandonment of both the market and the light cultural controls of the twenties did not come entirely from above. If Stalin, having consolidated his authority within the party, now came to adopt the program of the Left, he did not do so entirely on his own. As living standards began to deteriorate in the autumn of

1927, large numbers of workers, many of Moscow's soccer fans surely among them, were losing whatever limited patience they might have had with the semicapitalism of an era that had benefited nearly everyone but the revolution's purportedly most ardent supporters.

## The Great Turn

In April 1929 the Sixteenth Party Congress decreed the abandonment of the market in favor of a centralized, planned economy that was supposed to industrialize the Soviet Union swiftly. This was Stalin's "Great Turn." NEPmen who had benefited so abundantly from the market now had to find other avenues for their energies. The ambitious, often unrealistic goals of the first Five-Year Plan ended the conspicuous consumption of the NEP. Living standards declined in the cities. Food became harder to find. The pace of work in the factories became more intense and increasingly dangerous. At the same time, the social differentiation of the twenties gave way to an intense egalitarianism that included a leveling of wages and a variety of affirmative action policies designed to enhance the social mobility of workers.

The difficulties of daily life for the poor that had emerged in the cities were exacerbated when the disastrous decision to collectivize agriculture was made that winter. Peasant resistance proved massive. There was now a new civil war in which the city sought to impose its will on the countryside. With chaos in the villages and a massive labor shortage in industry, peasants flooded into the towns. They were joined in factories and at work sites by huge numbers of female urbanites. The Moscow workforce in industry, transport, and construction increased nearly 130 percent during the first Five-Year Plan.[85] The presence of so many new people changed the character and political role of the old proletariat in ways that were highly problematic. Was this a new working class or just an undifferentiated laboring mass? Did it have the same loyalty to the regime as the old proletariat? As Moscow's population exploded, there was no investment in housing. With few quick improvements in transportation and a deteriorating food situation, life in the capital became much tougher.

The first Five-Year Plan also witnessed a "cultural revolution" from above that put an end to the variety of NEP. Many successful creators of both popular and elite culture came under attack from the partisans of what was supposed to be a newly empowered proletariat.[86] In a broad variety of fields (not just culture), those with talents and knowledge acquired in the prerevolutionary period were discredited, attacked, and dismissed from their positions. Thousands of workers were recruited from factory floors into important functions in industry and the party. Their children found it easier to get into universities. Art, science, film, theater, and music were challenged and forced to revise their styles, practices, and goals in order to support these social changes and produce popular enthusiasm for the production goals of the state.

It is important to remember that not all of these changes took place simultaneously, nor were they fully consistent with one another. The signal for change may have come from above, but many of the period's campaigns struck a chord with Soviet citizens. A wide range of political, economic, and cultural struggles took place in these years of enormous chaos, confusion, and tragedy. Millions died, and other millions changed their social and economic roles overnight. Thrust into all manner of strange situations, those affected by these changes often had no idea of how they should behave.

Football was touched by the changes, but the effect was neither immediate nor entirely clear. The conduct of the games in 1928–1930 was similar to that of earlier seasons. Player movement continued unabated. One might think that a team such as Pishchevik, which operated so successfully in the entrepreneurial atmosphere of the NEP, would have experienced difficulties retaining players in the more controlled world of the first Five-Year Plan, but this was not the case. The party took a while to figure out what its attitude toward sport should be in the new era. It left football relatively untouched. Crowds grew. More weekday games were scheduled, causing large numbers of fans to skip work. As noted above, comradely games became more numerous and required trips farther from home.[87] In August, 1929, *Vechernaya Moskva* complained about the practice: "The basic goal of the majority of football journeys is to make money. They earn their money, divide it up and go home."[88] A ten-day trip by the army team earned each player three hundred rubles. The same newspaper reported, "They play cards, get drunk and spend time with prostitutes."[89]

Despite Pishchevik's success at the box office, the team's performance on the field fell off, and Dinamo came to dominate the Moscow league. As the role of the secret police expanded and as its activities received greater budgetary resources, its sports teams shared in the wealth. Dinamo now was able to attract a galaxy of stars. As the police presence became more onerous in its impact on the lives of ordinary citizens, resentments began to form among the civilian population. Games between Pishchevik and Dinamo became the highlights of each season, drawing twelve thousand in 1928 and twenty thousand in 1929.[90] Even more fans probably took in the 1930 match, held in Dinamo Stadium, but no information on attendance has survived. One newspaper noted that "games between these two teams are distinguished by their rough play."[91] Mikhail Iakushin, who would star for and coach Dinamo, described such clashes as "great events."[92] One must be careful, however, not to read too much into this early stage of the rivalry. The memoirs of players from both teams suggest that the Pishchevik-Dinamo relationship at this time was not as politicized as it would eventually become. Neighborhood and factory were still more powerful influences on team support than the political character of the teams' sponsoring institutions.

The spring of 1930 saw the establishment of a new, more powerful All-Union Council of Physical Culture (Vsesoiuznyi sovet fizicheskoi kul'tury, VSFK). The new organization was directly attached to the Council of Ministers, and its presidium included such stars of the Bolshevik firmament as Lev

Kamenev, Genrik Iagoda, and the Komsomol chief Aleksandr Kosarev—who would become Spartak's chief political patron. The VSFK was especially concerned with limiting the excesses that had crept into the practices of soccer. In 1931, it introduced a new rule that required all players on factory or trade union teams to be actual employees at their factories or members of those factories' trade unions.[93] The measure would prove devastating to such strong factory teams as Trekhgorka, which saw its players dispersed to a number of different clubs. Consistent with the greater advantages given to the structures of force, Dinamo and the new army club, called Tsentral'nyi dom Krasnoi Armii (TsDKA), were exempt from these limitations, which increased their competitive advantage at the top of the Moscow league. At the same time, the importance of trade unions in the larger economic process was reduced. Here the Pishchevik team was particularly challenged by the breakup of the food workers' union into numerous smaller groups.

The Starostins' club then came under the wing of an institution that was part of the Ministry of Trade.[94] This insufficiently studied body, called Promkooperatsiia, took upon itself the task of organizing those who had been unorganized under the NEP. Along with artisans, such once independent contractors as waiters, tailors, taxi drivers, barbers, and, most important, salespeople were forced into Promkooperatsiia. Eventually the new body's control would be extended to the always suspect retail trades, where it played a crucial role in the massively perplexing process of distribution during the Great Turn. Despite such a set of tasks and constituencies, Promkooperatsiia could scarcely be said to have occupied the apex of power and prestige within the changing structure of the Bolshevik regime. It was not part of the police or army, whose powers had been enhanced by harking back to the days of the civil war. Nor did Promkooperatsiia's members comprise a segment of the working class that had ever occupied an especially important position in the eyes of the party. Factory workers, especially male metalworkers, were thought to be the mainstays of the Communist project. By contrast, those who labored in the service sector and in trade had little prestige and were deemed marginal to the revived revolutionary process. In a sense, Promkooperatsiia had gathered the detritus of the NEP in one large, unruly, and politically suspect organization. In the eyes of the new authorities, a team supported by such folk was an imperfect carrier of official values.

Though Promkooperatsiia would eventually become immensely wealthy, it proved ill equipped to the task of sponsoring one of Moscow's stronger soccer teams. Pishchevik's longtime protector, Nikolai Pashintsev, moved from the trade union to the Dukat tobacco company, taking several players with him, most notably Isakov. The next year the Starostins, Leuta, and others came over as well, leaving Promkooperatsiia on the edges of the football scene during the period of cultural revolution. Many have assumed that Dukat (which replaced Pishchevik) took over the pre-Spartak mantle from Promkooperatsiia. In fact the Promkooperatsiia and Dukat were two completely different teams, and Dukat was by far the stronger.

**2.6** Football and industry were closely linked: Donetsk in the 1930s. Fotoagentstvo Sportekspress.

Ironically, though workers may have watched football, it lacked proper proletarian credentials in the eyes of those social levelers who were now on the offensive. The game practically disappeared from the pages of the nation's newspapers, and sport in general played a secondary role in this first frantic phase of "the socialist offensive." A high-performance sport played by an elite few and watched by a passive many (even though "the many" were primarily male working class), soccer undermined the egalitarian goals of this first period of Soviet industrialization. For fans, choosing teams was now trickier. Dinamo may have become suspect in the eyes of the football public because of its ties to the increasingly intrusive secret police. On the other hand, Promkooperatsiia, with its links to the NEP, had its own problems competing with a range of newly created factory teams that briefly won the allegiance of an audience largely preoccupied with the immense tasks of fulfilling the first Five-Year Plan.

Soon, however, it became clear to Stalin and many others in the party that the tasks set for the nation were so unrealistic and difficult that there were indeed some fortresses even Bolsheviks could not storm. Collectivization may have liquidated the kulak and fed the cities, but in many other ways it was a disaster. Faced with possible defeat, Stalin instead declared victory, pro-

**2.7** Football and the factory: Spartak vs. Torpedo, 1935. *Spartak Moskva: Offitsial'naia istoriia.*

claiming that the goals of the plan had been fulfilled in four years. A second Five-Year Plan was announced with more modest and realizable aims. The regime backed away from the abyss. What had been a time for work and work alone now was followed by a period of greater, if not extensive, leisure.

### The Birth of Spartak

As Nikolai Starostin has recounted the story, quite suddenly and unexpectedly, Pashintsev, the Dukat team's protector, was fired from his position at the tobacco plant. Starostin never furnished a reason for the dismissal, nor did he provide a date for this event, which most likely took place early in 1934. Following Pashintsev on his less than direct career path, the team had bounced around from sponsor to sponsor with damaging results for its performance on the field. Now it had lost its protector. Faced with possible extinction, Nikolai went into organizational overdrive. Thus began the family romance of Spartak's creation—a story with numerous versions, some by the same author.

Though club football had been in eclipse during the period of the first Five-Year Plan, both the Moscow selects and the national team continued to engage in a variety of important domestic and international competitions. The All-Union championship continued among city selects, and important trips were made to Sweden and Turkey by the national team. Nikolai was captain of both sides and in this capacity reported to a wide range of important figures in and out of the party, most notably Kosarev, who sought a greater role for the Komsomol in the administration and production of sport. Despite his fling with Dukat, Nikolai Starostin also had maintained good relations with the director of Promkooperatsiia, Ivan Epifanovich Pavlov, whose organization had mastered the game of retail trade under the new command economy and become extremely wealthy in the intervening years.[95] Finding a basis for agreement with Pavlov, Starostin brought the entire team back to Promkooperatsiia before the 1934 season. The Moscow City Soviet for Physical Culture automatically placed Promkooperatsiia in the top group of the city league, where it finished first in the spring season, while Dinamo triumphed in the fall. There would be other successes that year. All four brothers were now playing for their club, and all four were named to the Moscow select team sent to an international tournament in Paris. The honorific title of "Merited Master of Sport" (*zasluzhennyi master sporta*) was created in 1934. Petr Isakov and Nikolai Starostin were two of the nine footballers given the award.[96]

At some point during the summer, Starostin invited both Kosarev and Pavlov to hunt with him, making good social use of the skills learned from his father. Over spent bullets and dead animals, the three men agreed to form the first voluntary sport society since the creation of Dinamo. Kosarev promised to supply political support, while Pavlov, according to Starostin's account, pledged 15 percent of Promkooperatsiia's revenues to help recruit and pay the best available athletes in a broad range of sports.[97] Promkooperatsiia also provided the funds for the construction of a permanent training base at Tarasovka on the city's outskirts.[98] Competing with Dinamo required this level of investment. It was noteworthy that support for so extensive a sporting organization was to come from the civilian sector. The plan to create a voluntary sport society for the various workers under Promkooperatsiia was announced in the press on September 22, 1934.

Early in November, Kosarev called in Nikolai, whose career was winding down, and placed him in charge of the new group, which was to have thousands of members in cities across the USSR. The sport society would field teams in a broad range of sports, but, from the first, the Moscow football club was the organization's crown jewel and Nikolai's central interest. Kosarev also charged Nikolai with coming up with a name that could convey the spirit of the membership and its leaders. The brothers gathered such old friends as Petr Popov, Isakov, and Leuta, along with their close relatives, in Nikolai's new apartment on Spiridonov Street. After an all-night session, they finally agreed on the name "Spartak," for Spartacus, the gladiator and rebel slave of ancient Rome. To their dying days, the brothers would disagree about the source of the name. Nikolai recalled playing worker soccer teams named for Germany's revolutionary Spartacus League during a 1927 tour of Germany.[99] Andrei, on the other hand, claimed Nikolai had accidentally seen a copy of the popular Giovanoli novel about Spartacus on a bookshelf.[100] No one ever mentioned the earlier Spartak from Leningrad as a source of the name, despite the fact that Krasnaia Presnia had once played that team. Regardless of its provenance, the name of the new club, announced on November 14, was revealing. Many teams were named for factories; others had barely comprehensible acronyms. Still others, like Torpedo, Lokomotiv, and of course Dinamo, sought to convey an image of strength and power. Spartak, however, was the only Soviet sports club named after a revolutionary leader of the past and an athlete at that.

Thereafter, the organizational process continued with surface smoothness. The Council of Ministers granted final approval on January 28, 1935. On April 19, Spartak's charter was ratified by the VSFK, and the most powerful civilian sports club in Soviet history opened its doors. Soon thereafter, the last season of Moscow league football began. Very quickly, the new kid on the block provided a serious challenge to Dinamo, finishing second. Andrei recalled these years as the happiest of his life. At twenty-eight, he was a member of the Moscow and national selects and a star on the capital's most popular club. All his brothers got to play alongside him. He joined the Communist Party. He was the toast of Moscow's hippest intellectuals—handsome, well dressed, and highly cultured for a soccer star. Fine meals at the city's best restaurants in the company of the USSR's rich and famous were part of his regular routine, as were evenings at the Moscow Art Theater to see his buddy Ianshin. Postgame afternoons and evenings at the Sandunovsky baths were another ritual of the Stalinist good life.

Andrei had traveled throughout Europe, acquiring along the way more than a few luxury items, bartered for the cigarettes and caviar he had stuffed into his baggage before leaving home. In Paris, he made the rounds of local hot spots. This was, as he said, "a time of Soviet heroes," and he was one of them.[101] There seemed nothing especially dangerous about this kind of behavior. The second Five-Year Plan (1932–1937) was a time of relative prosperity after the turmoil of forced draft industrialization and collectivization. The midthirties also witnessed greater openness in popular culture, causing one highly informed Western specialist to refer to the period as a "Soviet Jazz Age."[102] Stalin had ended equality in wages during 1931. People with skills and talents could now be well rewarded, and there were places to spend those rewards. The Starostins were ready to take what was on offer, and it was clear they had a firm sense of entitlement.

In the existing sources, the creation of Spartak is portrayed as a relatively painless process from its genesis on a hunting trip to the official proclamation of its charter. Yet given the galaxy of contending political forces and the inevitable bureaucratic minefield that was Soviet reality, the establishment of the first voluntary sport society since 1923 cannot have been simple. Nikolai's talents, skills, and contacts were surely essential to completing this task. Moving from the entrepreneurship of NEP to the networking of the Stalinist command economy required the kinds of contacts Starostin had been able to acquire through his leadership position with the USSR's national team. Having a web of connections, characterized by favor-giving and back-scratching, known in Russian as *blat,* was, according to Sheila Fitzpatrick, the way things got done during the thirties (and later). She has described "complex social networks based on notions of friendship, mutual loyalty and reciprocal obligation. These were the networks of *blat* and patronage—usually considered, if they are considered at all, in a context of the second economy."[103] Alena Ledeneva described this system as "a reaction of ordinary people to structural constraints of the socialist system of distribution—a series of practices which enabled the Soviet system to function and which made it tolerable, but also subverted it."[104]

One way for the Starostins to advance their cause was to contribute to Soviet prestige at the international level. Soviet clubs had been trampling foreign worker teams for more than a decade, while such lesser powers as Turkey and Sweden had been dominated on the international level. Now both the sporting public and the party leadership were immensely curious about the capacity of Soviet teams to compete against the best foreign professionals, despite the official ban on professional sport. For some time, Nikolai Starostin had been among the loudest advocates of searching out the strongest possible opponents. Upon their return from Paris, the Starostins met with Kosarev at his office on Staraia Ploshchad' to discuss a forthcoming tour of Czechoslovakia by the Moscow selects. Beyond the usual meetings with worker teams, Kosarev raised the possibility of playing against professionals and asked Nikolai if they could win. Nikolai's cryptic reply was that while he could not guarantee success, it was possible to hope for it.[105] Aleksandr later described the reaction when the news leaked out: "People in the USSR don't know foreign football very well. Therefore, all sorts of legends have been created about the play of professional teams. Those sports fans given to panic predicted a complete defeat on the basis of these legends. . . . The very word 'professional' induced in them a sort of completely unfounded worship."[106]

Historic Russian feelings of inferiority, born of isolation, had surfaced once again, but the international situation had recently changed, enhancing the need for the USSR to engage internationally on all levels, including sport. The Nazi triumph in Germany during 1933 had discredited the earlier Soviet policy that derided others on the left as no better than Fascists. The Popular Front, uniting all progressive forces against Fascism, required broad engagement with the outside world.[107] As a result, the Moscow selects, dominated by Dinamo and Spartak players, stepped into a minefield of fears and hopes.[108] Their invitation had come from the Czechoslovak Communist Party. The Czechoslovak government was not particularly enamored of the idea of having a large Soviet delegation touring the country, but, in the spirit of the moment, they had agreed to the tour. In return, the delegation had to agree to eschew any revolutionary activity, a promise that was not entirely kept.[109]

The Czechoslovaks had been chosen not simply because of their geographical proximity. They were also then a football power. That summer they had gone to the final of the second World Cup in Italy, losing to the hosts 1–2. The leading Prague teams, Sparta and Slavia, were among the strongest in Europe but were not playing especially well at the moment. The Czechs, preferring that the Soviets play with the current league leader, offered a game with Zhidenice of Brno, which had just defeated Sparta 4–0.[110] After touring and defeating several worker teams by massive scores, the Moscow selects, captained

**2.8** The Moscow selects in Prague, 1934. *Sto let Rossiiskomu futbolu.*

by Aleksandr Starostin and coached by Mikhail Kozlov and Nikolai Starostin, prepared for the first meeting against professionals with great trepidation and nervousness. No one slept the night before the October 14 match. Possibly the Czechs underestimated their opponents. It is also possible they saw the match as a distraction from their main task of doing well in their league. Whatever the case, the men from Moscow exploded with the opening whistle and raced to a 2–0 lead at halftime. Thinking their work done, they went into a defensive shell, clearing any penetration of their territory with long, unaddressed passes. Panic had set in, and the calmer Zhidenice team was able to tie the score. Then with ten minutes left, the lanky and unpredictable Dinamo star forward Mikhail Iakushin received a long lofted pass on the dead run. Living up to his nickname of "tricky Mickey," Iakushin brought the ball down with his chest and, without waiting for it to settle, blasted it past the goalie to give his team a 3–2 victory.[111]

What, then, to make of this victory? Did the opponents offer a true test? Had shortcomings in their game been masked by the win? On November 22, 1934, the participants in the tour met at the VSFK. The matter was discussed extensively, with Aleksandr, Andrei, and Nikolai all speaking at length. Strong points and weak points were noted. A variety of suggestions for improvement were raised. Most of those present supported Nikolai's call for more such games, especially on Soviet soil. Beyond these concrete evaluations, the tone of the meeting is worth noting. By this time, the creation and naming of the Spartak Society had been announced, but there was no sense of any bitterness or intense rivalry between the professionals of Spartak and Dinamo who had been on the tour. Despite serious disagreements on a wide range of matters, the participants called one another by first names. No visible external political agendas were invoked.[112] Rather, the meeting reflected a sense of shared professional endeavor and mutual respect. Spartak's contribution to this important triumph was significant and duly noted.

While each club represented a very different kind of institution, the creation of the Spartak Society meant that the Starostins and their colleagues could now compete with Dinamo on an equal basis. Supported by the NKVD, Dinamo was undeniably a part of the state apparatus. Spartak, funded by Promkooperatsiia and the Ministry of Trade, occupied a more ambiguous position. Created with political support from an important party organization, it was organizationally tied to a consumer sector that was under siege throughout the thirties. In the 1935 season, Spartak provided a strong challenge to Dinamo's dominance, finishing a close second in the Moscow league's spring season. The team was also up to its old tricks on the barnstorming trail, playing twenty-three friendlies.[113] Now, however, this process was regulated, if lightly. Teams were required to get permission from the sports committee, a process usually completed relatively simply with an exchange of telegrams. In the fall, the stars of both teams again combined on select squads. A team of Czechoslovak all-stars returned the visit, playing various clubs in several Soviet cities. Although enormous differences would soon develop between Spartak and Dinamo, there was yet one more act of cooperation that would set the stage for fundamental change in the world of Soviet football.

# 3

# The Battle Is Joined, 1936–1937

The names of the French businessman Bernard Levy and the Russian émi-gré scholar Nicholas Timasheff do not usually appear in the same sentence, but one man touched off the most profound change in Soviet football history, while the other helped explain it. That moment came in May 1936 with the creation of a professional football league modeled after similar leagues in cap-italist countries. Knowing both Spartak and Dinamo were planning January tours against French worker teams, Levy invited a Soviet side to play his pow-erful Racing Club de France in Paris on New Year's Day 1936.[1] By doing so, he inflamed an ongoing debate inside Soviet soccer circles that led to the league's formation. Ten years later, Timasheff developed his concept of the "Great Retreat," demonstrating how a self-professed revolutionary state came to adopt the practices of the West, not only in sport but in a vast range of other areas of human activity as well.[2]

By replacing the chaotic local and national competitions with a clear and consistent All-Union structure, the newly reorganized VSFK provided the regime with a powerful force for nation building while giving Soviet fans what proved to be an immensely popular entertainment. What had been strong in-terest in football before 1935 now expanded exponentially. In a few years, ten million spectators, nearly all of them working-class males, were taking in games by sides euphemistically called "demonstration teams" (*pokazatel'nye komandy*). Dinamo Stadium was filled regularly, and big arenas (by the day's standards) went up in other cities. All this attention significantly raised the political stakes involved in the game, and success on the field became even more important to the various institutions supporting teams in the new league. When Nikolai Starostin had previously taken the lead in calling for profes-sional football, his views had clashed with some officials who still saw pro-fessional sport as un-Soviet. When he and other like-minded colleagues won the day in 1936, they proved particularly well set to take advantage of the new sporting order.

The Starostins' subsequent success made them hugely popular and famous. Moreover, they achieved their celebrity with a minimum of state support. This path to prominence gave them a measure of independence enjoyed by only the most talented and privileged segments of society. They were heroes, but heroes not created by the state in the manner of the miner Alexei Stakhanov, who had famously overfulfilled his work plan.[3] That independence, not to be confused with opposition, would threaten many in power and eventually put the men of Spartak in grave danger.

The second Five-Year Plan proved to be a time of tragedy. The famine of 1932–1933 killed several million men and women, and the 1934 assassination of the Leningrad party leader, Sergei Kirov, proved to be the first step in the massive self-destruction of the Bolshevik Party. Nevertheless, these years were less chaotic and socially disruptive than those of the first Five-Year Plan. Goals, measured in gross output, were reduced. At least initially, fewer people were arrested and fewer were executed. Having alienated much of the population, the party had come to understand the need to lessen the pressure. In 1935, Stalin made his famous declaration, "Life has become better, comrades. Life has become more joyous." The new Soviet constitution of 1936 stated that socialism had actually been achieved.[4] Yet the surface calm did not mean tensions within the party had disappeared. Nor can it be said that Stalin, Molotov, and others at the center felt secure in their positions vis-à-vis society.[5] With Hitler in power in Germany, the external threat had been heightened. War became a greater concern, and the secret police, in their eternal vigilance, made it clear to the leadership that moderation had not eradicated all discontent in the land.[6] Harsh measures could easily be revived and indeed soon were. If 1936 brought the good news of joyous soccer spectacles and a brand new socialist constitution, it also brought the greatest tragedy to befall the Soviet peoples. The "Great Purges" began with the show trials that same year.[7] In the midst of the Terror, the Starostins and Spartak would enjoy their greatest triumphs. As they won championships and glory for the USSR, employing what some called "bourgeois methods," hundreds of their sporting colleagues were arrested and shot. Attempts were repeatedly made to implicate the brothers and others at Spartak in all manner of crimes, some for things they did or said and some for things they could never possibly have done. Possessed of an extensive network of friends in high places, the Starostins were able to stay free for some time, but eventually they too were swept up in the purges.

## New Year's Day in Paris and the Mysteries of the "W"

It is not clear when the invitation arrived. News of Levy's plan appeared in *Komsomol'skaia pravda* on November 22, but according to Mikhail Iakushin, the players learned of it only early in December 1935. In the best spirit of the

Popular Front, Levy had invited a Soviet team to play his club, which was then leading the French first division. Well before the internationalization and globalization of football, Levy had assembled a cast that included players from England, Austria, Germany, Algeria, Yugoslavia, and Senegal. Led by an English coach, Dennis Compton (formerly of Arsenal), Racing had recently tied the Gunners, the reigning English champion, in a friendly at Paris.[8] The team was most certainly stronger than Zhidenice and a great deal more visible on the world scene. Most important for the Soviets, Racing played the "W" formation, which had been adopted by most of the leading clubs of Western Europe over the course of the previous decade.

In all sports, changes in rules produce changes in tactics. In the midtwenties, FIFA changed the always controversial and mysterious offside rule. Instead of three players, now two had to be between the most forward attacker and the goal when the ball was shot or passed. This change put more emphasis on speed and movement and diminished the importance of stagnant position play. To take advantage of the new rule, Herbert Chapman, the legendary manager of Arsenal, replaced the old system of "five in a line" with a new formation. Hitherto five attackers had been backed up by three halfbacks and two defenders:

```
                        A
                  D  H  A
            G        H  A
                  D  H  A
                        A
```

Chapman moved one halfback onto the defensive line and withdrew the inside forwards back from the other forwards:

```
            D                  A
                H        A
      G         D                  A
                H        A
            D                  A
```

The shape of the formation suggested a "W" (or "M"), hence the name of the scheme.

Like their colleagues in a vast range of technical fields, Soviet soccer specialists had been ignorant of the latest developments in the West. Later, when word about the W began to seep across the borders, many Soviet coaches were dismissive. With three players on the back line, the approach seemed too defensive. Soviet soccer had always stressed attack and goal scoring. More than a few specialists and sports bureaucrats went so far as to condemn the new formation as bourgeois. Especially in the thirties, when overtaking the West first became a priority, it was important to prove the superiority of Soviet methods. Conversely, borrowing from the West could be seen as politically suspicious. A few members of the national team remembered hearing about the W from their opponents during the Turkish tour of the USSR in 1933. Mikhail Sushkov recalled a 1935 friendly in Sverdlovsk against a Norwegian workers' team that played the W.[9] In both cases, the new method was ignored in the thoroughly mistaken belief that Soviet football had already staked out a leading position in the world. Scores of victories against worker teams and the sole triumph over the Czech pros had wrongly convinced many officials inside and outside the sports world of the power of their football.

Late in 1935, a Ukrainian select team, based on Dinamo Kiev, defeated the middle-of-the-table French side, Red Star, 6–1, providing further "proof" of Soviet excellence and underscoring the importance of the game with Racing.[10] Coming when it did, the challenge from Levy set off a raft of arguments in the world of Soviet soccer. Sentiment within the sports committee was mixed. Which team should be sent? Might a single Soviet club be too weak? Perhaps the national team would win, but that might have been seen as overkill going against a single French side. Given that the Soviet season had ended more than a month earlier, what kind of condition would the players be in? The possibility of embarrassment was real, and embarrassment was no longer tolerable, given the international political implications of such a meeting during the period of the anti-Fascist popular front. Whatever decision was made by those in charge of sports, the trip would have to be approved at the highest level. Although there is no record of the Politbiuro's deliberations on this matter, it appears to have been uncertain about the team's chances. Final approval of the tour was granted only on December 21, 1935, ten days before the scheduled match.[11] *Izvestiia* announced the game two days later, a month after it had been first mentioned in *Komsomol'skaia pravda*.[12]

It was finally decided to send a combined Spartak and Dinamo side, which would be called the Moscow selects. After the Paris game, each team would reassemble and tour France, playing workers' clubs. This seemed the best solution. Not only were these the two strongest teams in the Soviet capital, but many of the players were in relatively good physical condition because they were then in the middle of the winter Russian hockey season. This involved a version of the game called "bandy," popular in the Nordic countries and played in Russia since the nineteenth century. It was basically field hockey on ice. With little time to waste, men from both teams dropped their sticks and started training. They ran in the snow and did skills work in Dinamo's small gymnasium on Tsvetnoy Bulvar'.[13] In this mixed state of preparation, the team arrived in Paris on December 26, 1935.

During their training in France, they attended a four-team Christmas tournament, which included clubs from such soccer powers as Hungary and Austria. They left the stadium with the impression that they were no less talented than the professionals they had just watched.[14] Instilling confidence in this combined Spartak-Dinamo side may have been one thing, but deciding whom to start from each team proved highly contentious. The choice of goalie proved extremely thorny. Spartak's number one, Ivan Ryzhov, came down with a temperature. Evgenii Fokin, Dinamo's top goalie, was also ill. His inexperienced

**3.1** Moscow selects before the match against Racing Club de Paris. *Sto let Rossiiskomu futbolu.*

replacement, Aleksandr Krasnikov, had never previously been out of the USSR. The only remaining goalie was the twenty-year-old Spartak sub, Anatoly Akimov, a resident of Krasnaia Presnia with a lifelong love of the team but no experience in big games. The task of choosing the team fell to the troika of Konstantin Kvashnin, Nikolai Starostin, and the old Dinamo star Fyodr Selin. The three had to endure massive kibitzing from players, journalists, and delegation officials. After many hours and much shouting, the team was chosen with four Spartakovtsy—Akimov, Stanislav Leuta, Andrei Starostin, and Aleksandr Starostin, who played his usual role of captain. The other seven were from Dinamo and included the entire attacking five, led by Iakushin and Sergei Ilyin.

With the delights of New Year's Eve in Paris spread out before them, the Moscow selects retired to their rooms in the Hotel Cavour and went to bed before midnight, if we are to believe the Soviet-era accounts. The next day, their bus took them to the Bois de Boulogne, where sixty thousand fans filled the Parc des Princes Stadium. The anticipation for the game had been enormous. Even before the Politbiuro had given the final OK, the streets and kiosks of Paris had been covered with posters announcing the arrival of the "Russians." Once the match began, the Moscow men found themselves able to move easily against Racing. They ran all over the middle of the field, stringing passes together and dazzling the crowd, but once they approached the French goal, they were consistently met by defenders who seemed to appear at the last second. Even more problematically, their offensively oriented strategy had the disadvantage of allowing quick counterattacks, one of which led to a Racing

**3.2** Anatoly Akimov makes a save for Moscow selects against Racing Club de France, Paris, January 1, 1936. *Sto let Rossiiskomu futbolu.*

goal by Couard, their Senegalese center forward, who found the upper left corner at the fifteen-minute mark. Despite their dismay, the Muscovites came back within a quarter hour when Andrei Starostin set Iakushin free with a long pass. With the score 1–1 at halftime and the French crowd cheering their every move, the Moscow players might have felt some satisfaction, but instead they were puzzled by their difficulty in finishing, not to mention by the open space Racing had found down the middle of their defense.

The reason for their frustration was the W. With the center midfielder withdrawn to become a third defender, there was lots of room in the middle of the field. Yet when the Moscow side approached the goal area, that third defender made it far more difficult for them to get the ball in the net. They struggled mightily through the second half and held their own. Racing made repeated counterattacks, only to be thwarted time and again by Akimov's brilliance. As the game approached its end, the Russians' lack of conditioning began to show. A long pass into the corner was tracked down by Aleksandr Starostin, who fell down chasing his man. A quick cross into the box found Couard, racing forward untouched. The final score was 1–2. The Soviet players had put up a brilliant effort that won the hearts of the Paris audience, but their outmoded tactics had failed them.[15]

After a few hours of disappointment, the men of Moscow began to realize they had achieved something substantial. They had played one of the strongest teams on the continent away from home on even terms. The next day the *International Herald Tribune Reported:*

> The first [sic] Soviet football team to ever play an international match gave an unexpected display of fast, heady football to hold the strong Racing Club eleven to a 2–1 score yesterday afternoon. . . . From the start to finish the game was speedy and well fought with the Moscow team . . . measuring up to the French team in every department of the game.[16]

The Moscow men had reason to be proud, and that same pride may have dulled their attention levels when Racing's coach, Dennis Compton, a disciple of Chapman, showed up at their hotel the next day. He gave the players and all the members of the Soviet delegation a lecture on the W formation. He praised them for their individual skills and teamwork but explained that their inability to finish was the result of the defensive advantages of his system. The extra defender consistently thwarted them. Conversely, given the way all Soviet teams played, their two defenders guarded not individuals but zones. When the inside and center forwards flooded into the penalty box, Soviet teams were consistently outnumbered. According to the accounts of both Iakushin and Andrei Starostin, they all listened politely and, filled with their success, promptly forgot the lesson.[17]

It would take another year and a half for the leaders of Soviet football to understand the teachings of Herbert Chapman. In the meantime, there were rumors throughout 1936 of new meetings with professional teams. In April, the Politbiuro actually granted permission for the Komsomol to make overtures toward Chelsea, Manchester City, and Glasgow Rangers. The British International Football Board, however, refused to grant permission for any of these matches unless the Soviets joined FIFA, a move that was given serious consideration. Yet this dalliance with the capitalist football hierarchy did not last long. Less than two weeks after granting the sports committee permission to talk to the British clubs, the Politbiuro refused to allow a return visit from Racing.[18] As in the case of all the leadership's decisions, no reason was given.

### The League Takes Off

Nikolai Starostin realized full well that the match against Racing was a positive step. He made this clear in a statement to *Izvestiia* and was shrewd enough to understand that he could use the defeat for his own purposes.[19] This had not been Starostin's first trip to the West. He had seen many professional games and had spent countless hours with foreign colleagues. He respected Western methods and thought they could be adapted to the Soviet context. Back in Moscow, he revived his campaign for a professional league. At heart Starostin was a sporting impresario. He had learned how to run a football club during the twenties. Now he sought to create a bigger stage for himself and Spartak within the confines of the command economy. There can

**3.3** The Starostin brothers (Aleksandr, Nikolai, Andrei, Petr). *Spartak Moskva: Offitsial'naia istoriia.*

be no doubt he had the greater good of Soviet soccer at heart in arguing for professionalism, but he clearly was not averse to enhancing his visibility, comfort, and prestige in the process. Along the way he made a number of powerful enemies. The absence of strong opposition from state organs meant, however, that the call for a league of well-compensated, elite professionals was very much in tune with the tenor of the times.

Close to the end of the first Five-Year Plan, Stalin had moved sharply away from social leveling and wage equality. He had come to realize that the skills and judgment of so-called specialists with professional training acquired before the revolution were a necessary part of future progress. People with those talents expected to be rewarded appropriately. Starostin considered himself one of those highly skilled professionals and had no problem in accepting privileges in return for his skills. Hierarchy became a central feature of Soviet life from the midthirties on. The prerevolutionary Left's goal of social equality was abandoned.

Kosarev, who shared some of Starostin's showmanship, was his strongest ally. The Komsomol leader did not share the concerns of some party leaders who feared professionalism and wanted sport to be more clearly didactic. Rather, Kosarev believed that entertainment (sporting or otherwise) should, first of all, be entertaining.[20] It was important to the "leader of Soviet youth" that the "better and more joyous" life of the moment be filled with the kind of professional sport entertainments that had appealed to young workingmen

**3.4** The Starostin sisters. *Futbol skvoz' gody.*

throughout the world. Football was the modern, urban sport par excellence. It provided a shared discourse for the male members of the highly disparate new Soviet proletariat. With so many young peasants moving to the towns and forsaking more traditional versions of masculinity, football provided a modern form of male bonding—a manly game for the New Soviet Man. Kosarev was considerably less interested in the New Soviet Woman.

The richest account of the professionalization process has been provided by Barbara Keys in her history of global sport diplomacy. As she makes clear, while the Soviets were well behind the United Kingdom in making soccer into an element of mass culture, they did not significantly trail the continental countries in going professional. Austria had made the change in 1924, Czechoslovakia in 1925. Spain, where the sport was huge, went pro in 1928, while France did so in 1932.[21] Germany never was professional until 1963. Back from Paris in February 1936, Nikolai Starostin took up the cudgel at a meeting called by the Komsomol to discuss the defeat:

> We returned home and explained our opponent was good but that we were no worse. We lacked an awareness of tactical innovations. We needed to exchange experiences not just in away matches but at home as well. . . . [I said] our best players stew in their own juices. They play against each other once a year when the city selects meet. . . . In European countries, there are leagues where clubs play each other, but we naively believed that the climatic and territorial particularities of our country were insurmountable.[22]

Kosarev agreed and asked him to draw up a plan. Starostin's memorandum was on his desk in a week. A copy went to the chairman of the All-Union Council of Physical Culture, Vasily Mantsev. Starostin wrote:

> In the last two or three years, Soviet soccer has shown that it stands at the level of the best European teams. . . . At the same time an acquaintance with working conditions for foreign professional football players—and all the best teams in Europe consist of professionals—showed us that professional football has a number of advantages over amateur.

Starostin proposed an initial eight-team league that would play spring and fall seasons. This system, he noted without irony, would "legalize the professionalism that already exists in our football."[23] The VSFK accepted the proposal with minor revisions on March 22. It would take until early May to decide that twenty-eight teams would take part in the first Soviet championship, seven in the top flight, called Group A. The entire process had involved massive political infighting. Was the level of performance or the degree of influence to be the basis for inclusion in the new setup? In addition to the league schedule, a knockout tournament for the Soviet Cup open to every team in the entire USSR was to take place. This competition, too, followed Western example. With the backroom struggles settled, it was time for battles on the field, and the plan was announced to the public soon thereafter. The spring season began on May 22.

After reading Starostin's memorandum, one might well imagine a similar document produced by some Soviet Taylorist engineer on the wonders of the assembly line at Dearborn. As Keys notes, "The memo is striking for its uncritical admiration of Western, commercialized sport, the absence of any effort to distance Soviet sport from the Western version, and the assumption the best way to advance Soviet sport was to implant Western practices and structures."[24] When his enemies sought to have him arrested a few years later, Nikolai Starostin was accused of seeking to introduce "bourgeois morals into sport." Regardless of the justice of their claim, they did have some basis for such charges.[25]

From its inception, the league provoked a huge boom in football's popularity. Attendance grew to massive levels. Coyly calling the various clubs "demonstration teams," the press greatly expanded its coverage of the game. As had been the experience in many other nations, the number of friendlies dropped once a regular league schedule was established. By 1940, over ten million fans (many surely repeat customers) took in professional soccer at all of its levels.[26] Spartak and Dinamo spearheaded this growth in interest, which now approached that in the cinema as a form of mass culture. At the beginning of a soccer match, however, unlike a movie, no one knew how the story would end.

Once they came to dominate the league, Spartak captured the lead in attendance. Regardless of the numbers for either of the two top teams, these figures demonstrate that football was now a true phenomenon of mass culture and that Spartak had become the game's feature attraction. Its level of support, along with that of Dinamo, compared more than favorably with con-

**Table 3.1** Average attendance at Spartak and Dinamo matches, 1936–1940

|       | Spartak | | Dinamo | |
| --- | --- | --- | --- | --- |
| Year | In Moscow* | Away | In Moscow* | Away |
| 1936 | 29,500 | 23,300 | 30,000 | 24,000 |
| 1937 | 34,000 | 30,000 | 37,800 | 28,700 |
| 1938 | 27,700 | 19,500 | 22,300 | 18,900 |
| 1939 | 46,800 | 27,800 | 39,500 | 23,500 |
| 1940 | 53,900 | 25,900 | 44,400 | 26,000 |

*Source:* Figures derived from Eduard Nisenboim, *Spartak Moskva: Offitsial'naia istoriia* (Moscow, 2002), and I. Dobronravov, *Na bessrochnoi sluzhbe futbolu* (Moscow, 1999). All numbers are approximations, based on journalists' estimates.

\* Includes all games in Moscow, regardless of which Moscow club was the official home team.

temporary British teams. In the 1938–1939 season, Aston Villa topped the English league with 39,932 spectators per game. Arsenal attracted 39,102. Everton, the champion, was seen by 35,040 per home game, and five other teams averaged above 30,000.[27]

All this attention raises obvious questions. Why was this so? What made Spartak so popular? In no small part, Spartak was beloved for the simplest of reasons. It was good. Moreover, it had been good for many years. Its best players, particularly the Starostins, were already celebrities who had acquired their visibility through their own efforts rather than the state's. Dinamo had been the strongest football team in the USSR between 1928 and 1936. The antagonism between Spartak and Dinamo, dating to before 1935, intensified on and off the field with the establishment of the league. Between 1936 and 1940, the two teams shared the league championship evenly, establishing the great-

est rivalry in Soviet sport, which eventually outlasted the USSR itself. In the first year of league play Spartak was cofavorite with Dinamo, but the "Red and White" now needed to replace its older players. Nikolai Starostin was thirty-eight and had made the move to the front office of the Spartak Sport Society. Aleksandr was thirty-three and nearing the end of his career. Viktor Sokolov (1911–1999) was brought in from Dinamo to anchor the back line, which was the team's strength with Akimov in goal. Petr, the youngest of the Starostins, began to find a place in midfield, while the speedy Vladimir Stepanov (1910–1981) cemented a spot up front.

Among the new additions that came with the league were full-time coaches who handled matters on the field. Spartak's choice of leader produced some consternation in Soviet football circles for the simple reason that he was not a citizen of the USSR. Revealing what some saw as its worship of the West, Spartak had hired Antonin Fivebr (1888–1971) from Czechoslovakia. Before the war, Fivebr had played for Sparta Prague and after his retirement had gained extensive experience coaching in Italy and Spain. However, any high hopes were quickly dashed by the first match of the season, a 0–3 loss to TsDKA. Spartak went on to finish third in the six-game spring season, losing 0–1 to Dinamo before a crowd of sixty thousand. The players were then knocked out of the cup by Dinamo Tblisi, which defeated them 6–3 in a replay of the quarterfinal.[28] Fivebr departed for Dinamo Leningrad, replaced by Mikhail Kozlov, who had guided the team's preseason preparation.[29] Under his leadership, Spartak became champion of the fall season on the last day of competition. It defeated TsDKA 3–1 before a riotous crowd and edged out Dinamo, coached by Konstantin Kvashnin, the old friend from the Presnia.

As a reward for their victory, the Spartak players split a bonus of 10,000

**3.5** Inside Dinamo Stadium, 1930s. Fotoagentstvo Sportekspress.

**3.6** Outside Dinamo Stadium, 1930s. Fotoagentstvo Sportekspress.

rubles among themselves.[30] With ticket prices running from 1 to 5 rubles and average home crowds of nearly thirty thousand, their prize seems less than generous. After all, football was now big business. Paying players to free them from work had improved the quality of the Soviet game. Soccer players, not to mention team officials and coaches, were compensated at much the same level as top writers, academics, ballet dancers, and film stars. A model budget drawn up in the late thirties set players' base salaries at 800 rubles per month. This did not include bonuses for wins in the league and cup. Players on various select teams got additional compensation. Head coaches and top team officials were supposed to get 1,300.[31] The Starostins were reported elsewhere to make 2,000 rubles each a month. This can only be described as lavish, especially given all the other privileges they gained through Spartak, including the booty acquired on foreign trips and the use of dachas near the team's training base at Tarasovka.

Clearly people in the football world were at the top of the Soviet pay scale, and the Starostins were the best-compensated figures in the sport. Equally clearly, they saw nothing wrong with this. Why should the champions of the Soviet Union's most popular sport live like paupers? It was not as if they hadn't worked hard and well to earn their salaries and other privileges. Promkooperatsiia might have given mightily to get the Spartak Society going, but it was clear the soccer team itself was a profit-making enterprise. The model budget for a typical team included total costs at 637,365 rubles a year.

**3.7** An earlier episode from TsDKA vs. Spartak; note the primitive character of TsDKA's own stadium on Peschanaia Street. Fotoagentstvo Sportekspress.

More than half this sum went for wages. With ticket prices averaging 3 rubles, it should be clear that attendances in this era were sufficiently high to make most teams profitable.

Even if the players made much more than their fans, the Moscow workingmen who comprised the vast bulk of the football audience embraced Spartak. Moscow laborers of various sorts had always shown support for the club's predecessors, but now they had a team that could compete fully with Dinamo. The sports cliché "Enemies on the field; friends off it" may have applied to the players who shared a relationship as fellow professionals, but the leadership of the two societies and each team's supporters came to develop a sharp dislike for each other. This antagonism had roots in the fissures of Soviet society during the midthirties and later. As we shall see, off-the-field events that intersected with contemporary political tensions would exacerbate the rivalry.

Before the next season, Mikhail Kozlov announced his intention to return to teaching at the Stalin Institute of Physical Culture. Kvashnin, in the meantime, had been dismissed by Dinamo, and Spartak quickly snatched him up. His work with Spartak in just two seasons established the basis for the team's greatest successes. A multitalented sportsman and gifted musician, Kvashnin was a sports intellectual, constantly seeking to innovate. His approach helped establish a style for later Soviet coaches in a wide range of fields. They were supposed to be educated people with some semblance of culture, in the Soviet sense. Kvashnin had been with the Moscow delegation for the match against Racing. He had been present at Dennis Compton's lecture on the advantages of the W formation, and he now sought to introduce it into Spartak's play. The transition was not easy. Before the league season began, Spartak went out of the cup in the round of sixteen. Soon, however, it would achieve one of its greatest successes.

In late June 1937, an all-star team of Basque players, drawn from the powerful Spanish league, came to the Soviet Union to raise money for the embattled republic during the Spanish civil war. They were to travel the country and play a series of the best Soviet clubs. The Basques were professionals of the highest rank, far more talented than any other foreigners yet seen on Soviet soil. Spartak would be the only club to defeat the mighty Basques. Dinamo lost to them twice. Spartak was then rewarded with a trip to Europe, where it won two international workers' tournaments. From that moment, Spartak's popularity exploded. These were great successes. In the previous two years, both Spartak and Dinamo had achieved victories in a wide range of sports. For their efforts both societies received the Order of Lenin on July 22, 1937.[32] Twelve soccer stars received important awards; most prominent of these was Nikolai Starostin, who was given an Order of Lenin. Aleksandr got the Order of the Red Banner, while Andrei, along with Akimov and Leuta, got the Badge of Honor. Seven Dinamo players, from Moscow, Leningrad, Kiev, and Tblisi, got similar prizes. This was the most official form of recognition possible, and the Starostins, in a manner that had become obligatory, reacted in the most official of ways. Showing a well-developed ability to "speak Bolshevik" and pay the necessary fealty to the mighty, they sent a formal thank you note to Stalin:

> In this great epoch of the flowering of socialist culture, physical culture occupies an honored place in the lives of the Soviet people. We, workers of Soviet sport, refreshed by your care, promise all our strength to establish the leadership of Soviet sport and to powerfully develop our physical culture movement. . . . All hail our beloved leader, dear teacher and friend of Soviet physical culture—the great Stalin.[33]

Similar letters followed to Molotov and Vyshinskii. Upon returning home from Paris in August, Nikolai was no less fawning when he addressed a less than spontaneously assembled group of well-wishers, "We are glad that the appearances of our Soviet masters had such brilliant results. We are glad to return to our happy homeland. . . . All hail the great Soviet homeland. All hail the great Stalin."[34]

Despite these words of loyalty, Spartak's leaders soon found themselves accused in the press of all manner of crimes and malfeasance. Spartak's success had sowed jealousies. In the context of the show trials and the purges, these were not trifling matters that could be dismissed as the complaints of defeated rivals, particularly when Spartak's rivals had the right to arrest those who had defeated them on the field of play. The Starostins had already seen many friends and colleagues taken away, and they would soon have to mobilize their contacts at the highest levels of the party in order to defend themselves.

## More than "Us" and "Them"

There are many Moscow men who claim to have been at the match against the Basques. They date their love of Spartak from this defining moment, but was this the sole reason for the team's popularity? Huge numbers of people were coming to their games. Most of those fans were working-class males, but defining the term "working-class" as it was used in the midthirties has proved highly controversial. Spartak's sponsor, Promkooperatsiia, supervised the work of a vast array of people in the service and retail trades who performed physical work even if scarcely any of them actually were employed in factories. The capital's proletariat had grown enormously since 1929 and become highly heterogeneous. Hundreds of thousands had emigrated to the biggest of Soviet cities, and factory workers comprised only a part of this new group. Between 1929 and 1934, Moscow's population grew from 2.3 million to 3.6 million. Roughly one quarter of Muscovites were factory workers.[35] In the light of those developments, one can sustain only a broad definition of the working class, which includes workers in service, transport, and construction as well as the more traditional industries.

Those who watched football were not immune to the universal phenomenon of choosing a particular team to support. No one, not even at the height of Stalinism, could impose that choice on them. The regime may have preferred that the citizens root for Dinamo, the guardians of order and exemplars of official values. The government lavished far more of its budget on Dinamo than any other sport society, but the state's money could not buy love. In choosing to root for Spartak, Moscow fans came to call it "the people's team," but just who were "the people," and why did they choose Spartak? Who did comprise Spartak's fan base, and what were the political meanings of their choices? Answering these questions raises serious evidential problems. Aside from the team's impressive attendance totals and remarks in the press about its great popularity, there is little, if any, remaining contemporary evidence to explain the real reasons for Spartak's enormous support. Indeed, it is unlikely any such evidence was ever produced. This was a topic millions of citizens knew about but did not write about.

I have been going to the USSR since 1965 and have attended scores of games at which I have had scores of conversations with fans who, knowing I was American, openly discussed their love of Spartak and hatred for Dinamo. Had I known that some thirty years later I would be writing about Spartak, I would have taken notes. During the Soviet period, one could only infer from published accounts the reasons for the intensity of the fans' attachment, but time spent in the stands of Soviet stadiums and the kitchens of Soviet citizens clearly revealed the depth and character of feeling surrounding Spartak. These places were what James Scott has called "the social sites of the hidden transcripts" of a complicated and subtle form of resistance.[36] They were the spaces in which the unofficial histories of the game could be retold.

Only since the collapse of the USSR have we gotten published accounts that articulate what everyone, even outsiders, knew. The authors of these reminiscences can fairly be accused of thinking retrospectively, but the consistency of their themes is convincing. In a 1999 article published in the monthly *Sportexpress zhurnal*, Iurii Oleshchuk, a retired jurist, described rooting for Spartak as a preteen in the thirties:

> In our huge apartment house there were mainly communal apartments [*kommunalki*]. We were all working class, and in the courtyard [*dvor*], the kids all proclaimed they were children of a single class. Our rooting interests were basically one-half for Spartak and the rest for all the other clubs combined. In school it was the same. In Pioneer camp, the same. . . . Why? Today I understand most clearly that Spartak was the home team [*rodnaia komanda*] of ordinary people. Why? The name had meaning for us. Then all the kids and even the grown-ups knew the name of the leader of the slave revolt in ancient Rome. . . . It was studied closely in our schools—a story of the struggle of the exploited against the exploiters. . . . How could the names of the other teams —Dinamo, TsDKA, Lokomotiv or Torpedo compare?

Clearly, for Oleshchuk exploitation had not disappeared with the revolution, and his resentments found their way to the football field. Invoking a revolutionary discourse, he was using Bolshevik language to highlight the betrayal of the revolution's principles.

Spartak's sponsorship by Promkooperatsiia had a similar resonance. Although the organization was financially strong, for Oleshchuk it represented the ordinary people—barbers, waiters, tailors, salesclerks, and food workers who labored under its wing. Even industrial workers, who were formally outside Promkooperatsiia's institutional control and had their own factory teams, identified with Spartak. Among the team's supporters, only one club inspired real hatred—Dinamo. "The relationship of Spartak's fans to Dinamo," wrote Oleshchuk, "was highly antagonistic. Dinamo represented the authorities— the police, the organs of state security. The hated privileged elites. They ate better. They dressed better, and they certainly didn't live in *kommunalki*." Matches between Spartak and Dinamo were, in Oleshchuk's words:

> wars on the field and in the stands. There were lots of fights among the fans. Really huge battles were prevented by separating the supporters. Spartak's fans sat in the east tribune [of Dinamo stadium] where the seats were cheaper, while Dinamo's supporters occupied the aristocratic northern and semiaristocratic southern stands.[37]

In a 1990 interview, the late human rights lawyer and lifelong Spartak fan Boris Nazarov recalled, "In those years when I was growing up, when Spartak played Dinamo or TsDKA, you could hear from the stands 'get the cops' [*bei militsia*] or 'get the soldiers' [*bei koniushek*, literally 'the grooms'].''[38] Here, hatred of the structures of force (the police and army) was central to the fans' preference for Spartak. Conflating the army's postwar strength with its less mighty pre-1941 status, Nazarov continued:

> Through the draft, Dinamo and TsDKA could get the best players from the other teams. They served but never held a bayonet, never sat inside a tank, never worked in the organs of the MVD . . . and the public knew this. Spartak lost a great deal because of this, and the fans hated the players who left. . . . They [the fans] called them "traitors." . . . This was one very important reason for Spartak's popularity.[39]

Aksel' Vartanian, Soviet soccer's most informed student, places special emphasis on the role of the Starostins:

> Spartak was always popular. From the start of the league, they had very many fans. Some of it had to do with the Starostins, who had friends in the "bohemian world." . . . This team somehow belonged to society. Dinamo was the Interior Ministry. They were hated. TsDKA was the army. . . . Spartak was not a team that belonged to any single group. Maybe it was the Starostin brothers, maybe their friendships with the intelligentsia, but there was some kind of mark of democracy on the team. Giving your heart to Spartak, you hung on to some kind of hope that this team was somehow apart from all that surrounded it.[40]

Such views were not universally shared. Alexander Vainshtein, who coauthored Nikolai Starostin's 1989 memoirs, expressed doubts about social explanations of team support, but his final conclusion is similar to Nazarov's:

> The idea that Spartak was the "people's team" is a myth. Spartak wasn't the people's team. They were the most popular team. You can't say in terms of categories of fans that ordinary people rooted for Spartak and only KGB people rooted for Dinamo. Or that army generals rooted for TsDKA. Spartak was the most popular team for many reasons—first that it was not part of the structures of force.[41]

Vainshtein also stated that Spartak had its own support at the highest institutional levels, especially in the party. In that sense, he said, calling it the people's team made no sense since the people did not run the team. Of course, as has been noted above, nowhere in the world of elite sport do ordinary people run any team. The local soviet does not decide who should play goalie, nor does it set ticket prices or choose the colors of the uniforms.

Disrespect for the authorities could be exacerbated by the experience of attending one of Spartak's games. These were not exercises in order and organization. Getting to an important match on especially crowded transport did not enhance the serenity or obedience of spectators. Mounted police shoved the entering crowds into the stadium. Once inside, actually finding one's assigned seat often proved impossible. Overcrowding for big games was the rule,

**3.8** Fans crowd the field and destroy a goalpost: TsDKA vs. Spartak, 1936. *Spartak Moskva: Offitsial'naia istoriia.*

and gate-crashers, usually young boys, numbered in the thousands. Oleshchuk describes the process with a certain fondness:

> Only a fool tried to get past the ticket-takers alone . . . but there was another way—collectively. We had a reliable system . . . called the "steam engine." Thirty, forty, fifty of us without tickets formed a huge snake at one of the entrances and at an agreed-upon moment threw ourselves with incredible strength at the gate. The ticket-takers would scream, try to catch us with their hands, but they could not stop us.[42]

Begging older men to take them into the stadium was another technique. This did not involve possessing an actual ticket. Usually a man told the ticket-takers that the kid was his son. If, however, the boy had tried the trick with someone else a few minutes earlier and had been turned away, the police would ask his new benefactor if he knew his son had another father.[43]

Order was rare in the stands as well as at the gates, especially for games not played at Dinamo, where security was strongest. Writing in *Krasnyi sport*, Mikhail Romm described the season-ending Spartak-TsDKA match mentioned above. This wild scene took place on October 30, 1936, at the army's smaller, far more primitive ground:

> At halftime, spectators who had been behind the barriers began a general attack on the field. Thousands of people poured out like an avalanche and surrounded

the playing surface like a tight wall which went right up to the sidelines, surrounded the goals, and covered the corners, turning the rectangle into an oval.[44]

In the second half, the surging fans destroyed one of the goalposts. In the midst of this chaos, Spartak triumphed 3–1 to claim its first league championship. TsDKA protested the match, but its claim was denied. In addition, several administrators at the stadium lost their posts for failing to maintain crowd control.[45]

When the same two teams met in May 1937, there was more chaos. Schoolkids who were allowed in free pushed, shoved, screamed, and whistled as they pressed through the gates of Young Pioneer Stadium. When the match ended, they stormed the field.[46] In every season before the war, newspaper reports described further incidents involving Spartak players and fans.[47] Given the team's visibility, it is reasonable to ask whether Spartak supporters were truly more rowdy than the fans of other clubs. Recent archival research by Vartanian has shown disorders were common and by no means restricted to Moscow, nor did they begin with the introduction of the league.[48] The fact that press accounts involving hooliganism by Spartak fans and players were more frequent raises the possibility that certain newspapers were singling the team out for special attention because of its success on the field.

In the broadest sense, these antiauthoritarian attitudes and their accompanying rowdyism raise questions about public acceptance of the regime. Recent scholarship has demonstrated considerable dissent, disorganization, and grumbling in Stalin's Russia. This work has revealed that a broad social and cultural division had opened between what many Soviet citizens described as a righteous and exploited "us" and a privileged and self-aggrandizing "them."[49] Significant numbers of ordinary men and women made critical comments in a variety of forms and places. Although there were surely millions of true believers, it could not be said that the USSR under Stalin was a land of universal contentment. The first two Five-Year Plans had brought much misery, and the later thirties were still a time of scarcity and uncertainty, heightening the regime's fear of the masses.[50] Indeed, much of this complaining was closely monitored by the police. Therefore, it is interesting to note that the stadium was one of the few places in the Soviet Union where a person could utter the words "get the cops" and rarely if ever suffer serious consequences.

The reason for this island of comparative safety in a society otherwise characterized by extensive surveillance is not immediately clear. One finds no discussion of it in any Soviet-era source, published or archival. Here a comparative example, taken out of context, may help illustrate the nature of the stadium and the peculiar social relations it creates, regardless of the political system. In his celebrated memoir of Arsenal fandom, Nick Hornby remembers his first match on the hallowed terraces of Highbury. What impressed him most was not the Gunners' play but "the way adults [nearly all

**3.9** These two huge signs posted the football league standings and results. Fans gathered around them at all hours to talk soccer. Fotoagentstvo Sportekspress.

male] were allowed to shout the word, WANKER! as loudly as they wanted without attracting any attention."[51] Could it be that Nazarov's "get the cops" was the semantic equivalent of Hornby's "wankers"? Were the lads too focused on the field to take the words seriously?

A gathering of two or three people on the street could easily provoke police attention in Stalin's time, but thousands crammed into the stands was another matter. The police may not have liked it, but they had little choice but to permit sports events, especially football games, at which large numbers of people were crowded together under circumstances that raised their emotions.[52] Two large billboards—one with the latest results, the other with the league standings—were erected near Dinamo Stadium in Petrovsky Park. Even when there was no match, crowds of men gathered near these signs to talk of football and other things. Police spies were surely among those who took part in these gatherings, but for thousands of Moscow men the pleasurable male bonding of a shared passion created a community that was simultaneously temporary and ongoing.[53]

For decades, scholars argued that the workers' inability to change the system, despite their multiple dissatisfactions, was the result of the regime's use of repression to atomize possible opposition.[54] The authorities therefore found football problematic precisely because it brought people together to watch a highly unpredictable spectacle that created both social relations and discourses that undercut the impact of atomization. The British journalist Simon

Kuper noted a similar situation during World War II in Norway and Austria under Nazi occupation. As in Moscow, the stadiums of Oslo and Vienna became places for voicing anti-German feelings that went unpunished. Even within the Reich itself, writes Kuper, "the Nazis never quite trusted the game. . . . Football always had the potential to jump up and bite Nazism on the nose."[55]

It must nevertheless be remembered that sport's influence was limited. While it brought people together, it did not do so on a constant basis. Historically the stadium has been neither a public nor a private space but what Clifford Geertz, in the urtext of sport studies, has called a "focused gathering." For Geertz as well as Erving Goffmann, both the audience for a Balinese cockfight and, by extension, that for a soccer game are neither crowds nor organized groups but rather something liminal, or "in between."[56] The social relations created while going to the stadium, in the stands, and on the way home are complex but ephemeral. You can have a long conversation with your neighbors in the stands but never see them again. After the game, the excited and unified "we" may return to the otherwise atomized "I."[57]

Although fans discuss events among themselves and read about them in the press, they possess nothing that can be called power until they are once again gathered together. The episodic character of these moments makes them different from so-called ordinary life and creates the space for what would otherwise be inadmissible, even dangerous acts and utterances. As Eric Dunning has noted, the practices of spectator sport create "enclaves of autonomy" where "mass audiences" can evade "the goals of those who seek to control them."[58] Even in the highly repressive conditions of the purges, Moscow men used football in just this way. They had found in this particular sport a way to demonstrate a measure of agency denied them in other parts of their lives.

This does not mean that Soviet soccer games were truly carnivalesque. Even during a match rowdyism was the exception, and seating arrangements in which the privileged occupied more desirable locations undermined the possibilities for cultural inversion. If not the sites of Bakhtinian cultural role reversal, neither was the Soviet stadium the Circus Maximus. Football in the USSR was not a safety valve consciously created by the state. If it had been, the authorities would not have spent so much time complaining, publicly and privately, about the fans' bad behavior, nor would they have so heavily ascribed didactic aims to sport. Clearly, the evidence of tension between subordinate and dominant groups during the thirties is substantial, but it does not directly answer the question of whether the new Soviet labor force was an us or a them. Indeed, as we shall see, the very distinction may be too sharply drawn.

## The Struggle Assumes New Forms

The intense competition between Spartak and Dinamo that emerged with the creation of the league in 1936 was not limited to the field of play. That summer, after the spring season, the action moved from the grassy fields to the pavement of Red Square. Sports festivals were a significant part of the regime's arsenal of public rituals from the earliest days of Soviet power.[59] In 1931, the VSFK reinvented the tradition of Physical Culture Day. Mammoth sports parades were held each summer in the central plazas of the USSR's major cities. The biggest parade of all took place in Moscow on Red Square. Thousands of male and female athletes from the various sports organizations took part. Most marched in unison past the Lenin Mausoleum, saluting the leadership, who waved back happily. Others took part in mass gymnastic displays, while still more rode on all manner of floats with sporting themes.

In a previous book, I described these events as monolithic, even totalitarian in tone.[60] They can fairly be said to bear certain resemblances to sporting celebrations in Nazi Germany and Fascist Italy. They also were similar to the opening ceremonies of Olympic Games. As presented in photographs, newsreels, and documentaries, the parades of the Stalin era were supposed to symbolize the orderliness and controlled character of Soviet sports for both international and domestic audiences. It is important, therefore, to remember that Physical Culture Day was not a sports event but rather scripted political theater, supervised in 1936 by the stage director, Valentin Pluchek. Stalin never attended an actual sports event, but he was always there for Physical Culture Day. With their highly arranged displays of tanned and fit male and female bodies, the parades became the apotheosis of Stalinist body culture, projecting images of strength, order, and discipline.

Recent research by Karen Petrone has presented a rather different picture of Physical Culture Day. First, she has shown that this celebration demonstrated the social and cultural differentiation that characterized the Great Retreat. Not everyone could watch. Only ten thousand could be squeezed into the reviewing stands on Red Square. As Petrone has remarked, "The Soviet demonstration created hierarchies not only by ordering its citizens according to their relative importance, but also by moving them across a carefully defined geographic space and by creating a small but extremely important audience of Soviet officials to view the parade."[61] If the number of those who would gaze was limited, so too was the number who could take part in this grand display of human bodies. In many other Soviet parades ordinary citizens could amble through the square after the official ceremonies had concluded. To take part in Physical Culture day you had to be fit.

Surprisingly, the parades themselves were also far from orderly. Films and photographs do not show the stumbling and often drunk participants described in secret reports. Even the most talented participants made their share of mistakes, but only the trusted few on Red Square actually saw them.[62] Finally, what seemed on the surface to be monolithic turned out actually to be "contested terrain." Each group taking part in the parade fought for more time and for the right to present its segment as it wished. Struggles over content and slogans were constant, and not everyone was comfortable with the expected orderliness. As Petrone concluded, "What was promoted by the Soviet state as a universal and simultaneous outpouring of support for Soviet power was

**3.10** The famous match on Red Square. *Futbol skvoz' gody.*

in fact a complex mixture of local politics, individual rivalries, and personal preferences and ambitions that took on a state-decreed form."[63] Dinamo athletes were especially visible participants in these spectacles, and many of their floats driven through the square consisted of living sculptures of arranged, immobile female and male bodies.

The most spectacular challenge to this display of order and discipline was provided by the Spartak Sport Society, starting with the 1936 parade. In Nikolai Starostin's not always accurate account, the idea came from Kosarev. The Komsomol leader suggested playing an actual football game on Red Square. A giant green felt carpet the size of a regulation field would be sewn by Spartak athletes and laid down on Red Square's cobblestones. This was to be the first time that the "greatest friend of Soviet physical culture, the dear leader and beloved teacher" would see a serious soccer game. Some police officials feared injuries caused by the hard surface. Others were afraid of balls flying over the Kremlin walls or, still worse, into the faces of dignitaries.

Some three hundred Spartak athletes using shoemaking needles stitched together ten-meter sections of the felt at night when Red Square was closed to traffic. The rug was rolled up and stored in the vestibule of the GUM department store across the square from the Kremlin. The day before the parade, with the giant carpet rolled out for a rehearsal, Kosarev appeared with a General Molchanov from the NKVD. Molchanov declared to Starostin that the cobblestones were an unsafe surface for play. The general also announced that the police wanted no severe injuries in Stalin's presence. Seeing that Kosarev was reluctant to intervene, Starostin called over Aleksei Sidorov, a member of Spartak's reserve squad. Starostin ordered Sidorov to jump and fall on the "grass." Sidorov proceeded to do just that and quickly stood up. When Starostin asked him if it hurt, Sidorov said no and offered to do it again. At this point Kosarev jumped in, pronounced everything fine, and declared the match could go on. The next day Starostin saw Sidorov in the locker room, his thigh completely covered with bruises.

While it is not clear whether Dinamo was ever asked to take part in this first match, it was understood after Molchanov's attempt to stop the game that it would not be playing the next day. Instead the Spartak starters played the reserve squad in a match "according to scenario."[64] Seven goals were prearranged out of fear that Stalin would be bored. Kosarev stood next to Stalin during the match. He had a white handkerchief in his hand, which he would wave if Stalin lost interest. In fact, the day went well. What had been planned as a thirty-minute demonstration lasted a full forty-five-minute half. It was a triumph for Spartak that was then repeated every year. Eventually in 1939, Dinamo agreed to take part. The teams played only twenty minutes and tied 0–0. Prearranged scripts were not used in subsequent years, allowing Spartak to achieve its purpose of introducing an element of spontaneity, of real sport, into this otherwise highly planned event.[65]

In taking such different approaches to this consciously created celebration, Spartak and Dinamo were demonstrating two different versions of body culture—the disciplined military, Olympic style of Dinamo versus the more spontaneous professional-entertainment model of Spartak.[66] These approaches affected the subsequent practices of the two groups in a variety of activities beyond the parades themselves.[67] As already noted, the Soviets were torn between two models of sport, the Olympic and the professional. While they had refused to take part in the Olympics, the leadership came to favor a noncommercial competitive version of sport to be used for didactic purposes, particularly the goal of social improvement. The Dinamo Society, founded by the police, came to represent official Stalinist body culture, which embraced the statist Olympic model, if not its class and gender content, and the parades do bear similarities to the rituals and ceremonies of the Olympics.

Before the war, Dinamo athletes dominated the multisport Spartakiads that made the "civilized" sports on the Olympic program available to workingmen and women in the best tradition of "rational recreation."[68] By contrast, Spartak took a more spontaneous approach to leisure and sporting spectacles, emphasizing games rather than parades. The events it stressed in its own practice, as Oleshchuk, Nazarov, and Romm show, were less didactic. The primary rituals for Spartak fans were such male celebrations as the pregame metro or tram ride, the pushing and shoving to get to their seats, plus chanting, cheering, booing, drinking, and cursing—not to mention the occasional riot—practices more profane than sacred.[69] Press accounts extended the distinctions to encompass the two teams' playing styles. The famed children's writer Lev Kassil noted in *Izvestiia* that Spartak played with more "feeling," whereas Dinamo took a "consistent and planned" approach.[70]

These differences also tracked with the sponsorship of the two groups. Dinamo, supported by the secret police, was inextricably part of the state sector. Its athletes were to embody the virtues the regime sought to inculcate through sport—discipline, order, health, respect for authority, and social improvement.[71] Dinamo was part of an organization subject to military discipline, and the bodies it presented were supposed to give the impression of discipline.[72] By contrast, Spartak was sponsored by the retail trades, which made it more a part of the public. It was a producer of sport spectacles for the historically beleaguered consumer sector. Promkooperatsiia had become a wealthy organization that was more than willing to use its money to buy top athletes whom it presented to the public more often in athletic contests than in festivals.[73]

The body cultures of the two groups were tied to opposing types of masculinity. Here, too, differing understandings of what it meant to be male intensified rather than limited the class element of their rivalry. For Soviet men, like most others around the world, adopting sport, with its rules, organizational structures, and schedules was part of becoming modern and urban.[74] During the course of the nineteenth century, both professional and Olympic sports had been constructed in Europe and in the United States as male bastions, but each approach offered a different kind of manhood.[75] As we have seen, Spartak's supporters practiced a Soviet version of that rough British working-class masculinity that was often violent and little concerned with sportsmanship. It stressed hardness and toughness. As a group with a sense of grievance, these Soviet men considered winning very important. While Oleshchuk's characterization of the games as wars is overstated, he does succeed in conveying the seriousness with which Spartak fans approached the sport. The police may have ruled Stalinist society, but they would not rule football. By contrast, Dinamo, despite its own supporters' occasional lapses, offered a more respectable middle-class manliness.[76] Its publicly obedient athletes were presented as objects for emulation.

Finally, these different masculinities fostered different attitudes toward female sport, which was never hugely popular with the largely male sports audience. Dinamo and the army sports clubs at least paid lip service to women's participation. Spartak proved largely indifferent. The society's leaders cared most about football—a "real man's game" that Soviet women had long been forbidden to play.[77] Nikolai Starostin had little interest in female sport. He was an impresario with a passion for organizing sporting spectacles that attracted large numbers of ticket-buying spectators. Before 1941, football, and football alone, could produce such huge crowds.

**3.11** The mighty Basques at Vnukovo Airfield. Fotoagentstvo Sportekspress.

### Basque-ing in Glory

Along with the creation of the league, the Basque tour proved to be the pivotal event in the development of Soviet football before the war. Spartak's role in this historic moment was central. Following so quickly upon the league's first successful season, the presence of the artful Basques propelled the popularity of the game in the USSR. As Nikolai Starostin later noted, "Not before or since has there been that much excitement around football."[78] Much like the Georgians in the USSR, the Basques, a small ethnic minority, had taken to football with particular intensity and skill as a way of amplifying their separateness from central authority.[79] As in the case of Russia, the British had brought the game to the Basque country late in the nineteenth century, when many immigrants from all over Spain went to work in the region's growing steel industry. A strong case can be made that Atletic Bilbao, which played only residents of the Basque country, was Spain's strongest team before the civil war. Six of the tourists played for Atletic Bilbao.[80]

The Spanish national team for the 1934 World Cup had included six men who later came to Moscow. Spain was eliminated in the quarterfinals by the Italian hosts, having tied 1–1 and then losing a replay 1–0 the next day. Some have argued that the Italians were allowed to get away with exceptionally rough tactics, injuring the Spaniards' star goalie, Zamora, and knocking him out of the replay.[81] For many, Spain became the "unofficial champion of the world." On their tour of Europe to raise money for widows and orphans of the Spanish civil war, the Basques beat Racing twice in Paris and then defeated the French champions, Olympique Marseilles. Just before arriving in

**3.12** The Basques take to the practice field. Fotoagentstvo Sportekspress.

Moscow on June 16, they topped the Polish national team 4–3. Despite the elaborate publicity about the tour, the Politbiuro approved their appearance fee of five thousand U.S. dollars only one day before their arrival.[82]

Thousands met the Basques at the Belorusskii station and followed their bus to the swank Hotel Metropole downtown. An immense rally was held on Red Square in support of the Loyalist side in the Spanish civil war. Two million ticket requests came from all over the Soviet Union. Imagine, then, Spartak's disappointment when it was not included in the initial list of opponents, although the team had been league champions the previous fall. Instead, Lokomotiv, which had won the 1936 cup, was picked for the first match. Dinamo had just taken the 1937 cup and was listed second. After that, the guests were to take a tour of Leningrad, Kiev, Minsk, and Tblisi. In Andrei Starostin's 1964 account of the tour, the sports council made these decisions at a gathering of representatives of the teams in the top flight. Andrei had the grace to say that Spartak was not picked because of a poor performance in that year's cup competition. A far less generous Nikolai, writing in the more open conditions of 1989, simply called the failure to include his team "incomprehensible."[83]

For the first game against Lokomotiv, ninety thousand fans stuffed their way into Dinamo Stadium. With the metro still a year from completion, people were literally extruded through the open windows of trams. Gate-crashers numbered in the thousands as the Basques ran rings around Lokomotiv, winning 5–1 and displaying such virtuosic technique that the Moscow fans applauded them wildly. A few days later, the Basques faced the sterner test of

Dinamo. Some have described the first half of this match, in which three goals were scored, as the most exciting football ever seen in the USSR. Dinamo took the lead to great jubilation in the twenty-fourth minute, only to have this feat matched twenty minutes later by the "Golden Canonier," the great center forward Isador Langara. In the Basques' version of the W, Langara played a particularly advanced position, which put enormous pressure on Dinamo's two back defenders. Again, their outmoded tactics had damaged the Soviets' cause. A goal with one minute to go in the half then put the Basques in front for good. Many years later, the Basque players told the Soviet sportswriter Konstantin Esenin (son of the poet) that Dinamo had been the best team they faced. Writing in *Krasnyi sport,* the pro-Spartak Mikhail Romm wrote, "Scarcely at any time has Moscow seen play like that of the first half of Dinamo versus the Basques."[84]

A few days later, the hosts tried a different approach. The Basques moved on to play a side of Leningrad selects. On orders from Kosarev, the local department of the Committee on Physical Culture and Sport attempted to lure the Basques into a night of drinking and girl-chasing. A big party was organized at a restaurant the night before the match. Beautiful comrades, who had a strong interest in the success of Soviet football, were invited, but babes and booze did not succeed with the Basques. Some local organizers subsequently feared their honored guests from freedom-loving Spain would see this crude attempt to get them drunk as a lack of respect for their professionalism.[85] Even if they had not succumbed to the charms of certain captains and majors of the NKVD, the Basques might have been somewhat distracted. Perhaps it was the all-day walking tour of the old capital's sights or the long bumpy trip to Peter the Great's palace outside the city. Whatever the cause, they tied the Leningrad team 2–2. They were then scheduled to take off on their tour to Minsk, Kiev, and Tblisi. Soviet fans had been hugely impressed by the visitors, but there was also a sense of pain and disappointment at having been so badly outclassed.[86]

At this point, according to Nikolai Starostin, requests to organize two more Moscow matches came from the "highest authorities." The proposal did not please the Basques, who resisted at first. There is no record of why they ultimately agreed; perhaps newsreels of ships departing from Odessa with food for the Loyalist side changed their minds, or maybe Kosarev was up to his old tricks. Something may well have been added to their appearance fee. We simply don't know, but it was agreed that one more match with Dinamo and a meeting with Spartak would be scheduled for July fifth and eighth, respectively.[87] The Soviet sides were allowed to be strengthened with players from other teams. Dinamo added four club mates from Leningrad and Tblisi, appearing as the Dinamo selects. Spartak was permitted to take on anyone who had not yet faced the Basques.

The combined Dinamo team that opposed the guests was actually less effective than the regular Dinamo Moscow side, lacking the cohesion of a group that played together regularly. Within twenty-five minutes, Dinamo was down 4–0 but managed to pull back to 4–3 at the half.[88] Fairly quickly Vasily

Smirnov tied the game, whereupon Dinamo collapsed. Langara struck twice. The final score was 7–4. Spartak was now the last hope for Moscow and all of Soviet sport. The game had been scheduled for three days later. In that short time, it seemed that all of the famous and powerful in the capital had descended on the training base at Tarasovka. Several thousand fans watched every practice. Andrei's bohemian pals—Ianshin, Olesha, and Lev Kassil'— showed up. The team was inundated by letters, telegrams, and phone calls. Various big shots called in Nikolai Starostin, demanded victory, and reminded him of the importance of the game, as if he needed reminding. This was, perhaps, the single biggest moment of his professional life.

Spartak used a coaches' council that supported and advised Kvashnin, who appears to have been unthreatened by what others might call meddling. Nikolai Starostin, Petr Isakov, Evgenii Arkhangelsii, and a host of others met for hours on end each day, debating whom to invite from other teams, who to start, and how to counter the Basques' devastating attackers, particularly Langara. Kvashnin had begun partial installation of the W. He had scouted the Basques closely in their earlier matches. Specifically, he urged withdrawing the center midfielder into the defense to guard Langara. Others objected, and as a compromise the decision was made not to alter the offensive scheme in which the inside forwards were already playing behind the wings and center forward. Andrei Starostin was the individual who had to make the switch, and he was outraged.[89] Center midfield had allowed him to control a game. Eventually he was persuaded, but the position change was only one of his problems. He was also nursing a serious groin injury that, as is often the case with such injuries, had been extremely slow to heal. A week before the big game he was still in pain. Nothing had helped. Finally, on the advice of his wife, he visited his old hangout, the racetrack, where a trainer injected him with the drug Navikulin, usually reserved for horses. Despite some nasty side effects, the medicine reduced the pain sufficiently for Andrei to be ready for the great day.

The question of personnel was as important as tactics. To fill in what Nikolai Starostin referred to as "weak spots" in its lineup, Spartak had been allowed to strengthen the team with other players. It took full advantage of this privilege. Five were invited, and four started. The most important was Grigory Fedotov (1916–1957), a brilliant twenty-one-year-old outside left from Metallurg Moscow who would go on to become one of the most feared strikers in Soviet history. The Spartak that took on the Basques was scarcely the everyday Spartak. Fedotov's performance, in particular, was spectacular.[90]

On the big day, the team rented four huge but ancient Lincoln convertibles for the drive from Tarasovka to Petrovskii Park, but the timeworn machines soon broke down, necessitating a quick switch to a bus. Driving in from the north on Prospekt Mira, the bus turned right onto the Ring Road only to be confronted by what was most likely the first traffic jam Moscow had seen since the NEP. The capital had few private vehicles, but it seemed everything avail-

able with wheels had been c          ered and was headed for the stadium.
Realizing they would be lat          ers changed into their uniforms in the
bus. They arrived eight min          he scheduled seven o'clock kickoff and
went straight through the t          the field.[91]

Quite quickly, Fedotov               a weaving run down the left flank and
blasted a shot off the po            the Basques' attention. In the fifteenth
minute, he made a simila             time his shot, from an even more severe
angle, rocketed past the             sco, into the net. Not long thereafter, Andrei Starostin and Anato             miscommunicated, and Langara punished
their mistake to tie the             ad dash by Vladimir Stepanov quickly put
Spartak ahead, but ju                alftime a combination of several precise
Basque passes tied th                2–2. Spartak's defensive adjustments had
forced its opponents t               ch faster tempo than the one they preferred.
For the second period                r Starostin, who had turned his ankle, was replaced by Sergei Ar                  welve minutes in, the game turned. Fedotov
was tripped inside                   or certainly fell down convincingly—and a
penalty kick was av

The Basques pro                      lly. Many in the stands had their own doubts
about the justice c                  Martyn Merzhanov, who covered the game for
Pravda, later reca                   he ensuing goal was achieved "not without the
help of the refere                   nev."[93] It did not contribute to the legitimacy of
Spartak's case tha                   machev was also the chief of finance for the Spartak Sport Society                    ilovskii (1911–1973) was chosen to take the kick,
which he put ir                      kolai Starostin recalled choosing him because he
saw Shilovskii                       hile the Basques argued their case. From the sidelines, he called                     skii to take the kick. One may ask where the actual
coach, Kvashr                        en this decision was made. For the rest of the game,
the Basques c                        moan about the refereeing, but clearly they had gotten the message that good guest should allow his host at least one win. The
final score was 6–2. With the Basque defenders' eyes glued to Fedotov,
Stepanov was able to complete a hat trick. He supplemented his scoring with
a willingness to get back on defense and close the gaps at midfield created by
Andrei Starostin's move to the defense, where he succeeded in controlling
Langara the rest of the way. Soviet pride had been saved, and the press milked
every angle of the story. The game had been broadcast throughout the entire
length and breadth of the USSR. It was seen as a tactical triumph because of
the adoption of elements of the W and a victory of will, as all those who took
the field for the Red and White displayed great, even desperate energy against
the road-weary Basques. Ever politically adept, Nikolai Starostin wrote in
Krasnyi sport that Spartak had been instilled with confidence through the support of Kosarev and the then-sitting head of VSFK, I. I. Kharchenko, another
of Starostin's bureaucratic allies.[94]

Spartak was now an even bigger fan favorite, but the triumph did not please
the patrons of Dinamo. Perhaps ominously, Spartak had achieved its victory

**3.13** Spartak atop a float in the 1937 Physical Culture Day Parade. The score of the match against the Basques is written on a giant boot. Later Spartak would be accused of planning to assassinate Stalin from the float. *Spartak Moskva: Offitsial'naia istoriia.*

by adopting features of a Western system of play. Nikolai Starostin would note in his last memoir that Kosmachev was soon disqualified and expelled from the All-Union Collegium of Referees. The decision, Starostin claimed, was demanded by "high-ranking followers of Dinamo" in the NKVD.[95] It is a good story, but a perusal of several subsequent minutes of the referees' collegium shows Kosmachev present and voting. He had been disqualified but not for life. Starostin left the impression the Spartak-Basque game had been Kosmachev's last match.[96] Yet two years later, at a meeting of representatives of Moscow football teams, a comrade Serdiukov from Lokomotiv complained that the once-disqualified Kosmachev was still working.[97] In his final memoir, Starostin himself admitted that some could see Kosmachev's call as less than objective:

> Now many years later, it seems a bit funny to dwell on such small details. Nevertheless, recalling that penalty, I can repeat the words of a poet, "the tsar looked at everything through Godunov's glasses." I looked at everything through Spartak glasses. In my opinion the penalty was one hundred percent deserved.[98]

One could well understand Starostin's annoyance. Before Stalin's death, when the brothers were in labor camps, their triumph over the Basques went uncredited. In 1952 a memoir was published under the name of Grigory Fedotov. It is even possible that Fedotov saw the manuscript before publication, but it was common at the time for athletes' memoirs to be ghosted. In that volume Fedotov gave a detailed account of his great game against the Basques, but he never mentioned Spartak. His description of the tactic of using a third defender is quite detailed, but Andrei Starostin's name does not come up.[99] Andrei understood that Fedotov bore no guilt for this rewriting of history. He would later make clear in his own self-penned memoir that he and Fedotov had become good friends when they played together. Fedotov was a universally beloved figure who died quite young, and no one ever blamed him personally for the omissions no doubt demanded by higher authorities.

Despite its somewhat artificial nature, Spartak's victory over the Basques, the only one by a Soviet team, became perhaps the central chapter in the Spartak family romance. The Basques had revealed the stagnation of Soviet playing methods, but now Spartak was to be the leader in adopting what some saw as a progressive approach. Right after the game, Kosarev announced in the locker room that the team, guest players included, would be sent to Europe to represent the USSR at the Workers' Olympiad in Antwerp and at a tournament held in conjunction with the International Exposition at Paris.[100] Spartak won both competitions. The trip to Europe had been a grand reward, and there were surely even more tangible spoils of victory. Close to his death, Nikolai Starostin told his coauthor, Aleksandr Vainshtein, "After the game against the Basques we lived as if under capitalism."[101] Time in the stores and cabarets of Paris was a marvelous prize, but some of what the brothers did in those stores and cabarets would come back to haunt them.

As luck would have it, the Moscow Art Theater was in Paris at the same time as the football tournament. Andrei Starostin's friend Mikhail Ianshin was in the city as well. With the tournament over, it was time to relax. They were invited to a performance of Ianshin's company. The audience was composed largely of émigrés. Later, he and Ianshin went to an émigré restaurant and supper club called Martyanich, a branch of a prerevolutionary Moscow nightspot. They made no attempt to do this secretly. In fact, they went in the company of a cultural attaché of the Soviet embassy. Ianshin had wished to get to know the life in exile of his fellow performers. Many of them had, after all, come to see his show.[102] Still, given the accelerated pace of the Terror at home, this cannot be seen as a shrewd move. The show trial of Lev Kamenev and Grigorii Zinoviev had taken place the year before. That January, Karl Radek was in the dock.[103] Scores of the Starostins' colleagues had been arrested. In such an atmosphere, dinner with White Guardists was risky, something others could point to as one more proof of the Starostins' too admiring attitude toward the West.

Andrei Starostin recalled coming back from Paris in an ebullient mood, but his joy quickly dissipated. At the behest of the state sports committee, *Pravda* had published an article headlined "The Inculcation of Bourgeois Morals at the Spartak Society." Similar items appeared in the committee's own organ,

*Krasnyi sport.* One of the accusations concerned the "revelation" that Spartak "secretly" paid its players. In fact, Nikolai Starostin had received permission to do just that from Anastas Mikoyan, the minister of trade, who had authority over Promkooperatsiia.[104] Starostin was, however, a bit disingenuous, claiming that all that was allowed was an eighty-ruble-a-month stipend to the players. Given the extensive professionalism that had permeated the world of football in recent years, especially the evidence of player salaries of eight hundred rubles a month, the revelation that players were being paid cannot have carried overwhelming shock value.

Still other accusations appeared in *Komsomol'skaia Pravda,* the very organ of the party's youth organization supposedly controlled by Kosarev. It was charged that the Spartak Society had contracted with the Moscow Region Insurance Union to train eight thousand men and women to qualify for the national physical fitness standard (GTO, *Gotov k trudu i oborone*). Spartak was paid one and a half million rubles for this service, but only one-fifth of those supposedly being trained actually passed the norms. The money, it was claimed, went instead to pay large bonuses to Spartak officials, including some ninety-seven thousand rubles to the Starostin brothers. Here one may well ask why the Komsomol newspaper was attacking the very team the parent organization supported. Was Kosarev, given his close relationship with the Starostins, aware of the accusations before they were published?[105] Did the "friends of Dinamo" somehow plant a story in a publication one would have expected to be pro-Spartak? At a minimum, the lack of coordination would seem to demonstrate the sheer irrationality that surrounded this controversy. The Starostins had made their share of enemies who were not pleased by their success. There were other groups, specifically the secret police, then at work on reining in Spartak. At this stage, however, one finds a litany of complaints rather than the grand conspiracy that emerged later.

Nevertheless, the brothers had good reason to be worried and confused. Friends had been arrested. Viktor Prokof'ev, a former Spartak player and ex-husband of Nikolai's sister Klavdia, had been jailed. So had Viktor Riabokon' the head of the Lokomotiv Society, and the leader of Promkooperatsiia, Kazimir Vasilevskii. Nikolai was only slightly calmed by the fact that Vasilevskii's replacement, Mikhail Chudov, was a rabid Spartak fan who devoted a large percentage of his working time to the team. Chudov lasted a year and a half in the post before being taken in. The Starostins were particularly stunned by the arrest of their friend Vladimir Strepikheev, who had refereed the second Basque match against Dinamo.[106] Long family discussions ensued, and friends like Ianshin came by to assure them that all would be well. The brothers were less certain. By this time they must have come to understand that behaviors they had considered harmless were far more serious in the eyes of others.

They wrote to both Stalin and Molotov, admitting to "the greatest friend of Soviet physical culturalists" that "mistakes" had, indeed, been made in so young an institution as Spartak. The brothers noted, however, that they had defended the honor of the Soviet Union on playing fields the world over for the last fifteen years, proving their loyalty and patriotism. The charges, they argued, were the result of envy over their success.[107] The accusations, emanating from enemies on the sports committee, included (in their words):

1. living beyond their means
2. bringing numerous "presents" back from foreign trips
3. receiving apartments and dachas from the Spartak Society
4. awarding special prizes to motivate sportsmen
5. introducing bourgeois morals into sport

The brothers surely understood that such charges did have a basis in fact. At issue was the question whether or not such activities were criminal in the context of the Great Terror.

The Starostins realized this was a job for Kosarev and wrote him early in September after posting their letters to the great leaders. Kosarev received them in his office and promised the problem would be sorted out. At this point, the head of the Komsomol was at the height of his powers. He was also a close personal ally of the chief of the secret police, Nikolai Yezhov, who had taken the lead in the orgy of denunciation that fueled the purges. It is worth noting that the Starostins spoke fondly of Kosarev in their various memoirs despite the fact that the Komsomol leader had fully supported the worst excesses of the purge process. A few days later, *Izvestiia* ran an item saying the case against the Starostin brothers had been quashed.[108]

Yet the rumors about shady business practices at Spartak would not go away. For some, the Starostins were simply living too large. In the words of Aleksandr Vainshtein, "In the late thirties and early forties, Starostin was already a legend. . . . He already was a mammoth—from another life."[109] The eminent Soviet sportswriter and lifelong Spartak fan Lev Filatov recalled standing at the service entrance of Dinamo Stadium during the late thirties and seeing Nikolai, wearing a fur coat, "majestically" emerge from a giant Packard limousine.[110] Unbeknownst to the brothers, the "crimes" mentioned in the press were just the tip of the iceberg. Far more serious accusations were being secretly hatched at this time. The Starostins would learn of them only much later under considerably more difficult circumstances.

In the meantime, the league season had resumed in early August. Spartak returned to the capital from its successful European appearances only on the thirteenth. Weary from having played six matches in ten days, not to mention their nocturnal duties, the Starostins asked that their appearance against Dinamo Kiev, set for August 17, be postponed. Unfortunately, not everyone at the highest levels of the sports world seems to have been pleased by their efforts at raising the international prestige of Soviet football. Their request was denied.[111] Once back at Tarasovka, the tasks of training and competing might have diverted the Starostins' attention from the threats to their well-being. The immediate crisis might have passed, but a sense of foreboding enveloped their lives and affected Spartak's performance on the field of play.

# 4

# On Top and Bottom, 1937–1944

As the league season wound down in the fall of 1937, the Starostins sensed that the political stakes of their rivalry with Dinamo had been raised substantially. Decades later, the great sportswriter and passionate Spartak fan Lev Filatov learned from Andrei Starostin just how intense the pressure really was. On a sports tour through the provinces, the two men wound up sharing a room in one of the USSR's less glamorous hotels. Filatov did not give the time or place, but his description of the circumstances was vivid. They had returned to their room after dinner when the power failed in the entire building. This was hardly an unusual occurrence, and Andrei offered to tell Filatov a story as they lay on their beds in the pitch-black room. Typically, Starostin did not specify the date of his tale, but one can easily deduce the moment in question. On the eleventh of September 1937, the Spartak players had arrived at Dinamo Stadium to face their archrivals. The usual hustle and bustle of prematch activity was strangely missing, and the stadium workers who usually met their bus and helped them with their equipment ignored them. They walked in silence to their locker room, when Nikolai approached Andrei with ominous news.

Nikolai had learned that despite their victories, some higher-ups had not been pleased by their trip to Paris. It seems that while in Europe, they had independently taken on the mantle of the strongest Soviet team. One can easily imagine their hosts asking whether Spartak was the top club in the USSR, and one can just as easily imagine the Starostins answering yes. They had won the fall season in 1936 and beaten the Basques. Nevertheless, Dinamo, having come in first during the 1936 spring season and just taken the 1937 cup, was at least as good as Spartak if not better. Its irritation with its rival was understandable. By claiming to be the leader of Soviet football, even before their competitions had been completed, the Starostins had risked a blow to the nation's fragile prestige. Nikolai had learned that a defeat in that day's match would be taken as proof of the falsity of their claims. He told Andrei they would suffer consequences. Strangely, Spartak had proved their point eight days earlier by defeating Dinamo. Why, one may ask, was this second match so crucial? Whatever the case, they dominated play on this day, but the result was ambiguous—a 0–0 tie that bought them time but did not ultimately save them.[1]

Spartak was now under even greater pressure. Finishing the league schedule under these difficult circumstances, Spartak trailed Dinamo going into the last day of the season.[2] A year to the day from the previous season's triumph, it played the same team, TsDKA, which was now sitting in last place. A win would force a playoff. A tie would leave Spartak in second place, trailing by a point. Down 0–2 in the second half, it rallied to even the score on a goal by the irrepressible Stepanov in the sixty-fifth minute. The stage seemed set for more Spartak drama, but it was not to be. There was no riot, no broken goalpost, just painful and typically unexpected defeat. Only a few of the players had been informed directly of the political machinations behind the scenes, but surely all of them knew what had been going on and felt the pressure.

The end of the season brought a breathing space. Kosarev had made the charges against Spartak disappear, and the Starostins were now able to take on the task of preparing for next year. In the following two seasons, Spartak won the double, both the league championship and the cup, a feat that was never duplicated by another Soviet team. Indeed, until that moment the only other team anywhere to achieve something similar had been Glasgow Rangers. With its "double double," Spartak cemented its position as the strongest Soviet team and acquired legions of new supporters, eclipsing Dinamo as the Soviet game's biggest gate attraction.[3]

The coming of the 1938 season brought a change of generations to the team: Aleksandr retired and passed the captain's armband to the fiery Andrei, a true leader on the field. A nonstop talker and screamer during games, Andrei was now entitled to berate referees and opponents, which he did incessantly. Viktor Sokolov (1911–1999) took over Aleksandr's position on the right side of the defense. The striker Aleksei Sokolov (1911–1979) came over from Lokomotiv. He was soon joined on the left side of the defense by one of the team's all-time great stars, Vasily Sokolov (1912–1981), who had been plucked from the team of the Belorussian army garrison, giving Spartak almost as many Sokolovs (none related) as Starostins. Also coming from the army in Belorussia was the goalie, Vladislav Zhmelkov (1914–1968), who took over while Akimov performed his military service playing for Dinamo Moscow. These last two transfers would later become controversial, but they were clear signs that Nikolai had not lost his touch as a dealmaker.

## Double Double Brings Big Trouble

Even before the 1937 season ended, both football and political circles had begun a heated discussion about what form the next league schedule should take. In its first two years, this had been a small competition, of first seven and then nine teams. Yet if soccer was a marker of both the modern and the urban, it made political sense to expand the league throughout the USSR as part of the project of nation building. A cascade of proposals came from soccer people, the press, and the party. Some favored including twenty-six or even thirty-two teams in the top flight, giving each republic at least one team in the first division. While this plan was laudable in its sensitivity to the concerns of national minorities, the lack of good teams on the periphery threatened the quality of the competition and raised the possibilities for political meddling. Football professionals instead preferred what they called the "sporting principle," which favored the inclusion of the best teams based on performance, regardless of their location.[4] After some hesitation, the Starostins supported this latter approach.

The debates raged on through the winter. In the course of the arguments the newly retired Aleksandr Starostin was elected president of the toothless football section of the state sports committee (the VSFK). The section's lack of power became abundantly clear one month before the season opening when the new chief of Soviet sport, A. V. Zelikov, settled the question by decreeing a twenty-six team league with one round of competition (i.e., no home and away).[5] The new structure wound up doing little for minority nationalities. The sole previously unrepresented republic was Azerbaijan. Odessa, Stalingrad, Kharkov, Rostov, Stalino, and Baku got teams in the top flight, but the true purpose of the expansion was demonstrated by the fact that Moscow was now given ten teams, six more than in the previous year. Even as he went against the sporting principle, Zelikov did not replace it with a new national principle. Political rather than sporting criteria were used to decide who could be included in the top level of play, but this was not a politics guided in any way by ideology. Instead, the influence and ambition of powerful competing institutions determined the committee's choices.[6] Ultimately, Zelikov's approach pleased only those undeserving clubs that were invited to take part. Everyone else was disgusted by the ultimate results, whether they had won or lost.

Kvashnin prepared for the new campaign with a month of preseason training near Odessa. Though his extreme emphasis on conditioning precipitated a players' revolt, he succeeded in completing the transition to the W and retooled the offense to compensate for the formation's defensive emphasis. Spartak was ready to play, but the length of the new schedule proved an ordeal for both the players and the fans of Moscow. With the inclusion of new teams, the season was now dotted with a lot of unattractive matchups against weak opponents. Few attended Moscow derbies when one of the sides was seen as marginal. Stadia in cities now added to the top flight did not have the same capacity as those in the capitals. Finally, a season lasting from May into November ensured there would be plenty of games played in bad weather. All these factors caused a sharp drop in attendance, threatening the game's status as a popular culture attraction.

That year's cup competition, the biggest ever, was scheduled around the regular league calendar. On September 14, Spartak defeated Elektrik of Leningrad 3–2 before a crowd of seventy-five thousand to take the prize. For all its problems, the league saw a close contest for first place until the very end. TsDKA, now with Fedotov, and Metallurg, coached by the brilliant Boris Arkadiev (1899–1986), had the same number of points as Spartak going into the last two weeks. Spartak won its last games against the two teams at the bottom of the standings and completed the same double achieved the previous year by Dinamo. On the last day of the season, both TsDKA and Mettalurg lost under dubious circumstances. Metallurg went so far as to protest its loss to Dinamo Tblisi, and Spartak had to wait until the appeal was denied. The team was finally confirmed as champion nineteen days after the season's last match in a ceremony at Dinamo Stadium before thirty-five thousand freezing fans. In his capacity as team captain, Andrei Starostin, speaking his best Bolshevik, thanked "the best friend of physical culturalists, comrade Stalin." Dinamo Moscow finished fifth, plagued by internal bickering and a failure to adapt to the W. TsDKA was second and Metallurg third based on goal difference. Despite its triumph, Spartak was not immune to the dissension that had consumed Dinamo Moscow. Kvashnin, ever the maximalist, had worn out his welcome with both the players and Nikolai Starostin. He was replaced for the last two months of the season by the highly experienced Petr Popov (1898–1965).[7]

Under Aleksandr Starostin's leadership the league structure was revised yet again in 1939, this time for the better. Fourteen teams were to play a home-and-away schedule of twenty-six games from May to November.[8] It seemed like blessed normalcy. Popov approached the task of Spartak's repeating the double with an even stronger cast. Akimov came back from Dinamo and teamed with Zhmelkov to form a great tandem in goal. Together they gave up an average 0.8 goals per game in what was still an attacking era. In front of them, Andrei Starostin had become a ferocious central defender, flanked by the equally brilliant Sokolovs, Viktor and Vasilii. Sergei Artem'ev was joined in midfield by Konstantin Malinin (1915–1995), once of TsDKA. He had been one of the guest players in the match against the Basques. Up front, Vladimir Stepanov and Aleksei Sokolov composed a lethal pair of inside forwards. What had been a sluggish attack now improved. Although there was only one Starostin on the field (Petr had been rendered ineffective by a serious leg injury), this was the strongest team Spartak had yet put together. It won the league by a comfortable margin over a surging Dinamo Tblisi team, led by the brilliant Boris Paichadze.[9]

Dinamo Tblisi would also figure in the central event of Spartak's season. By the fall of 1938, the Terror, orchestrated at Stalin's behest by the insane Nikolai Yezhov, had gone completely out of control. With so many top leaders and useful functionaries arrested and executed in the party's orgy of self-destruction, the efficiency of the state itself was suffering severely. The army officer corps had been virtually wiped out. Hoards of innocents had disappeared, creating immense demographic problems. Given that war in Europe seemed imminent, it was essential to rebuild the country's defenses. Yezhov had to go. A man who truly knew too much, he was arrested and executed. Close allies of Yezhov, most notably Aleksandr Kosarev, were in grave danger. The new head of the NKVD was the Georgian Lavrentii Beria (1899–1953), who had held the same position in the Trans-Caucasian Republic.[10] This change proved good for the nation. At Stalin's behest, Beria presided over a massive decrease in the Terror. What had been hundreds of thousands of executions in the previous three years now fell to a "mere" two thousand. While overall arrests were diminished, Beria moved quickly to eliminate Yezhov's purported allies. Kosarev was arrested in November 1938 and executed soon thereafter. With Spartak's most powerful friend in high places gone, the brothers understood they too were in trouble.

It is worth noting that the Starostins never mentioned Kosarev's support for Yezhov in any of their memoirs. The Komsomol leader was instead described in the most positive of tones, even though he was every bit as ruthless as any other convinced Stalinist. He had supervised the bloody purge of the Leningrad party organization after the arrest of Zinoviev. Although the Starostins were surely ignorant of the fact, Kosarev alone had urged the execution of Bukharin when all others in the Politbiuro sought only to support Stalin's decision in the matter.[11] The brothers' airbrushing of Kosarev's historical image is important to note. Others would later ascribe "democratic" sentiments to the team and its founders, and there would be plausible reasons for making such claims. Yet it cannot be said the Starostins' worshipful approach to their great patron serves their own liberal image well. While Kosarev may not have been worse than any other leader of the era, he was surely no better.

It did not help Spartak that Beria was a passionate fan of football and a player of some ability in his youth. His position as head of the secret police put him on the presidium of the Dinamo Sport Society, and he took his duties seriously. While Beria's first loyalty was to Dinamo Tblisi, he was deeply concerned about the plunging fortunes of Dinamo Moscow. He became the Soviet equivalent of a meddling capitalist team owner, involving himself in the operations of many of the top Dinamo clubs. It was as if New York Yankee owner George Steinbrenner had been combined with former FBI head J. Edgar Hoover into one single human and given the powers of the chief of the Gestapo. Beria rarely missed a game any Dinamo team played in Moscow, and he and others in the secret police were not pleased by Spartak's ascendancy. If success on the field could soften the public's negative view of the police in the time of the purges, then failure at football could weaken acceptance of their authority and lower their prestige.

The Starostins now had an enemy in the highest of places. Nikolai Starostin later sought to explain Beria's antipathy in personal terms. In Nikolai's final account, he wrote that the two men had met on a soccer field in Tblisi sometime in the twenties. The professional Starostin claimed to have run rings around the chubby amateur, and he thought Beria retained memories of this humiliation. The next twenty-five years is then explained as a vendetta between the tall, talented, and handsome Starostin and the short, fat, awkward, and salacious Beria. As in other parts of the Starostins' memoirs, the story may be better than the reality. Neither the Tblisi-born historian Vartanian nor the veteran sportswriter Pavel Aleshin thinks such a scenario was likely, especially in a place as status-conscious as Georgia. Football at that time was not fully respectable, and, they say, an important functionary of the Caucasian secret police would not have risked his dignity by playing in such a match.[12] It can be safely said, then, that Beria's approach to the Dinamo-Spartak rivalry involved much more than a need to find compensation for earlier athletic failure.

In the last months of 1938 other ominous currents had emerged. The publication in the millions of the notoriously falsified short history of the Bolshevik Party intensified the process of ideological-political education in every Soviet entity. The study of this popularly directed volume was linked directly to the improvement of production, as if the knowledge of what Stalin did (or did not) do in 1917 could ensure the meeting of planned quotas. The carrot of education was soon complemented by the stick of a harsh new labor law. The December 28 decree aimed to inculcate discipline among the workforce. The rampant problems of absenteeism, tardiness, and job switching were now deemed criminal acts. The new proletarians, many of whom had just arrived from the countryside, were now forced to adjust to the tempos of industry.

Labor discipline had also bedeviled the soccer world. Players came to practice late, challenged coaches, drank too much, and fought on the field. Each team had its political officer (*politruk*), whose job was to drum a measure of culture and responsibility into the largely uneducated playing staffs. On Spartak, this task fell to a comrade Rabinovich, whose efforts the press criticized with unflattering comparisons to Dinamo Moscow, where the ideological training was supposed to have gone well.[13] It appeared that Spartak took its duties in this area much less seriously than did Dinamo. It later became clear that the Starostins were greatly disturbed by the new labor law, which they privately thought led to exploitation more severe than that found under capitalism.

It is not clear whether personal animosity, ideological education, or a simple will to win drove Beria's actions at this time, but his presumed interference in the regular sporting process soon precipitated one of the most bizarre moments in the history of world football. The cup competition took place in August and September along with the regular league schedule. Spartak advanced to the semifinal on September 8 in Moscow, where it took on Dinamo Tblisi, its strongest rivals in the league and Beria's favorite team. This was an extremely powerful side with excellent players who approached the game with great intensity. Known in the press as "the flying Uruguyans," the Georgians took an emotional and technical Latin American approach to the game that was distinct from the control and physicality of most Moscow clubs, including Spartak. Especially skilled dribblers and committed individualists, the Georgians vastly preferred attack over defense.

The semifinal, however, proved to be a defensive struggle, one that produced a single score. It came in the sixty-fourth minute after a scramble in front of the Tblisi goal. Dinamo's Russian goalie, Aleksandr Dorokhov, punched the ball away but directly onto the feet of Andrei Protasov. In Starostin's version, Protasov's shot crossed the goal line but failed to make it to the back of the net when defender Shota Shavgulidze cleared the ball away. Nevertheless, referee Ivan Gorelkin awarded the goal. Dinamo lodged a protest, which was quickly denied by the football section of the sports committee.[14] In distinction to past practice, the entire committee then affirmed the section's decision. Four days later Spartak defeated Stalinets of Leningrad 3–1 in the final and claimed its second cup in a row. Everyone went home and proceeded with the rest of the season.[15]

But some twelve days after the final, around September 24, Spartak team members and officials began seeing players from Dinamo Tblisi in Moscow. They learned from their Georgian guests that the disputed semifinal was to be replayed on September 30—three weeks after the final had taken place! The decision to overrule the sports committee had come from the Central Committee itself and had been announced in the Georgian press as early as the sixteenth of September. Given this degree of public knowledge, it is difficult to believe Nikolai Starostin and everyone associated with Spartak had been unaware of the order to replay the final. As head of the football section, brother Aleksandr may not have been happy with the ruling, but he probably knew about it. Nor is it likely the Central Committee would have informed only one of the participants in the replay. Spartak also had powerful friends who might well have known what was going on.[16] If the club was truly unaware of the decision, however, it was left with a mere six days to prepare for one of the biggest matches in its history.

Starostin sought to mobilize his political allies, but Kosarev was gone. No direct proof has ever been found to indicate that Beria personally demanded and got the replay, but one may well ask who else at that level would have cared enough about soccer. Even if Beria did make such a request, it is important to note that it found traction at the highest levels of the party. The Spartak leader was told the order had come specifically from the powerful party secretary, Andrei Zhdanov. In this light, the politics swirling around the 1939 cup appear to have gone well beyond Starostin's personal struggle with so perfect a villain as Beria.[17]

Going into the rematch, the Dinamo Tblisi players were surely tired from their long train trip back to Moscow, but Spartak was also in poor shape. Andrei Starostin had broken his hand, and leading scorer Aleksei Sokolov had been indefinitely disqualified for punching an opponent in the face. In the first half, Spartak was able to take advantage of Tblisi's halfbacks, who involved themselves too eagerly in the offense, allowing Spartak's outside right, Georgi Glazkov, to score twice. Dinamo's star, Boris Paichadze, came back with a goal before the half to make it 2–1. Almost immediately after the game resumed, Spartak was awarded a penalty kick, converted by Glazkov for a hat trick. The Georgians attacked furiously, but their best efforts were negated by Akimov's brilliance in goal. With four minutes left, however, they finally succeed in scoring off a corner. To add to the tension, Akinov was injured on the play and replaced by Zheml'kov.[18] The end of the game was played with the crowd of eighty thousand, nearly all pro-Spartak, in a heaving uproar.

Dinamo protested, claiming the penalty was not deserved. Two days later its claim was denied, and the cup stayed with Spartak. The victory was of immense importance to Spartak's fans. As Lev Filatov noted in 1997 in the last article of his life,

> There was a game played in 1939 that was more important for my younger generation than any that had ever been seen. . . . Never before and never again have I had to root so hard, breathing heavily, my knees trembling. . . . For us, what was being decided was not the fate of the cup or the fate of Spartak. What was being decided was the fate of football itself. Would it remain an island of justice or would we wave our hands as we passed the stadium and place a cross on our bliss?[19]

Along with the triumph over the Basques and the game on Red Square, the great victory in the forced replay became another chapter of the Spartak saga. The team had triumphed over arbitrary power and, thought Filatov, saved the game itself. The faithful had been rewarded. Writing his match report in *Krasnyi sport,* the great sportswriter (and Spartak supporter) Aleksandr Vittenberg returned three times to the phrase "Again, Spartak demonstrated its superiority."[20]

If we are to believe Nikolai Starostin, Beria left the stadium in a huff. Decades later Starostin told one of his favorite players, "I knew then we would be going on a long trip."[21] Beria's team had not defeated Spartak at football, but Stalin's favorite policeman had other, less than sporting tools at his disposal.[22] For all the political freight invested in this one match, however, it is by no means clear that Beria's frustration focused on Spartak's victory. The next season, Dinamo Moscow would right its ship, bringing in Arkadiev from Metallurg and winning the 1940 championship. Spartak finished third, losing 1–5 to its archrival before eighty-five thousand in a match some Dinamo players later recalled as the greatest of their careers.[23] One might have expected Beria to have been content, but as Aleksandr Vainshtein has suggested, his pursuit of the Starostins was about more than football.[24]

Despite Spartak's winning the double in 1939, there were still weaknesses in its on-field performance. Writing in *Vechernaia Moskva* during December, Nikolai admitted the players had not sorted out all their problems in attack. The team's strength remained the defense, especially with the tandem of Akimov and Zhmel'kov in goal. Spartak featured big and physical players in its back line. These men won through effort and strength. By contrast the offense, despite the presence of good athletes, did not cohere. Starostin suggested that the defensive orientation of the W formation had contributed to this problem, and he pledged that in 1940 his club would adopt a "new Soviet style."[25] This seemed a step back for a team that had prided itself on taking the lead in adopting the methods of the West. Yet by late 1939, World War II was already under way. With the Soviets tied to their new German allies by the Molotov-Ribbentrop Pact, there seemed little to be gained politically by playing in a style developed by professionals (the Germans were still officially amateur). Moreover, in an early sign of sporting xenophobia, there appears to have been pressure coming from outside soccer circles to abandon the W. The result on the field for Spartak in the last full Soviet season before the German invasion was confusion and defeat.

Spartak may have had millions of fans on the eve of the war, but it had also acquired enemies beyond Beria. Many of their colleagues in the football world were not admirers of the Starostins. Their opponents were jealous of their success, and more than a few were willing to voice professional complaints about their methods. At a 1939 meeting of Moscow team representatives, Lokomotiv's delegate (correctly) complained that Spartak controlled the referees chosen for its matches. He was particularly angry about Andrei Starostin's behavior on the field. Quite accurately, he noted that the fiery Andrei kept up a constant stream of complaint throughout games, and refs who drew his ire no longer worked Spartak matches:

> No one can do anything with Starostin. He's a big shot. But if he is such a big man, he should set an example with his behavior. Spartak wins referees to their side, reporters too. Things have come to such a state that what Nikolai Starostin says should be written gets written. The press is on their side too. They don't write about the other teams, even if they have some positive aspects to their work.[26]

Despite the presence of several pro-Spartak writers on its staff, the nation's main sports publication, *Krasnyi sport,* published by the sports committee, was not always well disposed to the Starostins. Elena Knopova, who succeeded the Starostins' ally I. I. Kharchenko at the head of the organization, pressured reporters into writing negative pieces on Spartak.[27] In a context other than that of Stalinism, these kinds of matters would, of course, not be causes for great concern, but during the late thirties any criticism of the Starostins was grist for their professional opponents' mills. These complaints could not, however, dent the massive support Spartak enjoyed among the laboring men of Moscow who composed the soccer audience.

## Spartak and the Soviet Working Class

In the previous chapter, I examined the political attitudes of Spartak's proletarian fan base using anecdotal evidence produced after the collapse of Communism. I want now to return to this matter and look at it more concretely in order to discover what team choice can tell us about male Moscow workers' attitudes toward the regime. If all workers were not fans, it can still safely be said that nearly all fans during the 1930s were workers. Scores of player memoirs and popular histories make this clear. In creating the chosen communities of team supporters described by Abramian, these lovers of football were exercising one of the few free choices Soviet citizens could make, choices that were not devoid of political significance. To support the civilian Spartak as opposed to the police club Dinamo implied a certain distancing from the party-state. Conversely, rooting for Dinamo suggested greater comfort with the forces of Soviet order. Yet this was a politics of the everyday in which citizens made what turned out to be highly ambiguous and swiftly evolving choices about their political and cultural identities. Not every Dinamo fan was a Communist, nor can it be said that those who supported Spartak were universally nonparty. There was instead, even at the height of Stalinism, this different, more diffuse kind of politics, one that had no immediate impact on state policy or on the careers of various highly visible actors. Rather, this was a much more amorphous set of lower-level power relations that ordinary people could use for some of their own purposes. The true nature of the Moscow labor force —and its view of Stalin's regime—is a subject that has been much debated by Soviet and Russian historians as well as an able cohort of their Western colleagues.[28]

Soviet cities, especially the capital, had grown enormously since the first Five-Year Plan. A quarter of the 3.6 million people who lived in Moscow in 1934 were factory workers. Some 649,900 more fit into the ambiguous social category of white-collar workers, called "employees" (*sluzhashchie*).[29] This huge increase had led to urban crowding and a massive reduction in living standards. As had been the case before the revolution, Moscow's labor force was quite heterogeneous, including thousands of urban women and peasants who took up work in the capital. Nearly all recent arrivals from the countryside—like peasants everywhere in the world—were little involved in the urban phenomenon of sport. Women, too, swelled the ranks of factory workers, but their involvement in prewar football was largely limited to watching men watch other men play football. In the little remaining documentary footage on early soccer (roughly forty minutes), women do appear in the stands. Yet nearly all the matches captured on film were cup finals or other important games at comparatively well-policed Dinamo Stadium. Those females shown on screen are stylishly dressed and usually young, and they tend to sit together. It is reasonable, given the prevailing patriarchy of the period, to think they may have been the wives or girlfriends of players, suggesting the absence of a female presence at most regular games.[30]

While one must be careful about making broad generalizations based on the paucity of solid evidence, it is clear that the workers who watched soccer had greater experience of urban life than did the newcomers. The men who had followed the sport before the revolution and during the NEP continued to do so into the late thirties. Many of them had raised families and passed on their love of the game to their sons. Additionally, several Soviet scholars claimed Moscow workers were becoming older and more skilled, a process that made them more likely to be drawn to the urban activity of sport. In the larger economy of the city, the shift away from female-oriented work in textiles toward more masculine metalworking can also be seen as a sign of an increasingly skilled workforce.[31] Under the third Five-Year Plan, announced in 1938, an even greater emphasis was placed on heavy industries, particularly defense.[32]

The chaos of the first Five-Year Plan had allowed little time for training, and the new recruits to the urban labor force were not highly skilled. Over the course of the decade, that situation changed. From the league's formation in 1936 up to the war, the capital's workers became more experienced, not only on the factory floor but also in the ways of city life. They were beginning to fit the sociological profile of football audiences in other nations, particularly Great Britain, where the relatively skilled segments of the working class were more likely to be involved in sports.[33] It should be noted that the precise meaning of the term "skill" (*kvalifikatsiia*), as used by Soviet historians, was ambiguous and not always like that of the British labor aristocracy.

To talk about Spartak and the working class, then, requires a clear understanding of how broadly or narrowly we are using the term "class." I have argued above for a fairly generous definition. Within that class, Oleshchuk's characterization of Moscow's football supporters as one half for Spartak and one half for everyone else corresponds to the preponderance of impressionistic evidence. This conclusion is not challenged anywhere in the literature, in archival material or in personal recollections. Yet this does not mean Spartak's following was socially and economically homogeneous or that one segment of the working class supported Spartak and another Dinamo, Torpedo, or even Lokomotiv. As noted above, Promkooperatsiia, Spartak's sponsor, represented primarily service and trade workers. Between 1928 and 1932, the organization grew from roughly 600,000 members to 1.6 million, while the percentage of workers involved in trade and distribution in the entire workforce increased from 5.3 to 9.2 percent.[34] Industrial laborers, who were not a majority in 1930s Moscow, may well have had different views and interests, but many of them rooted for Spartak along with their less successful factory teams. Thus it is best to adopt a broad approach to encompass thousands of workers outside the factory, including construction, transport, trade, and even entertainment.

Despite these caveats, we can say that a significant portion of Moscow working males made one of the few choices available to them, a choice that established in a limited but still meaningful way their independence from the regime. Romanticizing more than slightly, Nikolai Starostin noted this in his last book: "Football seemed somehow disconnected from everything that was going on around it. . . . It was, for the majority, the only, and sometimes the last, possibility and hope for maintaining in one's soul the smallest bit of sincere feelings and humane relationships."[35] The politics of the workers' choice were, however, far from clear, and it would be stretching the evidence to claim the team's following was anti-Communist or procapitalist.

The regime had sought to use sport to inculcate the rational values of health, punctuality, skill, and respect for authority. The state wished to see its "guardians of order" successful on the field and admired by the public. In a 1936 article in *Krasnyi sport,* the head of the state sports committee, I. I. Kharchenko, had remarked that Dinamo provided the best model for other sport societies.[36] Yet mass repression alone could never have achieved support for Dinamo. Chosen communities were just that—the people picked their own heroes. To be sure, many football fans did choose to root for Dinamo, and just as many of them were true believers in the system. Spartak's support may have been greater, but Dinamo was hardly bereft. Regardless of their specific sentiments, all of these communities were as episodic as the focused gatherings of match day. They were also, to use Benedict Anderson's now famous phrase, "imagined communities," culturally constructed without clear geographical boundaries.[37] The screaming fans in the stands (at least some of them) may have believed they constituted such a community, but this was so only for a moment.

During the late 1930s, male workers in Moscow used Spartak to make choices about their identities. To be sure, those choices were highly fluid. In the political context of the period, they could not have assumed organized form. Nevertheless, by choosing Spartak and supporting it in less than orderly ways, thousands of Moscow men kept their distance from much around them that was distasteful while maintaining a measure of personal dignity. This did not make Spartak, to use an anachronistic term, a "dissident" team. The club's supporters did not seek the overthrow of Communism. Oleshchuk recalled that he and his pals simultaneously thought Spartak great, Dinamo terrible, and Stalin an OK Joe.[38]

## The Case against the Starostin Brothers

Given the inescapably competitive nature of elite sport, it was inevitable that the Starostins made their share of professional enemies along the way. With Soviet teams supported by various important figures and institutions, some of which had the power to arrest their opponents, the possibilities for serious unpleasantness were considerable. From its very first moments, the Spartak Sport Society had inspired doubt and envy in equal measure. In 1935 the trade union newspaper *Trud* expressed concern about the Starostins' motives in creating so large and well-endowed an organization. A year later, several minor Spartak officials were required to appear in a local Moscow court to answer accusations of financial malfeasance, charges that were quickly dropped.[39] The first serious storm, as has been discussed, came in September 1937.

The accusations that appeared in *Pravda* and *Krasnyi sport* had been handled by Kosarev, but it turned out there had been still other forces conspiring behind the scenes against the Starostins and their closest friends. Having survived the schemes of institutional and professional enemies, the Starostins now had to deal with a threat much closer to home. On the 1937 trip to Paris, Spartak had been accompanied by an entire sporting delegation, which included the USSR's most famous distance runners, the brothers Serafim and Georgii Znamenskii. These men were prominent members of Spartak and neighbors of Andrei and Nikolai Starostin, sharing a stairwell with them in their new center-city apartment building on Spiridonova Street.

Holders of all Soviet records from 1,500 to 10,000 meters, the Znamenskiis were the sons of a rural priest. Despite their politically suspect lineage, they embraced Soviet power and became successful athletes. Georgii eventually got a medical degree. Both took part in the Great Patriotic War. Serafim died in 1942 and Georgii in 1947. In death, they became beloved figures, inspiring books and documentaries that transformed them into Soviet sport saints.[40] The Znamenskii Brothers Memorial Track Meet is still run today. Sadly, however, "stool pigeon" (*stukach*) turns out to have been one the skills listed in the job description of "Soviet sports saint." During 2000, on a program produced by the NTV television network entitled "Big Parents," Georgii's daughter, Elena, stated that both her father and his brother had worked for "the organs" and were well acquainted with Beria and Stalin. At no point did she directly label them NKVD agents, nor did she explain when they began the relationship, or whether they were working at Beria's behest. But Elena Znamenskaia had even more revelations: her uncle had not died at the front, according to the official story, but had instead killed himself while home on leave. She was unable to give a reason for Serafim's suicide, and we should not necessarily assume he acted out of guilt for his activities.[41]

In September 1937, well before Beria came to Moscow, Serafim sent the new head of the sports committee, Elena Knopova, a report on the Starostins' activities in France and at home. If the Znamenskiis were friendly with Beria, who took over the NKVD in 1938, for whom were they working in 1937? Did Knopova simply ask them to keep an eye on the Starostins, or were the great runners acting as concerned Soviet citizens? Regardless of their reasons, Serafim claimed in his report that Nikolai Starostin was altogether too friendly with the bourgeois types the delegation had met in France, acting like "the owner of a private sports club." Starostin, he argued, "spends all his time, attention and funds on football. He neglects the other sports and the preparation of members for the GTO badge. Only certain people are allowed to be involved with football, not like at Dinamo which is a true collective." The charge of neglecting mass physical culture in favor of elite sport would appear in the press again and again, and of course it was true that the Starostins found organizing high-level spectacles more compelling than teaching grenade throwing to factory workers.[42]

Serafim also reported that the brothers and their friends held nightly card games, accompanied by much drinking, shouting, and cursing: "I once asked

Andrei if he wasn't tired of these nightly drunks which broke up only at dawn. 'People will think you're some kind of playboy.' . . . Andrei replied ironically, 'You, Serafim, are a funny fellow.'" Although Znamenskii may have been exaggerating, Andrei was certainly no stranger to such activities. It also did not help the Starostins that Evgenii Arkhangelskii and Vladimir Strepikheev, two of their regular drinking partners, had recently been arrested. Serafim also claimed that each of these nightly parties must have cost around one thousand rubles, the equivalent of his own less than miserly monthly salary.

In France, the Starostins were said to have speculated in foreign currency while buying far more than their fair share of presents. Each member of the delegation, said Georgii Znamenskii, brought home a single suitcase. The Starostins arrived at the Belorusskii train station with four valises each. When a commission of the sports committee later examined the delegation's excursion, both Znamenskiis were called in. Learning of this investigation, Nikolai told Serafim the commission had been organized by those "scoundrels from Dinamo" and warned him to say nothing. Georgii related having received the same warning. If Serafim were asked how much the Starostins had brought back, he was to say, "As much as all the others." When it turned out the Znamenskiis did speak to the commission, Starostin threatened Georgii and temporarily cut off his salary. Echoing his brother, Georgii claimed these were the methods of the "entrepreneur of a private sports club."[43] Finally, the Znamenskiis stated that Nikolai Starostin had bragged about having army contacts who had helped him acquire two players from military teams (Vasili Sokolov and Vladislav Zhmel'kov), a charge that was true.[44]

Given the Znamenskiis' testimony, it surprising that Nikolai in his final memoir, written in the full glare of glasnost, does not have a bad word for them. Did he not wish to sully their reputation? Perhaps he understood and forgave them in hindsight. No doubt they had been pressured to produce their accusations, but there was a kernel of truth in what they had said. Still, charges of this kind could have been seen as criminal only in the context of the purges. Anywhere else they were a normal part of running a sports enterprise. At the time Starostin surely felt that his activities and those of his associates were more or less normal, since hundreds of other Soviet sportsmen and women, not to mention others who traveled to the West, behaved in much the same way. He was, after all, a sports showman. His team packed stadiums throughout the USSR, propagandizing sport and turning more than the odd ruble.

In retrospect, the "crimes" mentioned by the Znamenskiis were minor compared with what was being hatched at the same time, in this case without the Starostins' knowledge. In the same memoir, Nikolai related that Vladimir Strepikheev, Viktor Ryabokon', and others of his friends were arrested in the fall of 1937. Later, Strepikheev and Ryabokon' were shot. Nikolai did not write that they had been forced to accuse the Starostins of far more serious crimes than buying too many dresses for their wives. Although someone in the secret police may have been preparing a far bigger case against the Starostins, it does not seem likely that Yezhov, a Kosarev ally, would have been leading a grand conspiracy against them. Zealous underlings may have started something only to be called off by the Komsomol leader. Whatever the case, there does not seem to have been much interagency coordination at this time in preparing the case against the Starostins.

Nevertheless, the interrogation records of the arrested laid the groundwork for the most serious charges that the Starostins were forced to confront when they, too, were finally taken in during 1942. These documents (*doprosy*) were not truly stenographic accounts of police questioning of the accused. Rather, they were concocted stories the arrested were forced to confirm under various forms of pressure. In one case, the director of the Stalin Institute of Physical Culture, Sesan Fruman, repeated the old charge that Starostin came from a "family of traders" and was trying to "introduce the worst aspects of bourgeois sport." More elaborately, Vasily Steblev, a track coach at Spartak, alleged a conspiracy involving the German Embassy.[45] Steblev, who admitted to taking part in the plot, said he had set up meetings between Starostin and a German attaché. Starostin, said Steblev, "had organized an illegal, counterrevolutionary, fascist-terrorist spy organization among the physical culture organizations of Moscow."[46] The places and dates of meetings were stated with great specificity. Among the conspirators were Viktor Prokof'ev, Strepikheev, Ryabokon', and several others who worked at Spartak. The centerpiece of their conspiracy was the planned assassination of the leadership atop the Lenin Mausoleum during the 1937 Physical Culture Day Parade. The goal was to establish a Fascist state.[47] At the last minute, the plot was called off when one group of unnamed coconspirators was arrested.

Ryabokon' also admitted taking part in the plot and further implicated two former Spartak players, Stanislav Leuta and Petr Isakov. Ryabokon', who knew Starostin well, described him in ways that Ryabokon' must have known were false. "He is the son of a former house owner and is married to the daughter of a big tradesman. In the past he was arrested for speculation."[48] The original plan had been to shoot the leaders at "a sporting event at Dinamo Stadium." The Starostins' friend, the recently arrested "enemy of the people" Kharchenko, was in a position to give them advance notice when a big shot was planning to attend a match. Unfortunately, Stalin, the main target, never attended a real game in his life. Surely Starostin, who gave out hundreds of free tickets to Spartak games, would have known on his own if any important personage was planning to show up. Ryabokon' testified to gathering weapons, which proved a difficult process. Neither Ryabokon' nor Steblev went into specifics about the plot. Later, during his own interrogation, Nikolai Starostin was told that his accusers believed the Spartak players who were riding on a float shaped like an immense soccer boot were supposed to leap off the float, brandish revolvers hidden in their soccer shorts, and kill all the leaders. What would then happen was anyone's guess. The absurdity of these charges, made in 1937, must have been clear even to those who concocted them, for if the NKVD was so concerned about the Starostins' terrorist activities, one may ask why they were not arrested immediately.[49]

Although there is, at present, no way to know for sure, one can reasonably guess that Kosarev was able to keep the Starostins, if not their friends, out of jail in 1937. The Starostins may have been free, but this did not mean that suspicion about the brothers disappeared. At the beginning and end of 1938, *Izvestiia* carried reports of further financial irregularities at Spartak.[50] In May, the director of the Spartak Society's sporting goods store, Serafim Krivonosov, was arrested, and he further accused the Starostins of anti-Soviet attitudes and conspiracies.[51]

From 1937 up to the war, the Starostins were under close police surveillance. Some of the material produced by those spying on the brothers was clearly nonsense. In one report, Nikolai's father was said to have owned "an enormous slaughterhouse" before the revolution. Konstantin Kvashnin, who had coached Spartak, was said to have been the son of a tsarist general and the subject of several arrests. Another agent repeated the Znameskiis' charges of currency speculation and goods dealing during the French trip but went further, suggesting the brothers had arranged to have a car imported for Kosarev. Andrei was said to have given an interview to a "White Guardist newspaper," and Spartak was alleged to have received twenty thousand French francs for a match. Given that Spartak played no games other than official competitions during the tour, it is difficult to imagine what match this agent had in mind.[52]

Other reported comments, overheard by police spies, were more plausible and, with hindsight, reflect more positively on the Starostins. Late in 1938, one agent reported having been in Andrei's apartment, where Nikolai remarked that things would be more difficult without Kosarev—whom they praised, perhaps naively, as a principled person. In 1940, Andrei was reported to have commented on the new labor code in the presence of an agent:

> What kind of a ruckus would there be in any bourgeois country if such draconian laws were published? I have no doubt that such laws would be described that way in the foreign press. Just a year ago we shouted that only in our socialist country did a woman have a four-month vacation for a pregnancy, and now a single month is considered enough.[53]

The next year Andrei was supposed to have complained about the war with Finland. "We have scandalized the whole world with this Finland adventure. We have severed any kinds of ties with democratic countries and alienated any sympathizers from the socialist camp in Western nations. You can place a cross on the Popular Front."[54] It is possible to read these statements as reasonable disagreements among Communists on issues of Soviet policy. There is nothing in them to indicate opposition to socialism or even Communism. Yet it is a measure of the drastic narrowing of permissible discourse in the late thirties that the brothers were branded leaders of a "Rightist-Trotskyist" terror organization for these utterances.[55]

Sometime after the controversial replay of the 1939 cup semifinal, Beria called for the Starostins' arrest. We have no way of knowing whether Beria acted on the information in these reports or whether he had decided the only way to beat Spartak was to get rid of the Starostins. His biographers, it must be noted, omit any mention of soccer. Yet, Aleksandr Vainshtein was probably correct when he noted, "I don't think Beria wanted the Starostins arrested because he wanted Dinamo to be champions. I think the irritation was about their popularity and independence."[56] In the words of one police agent, "Nikolai Starostin enjoys enormous popularity among our youth."[57]

In fact, Beria had taken far more concrete and reasonable steps that winter to assure Dinamo's return to the top of Soviet soccer, hiring the erudite and innovative Arkadiev, who brought in new players, restructured the team's attack, and won the league championship in 1940.[58] That victory may have diminished some of Beria's earlier annoyance with Prime Minister Vyacheslav Molotov, who, according to Nikolai, had refused to sign the Starostins' arrest order in 1939. In his last memoir Nikolai attributed the refusal to a friendship between the daughters of the prime minister and Nikolai. Molotov, however, was not much of a sentimentalist. This was a man who did not object to the arrest of his own wife. More likely, this closest of Stalin's associates saw himself as something of a protector for elite academics, writers, musicians, dancers, film stars, and sportsmen.[59] The brothers were then free to move about, but they remained under surveillance.

In the summer of 1940, a strengthened version of Spartak, the reigning two-time champion, was selected to go on a brief two-game tour of Bulgaria. Iakushin and Fedotov had been added to the lineup along with several other stars. The resulting team was more a Moscow select side than merely Spartak. These games, which took place after the signing of the Molotov-Ribbentrop Pact, were the first matchups against foreign opponents since the Basque tour. Bulgaria, then a Nazi ally and good Russian neighbor, was a willing host. Andrei, still active and a star, was picked as the team's captain. Nikolai, on the other hand, was not allowed out of the country. In an atmosphere of enormous political intrigue and contention, this strengthened version of Spartak won both of its games by large margins as huge numbers of troops and police kept the players away from adoring local fans.[60] Later that year, the Bulgarians returned the visit, and Nikolai Starostin, of all people, was a member of the state commission that handled preparations for the tour.[61]

Suspicions about the Starostins persisted even after the outbreak of the war, although this was a time when police surveillance and restrictions on expression actually decreased. Nevertheless, in March 1942, Beria was able to get party secretary Georgii Malenkov's signature on an arrest order, and on the twentieth, the Starostins and several colleagues were taken to the Lubianka, the dreaded headquarters of the NKVD. What had happened in the intervening two and a half years to make it possible for Beria to achieve his purpose? Until now, all we have known of the Starostins' fate has come from their side, but it appears part of their story has been omitted. In his memoir,

Nikolai relates being accused of favoring bourgeois sport. There was also the matter of the 1937 Physical Culture Day plot. In responding to his interrogator at the Liubianka, Starostin noted correctly that he not been among those standing on the giant boot from which the attack was supposed to come. Moreover, there were two NKVD officers traveling inside the float.[62] Whether it was Nikolai's precise refutation of the charges or their outright absurdity, this particular accusation appears to have been dropped by the time the brothers were formally sentenced. Instead, they, along with Leuta, Evgenii Arkhangel'skii, and three other Spartak officials were given either ten or eight years at hard labor, with the Starostins getting the worse punishments. In the larger scheme of things, ten years was seen as a light sentence. In Nikolai's view, it was a tacit admission of their innocence.

Nikolai Starostin reported that the final charges for which they were sentenced were plundering a freight car and introducing bourgeois morals into Soviet sport.[63] The actual content of the sentencing document, delivered by the Military Collegium of the Supreme Court of the USSR on August 21, 1943, is different. The charges that can be deemed political were vague, involving "anti-Soviet statements" against the government and doubts about Soviet victory in the war (doubts that were shared by millions of their countrymen). The question of propagandizing bourgeois values in sport was mentioned only in passing.[64] There were, however, other charges, this time criminal. The conspirators were accused of stealing sporting goods from the Spartak Society's stores and selling them on the black market. They were also said to have charged well over the so-called official prices for items in the store while pocketing the difference. In total, they were said to have swindled the Spartak Society out of 160,000 rubles, Nikolai taking the lion's share with 28,000.

More seriously, Nikolai was charged with working out an illegal arrangement with the military commission of Moscow's Bauman region. In return for alcohol and foodstuffs, obtained through his contacts at Promkooperatsiia, Starostin was accused of receiving draft exemptions for his brothers and for members of Spartak. Additionally, those Promkooperatsiia workers who helped obtain the food—mainly vodka, sausage, and butter—were given exemptions as well.[65] At a time when many others were going hungry and serving at the front, these last accusations must be seen at a minimum as highly unflattering.

In the absence of any corroborating evidence, one can well question the reality of the state's claims. The sentencing document (*prigovor*) handed down by the military collegium cannot be deemed the product of any serious legal procedure. When one confronts documents with such charges, it is tempting to dismiss any such claims outright, and it could be that the economic charges were added by the police to make the Starostins appear to be common criminals. Yet if their aim had been to discredit Spartak, why were the accusations never made public? The Starostins' "criminal acts" were considerably more detailed and specific than the political ones. Here one might speculate that the political accusations may have been added to keep the case out of a criminal court, where a football-loving judge might have dismissed it.[66]

Despite the absurdities of the Stalinist system of justice, the criminal accusations are troubling. The charges in the sentencing document are consistent with the long series of other denunciations that had been made against the Starostins over the years, and they can hardly be seen as unusual given the extensive corruption that went on during the war. This sort of bribery was far from uncommon and often went unpunished.[67] Even as sympathetic a figure as Vainshtein has doubts. "I'm sure Nikolai Petrovich didn't tell the whole truth. There were various rumors going around about freight cars and other things. . . . No one," he correctly notes, "knows the whole truth."[68]

Guilty or not, the brothers and their coconspirators were dispatched to various parts of the labor camp system. Nikolai was first sent to Ukhta in Siberia. He recalled the work regime there as so harsh that as many as forty people died each day. He remembered seeing hills of corpses. Yet the founder of Spartak would be saved by football. Arriving at Ukhta after a three-month train journey from Moscow, Nikolai was met on the platform by several familiar faces—men who had played soccer in Moscow before the war. Some were prisoners. Others had been drafted and were serving in the Far East. They informed him that they were to take him immediately to see General Burdakov, commandant of the Ukhta camp. The general, a huge football fan like Beria, had plans for Starostin.

Burdakov had won an internal bureaucratic struggle for the right to "host" such a sport celebrity. During the war, the nationally organized soccer league closed down, but Soviet citizens, as was true all over the world, played wherever they could. Ukhta had a team sponsored by the secret police that played in the lower reaches of the Soviet league. Unbeknownst to Beria, Burdakov asked Starostin to coach it. In return Starostin received a twenty-four-hour pass to work outside the camp and permission to sleep at the team's training base rather than in the harsh barracks. Andrei, Aleksandr, and Petr all received similar proposals. All had success with their new teams and pleased their new "patrons." When the war ended, the brothers became salaried employees of the Dinamo Sport Society. Ultimately they did this with Beria's acceptance, if not blessing. Starostin would later claim that they had been saved by the "magic" of football:

> With the passage of time, I am no longer surprised that the camp bosses, responsible for the fates of thousands and thousands of people, perpetrators of the inhumanities and horrors of the gulag, related so positively to anything having to do with football. Their unlimited power over people was nothing compared with the power of football over them.[69]

Andrei was sent to a similarly northern clime, the still primitive mining town of Norylsk. Upon his arrival, the director of the city's largest works assigned him the task of directing physical culture and sport in the region. He also coached a Dinamo Norylsk soccer team that fielded several incarcerated former pros and an array of hard-drinking criminals. As he described it, Andrei's life in Norylsk was more settled than that of Nikolai, more like exile than imprisonment. The word "camp" is mentioned only briefly in one of his accounts. At one point late in his term, he was even allowed a visit from his wife. Aleksandr, who did not record his experience, was exiled to far-off Vorkuta but was quickly sent to the Urals city of Perm (then called Molotov), where he also coached. None of these activities were initially known to Beria, who, it was assumed, would have disapproved. Perm had become a central transfer point for prisoners moving from camp to camp, and it was there that Aleksandr was able to enjoy a month-long reunion with Nikolai. Less is known of Petr's whereabouts during the war, but his experience appears to have been the most arduous, seriously affecting his health thereafter. They were all quickly released in 1954 with the first, most privileged group of victims. All returned to their old apartments and resumed their careers.[70] All were eventually rehabilitated.

In their absence, Spartak played on in the diminished but far from barren world of wartime football. The league did not operate for the duration of the struggle, but the city championships were revived along with cup competitions. Without Nikolai's managerial talents, Spartak had difficulty hanging on to its players. By contrast, the army and Dinamo teams were able to keep their sides intact, evacuating them to the rear. Most of Spartak's players found jobs in war industries, but other clubs sought to poach their stars. More than one of these raids were successful. While Spartak fans did not know where the brothers were, nearly all knew they had been arrested. The Starostins were simply too visible to simply disappear. It was as if Pele had been jailed during his country's dictatorship. Despite these difficulties, things went well in 1942. Dinamo won the spring season; Spartak took the fall while defeating Dinamo 2–0 in the city cup final before thirty thousand spectators at Stalinets Stadium.[71]

The next two years were less successful. In the circumstances of war, the army soccer team emerged as the strongest Soviet side, winning the Moscow league in 1943 and finishing second in 1944. Dinamo was able to keep its players home as well and maintained its high standards. Still, there were also important moments for Spartak. Almost immediately after the liberation of Stalingrad in 1943, Spartak was invited to play a quickly organized city select team in a hastily rebuilt stadium. It had been invited because it had won the truncated Moscow Cup competition of 1942. To help deal with the destruction of the sporting infrastructure, the players brought with them a full complement of sports equipment. Because they would be flying close to the front, their journey was not without danger. When intelligence suggested a German counter offensive, their flight was postponed to the early morning of the game. They arrived in a state of exhaustion. With bands playing and a fighter-plane flyby overhead, the locals, who had to hunt down their teammates through the shattered city, won 1–0 before ten thousand fans. All those present shared the understanding that the tide had turned in the war and that eventual victory would be theirs.[72]

Exhibition tours to raise morale and establish some sense of normalcy were then undertaken by all the top teams. Spartak played thirteen games a year, including some in central Asia, where the players had done their preseason training. With regular seasons of fourteen games, they were kept busy. In the midst of the conflict, the game went on, as it did elsewhere in wartime. Lineups were fluid. Several Spartak players took the field for Zenit Leningrad, which had been evacuated from the front. For Spartak, the sporting highlight of the war came in 1944 when they faced Zenit in the final of the revived national cup competition. Dinamo Stadium had just been reopened, yet another sign of impending victory. Fifty thousand came to celebrate. People met friends at the stadium whom they had not seen since the war began. Amid these joyous reunions, the teams tied 2–2. The next day another fifty thousand showed up for the replay and saw Zenit triumph 1–0. It was, however, a day with no losers.[73]

———

The Starostin brothers missed this and many other football moments during and after the war. Despite the well-documented failings of what passed for justice under Stalin, the reasons for their wartime arrest and exile do raise questions about their prewar activities. In particular, the 1943 charges clash quite sharply with Nikolai's postexile reputation for probity. While he sought to tread carefully after his return home, he may have been less than fully honest before the war. Only those who would make him a saint could deny that something "on the left," as Russians say, may well have been going on. It later became clear, in the changed conditions of the Thaw, that corruption of this sort had been a significant part of wartime reality. In the Starostins' defense, these were difficult and terrifying times, and one must be careful about judging such matters as either good or bad. Otherwise good men and women may have been forced by circumstances to do less than honorable things, while moral monsters could, at times, commit acts of generosity. What, after all, does it mean to have broken the law at a time when law, in any proper sense, did not even exist? The case of the Starostins reveals all the ambiguities of what it meant to be human and to have lived in the USSR during history's most destructive war.

The same ambiguity applies to Spartak's prewar working-class male fan base. These men turned out to be neither uncritical supporters of the regime nor its innocent victims. Their identities may have been fluid, but it would be wrong to see them as cynics, using language to manipulate the system.[74] If anything, they found in Spartak a safe way to resist. To be sure, Dinamo had its fans. It also enjoyed support among a segment of the proletariat. Yet ultimately, the fact that a majority of Moscow laboring males favored Spartak undermines the view that acceptance of the regime was strong and universal among Soviet workers. During the late thirties, the team's fans, to use Stephen Kotkin's sporting discourse, "deployed" sport, among other things, as a "'field of play' in which people engaged the 'rules of the game' of urban life.'" This, too, was neither domination nor resignation but rather contested terrain, with the outcome undetermined.[75] Spartak supporters did not go so far as to seek the overthrow of Communism.[76] Instead of separating us from them, the rivalry with Dinamo was between two (of many) different ways of being Soviet.

# 5

# The Golden Age of Soviet Soccer

## Spartak in Eclipse, 1945–1948

For many, the truest picture of the USSR in the years after the Great Fatherland War has been the dystopic fantasy that George Orwell elaborated in *Nineteen Eighty-Four* (1949). As Abbott Gleason has noted, "No book was of greater importance in establishing the idea of totalitarianism (and its visual dimension)."[1] The totalitarian model, developed by Western scholars early in the cold war, equated the Nazi and Soviet regimes, focusing on their use of police terror to invade the most intimate aspects of their citizens' lives in order to realize full acceptance of their ideologies. Certainly, the USSR's self-presentation in those postwar years did little to dispel its image as the apotheosis of totalitarianism. Stalinism sought to portray, "itself as an ideologically governed and effectively controlled society."[2]

But what of the reality? Let us for a moment imagine that Orwell had been living in Moscow during the late forties (he did not) and had been a soccer fan (he most definitely was not). Had he decided to take in a match, he would have seen something that looked little like his famous creation. First of all, there was the fundamental matter of the destruction of war. Along with virtually everything else, the infrastructures of the USSR's mass culture industries had been severely damaged and could not have operated with the effectiveness Orwell ascribed to them. Paper shortages reduced the number of books. Film studios and their equipment were destroyed, as were thousands of cinemas.[3] Theaters were in serious disrepair. Stadiums, however, especially those in Moscow, had not been heavily damaged. Games had gone on throughout the conflict. Players were in shape. It was enough to print up tickets and open the gates. When those gates did open, the citizens of the capital came in the hundreds of thousands. With few entertainment alternatives, football became, as Soviet fans would later fondly but not entirely correctly recall, "our only spectacle."[4] Had Orwell wanted to take in one of the more important

5.1 German POWs clean the turf at Dinamo Stadium, late 1940s. Fotoagentstvo Sportekspress.

matches, he would have had to line up at the Dinamo Stadium box office a month ahead of time when tickets went on sale. Had he been serious about actually getting a seat, he would have gotten on line the evening before and spent the night outside the arena in the company of thousands of pushing, shoving, and arguing fans.

Orwell's fictional interest might logically have been piqued by Dinamo Moscow's wildly successful tour of Great Britain in November 1945 (he had, in fact, denounced the tour). Having just won the Soviet championship, a strengthened Dinamo team played brilliantly against such famous British sides as Arsenal, Chelsea, and Glasgow Rangers.[5] Millions of Soviet fans worshipped at the shrine of their radios as the great announcer Vadim Siniavskii related the triumphs of their comrades.[6] The Starostins, in their respective frigid exiles, shared this experience. The conclusion seemed inescapable. If Great Britain was the homeland of football and a Soviet team had held its own, then the regime's claim about the superiority of the "Soviet school" of soccer no longer seemed far-fetched. Moscow fans were now convinced they were watching a world-class spectacle, more entertaining than the boring movies, books, newspapers, plays, and music of the postwar era. This success had the added benefit of greater contact with the West when the USSR joined FIFA in 1946.[7]

To take in these spectacles, fans set out early on match days for Dinamo Stadium. Entering the metro as far away as the capital's southeast corner, spectators were already crowding the trains hours before kickoff. When they got to the stadium, they were extruded from subway cars and onto escalators, all of which went up. Mounted police herded the surging crowds through the

**5.2** Fans crowd the Dinamo Stadium box office in the late forties. Fotoagentstvo Sportekspress.

gates. As many as a half million came just to be near the action. The official capacity of Dinamo Stadium was fifty-five thousand, but it was common for attendances to be estimated as high as ninety thousand. Soccer supporters rooted passionately for their favorites and reacted to goals with ecstasy. These joyful and spontaneous crowds had come to the game to relax and celebrate their hard-won victory against the Nazis. In this, Muscovites had much in common with their counterparts all over the world. Everywhere, audiences for spectator sports expanded geometrically. New York, with three teams, became

**5.3** Overcrowded tram arrives at Dinamo Stadium, late forties. Fotoagentstvo Sportekspress.

the capital of U.S. baseball. Stadia throughout the United Kingdom were filled to record levels never achieved since.[8] As in so many other areas of life, Moscow, with several clubs in the top flight, was the center of the Soviet game. How then did all this fun track with our long-received notion of postwar Soviet history as the high-water mark of totalitarian rule?[9]

Some might argue that football is the rule-proving exception. By this logic, the people's game was consciously created by the regime as a safety valve that allowed citizens to let off steam in harmless ways. It may have been the carnivalesque atmosphere in which the exceptional moment of cultural inversion actually served to reinforce existing social relations. Tempting as it may be to ascribe such a special status to soccer, the published and archival evidence made available since 1991 does not support this view. The authorities continued to ascribe the same didactic purposes to football as to all other forms of popular culture. "Harmless fun" was never an intentional part of the Soviet mass culture menu. Both publicly and privately, sports officials and party ideologues constantly complained about the bad behavior of fans, players, team officials, journalists, and even referees.

Conversely, recent research has shown that postwar Stalinist football comports well with evidence about other cultural practices. Although it is too early to claim we have developed a fully elaborated alternative to the old totalitarian school's image of these years, it is clear that a new, more nuanced understanding of the period has emerged.[10] It is a view that helps us understand why "Orwell's Moscow" so confounded the picture of the type of state he had imagined in *Nineteen Eighty-Four.* Let us look more closely at the sources of the changes in Soviet society after the war, changes that would play an important role in the future development of football and other Soviet sports.

## Searching for Normalcy

The massive destruction of the Second World War left one-third of the USSR's territory in ruins. Like the other European war of the twentieth century, this one had been fought not only by armies but by societies.[11] In its wake, millions of Soviet citizens, who had sacrificed so mightily and endured enormous losses, now allowed themselves to hope the postwar world would be different.[12] Yet Stalin, after some uncertainty, sought a return to the practices of the thirties. His attempt to turn back the clock was, however, complicated, and in some particulars thwarted, by the dramatic changes in the society he ruled.

The enormous demographic change brought about by the carnage of war marked the USSR indelibly. The toll of war dead from all causes is now believed to have been twenty-eight million, three-quarters of them young men. By 1959, there were 633 men for every 1,000 women in the USSR. Millions of war widows never remarried. Millions of younger women never found a mate. Millions of Soviet men had to make little effort in order to find their own spouses. These dramatic changes were masked by the glow of triumph. What foreign observers called the Red Army had just marched through Eastern Europe. Many of them concluded that Stalin's Russia had replaced Hitler's Germany as the primary threat to postwar peace. Yet as it emerged from its death struggle with Nazi Germany, the Communist system in the USSR was far from the apogee of its power. As Moshe Lewin has shown,

> [The system's] absolutist features, befitting another age, were profoundly incompatible with the effects of a forced industrialization in response to the challenges of new times. The government that had summoned these forces was unable to accommodate the emerging realities, or interest groups, or constraints embodied in the social structures and layers generated by the developmental process.[13]

This situation, too, was a direct consequence of the war. In its catastrophic early months, Soviet citizens knew they were facing disaster, but the state media instead hailed great victories. In time the leadership came to understand that it had to level with the population or lose its support entirely. The innovation of accurate radio and newspaper accounts had a bracingly positive effect and led much of the population to expect that truth telling and openness would continue after the war. The dire situation confronting the country had obliged Stalin to make similar concessions in his dealings with the Soviet military. The unplannable chaos of the conflict, and in particular the rapid advance of German forces, had obliged him to abandon the early attempt to micromanage both the front and the rear. It was not possible in the heat of battle for the military to get Moscow's permission for every move. Having devastated the officer corps during the purges, the all-powerful dictator now allowed his generals to do their jobs. In the process, the army won considerable independence and prestige.[14]

Total war also required the imagination and work of men and women with a wide range of professional skills. They had to be able to think on their feet, take risks, act independently and, when necessary, spontaneously. The leadership had no choice but to stress the importance of skill and talent among engineers, scientists, and managers of all kinds. What had been a relatively small social group expanded swiftly over the course of the war. The very notion of professional autonomy, of being judged and rewarded for one's grasp of a task, changed the expectations of those with specialized education and training. These men—and they were primarily men—then came to hope they would play an expanded role in a new society.[15]

In the immediate postwar years the regime confronted a situation that would increase its reliance on the wide variety of educated professionals. Some of its largest cities and much of its transportation infrastructure lay in ruins. More than eleven million soldiers had to be demobilized. Five and a half million prisoners of war streamed home. Entire nationalities had been relocated away from their homelands.[16] In 1946 famine forced more peasants into Soviet cities, increasing the number of workers in industry and construction from eight million in 1945 to more than fourteen million by 1953. The influx of peasants and demobilized soldiers, combined with returning citizens who had been evacuated to the east, led to further deterioration in housing conditions. Workers, old and new, expressed open dissatisfaction with their living standards and with conditions on the assembly line.[17]

In response, the number of professionals with advanced secondary or higher education grew rapidly. Broadly referred to as an "intelligentsia," these highly trained white-collar employees differed from the historical intelligentsia, with its generally critical stance toward state power. Cowed by the regime's campaign for cultural conformity, this new intelligentsia tended to trade acceptance of the political status quo for privileges and comforts, following the logic of what literary critic Vera Dunham called the "Big Deal."[18] At the same time, however, this growing cohort of engineers, technicians, and other professionals "craved contact with the outside world" and were led by their "professional conceit" to believe that they should have a voice in policymaking.[19] Along with more traditional *intelligenty* these people were ready to work with a reformed state in order to make real the hopes and possibilities born of victory. Unquestioning loyalty was not part of this deal. Instead, the newly educated were ready to serve but not cringe. Indeed, recent research suggests that the Great Fatherland War weakened rather than strengthened the institutions of the state and the party. The regime's control was far from complete.

Many of the trends thought to have emerged between 1945 and 1948 were already developing during the war. Furthermore, it now appears that the cultural and political processes that characterized the post-Stalin Thaw actually emerged between 1948 and 1953. The flowering of youth culture, the appearance of contesting views in a number of scholarly fields, and the tentative signs of an aggressive public opinion were visible during the last four years of Stalin's rule.[20]

### The Futbol of Our Youth

The swiftly evolving social structure had a predictable effect on the mass audience for soccer. The growth in the size of the industrial working class meant the game's public was significantly larger—so large, in fact, that it overwhelmed the existing infrastructure for the sport. Dinamo Stadium, Moscow's only large arena, could not always accommodate all those who wanted to watch. At the same time, the audience for football became more various. Newly emergent professionals and specialists took to the game, as did many in the creative and scientific intelligentsia. For these men (and a very few women) attendance at big matches became something of a social necessity. Seen as effete by many inside the stadium, male intellectuals now became fans of the game in order to demonstrate their manhood. To make sure their point was not missed, many brought along female companions. Players brought their wives and girlfriends (sometimes both). Others took the cue, and women became a significant presence on big match days at Dinamo. Soccer, once a largely male proletarian pleasure, now became the pastime of all Soviet society. In the process, the popularity of one or another Moscow team could no longer be seen as a marker of the attitudes simply of workingmen. The game maintained its allure for male laborers, but it now gained new audiences, complicating the political, social, and cultural meanings one might attach to the game.

Reminiscing about the postwar years, Aksel' Vartanian claimed that "[football] was the only distraction for youth at that time. We didn't have these shows or concerts. Even the word 'jazz' was forbidden. . . . There weren't any of these genuinely popular, mass entertainments, only football."[21] This was true all over a triumphant but exhausted nation, but nowhere more so than in Moscow, home to several teams in the USSR's first division. "On the days of big matches," wrote Spartak's star striker, Nikita Simonian (b. 1926), "it seemed all of Moscow streamed toward Dinamo."[22] Aside from those who flowed from the metro, there were others who rode on the backs or roofs of trolleybuses. Excited fans arriving on trams did not wait for the doors to open, bursting instead through open windows. The capital was not a place of many vehicles, but on game days it seemed every car and truck in the city was headed for Dinamo Stadium along the Leningrad Highway. Only football could produce that then-rarest of events, a Moscow traffic jam. On the days of big games, the entire city was in chaos, as hundreds of thousands made the pilgrimage to the stadium.

**5.4** Buying season tickets at Dinamo, late forties. Fotoagentstvo Sportekspress.

The happiest of these pilgrims were those who actually had tickets. Fans who lacked such a prize could be heard begging for "a spare ticket [*lishnii bilet*]" at all points in the city.[23] Success in such ventures was rare, and, according to the director of Dinamo Stadium, most of those thousands of lovers of football who surrounded the stadium came with the intention of gate-crashing. This was especially true of young boys who made a science of the practice. They knew which gates were most guarded (closest to the metro) and those where one's chances were good. Many found it easier to get over the spiked fences if they first climbed onto the roof of the box office. Others begged older men to take them in, and many obliged. There was still the technique of the mass rush on a gate (the "steam engine") practiced by Oleshchuk and his friends before the war.[24] Once inside, there was the matter of finding a place to sit. Konstantin Esenin solved this problem for himself and his friends by buying a season ticket and making sure his seat was at the end of a row. He would then slide down a bit to allow one pal to join him. Another would sit on his lap and a third between his knees. "That way four of us got to sit for one season ticket." The aisles were filled. Ushers and police were powerless to evict the young boys and make way for the rightful ticket-holders.[25]

The stadium continued to be a place of happy reunions after so much tragedy and loss of life. Friends had been separated from each other during the war. People had lost touch in the chaos. News of a comrade's death often had not reached all his friends. Lev Filatov remembered how certain games in early 1941 would prove to be the last some of his comrades would ever see. More happily, many who had been separated since the beginning of the war

found each other on match day at Dinamo Stadium, where they would hug
and give joyous thanks that they had managed to make it through the great national ordeal.[26] To go to football was to embrace life, to take joy in the fact of
mere survival. The pleasure of unscripted excitement without the fear of death
was deeply moving for those who had just fought a real war. These were
mimetic rather than real battles with actual rules of the sort later described by
the émigré German sociologist Norbert Elias. The safety of strong emotions
without terrifying violence intensified the attractiveness of the sporting spectacle, not just for Russians but for all people who had gotten through the
war.[27] At Dinamo, spontaneity and the unplanned could be embraced, not
feared.

The epicenter of all this merriment (again, "carnival" would be too strong
a word) was the east end of Dinamo Stadium, where the tickets were cheap-
est. Although there were benches throughout Dinamo, the east end was the
cultural equivalent of the "terraces" on which working-class fans throughout
the world had stood for decades. As Oleshchuk related, before the war the
east end had been a scene of disorder and passion where young men could
openly express their emotions. After 1945, however, the section took on an
even greater aura. The north stand, with its government box and press bar,
was the roosting place for party leaders, NKVD officers, and assorted other
big shots. With the war over, the big shots were joined on this celebrity row
by writers, musicians, actors, film directors, war heroes, and the occasional academic. What Oleshchuk called the "semiaristocratic" south stand had a posh
restaurant beneath it. Male fans took their wives and girlfriends there to listen to jazz bands and consume the hardest of all commodities to find in postwar Russia, a decent meal. The west stand was close to the metro and had a
stronger police presence. The east end, in one of the eternal and universal
juxtapositions of spectator sport, was where the "real fans" hung out, separated from the action by the stadium's running track.

Filatov described this scene with feeling and insight. He claimed those who
inhabited the east end were the most "inveterate and noisy" of fans, who used
this special place to demonstrate a form of what he called "independence." As
a young man just back from the war, Filatov and his cohort, all Spartak supporters save one, regularly sat on the left side of the stadium's "curve" in row
twenty. This did not prevent them from attending the games of other teams.
They stood throughout all ninety minutes, cheered wildly, chanted in unison,
and embraced when goals were scored. Dinamo Stadium became a "nice place
where one wanted to spend time and each event was a pleasant way to pass an
evening."[28] They liked to get there early and leave late. Even after they began
working and could afford better locations, they always returned to the east end
unless they went with a date. They convinced themselves they comprised a select public whose chants, shouts, and whistles gave a tone to the rest of the
arena—which, as far as they were concerned, was made up of tourists who
were merely taking in the then-fashionable activity of football. At times the
east stand would be full while the rest of the stadium was half-empty.

Yet for all the energy they displayed, Filatov and his pals were certainly not hooligans. Fighting brought police attention and surveillance. No one was interested in doing prison time or worse. They were careful to eschew force, and they sought to control others who might resort to violence. Letting off a bit of steam that might otherwise be directed at the authorities was altogether too dangerous, nor were the police inclined to let the lads be lads. The stadium was a place for the open expression of emotion that discomfited the authorities, who had no choice but to allow the games to go on, but young intellectuals like Esenin and Filatov understood their part of the bargain with the police was never to let the expression of that emotion become unduly physical. This deal produced spontaneity and pleasure, which, combined with a bit of easily avoidable danger, made Dinamo a special place for young football fans. They had returned from war alive and victorious, and soccer afforded them the possibility of regularly reaffirming that fact:

> For Muscovites, Dinamo Stadium was as much a piece of home as Pushkin Square, Tsetnoy Bulvar', Kuznetskii Most or the Arbat. . . . For our group of friends . . . it was like the Maly Theater or MkhAT [Moscow Art Theater], used bookstores, the Metropole movie theater or the tram line called "Annushka."[29]

Who were these young *intelligenty* rhapsodizing so excitedly during the dark days of Stalin's last years? Were they true believers, even loyal Stalinists? Such was hardly the case. Konstantin Esenin's father was the famed poet Sergei, who had committed suicide in the twenties. His mother, the actress Zinaida Raikh, was arrested during the thirties and quickly shot. One day later his stepfather, the world-renowned theater director Vsevolod Meyerhold, was taken in and dispatched to a similar fate. Filatov's father had been arrested and exiled in 1935. His mother was sent into regional exile one hundred kilometers from Moscow. The fifteen-year-old Lev was taken in by an aunt. Eventually the great writer Maksim Gorky intervened on the mother's behalf, and she was reunited with her son, only to live the next eighteen years with the stigma of her husband's arrest. Filatov's father finally came back in the first wave of returnees soon after Stalin's death. Given their sufferings, it would not be correct to characterize either Filatov or Esenin as naive about the nature of the regime. They expressed a certain nostalgia about these years, but this did not mean they were comfortable with late Stalinism. At the same time, both men went on to have successful professional careers—Esenin as an engineer (and part-time sportswriter) and Filatov as a sportswriter and editor. Like the Starostins, they did not turn to outright opposition because of the arrest and exile of family members. Despite good reasons for their alienation, these men, like many others, found in both the sacred and profane rituals of football a sense of pleasure and affirmation that permitted them to survive these difficult times and later prosper within the system.[30] Their support for Spartak marked them as critics who were careful to choose life paths that would allow them to maintain their integrity.

Big matches at Dinamo Stadium were not simply festivals of male bonding. If the capital's biggest arena was scarcely a scene of order and calm, after the war it was still a place where female fans felt safe. If soccer games were sites for intellectuals to see and be seen, the same was true for women who came in numbers not seen before or since. This was, of course, particularly true for the players' wives, whose relationship to the game was not entirely independent. In 1984, the wife of Dinamo star Konstantin Beskov recalled:

> Then it was fantastic. You'd go to the stadium like it was a big holiday. We dressed up and tried to impress each other with how good we looked. We understood people were watching us. We were in the public eye. It was really fantastic when we won. There were flowers everywhere. We walked with our husbands to the [team] bus. The crowds were cheering.

Fans knew the players' wives as well. At times their presence was more compelling than that of their husbands. Esenin recalled being so bewitched by the beauty of Beskov's wife that he once stared at her for a full half hour before realizing he was at a football match. "These were the first postwar times," he recalled. "It was our youth."[31]

## The New Pecking Order—Spartak on the Outside

While the postwar period was a good time for Soviet football in general, it proved a very difficult time for Spartak. The political context surrounding soccer had changed, posing a huge challenge for Moscow's most popular team. Accordingly, it will be necessary here to examine the practices of the sport itself in some considerable detail in order to see how it was that Spartak was able to swim against the tide and survive. Because their athletes had already been in the armed forces and could be assigned to duties that did not compromise their ability to compete, Dinamo and TsDKA came out of the war with their playing staffs intact. In the words of Martyn Merzhanov, *Pravda*'s leading soccer writer, all other teams existed merely on paper.[32] It was easier for TsDKA and Dinamo to return to their full potential immediately, and they soon came to battle each other for supremacy. Matches between the two clubs became the highlights of each season's calendar. The army's crucial role in the triumph over Fascism enhanced its prestige. Victory made it easier to attract the best athletes. TsDKA took over Spartak's role as Dinamo's chief rival and dominated the postwar era, winning every championship but two between 1945 and 1951. Dinamo took the other two titles in 1945 and 1949.

Known facetiously as "the team of lieutenants," TsDKA was the more popular of the two postwar footballing powers. The *soldaty* were led by the powerful attacking tandem of Grigorii Fedotov and Vsevolod Bobrov (1922–1979), a young sensation from Tambov by way of Omsk. The two played together from 1945 to 1949 and terrorized the league. The great "Bober" may well have been the finest athlete produced by the USSR. At a minimum, he was the most

**5.5** The mighty Vsevolod Bobrov. Fotoagentstvo Sportekspress.

successful two-way performer in Soviet history—soccer's leading striker and ice hockey's top goal producer. So dominant was he in the new game of Canadian hockey that the sports authorities actually postponed the USSR's debut in the world hockey championship because he was injured shortly before the 1953 competition. Both Bobrov and Fedotov were affable and friendly in public, qualities that made them huge stars. The team was equally talented on the sidelines; its coach, Boris Arkadiev, had left Dinamo in 1944, no longer able to abide Beria's constant interference.

Dinamo's popularity rivaled that of TsDKA. The police team's reputation had been enhanced by its tour of Britain, where it had played the first professional teams faced by a Soviet side since the 1940 trip to Bulgaria. The impact of Dinamo's success, aided in no small measure by the addition of Bobrov to the traveling squad, is still well remembered in both Russia and the United Kingdom.[33] Even Spartak fans and officials took pride in these triumphs against the inventors of the game. Listening from their places of exile, the Starostin brothers were equally thrilled.[34] Vadim Siniavskii's live broadcasts (a risk taken by the party leadership) made an indelible impression on listeners who had just survived the trials of war. In the afterglow of their shared triumph, the tour encapsulated the hopes of millions of citizens of both nations for a peaceful future. For Soviet citizens, Siniavskii's reports signaled a new era of peace. According to the director Leonid Zorin, "Siniavskii's voice was the voice of a new day, of joy, of light, the voice of celebration."[35]

During the tour, Bobrov's striking partner was Konstantin Beskov (1920–2006), whose excellent passing skills abetted Bobrov's single-minded goalward drives. On the defensive end, Dinamo's great goalie Aleksei Khomich (1920–1980) won the hearts of the British public. Dubbed "Tiger" by the local press, he returned to the USSR a star and gate attraction of the highest magnitude. The prewar team captain, Mikhail Iakushin, replaced Arkadiev, and he, too, emerged as one of the great coaches in the history of Soviet football. With the best athletes, both TsDKA and Dinamo possessed great speed, endurance, and coordination, and one can fairly say their domination of Soviet soccer reflected the temporary dominance of society by the structures of force under late Stalinism. Surely the leadership was pleased with this state of affairs. It served the regime's purposes to have the public's heroes be policemen and soldiers. Still, the practices of Soviet spectating did not always lead the entire sports audience to a wholehearted embrace of the changes in the football food chain.

Under the new circumstances, Spartak found it difficult to flourish. In the first four seasons of postwar football, Dinamo and TsDKA left Spartak (and everyone else) in their wake. Spartak finished a catastrophic and unfamiliar tenth (out of twelve teams) in the first peacetime season of 1945. Vladimir Stepanov, hero of the victory over the Basques but now a double amputee who had lost his legs in an accident, coached a depleted group of players left over from the prewar heyday.[36] Such stars as the great goalie Anatoly Akimov had departed for Torpedo. Others had left for TsDKA and Dinamo. From the very first days of the new season, it became clear that Soviet soccer had evolved to become more maneuverable, with an emphasis on personal defenses that required enormous stamina. Spartak's veterans, most in their thirties, simply could not keep up. These failures did not occur because the new season had taken Spartak or anyone else by surprise. With victory near in the spring of 1945, it was clear well before the German surrender that there would be a full-fledged football championship. Approved by the Central Committee, the schedule had been in place since March, and the players had been training two months before that.[37]

The presence of so great a veteran as Vasily Sokolov at left back gave Spartak some strength in defense, but weak coaching led to poor team play, which in turn led to a number of early goals. Perhaps the most embarrassing such mishap took place June 10 against Dinamo Tblisi, which scored in the first minute of the match, leading to a 1–2 defeat at Tblisi in front of eighty thousand people. A 0–4 loss to Dinamo Moscow on July 29 before sixty thousand made clear the size of the gap between the two old rivals. In the stands, however, matters were more even. Huge crowds were common during those first months of peace. Memories of the double double of 1938–1939 brought thousands of old and new Spartak fans out on match days. The average home attendance for its games (forty-seven thousand) was still larger than that for Dinamo (forty-one thousand),[38] numbers that speak to Spartak's immense and long-standing residual popularity. Neither the disappearance of the Starostins nor mixed results during the war years had alienated the team's fan base. Nevertheless, the inevitability of an impending poor finish had a predictable impact on the size of Spartak's crowds as the season progressed. On the penultimate week just twelve thousand showed up at the smaller Stalinets Stadium (capacity thirty thousand) to take in a 2–0 victory over last-place Lokomotiv.[39]

In the wake of the war, the team's sponsor, Promkooperatsiia, which drew its revenues from the retail trades then constrained by rationing, could not support the club as it had done in the old days.[40] With its founders in the gulag and its fortunes lagging, Spartak faced the real possibility of relegation or even extinction. The president of the Spartak Society's central council, G. Mikhailchuk, came in for a good deal of abuse in the press. Nevertheless, during the off-season someone was at work trying to turn the team around. Stepanov was reassigned to the youth squad, and a broad search went on for a new coach.

Ultimately, Spartak took a step it had made before. The Czech specialist Anton Fivebr had led the team in the first half of the inaugural 1936 season. Now Spartak again looked to the west. Erik Bistrom, head of Spartak's Estonian branch, was in Moscow for a meeting and recommended Albert Vol'rat, who had played for Sporta Tallin in the early thirties. After retiring as a player in 1934, Vol'rat had worked as a physical therapist and assistant coach at then-powerful Ferencvaros of Budapest. Later stints at Barcelona and Arsenal also looked good on his resume, and Spartak took a chance on another non-Russian. This "liberalism" on the national question was in keeping with the club's traditions, and the faith shown in Vol'rat was rewarded. The Estonian stemmed the decline and laid the foundation for an eventual return to respectability by establishing a merciless training regimen and launching a renewal of the playing staff.

With the defense reasonably competent, the emphasis was placed on strengthening attack. Two new additions changed the tone on the field and in the locker room. Both twenty-one-year-old Sergei Sal'nikov (1925–1984) and thirty-year-old Nikolai Dementiev (1915–1994) were talented and creative players who rarely passed up an opportunity for a good joke or "morale-building" merriment. The tall, strikingly handsome, stylishly dressed, and intelligent Sal'nikov had grown up near the team's training base at Tarasovka. He had been part of Spartak's reserve squad, playing with Leningrad Zenit in 1944 and 1945 and scoring the winning goal against Spartak in the 1944 cup semifinal. Sal'nikov was a scorer and creator who possessed the rarest of all abilities for a Soviet player. He was good in the air. He was also good at the dinner table and at the bar, regaling his teammates with all manner of stories while pursuing levity with great purpose. Sal'nikov's glibness and charm also made him a favorite of Spartak's new fans among the creative intelligentsia, especially those in the theater.[41]

Dementiev came from Dinamo Moscow. Although his services were no longer needed on that team, Dinamo refused to allow his transfer until Spartak called on one of the Starostins' old high-level party contacts to intervene. Upon his arrival at Spartak, Dementiev found an immediate on-field understanding with Sal'nikov. Vol'rat tried to name him his captain, but Nikolai's reputation as a practical joker led team officials to oppose the idea. In protest, Dementiev, looking out a third-story window at Tarasovka, poured a bucket of water down onto the head of a Spartak Society official who had arrived to give the team a lecture on "ideological-political education." His masterpiece, however, involved an anatomy lecture for which attendance was mandatory. The lecturer was to demonstrate the parts of the human body on a cadaver that was covered with a blanket. Before things could begin, Dementiev had two teammates remove the cadaver while he hid beneath the blanket. As the lecture began, the blanket was removed and Dementiev jumped up and ran out of the room to much amusement. One can understand how so poor a role model could have worn out his welcome at an institution as rigid as Dinamo, but he lasted nine seasons at Spartak, retiring at the age of thirty-nine after having scored fifty-six goals in 186 games for his second team.

A 5–2 defeat to TsDKA in the 1946 season opener did not get things off to an auspicious start, but Spartak had many supporters in the sporting press, who, after the opener, found signs of hope. *Sovetskii sport*'s Aleksander Vittenberg, known to his readers as "Vit," applauded Vol'rat's lineup changes. All that was required was for the defense to return to its former standard, and the team's "thousands of fans will root for them out of something more than custom." Two weeks later, that shred of optimism was torn away in a 1–4 drubbing by Dinamo Moscow. Vit's headline read, "When the Spectators are Disappointed." Spartak, he wrote, showed no sign of "psychological or moral preparation." The newly demobilized prewar hero goalie, Vladislav Zhmel'kov, had a dreadful game—the coaching staff's first sign of alcohol's impact on his once-great skills. Spartak, Vit concluded, "was still far from its earlier form."[42] German Kolodnyi's report in *Vechernaia Moskva* took the same tone. Under the headline "85,000 Fans are Bored," Kolodnyi wrote, "Nothing took place on the field that will linger in the memories of yesterday's match."[43] It is, however, far from likely that all of those eighty-five thousand fans were disappointed or bored. Close to half of those in attendance must have been supporting Dinamo, and surely they were delighted and excited. They cannot have been pleased to read that the pleasurable spectacle they had witnessed was dull and uninteresting, nor could they have been happy with the obvious pro-Spartak bias of so many Soviet journalists.

Vol'rat's impact began to take hold soon after the difficult start to the season. The team rounded into physical condition, and the coach found ways to build morale. Sadly, Zhmel'kov continued to play poorly in goal and was forced to share the duties with Aleksei Leontiev (1918–1998), who had played all of Spartak's matches the previous season. Vasily Sokolov, who succeeded Andrei Starostin as team captain, found his game and led what turned out to be a respectable defense. Although he tired by the end of the season, Sal'nikov settled in well, finding a striking partnership with Ivan Konov (1924–1990). Each player scored nine goals in a twenty-two-game season. Eventually the team finished a respectable sixth, for which it was "rewarded" with a four-game tour of Albania. Although there had been progress, the 1946 result, combined with the tenth-place finish the previous year, did test the loyalty of Spartak's fan base. Attendance slipped to thirty-eight thousand per home game, compared with the newly popular Dinamo's average gate of forty-four thousand. Nevertheless, this slip was far from a collapse. When the occasion called for it, Spartak supporters could and did fill Dinamo Stadium beyond its capacity. One such moment, the season's highlight, now lay ahead.[44]

The 1946 cup competition, which came at the end of the season, was limited to twenty-four invited teams. All the matches took place in Moscow from October 8 to October 20. Spartak had an easy draw and advanced to the final, where it met Dinamo Tblisi, to whom it had lost twice in the regular season.[45] *Vechernaia Moskva* reported that a "huge traffic flow, a multitudinous stream of people from every end of the city toward Dinamo began at midday."[46] An estimated seventy thousand filled every seat and aisle on a cold, rainy day. The field was surrounded by soldiers and snowbanks. Although newsreel footage of the prematch excitement focused on the faces of women, Georgians, and well-known intellectuals, the crowd was overwhelmingly male and pro-Spartak. Many of them were soldiers.[47] At the time, field hospitals had been set up in Moscow to help rehabilitate injured veterans. According to Esenin, the stands were filled with wounded men on crutches—many with bandaged heads, others with casts. It seemed as if the stadium had become an enormous clinic. The pro-Spartak Esenin would later write that the soldiers who had suffered at the front empathized with Spartak, which had also fallen on hard times during the war.[48] If the venue and the moment gave Spartak an emotional edge, Dinamo Tblisi, with its great star Boris Paichadze, was a heavy favorite, having finished third in the league.

Spartak still had too many older players to maintain excellence over an entire season, but it retained sufficient talent and energy this one day to put forth its greatest effort since before the war. Vol'rat had made a number of tactical and personnel changes for the match, fielding a lineup that comprised the youngest and oldest members of his roster. The ancients, Nikolai Dementiev and Georgii Glazkov, assisted on the younger Konov's goal in the ninth minute, but Dinamo soon went ahead 2–1. When Glazkov, who had scored all three goals in the 1939 replay of the cup semifinal, tied up the game just before the half, Filatov and his friends found themselves flooded with memories of that most dramatic, politically freighted of matches. The entire stadium then seethed and shook through a scoreless second half and thirty minutes of overtime. In the ninety-ninth minute halfback Oleg Timakov (1920–1990) consummated a counterattack with a header. Spartak retreated into blind defense as Dinamo attacked with skill and determination. Ultimately, Vol'rat's intense emphasis on conditioning paid off for his team. Seeing Dinamo tiring, he chose to go back on the attack as time ran down.[49]

With the final whistle, hats, greatcoats, even crutches went flying into the air. For Filatov, it was as if he had been made whole again, knowing that his team could, at least this once, turn back the clock to its prewar glory. The team of moods now became a team of memories. Once again Spartak had shown the ability to challenge the teams supported by the structures of force, giving hope to those who dreamed their nation would take on new ways in the aftermath of the Terror of the thirties and the horrors of the war. Among those in attendance that day was Nikita Simonian, an eighteen-year-old Armenian striker who had come from his native Sukhumi to Moscow to play for Kryl'ia Sovetov. He later recalled, "I sat in the stands and was lost in conjecture. This can't just be luck but rather some kind of indomitable spirit. How to capture it?" Three years later Simonian would capture that spirit when he transferred to Spartak. At the time he had other options, but the events of that cold October day played a role in his choice of a new team.[50]

There may have been other reasons for Simonian's interest in Spartak. Each man had received an extremely generous three thousand-ruble bonus for the cup victory, and it appears they knew how to spend it. On November 5, the players, coaches, and officials of the Moscow Spartak organization gathered at the posh restaurant in the National Hotel to celebrate their triumph. The cup was filled with champagne and passed around. A jolly and noisy time was had by all, but once the heavily drinking group was ready for what Russians call the "second wind," they had run out of cash. The team then opened up a tab, offering the cup as collateral. All staggered home happy and sated, but a month then passed. The players had neither paid their bill nor reclaimed the cup, which lay in the restaurant's storeroom. The management of the National eventually protested to the state sports committee, which in turn demanded the team settle its accounts and immediately transfer the cup from the miscreants at the Moscow organization into the safer hands of the larger sporting society's central council.[51]

Spartak's reputation as a club that could rise to special moments was enhanced the next year when it defeated Torpedo 2–0 in a cup final contested in July. Vol'rat's team had played with maddening inconsistency, winning three, losing four, and tying three going into the cup competition. Again the players found the will at the crucial moment, dominating play but managing to get just two past their former goalie, Akimov. Their efforts won them the affection of the Moscow public, and each player received a brand-new Moskvich sedan along with a tidy bonus.[52] Soon, however, the team came unglued as Vol'rat lost control of his players. A week after their triumph, the same lineup faced Simonian and his young Kryl'ia Sovetov Moscow team, sponsored by the aviation industry. This side had been struggling along at the bottom of the standings. Coached by the highly capable Armenian specialist Abram Khristoforovich Dangulov (1900–1967), Kryl'ia held Spartak at bay for eighty minutes until the young Basque émigré Ruperto Sagasti (b. 1923) scored to give Kryl'ia what seemed a huge upset. Dangulov's team, in fact, had many talented players, as their 1–0 win over Dinamo Moscow showed a month later. Still, it seemed at the time that Spartak's letdown could be excused.

Soon, however, a series of defeats led to complaints in the press that Vol'rat was experimenting too much with his lineup while failing to instill responsibility in his players. For their part, team members told *Sovetskii sport* that they saw little reason in trying. With first place out of reach, they saw no difference between finishing fifth or eighth. There was no sign of effort in an early September 1–1 tie with Vasily Stalin's air force team (VVS), which occupied twelfth and last place. Spartak was now in eleventh place. Two weeks later a 1–2 loss to Dinamo Moscow did little to improve its situation, but as far as the press was concerned, the respectable effort only exposed Spartak's deeper problems. "After a series of poor matches," wrote *Sovetskii sport,* "Spartak showed they can play well if they want to. The coach, Vol'rat, must understand that only with a sober evaluation of his team's strengths and weaknesses, self-criticism and struggle with the star syndrome . . . can they escape these kinds of crude mistakes." The pro-Spartak sportswriter Yuri Vaniat', after a similar result with Torpedo, wrote, "Their play in this match shows that Spartak let several teams finish ahead of them simply because of their own carelessness. Let the 1947 season serve as a cruel but instructive lesson." *Sovetskii sport* headlined the season's final game, a 0–0 tie with Kryl'ia Sovetov, "A Sad Finish for Spartak" and accused the Spartak Society's chief officials of neglecting their soccer team. Not surprisingly, Vol'rat was relieved of his duties with the end of the season.[53]

## The First Steps Back

In the light of these troubles, it must be asked just who was minding the store when the Starostins were away. Not even the editor of the club's official encyclopedia can say for sure. None of the other leading Russian soccer experts are certain either. Yet important decisions were made during these years, the most crucial being that of a new coach. The choice may have been made by the former star Vladimir Stepanov and Nikolai Morozov (1913–1965), listed in the encyclopedia as "administrators" during this period. They were closest to the team's on-field affairs. It is also possible that the Spartak Society's top officers, Mikhailchuk and Vasilii Kuzin, took the next step. It is even possible Nikolai and Andrei Starostin, despite their exile, may have played a role. Neither mentioned this event in his memoirs, but it appears both brothers had access to telephones by 1948. Whoever made the choice must have been close to the team for a long time, as it was decided to bring back that old friend from the prerevolutionary Krasnaia Presnia neighborhood, Konstantin Kvashnin, who had earlier coached Spartak.

Kvashnin was deeply read and a talented musician. This made him unusual for a coach, and indeed, he was something of an eccentric. Truly great coaches are never "normal," human beings and Kvashnin fit the pattern of eccentricity, perhaps too well. He added few new players but made a conscious choice to give the young more playing time. The most important addition was a young Moscow defense plant worker named Aleksei Paramonov (b. 1925), who had been released by VVS (a sure sign of its incompetence) in the middle of the 1947 season. He had been recommended to Kuzin by Nikolai Ozerov (1922–1997), who would become one of the most important figures in the subsequent history of the Spartak Sport Society and all of Soviet sport. The son of a famous opera singer, the young Ozerov was simultaneously a Soviet tennis champion, an actor at the Moscow Art Theater, and an attacker on Spartak's reserve squad. Eventually he became the first great announcer of the Soviet television era, succeeding Siniavskii at the top of his profession. Paramonov would go on to become one of Spartak's greatest forwards ever, starring for the national team and winning an Olympic gold medal in 1956.[54]

The need for Ozerov's intervention was a sign of a broader malaise in the Spartak organization. On the eve of the 1948 season, *Sovetskii sport* ran an article by a provincial Spartak official headlined "Return Spartak to Its Former Glory." Its author remarked, "We old Spartakovites follow the unsuccessful performance of our football team with alarm." Yet the problem had been experienced across a wide range of sports contested by the society. Of the top ten nationally ranked athletes in each sport, only 6 percent were members of Spartak. By contrast, 34 percent of this sporting elite belonged to Dinamo. The blame for this sad situation fell on the beleaguered Mikhailchuk.[55]

Stepping into this difficult spot, Kvashnin seized the initiative. He established a training regime even tougher than Vol'rat's and introduced tactics used by both TsDKA and Dinamo.[56] Along with the speedy right-winger Paramonov, the coach gave added playing time to Konov and Viktor Terentiev (b. 1924).[57] The season began in early May with a stumble, a 1–2 loss to TsDKA, but it soon became clear that Spartak was on the road to better days. A 4–1 victory over Torpedo, marked by two early Paramonov goals, was followed three days later by a 7–1 wipeout of a strong Kryl'ia Sovetov Kuibyshev team. Vaniat' wrote in *Sovetskii sport* that Kvashnin had been able to reestablish the long-passing game that had marked Spartak's play in the late thirties. With its improved conditioning, Kvashnin's team could now compete with Dinamo and TsDKA.[58] Yet the very conditioning fostered by their maximalist coach held dangers for Spartak.

Proof of Vaniat''s assertion came in early July. With Dinamo in first place and Spartak in second, the clubs met at an overflowing Dinamo Stadium. Spartak won 3–0. Vaniat' was joined in his match account by Dangulov, still coaching Kryl'ia Sovetov Moscow. Both men praised Kvashnin for mobilizing his players and staying true to Spartak's tradition as a big-game team. At the end of the month, optimism gave way to euphoria. The team defeated TsDKA, then in fifth place. The victory put Spartak into first place for the first time since the war ended. The 2–0 triumph was the work of Spartak's young players. Sal'nikov scored early, and the match was clinched by a

Konov-to-Sal'nikov combination that was then headed in by an onrushing Paramonov.[59]

Sadly, Kvashnin could not maintain this effort. He still did not have the mix of generations on the team that would prevent fatigue as the season wound down. The old were a bit too old, and the young had not yet developed the strength and endurance they would need. Yet, Kvashnin in his fanaticism did not understand this situation. Things became unglued, as they so often did, when the team traveled south, where it suffered a 0–2 loss to Dinamo Tblisi. The usually reliable captain, Vasily Sokolov, had a bad game in defense.[60] This was a clear warning sign, and the fans' fears were confirmed a week later when Spartak was destroyed by Dinamo Moscow 1–5. Dinamo's Savdunin scored an early goal, and Spartak came apart. Sal'nikov and Paramonov, placed in unfamiliar positions by Kvashnin, were lost. So much, it seemed, for the "team of emotion" that was known for rising to the big moment.

Other losses followed, and Spartak fell to third place, overtaken by TsDKA and Dinamo Moscow. Eventually, the team of lieutenants beat its police rivals in the last minute of the last match of the 1948 season. Bobrov scored on a rebound off the post in what has come to be considered the greatest match of the postwar era. TsDKA would take the double, beating Spartak 3–0 in the cup final. Kvashnin was heavily criticized in the largely pro-Spartak press. He had continued to train his players as hard at the end of the season as he had at the beginning. Not only did this exhaust his team, but he lost its support. Despite his often counterproductive behavior, Kvashnin should have been thanked for bringing Spartak its first prize (third place) since 1939. Instead, he was let go. Nevertheless, the move set the stage for Spartak's eventual return to even greater glory.

### Legends, Branding, and "Spartak Spirit"

Before the war, Spartak drew working-class supporters (the so-called us) to their side. As Oleshchuk showed, those fans saw themselves as underdogs in the face of overwhelming police power (the so-called them), but both the Spartak soccer team and the larger organization had not been underdogs before 1941. Promkooperatsiia had supported them lavishly. After the Starostins' arrests in 1942, the team, severely damaged by the absence of its leaders, struggled, and its fans suffered. Throughout these years, it was no secret the Starostins had been sent away. They had been so visible during the thirties that their later absence could not help but be noted.[61] In the postwar period, their names disappeared from histories of the game and from information guides. Their goals were simply attributed to "others."[62]

Defeat, however, did not entirely drive their fans away. To be sure, attendance dipped to 38,000 per home game in 1946 and 1947, down from 47,900 in 1945, but this can scarcely be called a collapse. While there are no complete figures for 1948, it appears that big matches against principal opponents continued to be huge attractions, although less compelling games toward the end of the league season did draw smaller crowds.[63] Still, one can safely say that this sizable attendance provided a guarantee that Spartak, despite its difficulties on the field, would not disappear from the sporting scene. In the postwar period Promkooperatsiia's wealth had indeed withered, but ticket sales, money from below, provided more than enough to keep the doors open.

If anything, the identification of Spartak's supporters with their favorite club intensified in this era of shared suffering. The true test of the loyalty of any team's support always comes when it loses. Many of the team's fans saw themselves, rightly or wrongly, as victims. Now Spartak itself was seen as a victim of police power. In this trying context, Spartak's public came to believe their team had special qualities. The cup triumphs of 1946 and 1947 fed their faith that victory was always possible despite the odds. Eventually it became fashionable to speak of something called a "Spartak spirit" (*Spartakovskii dukh*). In service to this elusive concept, the club's new postwar legions of intellectual fans, none more loudly than Filatov, began to construct all manner of stories, myths, and legends.

If the team could not win consistently, at least it could be seen to play beautifully and thus embody the hopes and dreams of the postwar era. More than one pro-Spartak journalist bought into this idea. The club was supposed to represent all that was good about the game, whereas Dinamo was said to play an unattractive and somehow less humane soccer. Spartak was supposed to speak for the "healthy" forces in Soviet society, whereas Dinamo represented its darker side. This process of political self-identification through support for a particular team is in no way unique to the USSR, nor is the ascription of all manner of unattractive qualities to one's rivals. To Spartak fans it did not matter whether Dinamo really played inhumane soccer. These were simply the stories they told about themselves and their team. Some of those stories were actually true. Nikolai Starostin would later prove only too happy to invoke this Spartak spirit as a crucial part of the club's post-Stalin image. At its core was the tale of the Starostins' time in the gulag, when they truly were victims of the Stalinist machine. After his return, Nikolai never tired of regaling his players, coaches, journalists, and other football colleagues with stories of his "incarceration." Unmentioned was the possibility that he and his pals had done something that, to be charitable, was less honorable than being better at football than Dinamo.

Being "the team whose leaders had been sent to the gulag" became a central part of the Spartak family romance. Journalists, Western and Russian, have since taken this fact and run perhaps too far with it. After 1953, many in the USSR came to call Spartak a team of democracy or even freedom, without any clear sense of what those words meant in the Soviet context. If they were the victims of Stalinist repression, the Starostins never felt they were anti-Soviet. Soviet power had jailed them, but it had also provided the privileges that made their separate ordeals bearable. Eventually it was a different version of Soviet power that freed them. For fans, supporting Spartak may have been a small way of saying no, but this implied a carefully modulated resistance, not outright opposition or dissidence. When they were away from Moscow, the brothers made the best of a difficult situation, while their supporters railed against those who had exiled them.

After the war, Andrei Starostin remained in Norylsk. In time he found ways to carve out some comfort despite the harshness of a winter environment where streets were deep trenches dug in the snow in order to provide protection from Arctic winds. It was a place that Andrei later claimed allowed him "to fulfill the norm of a real man."[64] In time, visits from family and friends became common. His football and hockey teams enjoyed success, making him a local hero by the time he left in 1954. By contrast, Nikolai's postwar existence turned out to be something of an odyssey, one that would make its own contribution to Spartak's legend.

After a year at Ukhta, he was sent to a camp near the far eastern city of Khabarovsk. Although Ukhta and Khabarovsk were more or less in the same part of the USSR, Starostin was sent on a six-month journey that included ten intermediate stops. At the immense central transfer point for prisoners in Molotov, he met up with Aleksandr, and the two got to spend a month together. Nikolai eventually got to Khabarovsk on May 8, 1945, one day before the Germans capitulated. He soon learned he was to play the same role in his new home that he had in Ukhta. The commandant of the Khabarovsk camp, Colonel Goglidze, was as big a football fan as General Burdakov of Ukhta. The colonel was also a close ally of Beria, who now learned of the new status of the four Starostin brothers. Goglidze appears to have convinced his fellow Georgian to approve the brothers' relationship with the police, and they became official employees of the Dinamo Sport Society. Goglidze was, however, soon required to part company with Nikolai, who was now sent to Komsomolsk-na-Amur. The Amurlag camp was not without certain amenities, including stores, cafeterias, bathhouses, a movie theater, and a stadium. Its commandant, General Petrenko, was also a lover of soccer and an ally of Goglidze. As his new team enjoyed success, Nikolai was allowed to live outside "the zone," and his life became more like that of an exile than a political prisoner. Eventually, another admirer, the head of railroads in the far east, provided Starostin's team with its own semiluxurious, specially equipped railcar for road trips. Later, Nikolai's wife and daughter were able to visit him. At no point did he refuse these privileges in the name of any sort of principle.[65]

The most bizarre episode of this period (one that revealed the contradictions of late Stalinism) came some time in 1948 (as usual Starostin was imprecise on dates). According to Nikolai's version—and as in so many other instances it would be useful if we had sources other than his—he was summoned to the phone to take a call from Stalin's wastrel son, Vasilii, commander of the Moscow Air Garrison. Vasilii Stalin was a passionate sports fan and full-time drunk who was seeking to turn the VVS into a power equal to any.[66] Excellent facilities were constructed, and top coaches were hired, but instead of developing its own athletes, VVS sought to build teams in several sports by recruiting already successful players away from other sport societies. The air force soccer team had been promoted to the first division in 1946 but had languished at the bottom of the standings. Ignoring Nikolai's lack of achievement as a coach, Vasilii proposed that Starostin come to Moscow and take over VVS. A plane was dispatched the next day to take the prisoner Starostin to the capital.

On his arrival, Nikolai was taken to Vasilii's mansion and given his passport stamped with permission (*propiska*) to live in Moscow. Nikolai proceeded to his old home on Spiridonov Street for a joyous reunion with his wife and daughters. Their happiness lasted just a few days. Beria learned of his presence in the capital, and Starostin was given twenty-four hours to get out of town. Instead, he headed straight for Vasilii's house, where it was decided he would move in and never leave the young Stalin's side. If we are to believe Nikolai, this "closeness" involved sharing the same large bed with an often passed-out Vasilii, who, Starostin reported, kept a loaded revolver under his pillow.[67] This frisson of the homoerotic is surely tantalizing, but it could very well be yet another bit of Spartak apocrypha. After the collapse of the USSR, Vasilii's wife was quoted in a sympathetic biography of her sad and troubled husband. "And just where," she asked, "was I supposed to be at the time?"[68]

Perhaps it was Vasilii's snoring, or maybe it was a perfectly normal desire to share a bed with his wife that caused Nikolai to leave, but after two months, he sneaked out of Stalin's house one night and went back home. Unfortunately, he had been watched by Beria's men, who quickly interrupted his visit and put him on a train back to the far east. Vasilii brought Starostin back to Moscow one more time, but it soon became clear to both of them that Beria would have his way. Nikolai now headed to Kazakhstan, where he spent the rest of his exile, eventually settling in Alma-Ata to coach the republic's strongest team, Kairat. The club prospered, and he was given a comfortable apartment with a pleasant garden. He also enjoyed visits from his family during summers and school holidays. When Joseph Stalin finally died, it could not be said that Nikolai Starostin was suffering unduly.[69]

For twenty-five years of Soviet history, however, I sat in the stands of Moscow stadiums and heard scores of fans, nearly all male, state (with varying levels of sobriety) that Spartak was the "team of democracy." To this day I am not certain what these citizens of the USSR meant when they used this word. The fact that the team and its leaders had been victims of Stalinism was central to their claims, but it would be hard to argue that any of the Starostin brothers considered themselves democrats in the liberal sense of the term. Nikolai's coauthor, Aleksandr Vainshtein, by contrast with Filatov, is far less positive about his collaborator's political position:

> [Starostin] . . . tranquilly talked about a general of the gulag and spoke positively of a General Goglidze. He would say, "He was a great fan of football." He didn't say he killed millions of people or that he sent them to camps or that he

was a criminal. He said, "He was a football fan. He supported teams." . . . I am not sure he understood in his own mind that all those championships of the gulag and all the rest were built on the bones of people. He did not refuse to take part in them. Of course, it would have been stupid to refuse, even fatal. You can't judge that really, but I am not sure that he really understood you don't evaluate people by their relationship to football but by their relationship to more serious things. For him, if someone liked football and Spartak in particular, he was a good person. Those who did not like football were not good.[70]

Vainshtein's point is well taken, but it is necessary to bear in mind the distance between any team's leaders and its followers. If the followers constructed myths, legends, and benign images of Spartak, these discourses took on their own reality and had meaning for those who, rightly or wrongly, believed them. While we need to be aware of the ambiguity of the Starostins' own positions, their fans were still free to make what they wished of their heroes' lives.

The construction of founding myths that have only distant connections to actual historical circumstances has been a normal or at least widespread element of popular club loyalties and a significant part of sports fans' identity formation the world over. Indeed, congruence of attitudes and life situations between team owners and their customers has probably been the exception over time. After World War II, working-class baseball fans in Brooklyn saw the Dodgers, their local team, as emblematic of their own lives, but the club belonged to a callous millionaire named Walter O'Malley. Supporters of such giants as Arsenal and Manchester United, long run by social elites, have frequently evoked their club's origins as industrial teams. Barcelona is still the team of Catalan regionalism although in recent years it has had few Catalans in its side. More recently, we have seen the strange phenomenon of both Tottenham Hotspur of North London and Ajax Amsterdam being branded as Jewish teams, despite the fact that both teams currently have few traces of Jewishness on the field.

For these reasons, the story of Spartak spirit and the club's branding as the people's team should be seen as a contest of dueling myths rather than an accurate description of playing or management styles. Chronology presents the first difficulty in teasing out the veracity of any of these stories. We have come to learn the elements of the classically invented tradition of Spartak spirit over time. The memories of fans, even professionals, can be maddeningly imprecise, not to mention retrospective. What may have held true for the 1950s may not yet have appeared between 1945 and 1948. One often finds players and fans speaking glowingly of the "Spartak style," an improvisational, free-flowing, expressive even romantic short passing game that still characterizes Spartak's play, but the shift in this direction began only in 1949.

In the thirties Spartak had won with physically strong players who overwhelmed their opponents. The players on the 1945–1948 teams, who were holdovers from the prewar era, still played in that style, which required a high level of psychological preparation in order to perform with the necessary effort.[71] These men, in their early and midthirties, found they could now muster such efforts only occasionally. This simple demographic/biological reality formed the basis of the idea that Spartak was the team of emotion. After the war fans simply never knew which Spartak would show up, and this new unpredictability, most dramatically seen in the cup victories of 1946 and 1947, actually increased the team's popularity. Unexpected triumphs were combined with inexplicable losses to weak teams. In the words of Filatov, "They never left their fans indifferent."[72]

For intellectuals like Filatov, much of this Spartak ideology was self-referential. For creative professionals, the club's spectacular ups and downs mirrored their own struggles with their work at a time of what appeared to be growing political control.[73] Igor Netto (1930–1999), who began with the club in 1948 and became one of its greatest stars, would later remark on this tendency:

> The play of Spartak is much like that of a person of artistic bent. Such a person is not on an even keel but is one given to highs and lows that are hard to explain logically. They are capable of unexpected flights. . . . Even in the most difficult times, when they were assembling a new team, Spartak, which trailed several clubs, could suddenly destroy one of the leaders. They did this not by demonstrating a high class of play but by showing audacity and impetuousness.[74]

During the years of late Stalinism, Spartak fans were forced to embrace suffering and uncertainty. Intensifying these emotions was what insiders and outsiders saw as the fundamental cause of the team's vegetation: its founders had been arrested, and their leadership was sorely missed. While their names had been expunged from the record books, everyone knew what had happened.[75] Such sentiments gravitated from the training ground and the stands into a sporting press filled with Spartak sympathizers. Along with Filatov, others like Merzhanov, Vaniat', Esenin, Vit, and Ilya Baru romanticized the team. Taking cues from their fellow artists and intellectuals, sportswriters claimed Spartak players did not simply play football but rather *expressed* themselves. Those players, like members of other teams, had completed on average only seven years of education, but this did not prevent the growing legion of highly cultured football followers from ascribing a shared artistic creativity to their physically gifted heroes. Educated supporters claimed to find the same admirable characteristics in the players that they found in themselves. Often, as Filatov would admit, this involved emphasizing the irrational qualities of Spartak's play. "I would say that Dinamo's combinations were one move less than Spartak's and a meter longer. Dinamo's play was simpler, smarter and smoother. Spartak's play was more accidental, desperate and spirited."[76]

Many of the players actually came to welcome the interest of this new cohort of fans drawn from the creative intelligentsia as well as from the larger and growing ranks of professionals. Sergei Sal'nikov and later Nikita Simonian were often seen in the lobbies and dressing rooms of Moscow's leading theaters. In turn, the Moscow Art Theater, Maly Teatr, and Vakhtangov were all centers of Spartak support.[77] The film star and big-band leader Leonid Utesov was an intense Spartak fan.[78] These celebrities were following a pattern begun in the thirties by Andrei Starostin, who spent many an evening in the capital's leading salons, not to mention the Hippodrome and the circus. His friendship with the actor Mikhail Ianshin was well known, and Ianshin did not forget his comrade during Andrei's years of exile.[79]

Spartak's more articulate supporters sought to wrap the team in the mantle of what some saw as the USSR's best and brightest. Yet it cannot be said that all members of the expanding professional class were fans of Spartak. There were those among the talented and creative who sympathized with Dinamo, not to mention an array of other clubs.[80] There is simply no way to know what portion of this highly heterogeneous group supported Spartak. First, the very categories of "professional" and "intellectual" were broad and various. Clearly, the classic Russian intelligentsia of writers, artists, scientists, and academicians had attitudes different from those of midlevel engineers and factory managers. Second, no survey of fan loyalty was ever carried out. A reading of the literature on football leaves a clear impression that Spartak was the most popular Soviet club, but one needs to be cautious about accepting this part of Spartak ideology as truth. There were legions of articulate fans of other teams who were only too happy to dismiss such claims as mere image making.

Like Oleshchuk, Filatov maintained that half of Moscow's soccer fans supported Spartak, but if Spartak was still the most popular team, it must be noted that both Dinamo and TsDKA had much the same attendance between 1945 and 1948. The sheer excellence of these two clubs guaranteed large followings. There were, as Filatov had to admit, "no referenda." There certainly was no market research. Dinamo outdrew Spartak by a slight margin in the immediate postwar period. The primary point, as Merzhanov asserted, was that Spartak fans stuck with the club despite its travail. Fewer spectators might show up at less important games, but for the big matchups Dinamo Stadium was always overflowing.[81] It also was the case that many Spartak fans attended Dinamo and TsDKA games to root against their Moscow rivals. This massive level of attendance could have been maintained only by the continued support of those working-class males who still made up the overwhelming majority of Spartak's fan base. The presence of so many intellectuals may have changed the nature of Spartak's support, but there were not enough creative professionals to have compensated for any drop off in proletarian support. As Nikita Simonian freely admitted, not all Spartak supporters came from the ranks of "famous actors, writers and doctors. . . . There were plenty of inveterate Moscow hooligans during the postwar period."[82]

Rooting for Spartak had been one small way for the team's supporters to maintain a belief that they had carved out some measure of independence from the regime. The mysterious status of the club's sponsor, Promkooperat-siia, played into this element of the Spartak self-image. Fans knew to whom the other teams belonged, but few were exactly sure what it was that Promko-operatsiia did. It was said to play a role in the service industries and retail trades, two areas of the economy looked down upon by much of the rest of the population. This very uncertainty made it appear to the football public that Spartak belonged to no one, that it was somehow independent. The war years and the period of reconstruction had not been kind to what was once a very wealthy organization. The controls of rationing limited Promkooperatsiia's capacity to generate revenue on its own. As a result, the organization was no longer able to support Spartak as handsomely as it had done before the war.[83] When Torpedo sought to recruit Nikita Simonian from Kryl'ia Sovetov after the end of the 1948, it was in competition with Spartak for his services. Ivan Likhachev, the powerful director of the ZIS auto factory, told Simonian, "What is your Spartak? Promkooperatsiia? Here we are a huge factory."[84]

Much the same was true concerning Spartak's political support. Popular confusion about Promkooperatsiia's functions may have created an impression of independence, but it must be noted that Spartak was a team of the Communist Party. The club had always had powerful allies. In Vainshtein's estimation, "Spartak may not have been the team of a particular part of the bureaucracy, but it was like no other, a team of the party. If the 'organs' supported Dinamo and TsDKA, then Spartak was supported by the party, the KPSS . . . especially the Moscow city committee."[85] Vartanian concurred that Spartak was the team "of politicians."[86] Spartak's original patronage had come from Kosarev's Komsomol, but Kosarev was now long gone. The character of the party itself had been much changed by the war; so many prewar members were dead, replaced in large measure by millions of peasants and soldiers. Its influence and power had waned, well surpassed by the police during the late thirties and also by the army with the victorious end of the war. Thus, if Spartak still had friends in high places, these were no longer the best of all possible friends one could have.

With its financial foundation diminished and its political support marginalized, it is not surprising that the Spartak Society fell upon hard times in the first postwar years. The team was very much on its own, and it is fair to say that only its large ticket-buying fan base enabled it to survive through 1948. The very next year, however, would bring profound changes to both Spartak and the entire USSR. As the cold war set in, the USSR turned inward amid waves of chauvinism and xenophobia. These new circumstances seemed to promise the Spartak Society little good, but the team did not disappear from the game. Instead, it went on to lay the foundation for its greatest success.

# 6

# Spartak Resurgent, 1949–1952

Life in the USSR began to stabilize in 1948 as the most immediate tasks of reconstruction were accomplished. This improvement on the domestic front occurred just as the international scene was growing more complex and dangerous. Cold war tensions increased with the Soviet rejection of the Marshall Plan and the failure of peace treaty negotiations concerning Germany. Those moments were followed by the blockade and subsequent airlift of Berlin. These changes in the international situation weakened Zhdanov's position and played into the hands of his rivals. By 1949, Malenkov and Beria, with their new ally Mikhail Suslov, had made a political comeback. Along with greater international truculence, anti-Semitism intensified, as did the related sentiments of Great Russian chauvinism and xenophobia.[1] Contact with the West diminished dramatically, and the USSR entered a period of isolation that had an enormous impact on all forms of sporting activity. Participation in international competitions, with their anodyne messages of peace, understanding, and friendly competition, virtually ceased. Turned inward, Soviet sport, so vital and dynamic in the early postwar years, stagnated.

The economic comeback during the last period of Stalin's rule (1949–1953) brought many of the trappings of a long-sought, if rather strange, normalcy as the nation entered a period of attenuated recovery. Economic growth, extensive for decades, now became intensive. Nevertheless, low living standards persisted, dampening any lingering postwar optimism. In the light of the new circumstances, hopes for something better gave way to satisfaction that nothing worse had been visited on the population. Housing and transportation continued to be huge problems, but no longer were the Soviet peoples perpetually on the edge of subsistence crises. Rationing was ended precipitously late in 1947. At the same time, a draconian currency reform sharply reduced the amount of money in circulation and filled the stores with consumer goods set at market prices. Material comfort for anyone but the highest elites, who benefited from the new situation, had to wait until the midfifties. Life, a bit better if not exactly more joyous, was still pinched for the masses, whose postwar hopes for a better life had to be scaled back.[2]

Faced with challenges along a broad front, Stalin fell back on repression, intimidation, and a muted return to terror. Along with the restoration of the death penalty in 1950 came an increase in the prison population, which swelled from 1.7 million to 2.5 million. The new purges, while unpredictable, were considerably less extensive than those of the late thirties. Executions were largely limited to elite intellectuals and losers of political struggles, while ordinary folk accused of crimes were incarcerated or sent to labor camps. There were notable atrocities. The 1948 murder of the world-famous Yiddish actor Shlomo Mikhoels, the 1950 purge of the Leningrad party organization, the "Mingrelian Affair," and the so-called Doctors' Plot of early 1953 all had the intended effect of intimidating much of society into submission.[3] This renewed reliance on repression was but one of the methods employed by the regime to put the Humpty-Dumpty of the system back together again, but Soviet society was now different. The most elementary, even vulgar, of Marxists had no difficulty in drawing the conclusion that a political system that sought a return to the past could not paper over new realities. Indeed, reliance on old methods involved real dangers for the system's stability. It was one thing to employ massive terror on the eve of history's most destructive war. It was altogether another to revive it at a postwar moment when people still yearned for some possibility that life would actually get better.

The horrors the new turn evoked were so visible and disturbing to outsiders that, quite properly, they became the basis for the West's indictment of Communism. Yet the attempt to reassert the old controls appears "more haphazard and less successful than once thought."[4] According to Julie Hessler's rich and nuanced account of Soviet trade, Stalin's last years may have had more in common with what came after 1953. "The late Stalin era," she argues, "formed a transitional phase between the extreme, survival-threatening privations and crises of the period from 1917 and 1948 and the mundane shortage economy of the later years."[5] Eric Duskin describes these years as a "passage from convulsion and disorder to routinized professionalization common in most industrial societies."[6] The rapid growth in the number of educated workers that he described would ultimately have an important impact on Soviet society. Repression had thwarted the constructive forces that emerged from the war, but the struggle against Nazism had revealed the fundamental inadequacies of the system.[7] Restoring the prewar order did little to solve those problems, which lingered well after Stalin was gone.

Postwar society's response was certainly one of fear and intimidation, but around and within the cracks of institutions and formal organizations, the Soviet population was drawn to a variety of liminal activities, many of them pleasurable, that did not fit the older pattern. The spontaneous, fun-loving soccer crowds that continued into Stalin's last years can properly be seen as a sign of other forms of spontaneity that, as Lewin reminds us, should also be the "legitimate—and sometimes central—topic[s]" of our study.[8]

Official policies, even if fully executed, could also contradict one another. Often the regime was not even on the same page with itself. In December 1948, the Soviet government was advancing policies that turned the USSR's back on the outside world. At the same time it issued the famous proclamation calling for world dominance in sport, which inescapably involved active participation in the international sporting scene. There had been extensive internal discussion about taking part in the first postwar summer Olympiad (1948), held in London. As had been his wont, Stalin demanded to know whether victory could be guaranteed. When the sports authorities said no, the decision was made to stay home. At the very same moment the USSR was joining a broad range of international sports federations, it was shutting out the capitalist world. In the climate of increased xenophobia, participation in international events was reduced. Soviet soccer suffered as a result. Young players failed to develop, while the skills of the older generation eroded. The eventual result of this sporting isolationism was an embarrassing and unexpected defeat in the 1952 Olympic football tournament at the hands of the politically defiant Yugoslavs.[9]

## Ideology and Football Redux—Suslov's Penicillin

Late in 1947, even before Zhdanov's death, Mikhail Suslov and his protégés assumed control of the Central Committee's Bureau of Agitation and Propaganda. This institution, known as Agitprop, was responsible for matters pertaining to culture, including physical culture and sport. Zhdanov, whose career had been in decline well before his passing in August 1948, had accused Malenkov and Beria of ideological laxity in 1946. This charge, however, could scarcely be said to apply to Suslov, who sought to impose a rigid and simplified version of Marxism-Leninism on the citizenry through a process called "ideological-political education."

This was not a new term, nor was it a new practice. It had long been employed in a broad and general way. Readings of such "classics" as Stalin's biography or the short course of the history of the Communist Party were now combined with public lectures on topics of the day and excursions to sights of political and cultural importance. The purpose was not only to create true ideological believers but, more important, to improve their performance at work. This form of brief and superficial training was supposed to solve the system's problems and make it function better.

With Beria closely tied to Suslov and both men free after 1948 to implement their policies, it was inevitable that the struggle for ideological-political education should turn to football. Here, however, the campaign became ridiculous. Its purpose was not only to improve the players' behavior but also to enhance their performance on the field.[10] Soccer professionals, however, saw ideological-political education as a huge annoyance. The idea that Stalin's

**6.1** The impish Nikolai Dementiev receives his runners-up diploma after the 1952 cup final. Fotoagentstvo Sportekspress.

biography could help them win games seemed thoroughly absurd. In 2001, Nikita Simonian told me the players hated the lectures.[11] Perhaps their attitude was best expressed by Nikolai Dementiev's aforementioned bucket of water directed at the presenter of one ideological-political lecture. The entire campaign can be seen as a precursor of Mao's Little Red Book. No doubt it had roughly the same impact on sporting performance. Nevertheless, lip service both publicly and secretly had to be paid to Suslov's remedy.

During the thirties calls for the political education of the Soviet soccer player had been uttered at various congresses of football specialists. In truth, any education at all would have helped Soviet footballers, who averaged seven years of schooling. This cultural and educational issue had from time to time been raised in both the sporting and the general press. During Zhdanov's ascendancy, a period known as the Zhdanovshchina, some attention had been directed to widespread ideological laxity in the Soviet soccer world. An order (*prikaz*) of March 10, 1948, addressed the failures of ideological-political education in football.[12] The next month, Suslov raised the matter at a meeting called to discuss several failures by Soviet athletes in recent international competitions.[13] The return to favor of Malenkov, Beria, and Suslov was marked by a full campaign of interference in the sporting process, particularly as it applied to football. Ideological-political education became the cure for all the ills of Soviet soccer, fictional and real. The campaign, long a matter of secret concern to party officials, took off and became a public obsession. Starting late in 1948, ideological-political education was repeatedly mentioned in newspapers and other periodicals. Teams were required to pay serious attention to the matter.

In an earlier work researched before 1992, I described this phenomenon without the use of archival material.[14] At that time, I focused on the authorities' fear that bad on-field behavior by players would set a poor example for spectators, an example that could and did lead to violence. A perusal of the annual reports of club coaches, now available in the archive of the state sports committee, reveals several points of further interest. Before 1949, coaches, who prepared the reports, paid little attention to matters cultural and educational. Mikhail Iakushin, coach of Dinamo Moscow, best summed up their attitude late in 1948. Speaking before a plenum of the Football Section of the Sports Committee, he noted that ideological-political work was fine as long as it did not interfere with football.[15]

On a certain level, however, Suslov's approach could be seen as less menacing than earlier methods used to maintain labor discipline. At the same meeting, Viktor Dubinin, a coach and sports committee official, complained that players were routinely late or absent from practice. He urged that they be punished according to the Soviet criminal code, particularly the labor law of 1940, which called for severe penalties in such situations. Suslov replied, "Why introduce the criminal code? We should be talking here about educational work." Dubinin answered, "Up to now, no such activity has been put in place." Things would soon change, but in Suslov's defense it must be said that being forced to read Stalin's biography was a good bit more pleasant than spending time in jail.

Starting in 1949, each team's report featured a detailed list of readings, lectures, and excursions. Some coaches even mentioned the players who responded to these lessons and those who ignored them. Different teams took different approaches to fulfilling Suslov's requirements. Even the reluctant Iakushin, whose report may have been prepared by an assistant, cited a full catalog of activities that may or may not have actually taken place. By contrast, TsDKA's highly cultured coach Boris Arkadiev had long made a point of taking his players to museums, plays, and films. He did not consider such work a burden but took a more casual and less detailed approach to describing it. Indeed, one can be fairly certain that the activities described by Arkadiev, as opposed to those of Iakushin, actually took place.[16] Spartak's reports, prepared by several different coaches, fell between those of Dinamo and TsDKA in their level of detail. The players were less than thrilled to have these tasks imposed on them, but certain features of the team's program were taken up with great enthusiasm. Those activities in turn had a significant impact on Spartak's relationship with the new, cultured segment of its fan base.

During the 1952 season, Dinamo began its educational activity with once-a-week classes as part of winter training. There were lectures on "How to Work with a Book," "Hygiene and the Regime of the Football Player," and "Training the Athlete in Light of the Work of Academician Pavlov." Iakushin here was slanting the program to topics that could in fact improve player perfor-

**6.2** Matinee idol Sergei Sal'nikov at the beach. A. Soskin, *Sergei Sal'nikov.*

mance. Trips to the Tretiakovskii Art Gallery, the Lenin Museum, and the museum of presents to Stalin were less tied to results on the field. Starting with spring training in the south, classes were held two times a week, a pattern that continued throughout the season. Topics shifted toward the political and cultural and included "Great Communist Construction Projects," "The Economic Situation in Rumania and Bulgaria," "Anglo-American Adventurism in Korea," and "Football in Austria." Iakushin claimed the players were attentive during the classes. On the other hand, Sergei Sal'nikov, now with Dinamo, and the great goalie Lev Yashin (who would go on to become a model of Communist propriety) did not approach the process seriously at all. Both men, Iakushin suggested, demonstrated a "parasitical attitude."[17]

That same year, Spartak, coached by its former captain Vasilii Sokolov, also held one class a week during the winter. Lectures, contracted out to the Moscow Lectures Bureau, began in spring training. Of twenty-eight presentations only five were on international affairs; four dealt with domestic developments. The rest were concerned with cultural, educational, and sporting matters. Lectures were supplemented by frequent trips to the movies. Yet the activities most popular with the players were frequent visits to the Moscow Art Theater and Maly Theater. The athletes got to mix with the actors and compare notes on the differences among their respective kinds of performances.

The actors, male and female, were often fans. Friendships formed around their shared celebrity, much as elsewhere in the world. This exchange between Spartak and the world of theater had been going on for many years, dating back to Andrei Starostin's prewar (and continuing) friendship with Ianshin. Simonian, Paramonov, and Sal'nikov had been the most popular players with the theatrical crowd, and all three men used these contacts to raise

**6.3** Mikhail Ianshin, actor of the Moscow Art Theater and Andrei Starostin's best friend. *Futbol skvoz' gody.*

their own cultural levels. Spartak's players, in general, had received as little education as their counterparts on other teams. To be sure, support by the highly cultured was not exclusive to Spartak. Dinamo, TsDKA, Torpedo, and Lokomotiv had their own supporters among the creative intelligentsia, but their organized visits to the theater were far less frequent.[18]

A link appears to have formed between Spartak and a particularly visible segment of the intelligentsia. Ironically, Suslov's ideological obsessions served to intensify relationships that previously had involved only a few select individuals. The connection to the world of the creative arts, formed during this most repressive period, would bloom after Stalin's death and mark the team as different from others. More generally, the attentions of the Central Committee's Bureau of Agitation and Propaganda were not welcome in the world of Soviet football. This antipathy extended well beyond Spartak, and there is little evidence that Dinamo, army, or any other athletes, with a few exceptions, responded any more positively to the campaign. Rather, ideological-political education was one of many signs of the repression imposed on society by the state after 1948. Soccer had attracted the attention of millions of fans. Their spontaneous pleasures in turn stimulated the concern of the authorities, who saw the dangers of uncontrolled football. If the game had been, as some might argue, only a safety valve, the authorities would never have bothered with such a program.

## The Non-Russians Are Coming!

The off-season in the winter of 1948–1949 produced changes that laid the groundwork for Spartak's eventual return to greatness. Overly demanding as he might have been, Konstantin Kvashnin had begun a transition to younger players that had won the club a third-place medal (along with accompanying secret bonuses). Still, the team's comparative weakness in the first four seasons of postwar soccer was emblematic of larger trends during this period. It seemed logical that after the war, teams representing the structures of force should dominate the game. On the other hand, it is surprising that as political conditions actually got worse and more repressive beginning in 1949, Spartak found a way to prosper while going against the grain. The Zhdanovshchina had promoted a Great Russian nationalism in cultural matters that grew even worse after 1949. Anti-Semitism intensified, as did disregard for the concerns of national minorities. Faced with a variety of partisan struggles in several borderlands, the regime did not look kindly on the needs of those who were not Russian.[19]

Moscow teams had historically been dominated by Slavic players. This was not the result of any consciously exclusionary policy, such as the baseball color bar in the United States. At the end of the war, however, Stalin, ignoring the inclusive discourses of wartime, made clear his belief that Great Russians had made the largest contribution on the battlefield. While nothing was decreed, it followed that they would play leading roles on the football field, a manly activity that had, far from correctly, been seen by many inside and outside the USSR as a surrogate for war. Just as there were hundreds of African American celebrities and successful professionals in the United States, many non-Russians who lived in the capital had made careers in a number of fields. Yet the intensely masculinized bastions of each nation's most popular game had, in their largest city, been among the last places to accept such outsiders into their ranks.

In 1949, however, Spartak took a different turn, recruiting several non-Russians to its playing and coaching staffs. Already, the team had employed non-Russians as coaches, the Czech Fivebr in 1936 and the Estonian Vol'rat in 1946 and 1947. Having "gone Russian" in 1948, they again looked outside the Slavic heartland for a coach. Minorities were also recruited as players. It is not clear why these choices were made. There is little evidence that this trend signified a consciously inclusive "nationality policy." One might speculate that the Starostins' openness to what had been called "Western methods" still imbued the organization, but professional rather than political agendas appear to have driven the search for talent.

Professional actions could, however, have political consequences. By casting its net widely, Spartak expanded the size of the talent pool for elite soccer. Dur-

**6.4** Nikita Simonian. Fotoagentstvo
Sportekspress.

ing a period of extreme Russian chauvinism, Spartak was not marching in step.
This willingness to buck larger trends, if not fully conscious, is worth examining in some detail. Spartak's disposition to multiculturalism, whether or not
intentional, had a profound impact on the club and eventually all of Soviet soccer. In 1949, Abram Dangulov, Kryl'ya Sovetov Moscow's coach, born in the
town North Caucuses town of Armavir, was named coach of Spartak.[20] He was
joined by another Armenian, striker Nikita Simonian, from the Black Sea port
of Sukhumi. The next season, midfielder Igor Netto, the Moscow-born son of Estonian parents, became a regular in the Spartak lineup. All three men fit in perfectly with the veterans Sokolov and Dementiev as well as the young stars
Sal'nikov, Paramonov, and, in 1950, Anatoly Ilyin (b. 1931). Together, they laid
the foundation for Spartak's return to greatness, using new methods of finding
talent, developing an original style of play, and, finally, overcoming political
and institutional roadblocks to emerge as champions in 1952.[21]

Dangulov built on Kvashnin's changes in personnel, but he introduced an
entirely new playing style. His soccer journey had begun in Krasnodar during
the civil war. He had then spent the rest of his career as a crafty midfielder in
Armavir, retiring in 1934. Coaching spells in Piatigorsk and Stalino (now

**6.5** The unorthodox but brilliant Igor Netto. Fotoagentstvo Sportekspress.

Donetsk) led to an appointment as head coach of one of the aviation industry's teams, Kryl'ya Sovetov Kuibishev. Success there led to the reins of Kryl'ya Sovetov Moscow, which won a place in the Soviet first division after the war. In the capital, Dangulov had put together a competitive side with few resources at his command. He found it necessary to employ not only non-Slavic but foreign players as well, including two refugees from the Spanish civil war, Augustin Gomez (1922–1975) and the Basque Ruperto Sagasti. Dangulov's skills and innovations had attracted favorable comment from the press, and Dangulov in turn developed close relations with leading sportswriters. His byline often appeared above match accounts in *Sovetskii sport.* When injuries swept Kryl'ya Sovetov in the 1948 season, causing the team to finish last and be relegated, Dangulov was far from an unknown quantity. Yet he was out of a job when the aviation industry broke up its soccer team rather than accept assignment to the second Soviet division.[22]

As it happened, Spartak was out of a coach. One stop down the Yaroslavl railroad line from Kryl'ya Sovetov's training base was Tarasovka, home of Spartak.[23] On more than one occasion, Kryl'ya had been required to make use of Spartak's facilities for its own practices. Nikolai Morozov and Vladimir Stepanov, both now Spartak administrators, had observed those sessions. Other team officials may have done so as well. No one seems to know exactly who at Spartak made the decision to engage Dangulov. It may have been Morozov, or it may have been the much criticized Vasilii Kuzin, head of the Spartak Society's Moscow council. Whoever came up with the idea, the choice proved to be inspired.

It appears the decision had little to do consciously with Dangulov's nationality. The fact that he was Armenian was clearly not a problem for Spartak's leaders. No one stood in the way of expanding playing opportunities for minorities on the game's biggest stage. Multinational inclusiveness had been a big part of the war effort worldwide. The Brooklyn Dodgers had gained international attention by taking on Jackie Robinson, U.S. baseball's first African American. The team's general manager, Branch Rickey, was obviously looking to gain advantage by mining a new source of talented players, but he was also trying to make a larger political and cultural statement. Spartak was similarly inclusive, but it did not advertise the fact. The team was not looking for "one good Armenian" as the Dodgers had been searching for "one good Negro." Quite simply, Dangulov was a highly competent and visible professional who happened to be available.

The new coach changed Spartak's approach to the game forever. His style can still be seen in the team's play despite enormous changes in the way football has come to be played. He was a champion of the quick run into empty space and a short passing game, with technically brilliant players forming constantly changing triangles as goals were built with an artistic, highly improvisational but structured style—a style Spartak's fans, not entirely correctly, came to see as "romantic." This team approach was then augmented with skilled dribblers who could break down defenses on their own when needed. As one of those dribblers, Nikita Simonian, described it, "We had to construct our play in a rational manner. The players who controlled the ball had to see the next player in order to make a precise pass. The guy who got that pass is already looking for the next free player."[24] For Filatov, Dangulov brought a "southern style" to Moscow football. Caucasian players—Georgians perhaps more than Armenians—had been known as great masters with the ball who played with fiery southern passion and commitment to attack. Those who characterized them this way did so with keen awareness of Latin American playing styles. Press accounts had long described Dinamo Tblisi as the flying Uruguyans, and Uruguay, along with its neighbor Argentina, had been among the world's dominant teams before the war.[25]

By emphasizing the short and medium pass, Dangulov minimized the number of mistakes to which southern Soviet teams had always been prone. Spartak now became the southernmost of the northern clubs. Before the arrival of Dangulov, Spartak had been a strong defensive team with big, physical players who triumphed through effort, will, and confidence. They played, more or less, like the other Moscow teams, only better. The new Spartak side was smaller, faster, and more technically skilled. The players looked different and played differently. Pictures of the 1949 team are revealing. The five-foot-eight Paramonov stood in the middle of the team portrait. Five of his comrades were even shorter. Dangulov's novel strategies and unorthodox preferences in personnel created the basis for what came to be known as the Spartak style, and Spartak style eventually took its place alongside Spartak spirit as an element of Spartak ideology. It was not only the players who bought into Dangulov's system; so did the fans, who came to see these innovations as one more proof of Spartak's progressive approach.[26]

Was any of this a conscious choice in favor of Soviet socialist internationalism, even cosmopolitanism, at a time of xenophobia? Certainly, no one articulated anything like that at the time. To do so would have been suicidal. Yet the differences between Spartak and its Moscow opponents were striking and highly visible. Smaller, faster men—like Paramonov, Simonian, and Ilyin—and lanky, more graceful men—like Netto and Sal'nikov—were playing a different, less physical kind of football. In doing so, they exhibited a different kind of body culture. None of them looked like the classic Russian muzhik, best typified by the rugged Bobrov. Spartak did not practice a hard-charging, long-passing and running game like that of the British, with its overtones of Victorian middle-class "rational recreation."[27] Other Soviet teams did.

The not entirely conscious model for Spartak, by contrast, was the Creole soccer of the River Plate. That approach had given Argentina and Uruguay great success during the twenties and thirties. This was the football perfected by millions of Italian and Spanish male immigrants to Latin America—a football of cunning and wiliness, of touch and artistry. These same men, together with their women, gave the world another exotic cultural form—the slinky and sexy tango. For them, football and dancing were closely linked—bodily practices that could express what the mind could not.

It turns out Spartak players, too, were dancers, both on and off the field, and they did not eschew those other bodily pleasures to which dancing could lead. Most important, they shared these joys with their fans. In 2001, Simonian told me:

> We were not isolated. We didn't have bodyguards and security. At that time [after 1949], entrance to our training base at Tarasovka was free and open. People came to the practices. They watched scrimmages and games between the first team and the reserves. They came and interacted with us. It was completely open, especially for the fans. There was a pavilion at Tarasovka with a dance floor, and a jazz band played there. People came from Moscow to dance. Pretty girls came. There could be a game the next day or the day after, but the fellows made use of the possibilities [of this situation]. For us there was no control. For Dinamo, there was control.[28]

In a separate interview, Simonian's friend Aleksei Paramonov confirmed this account without prompting.[29] Given that the Orwellian image of late Stalinism had not included much dancing, I asked Simonian (a trumpeter in his youth) what he meant by "jazz." He replied that it included fox trots, Glenn Miller, and the tango. Since for years we had been told the saxophone had been banned during Stalin's last years, I asked whether the band included saxophones. He looked at me as if I had lost my mind and said, "Of course, they had saxophones. It was jazz."[30]

By 1949, posh restaurants in downtown Moscow were no longer advertising jazz bands as part of their entertainment (although some jazz was still played). Recent research, however, indicates that Soviet youth generated their own dance craze, which spread far and wide across the nation from hundreds of villages to the hip dance hall inside Gorky Park. Like football, dancing was an entertainment that was easily and quickly resurrected, and the kinds of music driving this passion of the young were far more extensive than jazz. Juliane Furst has discovered that such activity was not furtive: "At any occasion and in any place young people set up makeshift dance floors and spent their time turning to waltzes, foxtrots and tangos. The post-war dance craze embraced all sections of society." Whether it was soccer or dance, both activities were manifestations of a global desire to "escape the seriousness of war."[31] The quality of the music at Spartak's training base may have been much higher than on local dance floors, for Utesov and other stars were said to have played there. Yet the spirit at the thousands of other smaller sites surely must have been much the same.

To any student of global soccer history, it should not be shocking that male footballers, dancing, and pretty women often went together. It is, however, interesting that the USSR between 1949 and 1953 was no exception to this seemingly universal rule and that Spartak seemed to be in the vanguard of such pleasureseeking. In particular, the dashing and stylish Sal'nikov was often accused of playing "to the ladies [na devushkvi]." It turned out that here, too, Spartak exhibited a body culture different from that of its opponents, part of a different, more cosmopolitan (to use a loaded word) form of masculinity. To be sure, the lads from Dinamo and TsDKA did not shun the female attention that resulted from their celebrity. The great Bobrov was a famous playboy who enjoyed the nightlife, but the public display of the various Moscow teams differed in interesting ways. Clearly, Spartak's particular body culture and its own version of manhood were not practices of opposition or even resistance. Openly oppositional sexual politics were obviously not part of late Stalinism, but it is fair to say these were ways in which Spartak, intentionally or unintentionally, differentiated itself from the rest of Soviet soccer and simultaneously maintained a distance from the norms of the era.

In allowing his players to have sex the night before games, Dangulov was hardly a typical Soviet soccer coach. Otherwise, however, he shared the idiosyncratic character of all great team leaders. He was a man of few words with his players, who were addressed correctly and respectfully, with the polite form of "you" (vy, not ty).[32] Along with his assistant and garrulous alter ego, Vladimir Gorokhov, Dangulov spent a great deal of time working with his players individually on the technical skills required to execute his system. A chain smoker, he would light up and drift into another world while watching a match, not saying a word, only to return to the land of the living with the final whistle. Yet his quiet concealed great emotional involvement and generosity. In particular, he understood that a team could not play in his system without a high level of harmony. To enhance this internal club atmosphere, he organized many group evenings and visited his players in their homes to learn about their families. He displayed a similar generosity in his relations with the press, explaining his decisions at length and inviting reporters to his apartment for evenings of "southern hospitality."[33]

It was the southern connection that brought Dangulov his greatest player, the aforementioned Simonian. Like his coach, he was born in Armavir, to which his parents had fled from western Armenia during the genocide in 1915. Simonian moved with his cobbler father and housewife mother to the multiethnic city of Sukhumi, capital of the Abkhazian region of the Georgian Republic, in 1931. Russian was the lingua franca in this polyglot port town, and much to the consternation of his traditionalist father, the young Simonian spoke Russian. Discovered playing in the streets and empty lots of the city, Nikita became a member of the Dinamo Sukhumi youth team. In 1945, Dangulov and Gorokhov brought the Kryl'ya Sovetov first and reserve squads to Sukhumi for spring training. Simonian's side played both teams. He scored three goals in each game and was summoned to the Hotel Abkhazia to meet Dangulov and Gorokhov, who invited him to come to Moscow and play for them. Simonian's parents resisted so drastic a move, but a long conversation conducted in Armenian between the father and Dangulov changed their minds.[34]

Shortly before the 1946 season, Nikita showed up in Moscow, where he lived in Gorokhov's cramped basement apartment in the center of the city. Assimilating quickly with the help of Gorokhov's generous family, Simonian learned his way around the capital, taking in movies, the theater, and as many big games at Dinamo as he could. Alert and intelligent, he had little difficulty adapting to the pace of big-city life. He also has written (post-1991) that he did not confront ethnically motivated insults or incidents of discrimination. Simonian did mention hearing cries from the stands of "C'mon, Simonian. You've got to run," but he did not interpret such fan interventions to be directed at his national origin. The first three years with Dangulov were a learning process. Simonian was considerably younger than anyone else in the top division. His first goal, against Dinamo Minsk, was a headline story in *Sovetskii sport*.[35] A talent of his sort could not slip under the radar. In each of his first two years he played a full schedule but scored just three goals each year. His last season with Kryl'ya yielded the same total of goals but, due to injury, in just ten games.[36]

From the first, the secret police in the Republic of Georgia, sponsors of Dinamo Tblisi, had been displeased by Simonian's decision to move to the capital. Quickly, they resorted to their own special brand of persuasion to get him to return. Simonian came home with his team for a friendly against Dinamo Sukhumi. With a positively Starostin-like disregard for chronology, he did not specify in his memoir account precisely when this happened, but most likely it occurred on the eve of the 1947 season, when Kryl'ya again trained in Sukhumi. Upon his new team's arrival, Nikita learned the police had searched his house and arrested his father. Their aim was to pressure the son to come back to Georgia. Dangulov was told Simonian would be arrested as well. When the match ended, Nikita was surrounded by the entire team and escorted back to the hotel. From there, he and Dangulov made a beeline for the Russian border and safety in the nearby Black Sea resort of Sochi. Two days later the elder Simonian was released.

The "best friends of Dinamo Tblisi" did not take this for an answer. When Simonian was again back home, most likely after the end of the 1947 season, he was called in to see the head of the Abkhazian Ministry of Interior, who asked him how a product of Georgia could wind up in Moscow. "In Georgia we think you should play for a team in the republic and you should discuss this immediately in Tblisi." This time the family decided it was best to answer the minister's summons. No less a figure than Boris Paichadze, now retired, met Simonian at the train station in Tblisi and ushered him into the inner sanctum of the Georgian secret police. We have only Simonian's account of his meeting with the head of the local NKVD, a figure he either neglected or chose not to name. This time he was offered carrots, not sticks. "Listen," he was told, "why are you living in Moscow? You are an Armenian. Armenians and Georgians are brothers. The Russians call us 'Turks.'" Simonian responded politely and perhaps naively that he had been in Moscow for more than a year and had heard no anti-Armenian or anti-Georgian remarks. Furthermore, he claimed to feel no difference between himself and his Russian hosts. After agreeing to think over the proposal, Simonian returned to Sukhumi, discussed the idea with his family, and turned down a transfer to Dinamo Tblisi. Yet every day until he retired from Spartak, Nikita's father continued to fear another arrest. "He felt," wrote Simonian, "the defenselessness of the people before the illegal and evil will of officialdom."[37]

When Dangulov and Gorokhov signed with Spartak, Simonian did not follow them immediately. Torpedo, sponsored by the giant ZIS auto factory and its powerful director, Ivan Likhachev, made a serious bid for his services. Its star center forward, Aleksandr Ponomarev, stressed the team's massive support from the factory's workers, and Likhachev added, "The working class loves football and lives for its team." As it turned out, Ponomarev would have been better served to remain in the shadows. Simonian saw himself as a center forward and feared he would not be able to displace Ponomarev. Spartak's incumbent center forward was weaker, and Simonian felt he could win playing time. Although he respected Dangulov and loved Gorokhov, Nikita's reason for joining Spartak was simple. He wanted to play. True, the great cup victories of 1946 and 1947 had been inspiring, but his spurning of Torpedo was based on the most basic of professional considerations.[38] Placed alongside such talents as Dementiev, Sal'nikov, and Paramonov, Simonian blossomed. His appearance was timely. Seduced by the offer of an apartment, Ivan Konov had left the team for Dinamo. He had scored fifteen goals, which would normally have been hard to replace, but Simonian's twenty-six goals in his debut Spartak season more than made up for the loss of Konov.[39]

Success did not come quite so quickly to the other important addition to Spartak, midfielder Igor Netto, who played in only eight games during 1949.

A native Muscovite, Netto was considerably less exotic than Simonian. His Estonian last name and his style of play were the primary elements of non-Russianness he contributed to Spartak's image. Tall and lanky, with a hatchet face and big nose, Netto did not look like a central casting Slavic hero. At the age of nineteen, his gifts, first honed in the courtyard of his apartment house, had already been noted by the press and other observers, but Netto did not grow up dreaming of playing for Spartak. The first match he witnessed when he was ten had involved Dinamo, solidifying an early loyalty to Spartak's chief rival. Luckily for Spartak, no coaches could be found when he showed up at Dinamo Stadium looking for a tryout. Finally, in 1947, his friends urged him to contact Spartak. Greeted and received by Vladimir Stepanov, now coaching the youth team, Netto was quickly accepted and found a place at left halfback in the reserves.[40] Two years later, Dangulov began the process of turning him into one of the all-time greats, not only for Spartak but for the Soviet national team as well.

Highly intelligent but also irascible, uncompromising, and thoroughly idiosyncratic, Netto somehow fit in well with the new Spartak. A proponent of the short and medium pass, Netto, like the chess player he was, thought three moves ahead. This talent proved to be an ideal fit for Dangulov's system. A magnificent passer and responsible defender, Netto was a perfect midfielder who, for all his character flaws, was a born leader on the field. His teammates came to accept his constant stream of criticism, which was accompanied by an even less attractive unwillingness to take criticism himself. Neither coaches nor administrators, including the Starostins themselves, were immune to his acid tongue. The often cavalier Sal'nikov was one of Netto's favorite targets, but although Sal'nikov was popular with his teammates, they also understood the fairness of Netto's views. In time, Netto became Spartak's captain, eventually occupying the same post with the national team.[41]

With new players, a new coach, and a new approach, Spartak began the 1949 season with optimism. In a season preview in *Sovetskii sport,* even Boris Arkadiev went so far as to predict a bright future for the team. An April third friendly against TsDKA in Sukhumi may have been the first sign of things to come. Playing in front of his home fans for the first time as a Spartakovets, Simonian scored the winning goal in a 2–1 victory. Yet these hopeful portents did not lead to immediate results. It was six weeks into the season before Spartak scored, but then things changed radically for the better. Four goals against Neftianik Baku were followed by a 5–0 thrashing of Kryl'ya Sovetov Kuibyshev. More victories produced positive press commentary by noted savants. Sergei Savin, a referee and sports bureaucrat, remarked in *Sovetskii sport* that the team was playing with great togetherness and effort. The new lineup, which Dangulov had consistently put on the field, yielded results. In *Vechernaia Moskva* the aforementioned Viktor Dubinin attributed the players' success to a revived attack that had compensated for unusual defensive weaknesses, especially in goal. Soon, however, defeats to Dinamo and TsDKA, plus a 5–0 drubbing at the hands of Zenit Leningrad, cooled the excitement. The season's halfway point found Spartak in fifth place.[42]

Dangulov's system began to take hold in the latter part of the season with a string of victories, interrupted only by three defeats during the always troublesome (and distracting) tour of the Caucasus. Once back in the north, the team continued its wins. The excitement was barely interrupted by a 2–1 loss to TsDKA in an intense, well-played game that *Vechernaia Moskva* dubbed "a match of equals."[43] The anticipation was enormous leading up to the next confrontation with Dinamo on October first. The day found Spartak in second place and Dinamo in a catchable first. The game did not fail to live up to expectations. Those who do not consider the season-closing TsDKA-Dinamo match of 1948 to be the greatest game of this era invariably point instead to Dinamo-Spartak in 1949 as the peak of Soviet football's Golden Age.

Although Spartak did not triumph, this game also became part of the team's legend. Win or lose, the team was, as always, never boring. Sal'nikov opened the scoring in the thirty-fourth minute when the great Dinamo goalie, Aleksei Khomich, was screened by his defenders. Just before the half, the former Spartak attacker Ivan Konov evened the score. The fireworks began in the fifty-third minute when Simonian scored on a pass from Sal'nikov. Soon thereafter, Dinamo's Vladimir Savdunin tied things up, and a minute later Vasilii Trofimov put Dinamo ahead. In two more minutes, Terentiev tied the match, and a minute later Sal'nikov put Spartak ahead. Five goals had been scored in ten minutes. Dinamo replaced a shaky Khomich with Val'ter Sanaia. With the crowd beside itself, the match flowed back and forth. Konstantin Beskov tied the game yet again in the seventy-sixth minute, and with no one able to imagine what would happen next, Savdunin ended what he had begun with a goal three minutes from time. The goalkeepers may have taken the day off, but the game had been thrilling for all who watched and participated. The former Lokomotiv great, Valentin Granatkin, wrote in *Sovetskii sport* that the match had demonstrated the best (and worst) qualities of Soviet soccer. It remains a game that fans of a certain age still remember vividly.[44]

Two weeks later, the season ended with Dinamo as champion and the army team just nipping out Spartak for second. The third-place finish was the same as the year before, but team officials and fans saw Dangulov's achievement as more significant than that of 1948. A new path had been pointed out. It was not only a matter of being successful on the field but a matter of how that success was achieved. Once again, Spartak supporters could believe there was something special, even original, about their club. In his annual end-of-season report in *Sovetskii sport,* Sergei Savin complimented Dangulov for instilling a high level of technical mastery in his players. The young players had meshed well with the holdovers to produce an exciting team that still was handicapped by the lack of a consistent goalie. Each year, Savin's article had been supplemented by a team portrait of that year's league winner. So great was the optimism and excitement of *Sovetskii sport*'s Spartak-loving

**6.6** Spartak fans celebrate a victory. Fotoagentstvo Sportekspress.

football section that 1949's bronze medalists, not the champions, graced its pages.[45]

The season's final chapter, however, was yet to be written, and it turned out to be a chapter that would remind Spartak of the obstacles still standing in the way of eventual success. On October 30 the two great rivals met yet again, this time in the cup semifinal. Sixty thousand showed up on a cold and cloudy day to take in what turned out to be an extremely rough—indeed, dirty —contest that quickly slipped out of the control of the experienced referee, Mikhail Dmitriev (1907–1965). Early in the match Dinamo's Savdunin punched Spartak defender Anatoly Seglin in the face. The transgression, which went unpunished, touched off an orgy of physicality. When matches spiral out of a referee's control, as this one did, the advantage always goes to the stronger, more physically powerful side. Spartak's lighter, faster, more technically skilled players could not play their game. Despite these difficulties, Simonian opened the scoring with a pass from Sal'nikov in the twentieth minute. Six minutes later, Konov struck his ex-teammates for two goals within two minutes. With players falling right and left and Spartak fans calling for Dmitriev's immediate removal from the field, it was left to Sal'nikov to even the contest off a corner. Only twenty seconds remained.[46]

With the match over, the backroom games began, much to Spartak's disadvantage. The replay was scheduled for the very next day, hurting the chances of the team with the shorter bench—Spartak. Having witnessed Savdunin's act of aggression, the disciplinary committee of the sports committee disqualified him for the next day's match. This decision was then verified by two assistants of Arkadii Appollonov, head of the sports committee, who thereupon overruled their advice. Not only did he declare that Savdunin could play in the next day's replay, but he assigned the much-maligned Dmitriev to work the match. As an NKVD colonel, Appollonov had risen through the ranks of the Dinamo organization, and it is fair to say his decisions showed considerable sensitivity to what surely were Beria's preferences for dealing with the matter. Spartak could only protest. Memories of the 1939 semifinal replay surely must have come to mind, but that famous victory was not to be repeated. Simonian scored at much the same time as he had the previous day, but in the second half Dinamo eventually wore Spartak down. Again, Konov evened the score, and two minutes later, in the seventy-seventh minute, Mikhail Semichastnyi sealed Spartak's fate. This time there were no late Sal'nikov heroics. Dangulov and his men did, however, get to indulge in a measure of schadenfreude when Dinamo lost the final 2–1 to Torpedo.[47]

In the weeks that followed, newspapers were deluged by letters of complaint. Agitprop received many similar messages, as did individual Central Committee members, including Stalin himself. So intense was the rage expressed by fans that middle-level operatives at Agitprop felt it necessary to report on the matter to their superiors, in this case Georgii Malenkov. These particular functionaries—A. Sushkov and K. Kalashnikov—performed their duties with a considerable level of professionalism and objectivity. They noted, quite correctly, that nearly all the letters sent to newspapers and high officials were from Spartak fans and had a "tendentious character." Additionally, they stated that the first semifinal was "a tough sporting struggle which Dinamo won fairly." There was no reason, they argued, to order a second replay.

On the other hand, Sushkov and Kalashnikov asserted there was merit to the petitioners' objections. Typical of these fan complaints was a letter sent to Stalin by one A. A. Khakhamov, a party member from Moscow. Khakhamov was particularly exercised by the behavior of Dinamo players during the replay, claiming they had taken Appollonov's decision as a sign of permission to engage in dirty play. Konov, in particular, had knocked Spartak's goalie, Chernyshev, unconscious but was not charged with so much as a foul. Khakhamov continued to address Stalin:

> Perhaps you were listening on the radio. For a long time you could hear fans shouting "turn the referee into soap [*sudia na mylo*]" and claiming that Dmitriev, not Dinamo, had won the game. In the entire history of Soviet refereeing there has never been such massive indignation. The fans were shouting for the referee to be removed. . . . As a Communist, a political worker in the Soviet Army reserve and a patriot of the physical culture movement, I am outraged to the depths of my soul.[48]

One must note here that the suggestion that Stalin was listening to the match is simply ridiculous. He was completely indifferent to matters of sport, football in particular. Beyond this, the claim that such cries from the stands were in any way novel in the history of Soviet soccer is preposterous. Taunting of referees had been a regular feature of fan byplay from the first days of the revolution, indeed from the very first days of football. "Sudia na mylo," the Soviet version of "kill the ump," was hardly new. Yet writing to the leader of world socialism to protest the result of a soccer game was scarcely a typical act for a Soviet citizen. The idea that Stalin would take time from his busy schedule to assure that Dmitriev never worked another game, as Valentin Dubrovitskii and Vladimir Anisimov separately requested, is a measure of the seriousness, perhaps a trifle deluded, with which many fans took this issue.[49]

Sushkov and Kalashnikov took the complaints seriously as well. They conveyed to Malenkov that the evidence from the letters and other materials suggested that Appollonov did indeed favor Dinamo:

> The mood of the fans at the stadium during matches with the participation of Dinamo . . . demonstrates that among a part of Soviet sporting society, Dinamo has little authority or affection. His [Appollonov's] unobjective attitude . . . discredits this team. He often ignores public opinion, not hiding his sympathies for Dinamo.

Sushkov and Kalashnikov also urged Malenkov to suggest to Appollonov that the decision concerning Savdunin's attack on Seglin "flew in the face of public opinion."[50]

This would not be the last time Sushkov and his colleagues would raise the issue of public opinion, but placing this question before their superiors can only be seen as unusual. I have found no documents prepared by any other functionaries in the sport bureaucracy that pay such direct attention to the impact of soccer on society. It is safe to say that the most powerful leaders of the Soviet state did not make a practice of consulting or being influenced by public opinion when making policy. If they wanted to know what was happening in society, they consulted the secret police, not the fans who regularly gathered outside Dinamo Stadium to discuss football and related matters.[51] The NKVD surely had spies among those who frequented these gatherings, but they were unlikely to report to superiors that Dinamo was Soviet soccer's most hated side. On the other hand, here we had Malenkov, the second- or third-most-powerful man in the USSR in 1949, being urged by subordinates to pay attention to the views of what Sushkov and Kalashnikov also referred to as "sporting society."

It is difficult to think of more convincing proof that football had become thoroughly enmeshed with the realities and unrealities of the everyday lives of ordinary Muscovites. The game's very liminality had made it possible for soccer to occupy the cultural spaces in between official Soviet institutions, and it was in such spaces, not formal institutions, that those parts of life that most concerned Soviet citizens could be found. Here again, Kuper's metaphor of the slippery tool is apt. Football was not simply a weapon deployed by the state to control the masses. In fact, the game could have political consequences for the regime. After 1949, workers found it more difficult to air their various shop-floor grievances, but one could write to Stalin and complain about refereeing in a cup match. If those letter writers had been merely letting off steam at a sporting spectacle, they would not even have bothered to write to their political leaders, not to mention the press. Instead, they would have knocked back another hundred grams of vodka and gone home, more or less quietly. One can only speculate what other grievances, of a nonsporting nature, may have been felt by these angry Spartak fans. In this case, football's unpredictability, emotionality, and considerable potential for disorder forced the leadership, as Sushkov and Kalashnikov argued, to pay attention to the concerns of the fans in the stands.

## The Sal'nikov Affair and the Talent Wars

Spartak had returned to the heights of Soviet soccer, but in the last days of the season it had been reminded of the continuing capacity of arbitrary power to thwart its desires. That winter, when one of its stars transferred to Dinamo, the team again faced an enormous challenge to its ability to put its most talented players on the field. In the world of global soccer, this was hardly exceptional. At virtually every level in virtually every team game, the question of player movement has been one of the most controversial and vexing. The control of this process in elite soccer has always posed problems for the game's organizers. Until the advent of free agency relatively late in the twentieth century, players under contract to a particular team were traded, bought, or sold. In the USSR, however, all athletes were formally amateur, without contracts. Additionally, the few remnants of Marxist ideology pertaining to Soviet labor relations militated against treating athletes as if they were commodities.

From the earliest days of Soviet power, there were few rules governing player movement, and those that did exist were never enforced consistently. In reality, Soviet soccer stars were relatively free to move to new teams. Nevertheless, the practice, while widespread, was frowned upon in some quarters. Loyalty to the sport society that had trained players as youths was seen as admirable. Searching for better living conditions and higher salaries was a sign of a selfish professional. On the other hand, sport societies that recruited rather than raised their own athletes were accused, as the Starostins had been, of introducing bourgeois morals into sport.

When the rumor began to spread during the winter of 1950 that Sergei Sal'nikov had submitted an application to join Dinamo, it touched off what proved to be the most controversial and scandalous player transfer in the history of Soviet football. A weakened Spartak had been under siege for several years. Its athletes in several sports had been recruited by wealthier, more powerful clubs, primarily Vasilii Stalin's air force sport society and, of course, Dinamo. One local Moscow Spartak official named E. Rogovskii wrote to Stalin, "Some physical culture organizations have entered on the path of shifting leading masters of sport from the organizations where they were trained to their own collectives for sporting glory."[52] This process had been going on at least since 1948, when Konov left for Dinamo. At the same time, the entire starting lineup of Spartak's hockey team had been recruited by VVS. The incentive, a Promkooperatsiia official wrote to Stalin, was "improved material conditions" that were higher than the norms established by the government. Specifically, Rogovskii charged that significantly better wages were the main draw, a practice that undermined the principle of "equal pay for equal work."[53] Groups of fans, described as "Moscow workers," sent letters to *Pravda* and *Sovetskii sport*. VVS and Dinamo were described as having "unlimited resources," while Spartak had "limited means."[54] The raids on Spartak had been approved by the sports committee, led by the old Dinamovets Appollonov. Indeed, early in 1949, writing in defense of his personnel policies, Vasilii Stalin reminded Appollonov, "You yourself know that not one person came into our sporting collective without your agreement."[55]

Sal'nikov had been a special darling of Spartak. Raised near the team's Tarasovka training base, he was even rumored to be Nikolai Starostin's illegitimate son (a charge no longer believed).[56] How could he, of all people, go over to the "old enemy"? Spartak fans felt embattled. Losing a star attacker had now become an annual event. First it had been Konov, now Sal'nikov. Having finally achieved some level of equality with Dinamo and TsDKA, the rug had been pulled out from under them. In truth, the regime's power to influence the sporting process was complicated and by no means absolute. Nevertheless, ordinary Muscovites who supported Spartak interpreted Sal'nikov's transfer as yet another case of the old, mighty them keeping down the long-suffering us.

The sports committee initially turned down Sal'nikov's request in January, but on March 3, on the eve of the 1950 season, it approved his move to Dinamo. When word got out, letters and protests flooded into newspaper offices and Agitprop headquarters. Neither the powerful nor the ordinary hesitated to express their written outrage to the USSR's highest officials. In reporting to Malenkov just after the eruption of the *skandal,* Sushkov and Kalashnikov mentioned that after being turned down, Sal'nikov had turned to Beria and Politbiuro member P. K. Ponomarenko for help. Tantalizingly, they said nothing about when and why Sal'nikov had contacted these men. Their information about Sal'nikov's attempts to move may or may not have been correct, but Sushkov and Kalashnikov did not go so far as to suggest annulling the transfer. Nevertheless, they also wrote, "We also think it necessary to suggest to Comrade Appollonov that he provide help in strengthening Spartak, which recently has definitely gotten weaker."[57]

At much the same time, Suslov received a letter from the editor of *Komsomol'skaia Pravda*, D. Goriunov, who suggested this stacking of the deck had larger political consequences:

All of this disgrace is known to the players against whose morals the fans protest during sports events. At stadiums, especially those in Moscow, when teams composed of these "rolling stones" appear, rotten apples are thrown. Fans whistle and boo these "turncoats" and loudly defame them with all sorts of offensive nicknames. This kind of reaction has not been seen previously.

Goriunov protested to Suslov that his paper had not been allowed to publish an exposé on the Dinamo Society official, Konstantin Morar', who, according to Goriunov and his staff, had been behind the transfers of Konov and now Sal'nikov. The bait, they claimed, was not just a higher salary but an apartment.[58] Sushkov and Kalashnikov, acting with their characteristic caution, suggested to Suslov that the exposé not be printed but that Appollonov should again be warned to put a stop to such practices.[59]

Marshal of the Soviet Union and Politbiuro member Kliment Voroshilov received a flood of letters from various citizens complaining about Sal'nikov's transfer. A group of rubber workers from Moscow protested that Spartak was the most beloved team of the city's fans, but, "although in recent years it has occupied decent positions, it cannot compete for first place. This is because each year players the team develops leave for Dinamo. Last year it was Konov, now it is Sal'nikov. We protest this annual weakening of this team." An E. Smirnov raised this question with Voroshilov because of its "social and political character." He continued, "The sporting society of the capital is deeply convinced and disturbed that the products of the Spartak school—Sal'nikov (and Konov before him) are transferring for 'egoistic goals' to Dinamo, which has not been preparing replacements for many years but instead recruits players from other teams." This state of affairs had emerged, argued Smirnov, because "Appollonov did not take public opinion into account." He urged that Sal'nikov be returned to Spartak "in the interests of justice and to pacify public opinion."[60] Voroshilov also received a letter to the editors of *Pravda* from "a group of Moscow sportsmen and sports lovers" who complained about "morals that dominate in bourgeois sport" and players pursuing "better material conditions and the long ruble." Dinamo, they asserted, "despite its great sporting successes does not enjoy much popularity among the fans."[61]

Even more complaints, letters, and petitions, some arriving as late as August, had been sent directly to Agitprop, and Sushkov passed on a summary of several of these communications to Suslov. There were general complaints about the disorderliness and ugliness of the entire transfer process. Not only had Sal'nikov moved to Dinamo, but Anatoly Akimov and Vsevolod Bobrov had switched to Vasilii Stalin's VVS—moves that produced far less public outcry. A group of engineers decried players' pursuing "egoistic goals" and claimed that the purchase of "stars could take place in Truman's America but not in our socialist homeland." At the end of his digest of letters to the press, Sushkov reminded Suslov that this question "worries Soviet society [*obshchestvennost'*]," as revealed by the vast number and variety of communications to many different newspapers and to the Central Committee. Despite all the messages from the masses, Appollonov had allowed the transfer of Sal'nikov to Dinamo to go ahead. Sushkov urged Suslov to deal with this problem, particularly the lack of any order or consistency in the movement of players.[62]

The sheer magnitude of open protest over Sal'nikov's move was unprecedented in the history of the nation's most popular game. Citizens expressed outrage through letters to the press. They also wrote directly to their political leaders, demanding that a decision made by top governmental figures be changed. In the process, men at the highest level of both the state and the party structures were urged by competent and sensitive subordinates to pay attention to these expressions of public opinion. Moreover, it was suggested by these midlevel functionaries that ignoring public opinion posed political dangers for the regime. Of course, one might well argue that all this unhappiness was so much talk, but in expressing outrage over the destruction of their favorite team, these Moscow male sports fans were using the kinds of mechanisms for protest that had long been available to citizens of liberal democracies with flourishing civil societies. On the other hand, it does not seem unfair to suggest that the complaints raised in the course of the Sal'nikov affair are more than a bit reminiscent of the rage and anger that characterize the content of contemporary sports-talk radio, a discourse that exploits what some might call freedom of speech. One could certainly dismiss all the discourses in the Sal'nikov case as meaningless. They did nothing to change the decisions of the authorities, just as the cries of pain from fans over the firing of a popular manager by an ignorant and supercilious baseball or soccer team owner have never had an impact on the powerful figures who control the sporting process.

For all the intriguing elements surrounding the debate about Sal'nikov, the real reason for his desire to leave Spartak does not represent a protesting civil society at work in microcosm. Rather, it was a classic case of arbitrary power interfering in the world of sport. Sal'nikov took a public roasting for his perceived selfishness and egoism.[63] He was taunted from the stands in every game he played during the 1950 season, but it turns out he was forced to join Dinamo for the most unselfish of reasons. Rumors and myths surrounding this bit of Soviet soccer history swirled for decades. Interestingly, there is only the barest hint of what really happened (the reference to Beria) in the archival material concerning this case. Only in 1995 did Nikita Simonian reveal in his memoir that Sal'nikov had moved to Dinamo to lighten the sentence of his stepfather, who had been arrested.[64] With no further proof, others repeated the story, which became what passed for established fact in post-Soviet Russia.[65] More recently, however, new research has indeed confirmed the general correctness of Simonian's account.

A 2004 biography of Sal'nikov by Aleksandr Soskin and an unpublished investigation by Pavel Aleshin, both veteran sportswriters of considerable distinction, revealed that the stepfather, Vladimir Ermolaevich Sergeev, had been imprisoned in an Arctic camp for economic, not political crimes. Sergeev's sister, the well-known actress Galina Sergeeva, had allegedly received a visit late in 1949 from an unnamed police official who informed her that Vladimir was in poor health and might not survive the strict regime and freezing winter in the northern camp. According to this account, Sergeeva then passed this information to Sal'nikov's mother, who in turn related it to him. Sal'nikov took it upon himself to visit his old teammate, Ivan Konov, who was now playing for Dinamo and who had good contacts with "the organs." Shortly, after their conversation, Sal'nikov was said to have received a phone call with the proposal that a move to Dinamo could improve his stepfather's circumstances. This version of transfer by blackmail was similar to the tactics Simonian had faced, but unlike Sal'nikov, Simonian had been in a better position to reject the threats of the secret police. The 1950 season then began with Sal'nikov as a Dinamovets and his stepfather ensconced in a regular prison just outside Moscow at Elektrostal'. Vladimir Sergeev could now be visited often by his wife. He survived his sentence, while his stepson played the next five seasons for Dinamo. Sal'nikov chafed at its rigid discipline, and the team's leadership was less than pleased with his character. On the field he achieved solid but far from spectacular results.[66]

The minds of Spartak fans may have expressed themselves in ways that mimicked the citizens of the West, but the body of Sergei Sal'nikov was, nevertheless, now covered in Dinamo blue. This reality is a perfect expression of the enhanced repression during the years when Beria and his allies could impose their will, at least episodically, on a human activity that had otherwise shown considerable, but far from complete, autonomy. Clearly this set of events has more than the aroma of totalitarianism, and, it must be noted, the Sal'nikov affair demonstrates the limits of the quasi-democratic discourse that had emerged, if fleetingly, within the world of sport. This was not, however, the final chapter of Sal'nikov's career. The sentiments and words uttered and written about the "great Salo" in 1950 were not forgotten after Stalin's death. When Nikolai Starostin returned from exile in 1954 to resume leadership of Spartak, his first task was to get Sal'nikov back to his old team, and sure enough, as the 1955 season began, Sal'nikov returned to wearing Spartak red. For the next six years he was a massive and happy contributor to the team's Golden Age.

## Warmth before the Thaw? Groundwork for New Glory

The 1950 season was greeted not with the optimism of the previous year but instead with dread and uncertainty about the Spartak Society's diminished capacity to sustain the necessary support for its athletes. Under the headline "Return Spartak to Its Former Glory," *Sovetskii sport* again lamented the decline of an organization that had won so much international glory before the war. It was true, the paper admitted, that Promkooperatsiia was no longer able to support Spartak as lavishly as it had in the past, but most of the blame fell on Mikhailchuk and Kuzin, who still headed up Spartak's Moscow council. While lamenting the unwillingness of the sports committee to follow a consistent line on the matter of athlete movement, *Sovetskii sport* also expressed the view that Spartak itself was not doing enough to keep its people at home.[67]

For all the worry, the season started brilliantly with six wins and four draws in the first ten matches. Moreover, the team was winning with style, specifically, as it was noted in the press, "Spartak style." Best of all, the big crowds started coming back. Eighty thousand jammed into Dinamo when mighty Dinamo Tblisi came to town on May 22.[68] Netto settled seamlessly alongside Oleg Timakov in midfield to form a powerful force. Vasilii Sokolov found new life in defense. Anatoly Ilyin assumed Sal'nikov's position at outside left, while Terentiev, Paramonov, and the ever-young Dementiev picked up their goalscoring.

Yet the central force behind the early success was Simonian, who had seven goals during the ten-game streak. In fact, he was on his way to a season unprecedented in the history of Soviet soccer. Already a star, he now became a superstar, the first non-Russian to achieve this status in Moscow. He was headed for a goal-scoring record (thirty-four goals in thirty-six matches) that would stand for a quarter century. This was one of those brief but often passing moments when the perfect player in the perfect system with the right coach and able complementary players creates football perfection. Press accounts frothed about Spartak's "wonderful play," its "fast attack with quick, short passes." The men executed their plays at high speed, often changing positions. Simonian's winning goal against VVS, which now featured Bobrov and Akimov, was touched by all five attackers before it returned to him.[69] Mikhail Sushkov and Petr Isakov, writing separately in *Vechernaia Moskva,* attributed the success of "the favorite team of Muscovites" to the emergence of the young players. Vladimir Chernyshev contributed much-needed stability in goal. Parshin, Netto, and Ilyin came in for praise.[70] Sergei Savin wrote in *Sovetskii sport* that Spartak had its own style of play, which was "possible only with the complete interaction of the entire team."[71]

The praise may have been intoxicating, but reality set in soon enough with a 2–1 loss to TsDKA and a 1–1 tie with Dinamo. The weakness of Spartak's opponents, it turned out, had as much to do with the team's good play as its own talents. The old ghost of inconsistency had returned. Despite these speed bumps, Dangulov's team was in third place, well positioned for serious success when it set off in August on its annual road trip to the south. The otherwise hospitable Caucasus had always been less than welcoming for Spartak. This year was no different. The team lost four straight. The final humiliation came with a 2–1 loss to its Tblisi club mates, led by the old Spartak hero-goalie Zhmel'kov. Dangulov had begun to experiment frantically with his lineup, putting defenders up front and attackers in the rear. Discipline problems emerged. Some players had partaken too heartily of southern hospitality, and others got into the habit of showing up late for practice. They returned to the capital in seventh place. A 2–0 victory over VVS stopped the slide but revealed considerable fatigue among the younger players. Opponents were figuring out how to combat the short passing game. Spartak's first postwar season without Sal'nikov wound up bringing a disappointing fifth-place finish and doubts about Dangulov's methods.[72]

Spartak's achievements did not go unnoticed by the sports leadership. At a time when international competitions had been severely reduced, the team, with a few additions, was sent on a goodwill tour of Norway, not one of the world's soccer powers but a capitalist fleshpot nonetheless. Three easy victories against Norway's best before large crowds gave the players reason to celebrate, and some, it appears, celebrated too intensely.[73] Worse yet, much of the drinking and carrying on had been quite public. On a flight between Helsinki and Stockholm, Netto and several others had gotten thoroughly drunk. According to Agitprop, "The reactionary press in Sweden learned of this and used it to publish provocative threats against Spartak." One of Netto's fellow revelers, the veteran Konstantin Malinin, was summarily kicked off the team after twelve seasons of service, while the young superstar got off with a warning.

The season was not yet finished, however. The cup competition remained. Again, Spartak would reawaken Spartak spirit, giving its fans one more reason to believe that however bleak the outlook, their team was always able to achieve moments of greatness. The competition was restricted to sixteen invited teams. All matches took place in Moscow. Two easy victories put Spartak into the semifinal against the champions, TsDKA. A close loss and a tie during the season augured well for Spartak's chances. The result was a convincing 4–0 victory on November 1 before seventy-five thousand, with Simonian scoring two goals while assisting on the other two. Second-place Dinamo won its game, setting up a dramatic final five days later. The controversial semi of 1949 and the defection of Sal'nikov made this more than a matchup of two old rivals.[74]

Early November has never produced ideal football weather in Moscow, and this day was no exception. It was cold and rainy. The field was muddy and covered with puddles. Spartak began the match with commitment and energy. Netto and Timakov, with the help of Sokolov, neutralized Sal'nikov and Beskov. Chernyshev played brilliantly in goal. Meanwhile, Simonian and Terentiev, despite the conditions, were able to execute the Spartak style. Each scored a goal, as did Oleg Timakov (who had also scored in the 1946 and 1947 cup victories). It was a 3–0 payback to Dinamo for all the suffering that had been inflicted on Spartak by its rivals with friends in high places.[75] Again, Spartak had convinced its supporters that, on a given day, there was no fortress it could not storm.

Another victory, this one backroom, appears to have occurred around this time. The sources are unclear on the timing of the event, but Appollonov was relieved of his duties as head of the sports committee in favor of Nikolai Romanov, the man he had replaced in 1948. Romanov would go on to become a respected professional who developed a measure of independence in dealing with the political leadership. Instead of enforcing decrees against those in the sports world, he became an advocate for the athletes and coaches whose work

**6.7** Scene from the 1950 cup final, Spartak vs. Dinamo. Fotoagentstvo Sportekspress.

he supervised. In particular, he lobbied hard for participation in the 1952 Olympics, at which the USSR made its debut. Romanov was not a partisan of any particular sport society, and under him the annual raids on Spartak's soccer team stopped.

Nevertheless, the removal of a major institutional impediment to Spartak's success did not produce positive results on the field. The next season, with the same cast of characters, the wheels came off. Just one new player, defender Nikolai Tishchenko (1926–1981), came in to replace the dismissed Malinin. As in the past, depth was still a huge problem. Only twelve players received significant playing time. Simonian was not his old self. Five consecutive losses at the beginning and a position in next-to-last place led to Dangulov's dismissal.[76] Problems with internal discipline and breaking of training had persisted.[77] For all the great coach's virtues, he had not been a powerful motivator. Gorokhov then held the fort for two games until early June, when Georgi Glazkov, one of the great Spartak heroes of the thirties, was brought in from Spartak Vilnius.

The old forward restored some stability and effort. Simonian and Netto, who had struggled earlier, came back to life. A 2–1 victory over Dinamo in late August put Spartak in fourth place.[78] Eventually the team came in sixth, one place behind Dinamo, which had also suffered through a difficult campaign after losing its great coach, Iakushin. The army team, now called TsDSA, took the championship without the departed Bobrov in its ranks. For the first time three provincial teams—Dinamo Tblisi, Shakhter Donetsk, and Krylia Sovetov Kuibishev—occupied the next positions. Despite the disappointing result,

Spartak's attendance (approximately 46,600 per home game) climbed back to the high levels of the first postwar seasons, slightly surpassing that of Dinamo (approximately 46,400 per home game), which had been doing slightly better at the gate. The solidity and loyalty of Spartak support among the public was again demonstrated convincingly. Once more, ticket sales, rather than institutional support, continued to keep the team afloat.

Changes were clearly in order for the next season, which proved to be one of the strangest in Soviet soccer history. The USSR had decided to enter the 1952 Olympic Games in nearby Helsinki. Great attention was paid to the football competition. Many of the Eastern European teams, now formally amateur, had deep roots in the prewar professional game. Hungary, now socialist, was thought by many to have the world's strongest team. Yugoslavia and Czechoslovakia were also highly regarded. Despite the strong opposition, Soviet political officials had great but completely naive expectations.[79]

In every footballing nation there is always a tension between the domestic needs of the clubs and the demands of international play. In the USSR, not surprisingly, the demands of country always took precedence over those of the teams. The 1952 league season was truncated to thirteen games, all of which were scheduled to take place after the Olympics. Boris Arkadiev of the army club was put in charge of the national team, leading to the assumption that the *sbornaia* (national team) would be composed of his championship army team, but in fact only half the players came from TsDSA. The pre-Olympic training camp proved chaotic. Players came and left. Some few Spartak representatives were invited to try out, but only Netto stuck. No Soviet coach had ever prepared for such a competition, and even the brilliant Arkadiev was not certain how to proceed. The result, after a replay, was a shocking and dramatic second-round exit to a Yugoslav team that eventually lost in the finals to the Mighty Magyars of Hungary, a team that the next year would thrash England 6–3 in London.

For the inexperienced Soviets, losing to Yugoslavia on the worldwide Olympic stage was no embarrassment in football terms, but a political defeat at the hands of the representatives of the defiant Marshal Tito was intolerable. Soon thereafter, Malenkov called a meeting of Central Committee and sports committee members to discuss the Soviets' generally positive results at Helsinki. The USSR had startled the world, barely losing out to the long-dominant Americans in the final point standings, but defeat at soccer could not be forgiven. According to Romanov's memoirs, Beria succeeded in convincing Malenkov that the army team and especially Arkadiev were to blame for the fiasco. This was, of course, nonsense. There had been numerous representatives of other clubs as well, including Dinamo Moscow and Dinamo Tblisi. Yet ordinary fans, reading *Sovetskii sport* in August, would soon find TsDSA's name missing from the league standings. The team had been disbanded in a decree of August 18, 1952, signed—reluctantly, as we now know—by Romanov at Malenkov's behest. There is no evidence that Stalin demanded this step or signed off on the matter. At a time when Dinamo Moscow was struggling, Beria succeeded in eliminating his team's greatest rival with one mendacious stroke.[80]

In subsequent years, there have been many other explanations of these events that do not support the standard version I have presented here.[81] While several players lost their master-of-sport titles after the Olympics, including Dinamovtsy such as Konstantin Beskov, no one was arrested or sent to Siberia. Arkadiev was subjected to several sessions of public criticism but did not disappear from the soccer profession. A rump version of TsDSA continued to play as the team of the Kaliningrad garrison. Other players caught on with other clubs. Anatoly Bashashkin (b. 1924), would play twelve games with Spartak the next year.[82] By then Stalin had died. Beria was subsequently arrested and executed. Football, not to mention life, went on. As early as 1954, TsDSA could again be found in the league table. On the other hand, Vasilii Stalin's VVS was disbanded once the 1953 season began. He was arrested, and the army club took over control of VVS's facilities. VVS players were dispersed, with Bobrov playing four games for Spartak in his final season. TsDSA, later renamed TsSKA (Central Sports Club of the Army), would not win another league title until 1970. The powerful army sports club, with its impressive campus on Leningradskoe Shosse not far from Dinamo Stadium, went on to great success in virtually every sport, with the notable exception of football.

With TsDSA gone and Dinamo Moscow still struggling, an enormous opportunity opened up for Spartak in the shortened 1952 season which took place after the Helsinki Games. At the age of forty, the great defender Vasilii Sokolov retired and became head coach. Hard-driving and demanding, he was the kind of psychological force the team needed. Dangulov was brought back to handle the technical issues, which, it must be assumed, were Sokolov's weak point. Together they would serve three seasons. No other significant personnel changes were made. While the depth problem was not addressed, it was assumed that with the thirteen-game schedule that year, the lack of able substitutes would be less of a problem. While the national team prepared in semisecrecy for the Olympics, an informal tournament was organized. Spartak finished next to last. Expectations were minimal.[83]

All that changed three weeks into the season when the breakup of TsDSA was formally decreed. The most dominant Soviet team of the era, suddenly disappeared. While some U.S. citizens might wish such a fate for a perennial leader like the New York Yankees, the possibility of a nation's greatest team vanishing overnight cannot even be imagined anywhere else in the world. The only similar situations that come to mind are the plane crashes involving Torino, Manchester United, and later the Zambian national team. A similar tragedy, also never explained publicly, had actually happened to the VVS hockey team. Suddenly, the remaining Soviet football clubs felt they had a chance, especially in light of the truncated season. Swiftly and decisively, Spartak seized the opportunity, clinching the title with nine wins and two draws in the first eleven matches. Its only two defeats came after the championship had been won. The team also did well in the cup, making the final, where it lost 1–0 to an excellent Torpedo team.[84]

While Spartak could claim to be back on top, it is clear that its triumph was somewhat tarnished. Nevertheless, it had managed, despite enormous obstacles, to create the core of a new team, which it was now able to keep together. In the midst of the most repressive part of the late Stalin era, buoyed by a now more socially varied ticket-buying public, Spartak had laid the groundwork for what would be its greatest era. The players gathered and trained by Dangulov would go on to great glory for both club and country after Stalin's death. That they were able to lay the foundation for that glory at a time of repression, surveillance, and control is remarkable. Even in harsh times, football's liminality made it an unreliable tool in the hands of even the most repressive of dictatorships.

This was not true for most of the other events on the Olympic program, which lent themselves more easily to the Soviet state's attempt to use sport for diplomatic and domestic political goals. In individual events like track and swimming, it proved easier to manage the athletes away from the sometimes troubling group dynamics of the team experience. It was easier to ascribe political slogans and meanings to multisport festivals like Olympiads and Spartakiads than to football, with its unpredictability and violence. Spartak, especially when it began operation after 1935, did take its multisport function seriously, but the Starostins, impresarios to the core, had always preferred soccer, the world's most professionalized and popular sport. The Olympic Games were about education. Their purpose had always been didactic, an approach that was thoroughly consistent with the goals of Soviet sporting practice. Soccer, on the other hand, was about entertainment, even during Stalin's last years.

By the time preparations for the Helsinki Olympics effort had begun in earnest, the larger Spartak Sport Society was in eclipse. Dinamo and the armed forces sports clubs had become the main pillars of the system. The Spartak Society was less involved in participating in the state's new cold war campaign for international prestige through sport. On the eve of the Games, according to a report to the Central Committee, there were 602 athletes on lavish stipends in training camps around the country; 200 were from Dinamo, while 180 were in the armed forces. Only forty-two sportsmen and women came from the Spartak Society.[85] Thirty-one Dinamovtsy won medals at Helsinki; only one Spartak Society athlete made it to the podium. Support of female sport was an important part of the Soviet effort. Forty members of the 250-person Soviet contingent were women, but only three came from a Spartak organization, which had shown little interest in female athletic activity. Here, too, Dinamo and the army had been much more active.[86]

The multisport Olympic system had its origins in the sports festivals and parades that had flourished under Stalin during the 1930s. When previously unknown Soviet athletes burst upon the world sporting stage after the war, the structures and processes that produced them had been in place for more than two decades. Even after Stalin's death, the organizational approach to sport developed under his aegis continued to function without significant change. Football never fit in well with this version of state sport. It should not be surprising that its sporting and cultural practices clashed so sharply with the picture drawn by Orwell in 1949. Throughout its history, Spartak had been devoted to the concept of pleasurable entertainment. If its struggle to give their fans pleasure became particularly difficult during late Stalinism, the pursuit of that pleasure, as Lev Filatov would assure us, was nearly always fun.

# 7

# Thaw, Change, and Resurrection, 1953-1956

Nick Hornby has lamented the great length of a soccer season. This fact alone, he wrote, has meant most people die without knowing their team's final place in the standings. Such was the fate of Joseph Stalin, who expired on March 5, 1953, a month before league play began. If truth be told, the "greatest friend of Soviet physical culture" couldn't have cared less. His interest in football was at best episodic, limited to the sport's possible political uses. Beria, whose relationship with Stalin had deteriorated in the year before the leader's death, was another matter. By mid-June, the dictator's favorite policeman was under arrest, and his absence had a direct impact on the final result of the season. Beria would be executed in December, having seen the title snatched from his beloved Dinamo Tblisi by Spartak under circumstances that proved more than a trifle dubious. Not only did his political opponents kill Beria, they taunted him on the way to the grave by cooking the final results of the 1953 soccer season. Regardless of how the victory was achieved, Spartak's triumph did mark the club's return to the top of the Soviet game. With newly powerful friends now in the highest of places and old enemies removed from the scene, Spartak could no longer consider itself an outsider.

After Stalin's death and the eventual consolidation of power by Nikita Khrushchev, the Soviet Union began a multisided struggle to overcome the consequences of a quarter century of turmoil, war, and terror. The next eleven comparatively peaceful, if not entirely normal, years witnessed a complex set of processes, variously described as de-Stalinization, liberalization, and reform. These trends were resisted by a variety of entrenched interests. The uneven and incomplete relaxation of cultural controls, known as the Thaw, was but one of these many interrelated processes. One aspect of the Thaw was the emergence of a definable and active public opinion, composed primarily of intellectuals, students, and white-collar professionals. At the same time, laboring men and women manipulated the system. Absenteeism and shirking on the factory floor were part of their repertoire, along with occasional violence.[1] Both intellectuals and workers contended with confused and uncertain authorities who could not find a consistent approach to the demands of the various segments of increasingly various publics. Given those ambiguities and uncertainties, the Thaw ebbed and flowed.

This same period turned out to be Spartak's Golden Age. Nikolai Starostin and his brothers returned from their exile to do battle once again with Dinamo. Although TsDKA was resurrected in 1954, it never returned to its former glory, and so the Dinamo-Spartak rivalry again became the centerpiece of Soviet soccer. Neither team could dominate the other. Between 1952 and 1959, one or the other took top honors. Strangely, Spartak's ups and downs on the playing field seemed to track with the ups and downs of cultural liberalization. When Spartak won championships (1953, 1956, 1958, and 1962), things were more or less good for those who benefited from the Thaw. When the team's fortunes ebbed, it seemed repressive tendencies had gained the upper hand. Was this a coincidence? Most likely it was, but could a hypothetical Soviet sports bettor (not a sizable group) have gained an advantage by reading the cultural press of the time? Could it have been that provocative material in the period's leading literary journal, *Novyi Mir,* was a sign of forthcoming success on the field for Spartak and dull material an omen of failure?[2] Needless to say, it is hard to imagine any such claim would be sustainable. Rather, it is best simply to say that Spartak and its supporters swam in the same cultural/political waters as students and intellectuals, not to mention those groups of workers who were most sympathetic to reform. All were part of a society once again undergoing profound but contested change while renegotiating its relationship with the state. In the process, the very boundaries between state and society, never entirely clear, were blurred even further.

The USSR confronted new circumstances after Stalin's death. Quickly the party restored its authority over the police.[3] In part, this was a tactical measure taken by Khrushchev, who became party general secretary. Malenkov, following Stalin's course, had based his power in the institutions of the state, including the secret police, a political liability after the arrest of Beria.[4] With the NKVD no longer rampant, the Terror came to an end, and in time the gulag was greatly reduced in size. The secret police could still arrest citizens but lost the power to judge and punish them as well. More broadly, continuing economic and social change produced a still more complicated social structure. The pace of urbanization accelerated further. As cities became ever larger, the industrial working class continued to grow in both absolute numbers and segmentation. At the same time, proletarians made up a smaller percentage of the total population.[5] Millions now worked outside the factories, mines, and farms, creating a broad variety of often competing interest groups.

Internationally, the postwar Soviet Union became thoroughly enmeshed in global politics, which after 1953 hardened into the long and dangerous confrontation of the cold war. With the Soviet acquisition of thermonuclear weapons, the United States of America and the Union of Soviet Socialist Republics embarked on a resource-devouring, terror-filled arms race that was in turn accompanied by global competition on the political, economic, scientific, and cultural fronts. Military preparedness and the need for an expanded defense industry skewed the USSR's subsequent development, making it difficult to provide badly needed and much desired consumer goods of all sorts to an eager and newly expectant Soviet population. In all the years of the struggle with a mature and successful postwar capitalism, the USSR was always at a marked disadvantage with the United States, not really capable of combining guns with butter.

All these changes had a profound impact on sport. The xenophobia of Stalin's last years had evaporated almost overnight. As the USSR embraced sport as a diplomatic tool, the meager dog's breakfast of international friendlies gave way to a banquet of foreign matchups.[6] What formerly had been domestic entertainments were now a highly visible part of the battle for political prestige with the capitalist West. Soccer, however, did not occupy center stage in the sporting struggle that emerged during the cold war. The chief enemy was the United States, which was not a soccer nation. Rather, the fight against the Americans was played out primarily on the stage of the Olympics. Starting in 1956, the Soviets came to dominate both the summer and winter games, seeming to specialize in a wide variety of unprofitable and unpopular sports and events that had never generated much interest among the U.S. public.

Reasoning from the market model, Westerners tended to assume that the Soviets were good at kayaking, gymnastics, biathlon, and Greco-Roman wrestling (to name just a few) because thousands of Soviet fans flocked to arenas to watch such sports. In truth, these activities had small audiences. Rather, the sports committee came to realize that the best way to win the games was to contest virtually every discipline, regardless of the size of the sport's domestic public. In a command economy, it proved possible to direct resources toward events that presented opportunities for victory, not because of their sizable audiences but rather because of the indifference of capitalist nations. Nowhere was this more true than in the case of female sport.

Soccer was another matter. By far the USSR's most popular sport, football influenced relations with all those other nations that paid attention to the world's most popular game. Here the record was decidedly mixed. Comradely matches against Western professional clubs were treated by the leadership as examinations of the Soviet school of football. Spartak played a leading role in these contests. It also became increasingly involved with the performance of the national team. After the debacle of the Helsinki games, the Soviet team was revived in 1954, and Spartak players composed roughly half its membership. In 1958, the USSR entered its first World Cup, and in 1960 actually won the first European Cup. Throughout this period, training and preparing players for international competition became an important part of Spartak's responsibilities. When things went well, there was glory all around. When things went poorly, Starostin and his colleagues took much of the blame.

How, then, to square this new importance with the carefully cultivated Spartak ideology of the team of underdogs? With their strong support from a reinvigorated Communist Party, Starostin and his colleagues could scarcely continue to play the victim, but in seven memoirs published between 1964 and 1989 Andrei and Nikolai drew a picture of suffering at the hands of the Stalinists. During the Thaw many of their fans went so far as to describe Spartak as the team of democracy, but what did the word mean in the Soviet context? Spartak drew its resources from the Moscow branch of a political party that did not take such a term seriously. Was this a contradiction, hypocrisy, or simple confusion? Writing on the ways soccer generated identities, the Argentinean anthropologist Eduardo Archetti noted that the game, like many other cultural forms, was simultaneously a mirror and a mask of reality. Spartak fans could cling to the image of the victim, while others saw this as a way of hiding the club's connections with powerful patrons.[7]

Here the ambiguities of Spartak's position in the post-Stalin world reflect many of the complexities of the struggle for and against the renunciation of the Stalinist legacy. It was still the strongest civilian team. Dinamo was still the child of the secret police. Yet Spartak had no shortage of powerful and important friends. Before the war, there had been a tangible if imprecise social basis to the rivalry. We can be fairly certain that roughly half the Moscow male working class supported Spartak before 1941, but their confrontation with Dinamo was now less about the present and more about the contested terrain of recent history. In the post-Stalin world, realities and truths became even more elusive. In this new context, it became more difficult to describe a righteous and underprivileged Spartak us taking on an evil, well-off Dinamo them.

## Change and Its Sources

Even before Stalin's death, it had become clear to many inside and outside the USSR that the system that had quickly industrialized the nation and enabled the victory over the Axis was archaic and in crisis. While there was fear among the leadership and in society about the chaos a future without Stalin might bring, there was also a sense of the necessity of change. Many of what appeared to be new kinds of concerns, demands, and ideas had in fact emerged during the dictator's last years. Citizens had been rehearsing new roles for themselves well before Stalin left the stage. After 1953, a definable and audible public opinion became active and aggressive. The voice of the people, which was manifested in so constrained a manner during the Sal'nikov affair, now took on much bigger questions. No less a loyal Stalinist than Beria had emerged from the dying leader's bedchamber to declare an entire series of political reforms along with amnesties for more than a million prisoners of the gulag.[8] Three months later, his opponents in the new collective leadership moved to arrest Beria as a first step in reasserting the party's authority over the police and ending the terror of the previous quarter century.

More change would soon be on the way. As Stephen Cohen has written:

Virtually every area of Soviet life was affected by the changes of 1953–1964, however contradictory and ultimately limited—from the end of mass terror and freeing of millions of prison camp victims, the measures introduced to limit some of the worst bureaucratic abuses and privileges, the civic awakening and growing political participation of educated society, and the array of economic and welfare reforms, to revisions in Soviet foreign policy that we now call detente—occurred without protracted violence or upheaval.[9]

Similarly, in listing changes in the legal system, Moshe Lewin argued that "we are dealing with a different type of regime." The show trials and mass executions were a thing of the past.[10]

In economic matters, Khrushchev introduced reforms that attacked some of the imbalances of the Stalinist structure by decentralizing power away from the giant government ministries to regional councils (*sovnarkhozy*). Planning was to become more realistic. If raw materials were produced and consumed in the same locale, the center no longer controlled their production and distribution. In an attempt to improve agricultural production, Khrushchev brought previously unused land under cultivation. With Stalin-like fanfare, huge swaths of Kazakhstan and other regions (the so-called Virgin Lands) were planted. Thousands of young people were induced, even inspired, to move to forbidding climes to join in the campaign. Initially this program was successful in raising overall yields. It allowed Khrushchev to make claims about his contributions to the long-suffering rural sector.

There were, however, even deeper forces pushing change, and state policies turned out to have consequences that were not always intended or understood. The massive movement of peasants into the cities during the thirties and forties became a flood after 1953. By 1959, half of the Soviet population had come to live in cities. This shift would change almost everything. "Urbanization," as Lewin has demonstrated over the course of his career, "is the commanding fact in the history of the USSR."[11] The process was highly spontaneous and relatively unplanned. Soviet society became extraordinarily more multifaceted as the tasks facing the economic system became more difficult and various than the relatively clear-cut campaign to fulfill certain gross output goals.

As we have seen, this process had begun even during the war. Skilled managers, engineers, and others with education and ability were required to handle the even more daunting tasks of postwar reconstruction. Internationally, the cold war imposed a military imperative on the Soviet industrial infrastructure. Production of advanced weaponry, conventional and nuclear, could not be left in the hands of enthusiastic amateurs. These new people were initially politically quiescent, but after Stalin their political positions changed, and they became more assertive.[12] Significant numbers of Soviet scholars, scientists, and engineers rose to positions of international eminence. Aside from privileges and tangible rewards, they expected to be taken seriously, listened to, and judged for their accomplishments in their particular fields of expertise.

This new embrace of citified modernity had a predictable impact on popular culture in general and football in particular. Focusing on the young, the majority segment of the stadium-going soccer public, Hilary Pilkington has suggested that "like Western societies, the Soviet Union experienced a postwar 'boom' which expressed itself in the most comprehensive urbanization drive to date. . . . Moreover, the cultural thaw associated with the Khrushchev period reduced the political costs of non-sanctioned cultural activity."[13] Football had always been played in the cities. As urban centers expanded, so did the reach and grasp of the game. In the fifties and sixties, soccer became an even bigger spectator attraction with larger and larger audiences. The televising of games, which started in the midfifties, further expanded interest and provided a new, more private space for fans to experience the game. Soccer matches, to be sure, were officially sanctioned events, but they did in turn produce many nonsanctioned activities, not least a healthy dose of hooliganism, drunkenness, cursing, and joke telling.

Industrialization had been achieved with the archaic methods of force and repression, but such measures would not serve further modernization. Not entirely unlike serfs, Soviet workers had been legally bound to their places of employment under Stalin. Changing jobs was deemed a criminal act, even if there were frequent instances of it.[14] The massive use of prison labor provided by the gulag had been shown to be inefficient and, perhaps even worse, unprofitable. The new leadership removed restraints on worker movement, thereby facilitating the emergence of an authentic labor market.[15] If the state now wanted to move working hands to uninviting climes, it had to offer so-called normal incentives in the form of higher wages and better working conditions.

A burgeoning and quite various white-collar population became a significant presence in the cities, especially Moscow, the administrative center of the nation. Ranging from office workers to engineers and scientists, these men and women had their own concerns. Along with the creative intelligentsia who reveled in the greater freedoms of the Thaw, these increasingly numerous non-manual workers came to constitute another part of a newly vigorous public opinion. To be sure, the very variety of this expanding layer of professionals worked against their ever becoming an organized alternative to the regime, but Khrushchev understood that these groups had to be courted, if not always obeyed.[16]

The fifties and early sixties turned out to be a time of rapid economic expansion, and this progress produced optimism and rising expectations among the population.[17] In particular, Khrushchev attacked the enormous housing problem, providing apartments for more than a hundred million families.[18] By contrast with 1935, when Stalin first made the claim, life really did get better in the Soviet fifties. Soviet citizens were no longer subject to the horrors of war, terror, and coerced exploitation; it was possible to have many of the trappings of a normal life. Millions lived relatively long lives, had decent careers, raised families if they were lucky, and died in their beds. Yet rapid urbanization had its stresses and strains. It was essential to forge a new approach to the tattered relationship between state and society, but few had any clear vision of what such a relationship would look like or even whether the very notion of a relationship made sense. Outsiders came to call these processes de-Stalinization.

## Which Side of Which Side Are You On?

Contemporary Western journalists tended to divide the post-Stalin USSR into clear camps of hawks and doves, hard-liners and moderates. As archives have come open and scholars have examined the history of the Khrushchev period, these earlier categories have begun to melt away. The great poet Anna Akhmatova, who had suffered persecution and criticism under Stalin, later remarked that with the flood of returnees from the camps, two Russias faced each other—the jailers and the jailed. There was, however, a third Russia that neither "went nor was sent. . . . Soviet society did not consist only of convicts on the one side and the executioners on the other."[19] This third group is of the greatest historical importance. Spartak, its leaders once jailed but now returned to privileged positions, once again reflected all the ambiguities and uncertainties of Soviet life as lived by the overwhelming majority of the population.

Most crudely put, the nation embarked on a struggle between an uncertain path of change and a fearful return to a discredited and cruel past. The battle lines of that struggle were by no means clear. There were no clearly organized camps with fully elaborated programs. People shifted sides continually. So-called good people could do bad things, and the supposedly bad were often capable of acts of generosity. What contemporary observers inside and outside the academies of the West described later as a struggle between the "official" and the "dissident" never captured the deeper and broader realities of the period. In a certain sense, the tensions existed not among various groups but rather within the minds of all citizens from the bottom to the very top of the social structure. The new leadership, perhaps Khrushchev most of all, understood the necessity of a break from the past. At the same time, it feared that the loss of continuity could lead to chaos.

De-Stalinization was an unstable concept that involved much more than the limited rejection of the cult of personality, which had been the centerpiece of Khrushchev's famous Secret Speech in February 1956. Ending the terror at the highest levels of the party-state and reducing the magnitude and cruelty of the camps were only first steps in a process that would not be complete by the time of Khrushchev's ouster in 1964. It was also necessary for a different kind of regime and a society in continuing flux to adjust their relationship. As Vladimir Kozlov has written, "Both the common people and the elites formed new models of the world, both the 'bosses' and the populace adapted to the new historical reality."[20] Those who after the war had wished to serve but not cringe were now called upon to do just that. Those who did not wish even to serve could do that as well.

After Stalin, individuals could have private lives, but finding the spaces in which to live those lives was not a simple matter.[21] If citizens were still trying to find small ways of saying no, knowing where and when to say no was still tricky. In a swiftly changing world, the subjective processes of identity formation became even more slippery. If football was still a place where people told themselves stories about themselves, what sorts of stories were the old and new fans of Spartak telling themselves in the fifties and early sixties? Chanting "get the cops" in a stadium could still be done with impunity. Doing the same thing right after the game in a metro station filled with police continued to be unwise.

The Thaw was thought to have benefited the creative intelligentsia most of all, allowing them to find their voices and giving rise to bursts of public opinion.[22] The new labor market, reforms on the shop floor, shorter workdays, and extensions of the welfare system benefited ordinary working people. Improvements in living conditions, especially in matters of housing, were extended to all social groups. Individual citizens came to interact in different, more trustful ways.[23] In the very broadest sense, all these trends seemed to be related, but it cannot be said that they moved in lockstep; the entire process was uneven, uncoordinated, and unpredictable.

Spontaneity, the most central part of all sport, was also fundamental to the flowering of public opinion once Stalin was gone. The writer Ilya Ehrenburg, whose novel gave the Thaw its name, wrote, "Critical thought simply spilled out, stimulating the wish to find out about one thing, to examine another."[24] The quickness with which such thoughts emerged could only mean that these ideas and feelings had been harbored by many for some time. In the last issue of the aforementioned *Novyi Mir* for 1953, the critic Vladimir Pomerantsev published a provocative piece entitled "On Truthfulness in Literature." "The controversy that Pomerantsev's article had initiated soon developed into a discussion of public problems, acquired a political nuance and revealed issues that had been maturing in the minds of thinking people for some time."[25]

It is hard to imagine that Spartak players, with what were now ninth-grade educations, were exposed to Pomerantsev's article in their political education classes, but it is fair to say that intelligent and cultured individuals such as Sal'nikov, Simonian, and Netto, who numbered writers, musicians, and actors among their friends, were probably well aware of the ferment of the moment. Upon his return late in 1954, Andrei Starostin was met at the Yaroslavl train station by his literary friends and quickly stepped back into the cultural mix from which he had been torn twelve years earlier. It is difficult to believe that the issues of the day never came up during the team's many visits to the Maly and Moscow Art theaters, which often invited them for shared evenings of gaiety and discussions about the "creative process."[26]

Above all, it is important to remember the fluidity, ambiguity, and uncertainty of the fifties and early sixties. Polly Jones has noted, "De-Stalinization was improvised from a mixture of old and new mentalities and policies, belying the sense of finality implied in both the Russian and English renderings of the term."[27] One cannot view all criticism of the state during this period as necessarily anti-Soviet. Similarly, little sentiment in favor of a return to capitalism emerged in the course of the period's many debates. Ultimately, the process of liberalization proved to be neither broad enough nor deep enough.[28] When Khrushchev was forced to retire, no one mourned his exit. It would fall to his successors to fix all the problems he had failed to solve. It cannot be said their efforts were much more successful.

### Football without Stalin (and Beria)

The turmoil, anxiety, and uncertainty of the Thaw affected all aspects of Soviet life. The football world could not escape the changes, nor would it have wanted to.[29] Life got much better for the men of the Soviet soccer world, none more so than the men of Spartak. On the eve of 1953, N. N. Romanov announced several new measures that enhanced the profitability of the football industry and the wealth of its players and coaches. Salaries now ranged from 1,200 to 2,000 rubles a month. Bonuses for victories were set near 300. To make more money available for the clubs themselves, the sports committee now gave 70 rather than 60 percent of gate receipts to be divided between match participants.[30] Flush with cash, the teams were able to provide copious nutrition for their players. Spartak fed them an average of five thousand calories per day at a time of shortage and insufficiencies for ordinary citizens.[31] Finally, trade union and other nonmilitary teams were to have access to a pool of fifty to sixty young players who were exempted from military service of any kind.

With the Communist Party reasserting its ascendancy over the police, civilians once more assumed domination over the structures of force.[32] This worked to the advantage of the civilian sports clubs. Romanov's measures were a sign of this shift. Spartak, even during its internal exile, had always been the most popular and successful civilian club. More than the trade union teams, it was the darling of the party. The tie to Promkooperatsiia remained, but more than ever Spartak came under the less than fully separate wings of the Moscow city party committee (*gorkom*) and the Moscow city council (*Mossovet*).[33] The competitive advantage of this arrangement was straightforward. With millions being invested in new housing, an apartment became the greatest reward to which a player could aspire. The gorkom and Mossovet had control of much of the new housing stock in Moscow, and their doors were always open to Nikolai Starostin. In 1990, the legendarily cantankerous sportswriter Arkadii Galinskii told me with his usual hyperbole, "Spartak is the team of the Moscow city party organization and Mossovet. It is a very wealthy team. If you put together all the apartments they have given out over the years, you could construct an entire region."[34]

Despite their differences, both Malenkov and Khrushchev shared a belief in the importance of expanding the consumer sector and raising living standards. Entertainment, one significant part of the consumer sector, revived quickly after Stalin's death. As a populist gesture, the Kremlin was opened to the public for the first time since 1930. On the goods front, the giant GUM department store on the north side of Red Square reopened late in 1953. On the food and frivolity front, the equally immense Praga restaurant again opened its doors in 1955.[35] Jazz, or something like it, reappeared in other eating places and was even more listened to in the homes of the young. The Starostins, with their many connections to the world of Soviet show business, saw themselves as but one segment of a newly unshackled popular culture, and they flourished in the post-Stalin moment. The northern stand at Dinamo Stadium took on a different hue when Spartak played. Army officers, top cops, and party bigwigs were joined by writers, composers, and the stars of Soviet stage and screen.

With Beria gone, the most egregious forms of government interference disappeared as well. Players were no longer blackmailed, nor were their parents arrested in order to encourage transfers to Dinamo. Cup semifinals were definitely not replayed after finals. Opponents were not sent away to the camps. In the years before Stalin died, Dinamo Moscow's performance had fallen off. The club faced a change of playing generations, but Iakushin had resigned. Much like his predecessor Arkadiev, he was unable to bear Beria's constant meddling. Iakushin worked instead for Dinamo Tblisi, also an object of Beria's attention but harder to control since it was far from the capital.[36] Once Beria had been removed, Iakushin came back to Dinamo Moscow and led it back to the top in 1954.

This last point raises the larger issue of professional autonomy in the post-Stalin Soviet Union. Professionals of all sorts, especially elite scientists and the cream of the creative intelligentsia, drove the Thaw with their new assertiveness. Soccer players, coaches, and officials also saw themselves as professionals. Like other professionals, those who labored in the sportsworld sought independence and respect. This desire for a football professionalism free from outside interference is indirectly reflected in the memoirs and popular histories that cover the post-Stalin period. Whereas accounts of the prewar years are thoroughly intertwined with high political matters, the later literature focuses almost exclusively on the field of play. There is not even much to be learned about backroom struggles or the social world of the footballer. In this case, the silence on traditionally understood political questions speaks the proverbial volumes. Political subtexts did not disappear, but their impact became less obvious. Following such logic, this chapter will concentrate on the game itself, which, thankfully, was now the soccer world's primary concern.

The surface apoliticism of these accounts does not mean, however, that the powerful now kept their hands off the game. With the tensions between the police and the party resolved in favor of the party, football teams became the objects of internal rivalries within the party itself. Each region, factory, and institution demanded preeminence for its team. Coaches of nonperforming teams were called on the carpet. Many were summarily dismissed. Some players were coddled, but many others found their careers ended by an untrained party big shot's tirade. Local chiefs sought bragging rights and solicited the help of a broad range of patrons when funds were needed.[37] The competition for support led eventually to corruption. Not only could the party not control football, but its members could not control themselves when it came to football.

While clearly appalling, this tyranny of the ignorant but powerful was hardly limited to Soviet soccer. Rather, it has long proven normal throughout the world of professional sport. Wealthy team owners, who have made their fortunes selling real estate, aluminum siding, or plastics, have always made decisions that reflected their limited knowledge. High-handed treatment of hired professionals was scarcely limited to Soviet Communism. If Ivan Likhachev, who headed the ZIS (later ZIL) Auto Works, took a hands-on approach to his Torpedo team, was this so different from the behavior of the Agnelli family, founders of both Fiat and Juventus, Italy's most powerful club?[38] Are the owners of the U.S. media giant Cablevision, who control the New York Knickerbockers basketball team, any less inept than their Soviet counterparts?

Despite the less oppressive post-Stalin climate, the army and police did not lose all their advantages in obtaining top talent. The appropriate commissions did not rubber-stamp all the transfers Dinamo and TsSKA wished for, but the ministries of Defense and Interior could still draft promising young athletes and place them in their ranks with many of the privileges and advantages accorded to military officers. Scores of young players would find themselves escorted from practice into waiting cars by uniformed men, never to play for their old teams again. Perhaps not surprisingly, this practice, with its aroma of the Terror, proved controversial. Trade unions and other organizations protested to the Central Committee, which found itself constantly trying to balance the needs of the various elements that composed the sports system.[39]

It could no longer be said that the authorities favored Dinamo and TsSKA. On the one hand, Spartak had directly benefited from the new state of affairs when in 1954, the Starostins were four of some twelve thousand prisoners with political connections allowed to return to their homes and restart their careers.[40] On the other hand, the continued micromanaging by party officials proved a brake on the unfettered professionalism that Spartak officials, among others, wished to see strengthened. Again, Spartak's reliance on the party undermined its well-cultivated public image of independence. The ambiguity of the club's situation reflected the broader uncertainties facing all professionals during the Thaw.

## Interregnum

First place for Spartak in 1952 marked a return to Soviet soccer's elite, but it cannot be said that the victory was, as the Soviets said, "fully merited." As we have seen, the calendar had been shortened to thirteen games, all played in Moscow. Dinamo was in a down period, and TsSKA had been disbanded. The 1953 season, with a full schedule, would be a much more serious examination. The great defender and team captain Vasilii Sokolov was now in charge. His assistant was Dangulov, whose quiet and respectful manner had been deemed insufficiently motivating. Sokolov, whose playing career had ended, brought the very opposite managerial style to his task. In order to assert his authority over players with whom he had recently shared the field, Sokolov was harsh and demanding, a screamer who did not spare the feelings of either players or management.[41] Conflicts, especially with experienced comrades, were many. While this approach may have suited the team's needs, it was not a recipe for Sokolov's longevity in the post.

The core of the "new" Spartak, which had been growing since Dangulov's arrival, remained intact. Yet there were important changes. With the breakup of TsDKA, the great defender Anatoly Bashashkin (b. 1924) came over to anchor what had been a weak spot.[42] Vasily Stalin's air force club had by now been disbanded, and Vsevolod Bobrov, who had left TsDKA for VVS, settled in for what would prove to be a cameo appearance with Spartak.[43] Bobrov brought along his personal discovery, attacker Anatoly Isaev (b. 1932). A Muscovite, Isaev had taken a long and difficult path to elite soccer and would not solidify his position in the Spartak side until the next season. The emergence of the twenty-year-old Boris Tatushin (1933–1998), a right-winger from Moscow who had joined Spartak in 1951, was one of the highlights of the season.[44] Tatushin's speed and his gifted right foot (his left foot was useless) won many a ball and set up many a goal. His ability to send in crosses from the right flank led English observers to call him the "Russian Stanley Mathews." Tatushin's talents allowed an aging Paramonov to move to right halfback, where he joined Netto and Oleg Tinakov to form a strong midfield.

Despite a slow start, Spartak climbed to second place, two points behind Dinamo Tblisi by the end of the first half of the season. Soon thereafter, Tblisi came to Moscow. Spartak was just beginning to peak, having improved the link between its forwards and midfield. In the game, Netto continually found a hard-running Simonian, who easily eluded the Dinamo defenders. Netto then set up goals by Anatoly Ilyin and Nikolai Dementiev. Simonian, who had scored himself, set up Paramonov for a 4–1 result over the demoralized Georgians. Tblisi had clearly been outclassed, and Spartak's improvement was duly noted by the vice minister of sport K. Andrianov, writing in *Sovetskii sport*.[45]

On July 15, Bobrov made his first Spartak appearance, coming on as a substitute against Lokomotiv. He had two goals in league play and one in an international friendly before starting against the powerful Hungarian club Honved in Budapest on August 20. It proved a bad day for Spartak, which lost 2–3, and a worse day for Bobrov. The great man hurt one of his oft-injured knees and was forced to retire from football. Thereafter, he devoted all his energies to ice hockey, which was easier on his painful legs. The loss to the great Hungarian side was but one of three major internationals played during the midseason break. The others were a 2–0 victory over the Czechoslovak national team and a 1–1 draw with the club Swedish club Djurgardens.[46]

The season then resumed with Dinamo Tblisi still leading by a point. On August 27, Spartak faced Dinamo Moscow. The game was as intense as always. An early goal by Dinamo was disallowed for offside, but soon thereafter Sal'nikov scored against his old teammates with a low shot from the right flank that just found the far left corner. Despite tight marking by Dinamo, Tatushin evened things up in the thirty-fifth minute. Spartak continued to threaten, but the great Lev Iashin (1929–1990), just emerging as Dinamo's number one in goal, parried all attempts and the match ended 1–1.[47] Dinamo Tblisi remained at the top of the league table, closely trailed by Spartak.

On September 4, a week before the close of league play, Dinamo Tblisi prepared to end its season in Moscow against a powerful and exciting Torpedo team that would finish third. A victory would give the Georgians twenty-nine points, clinching a tie for the title. A one-game playoff would be needed only if Spartak won its final two matches against Zenit Leningrad and Zenit Kuibyshev. By this time, Iakushin had returned to Dinamo Moscow. He was replaced at the helm of Dinamo Tblisi by Boris Paichadze, and there were now problems for the club off the field as well. Dinamo Tblisi had lost its Georgian protectors at the apex of state power, not only Stalin but, more important in terms of soccer, its hyperfan Lavrenti Beria.

I must note here that my account of what then ensued is based on a single oral source—namely, Aksel' Vartanian, a Russian-speaking Armenian originally from Tblisi, who is the most archivally informed and scrupulous student of the Soviet game. Though the well-known Russian journalist Aleksandr Nilin has hinted at foul play in his post-1991 history of the Soviet game, I have seen no printed source, archival or published, that speaks to these events. In any case, Dinamo Tblisi won its match against Torpedo. When it was over, the official protocol was signed by both captains, neither of whom noted anything untoward in the document, which Vartanian has examined. Despite Torpedo's acceptance of defeat, some of its fans did not take the result so peacefully and attacked the locker rooms of the referees and Dinamo. Police intervened, and after some time the players were finally able to return to their hotel to celebrate what they thought was a great triumph. For the first time in the history of the Soviet game, a provincial team was the likely champion.

The next day, as they prepared to go their separate ways, the men from Tblisi were informed a protest had been lodged and accepted. A replay would take place on September 7. Paichadze complained loudly but was told to keep quiet and prepare for the game. At this moment, the Georgians realized that Spartak was meant to win the title and everything was stacked against them. This became even clearer when the USSR's most famous referee, Nikolai Latyshev, was named to work the game. A Muscovite with whom the Georgians had had run-ins before, Latyshev was president of the USSR's college of ref-

erees. The players spent the next two days crying, agonizing over their pow-
erlessness and drinking mightily. They had been so close to the championship
but had been crudely pushed away. On September 7, a disheartened Dinamo
Tblisi, unlike Spartak in 1939, went out and lost 4–1. It had to settle for twenty-
seven points. Four days later, Spartak had won its two last games. The people's team had twenty-nine points to finish in first.

Right after the September 4 match a protest had been filed, citing the usual
reasons for such complaints—goals that should have counted, dubious off-
sides that should not have been called, penalties that should have been given
—complaints of the sort that had nearly always been ignored by the state
sports committee. Even stranger, matters of this sort usually took three months
to adjudicate. The discussion of this protest had taken one day. Vartanian as-
sumes the order to replay came from the highest levels of the party. The point,
he notes, was not to help Spartak. Any Russian team would have done. Rather,
Beria's enemies aimed to make sure no Georgian club took the title. The team
that had benefited from Beria's influence in 1939 now suffered the fate that
had once befallen Spartak. The difference was that Spartak had won its replay in 1939. Fourteen years later, Dinamo Tblisi succumbed to Torpedo. Had
the greatest friend of Soviet physical culture managed to hold on for another
seven months, Dinamo might well have won the title.

If this attempt at controlling the sporting process was farcical, the next meeting of the two teams would end in tragedy. After Stalin's death, there had been
riots in Tblisi protesting the course of the new leadership. Georgian nationalism was surely fanned by what had happened to their team in September.
As was the custom, the first game of the 1954 season saw Spartak play Dinamo in Tblisi. As was also its custom, the football section of the sports committee failed to see the potential danger of this situation. A quarter of a million
ticket requests flooded in for the forty thousand available places. In the minds
of the Georgian nation, this match was the true championship of 1953. One
can well imagine the sort of reception Spartak got on its arrival in Tblisi. The
famously exceptional hospitality of the Georgians must surely have been tempered by the presence of those who, rightly or wrongly, were perceived as
having stolen the championship from their local heroes. Although it was impossible to get a ticket, on the day of the match enormous, angry, revenge-dri-
ven crowds stormed the stadium. There was massive disorder and rioting.
Some twenty people were killed and scores injured. Blood flowed in the
streets. By the time the game had ended, with Dinamo Tblisi a 2–1 winner,
NKVD troops had surrounded the stadium, cleaned up the blood, and set up
checkpoints stretching a kilometer from the arena in every direction. In the
next week, according to Vartanian, there were many more than the usual number of death notices in local Tblisi newspapers.[48]

To be sure, it is possible Vartanian's account is not correct in every detail,
but it does ring true. Could the Georgian police not have expected trouble, especially in the light of the other forms of unrest that occurred after Stalin

passed on? They knew what had happened in September the year before. Such incompetence was hardly surprising, and the Moscow and Leningrad authorities were hardly any more prescient when it came to predicting violence at soccer games. In any case, Spartak did go out and win its last two games of 1953. As far as the players and coaches were concerned, they had played well enough throughout the entire season to be in a position to snatch victory from their closest competitors. The enemies of Stalin and Beria had used Stalinist methods to ensure the defeat of the Georgians, but it is fair to say Spartak's triumph was merited, even if it was stained by undue, if not fully proven, influence from the top.

Whatever the circumstances of its victory, Spartak went on to justify the support of its benefactors. With the league season completed, the newly crowned Soviet champion launched a series of friendlies against foreign competition. Rapid Vienna, with its long and distinguished tradition, came to Moscow on October 13 and was dispatched 4–0. Eight days later, Dosza of Budapest, not the best of clubs from the great footballing nation of Hungary, was crushed 5–0. Both games filled Dinamo Stadium with estimated crowds of eighty thousand.[49] These triumphs were followed by three games in Poland and four in Bulgaria, the only blemish a 1–0 defeat to Bulgaria's army team in the last match of a long tour.[50] Vasily Kuzin, president of the Spartak central council, and team officials such as Vladmir Stepanov and Nikolai Morozov could take pride in having constructed the top club in the Soviet Union.

They had achieved this success without the help and wisdom of the Starostins. The stars of the team, the non-Russians Simonian and Netto, had been brought on during their watch, and it had most likely been their decision to hire Dangulov, who set Spartak in the right direction before turning the reins over to Sokolov. Netto now succeeded Sokolov as captain. To outsiders, this may have seemed a curious choice. Netto was often a feisty and undiplomatic character on the field. His role inside the team was, however, a different matter. As Simonian would later explain, "Although the captain's character was far from pleasing to everyone, they understood that he was fair."[51] Those same character traits served him well on the national team, which he also soon captained. Perhaps more than any of his teammates, Netto was a patriot of the short passing game. As Simonian told me, "He completely refused to recognize there was such a thing as a long pass. . . . He was very self-confident and never wanted to make a mistake with a pass. He never took a risk . . . and if any of us made a long pass, he would shout, 'What's with you? Are you playing village football?' "[52]

When the 1953 season ended, Nikolai Starostin was still in provincial exile in Alma-Ata coaching the local team, Kairat. Andrei continued to run sports in Norilsk.[53] At some point near the end of 1953, Nikolai, according to his final memoir, received a phone call from his wife, who had been visiting him regularly during summers and school vacations. She informed him that it was

now possible, as one of a small group of privileged exiles with political connections, to apply for a release and return home. She urged him to write
Khrushchev, and Nikolai did so the same day. The initial request was granted,
and at some point the next year (once again Starostin is imprecise on dates)
he flew home. There he visited Dmitri Pavlovich Lebedev, one of Khrushchev's close assistants, who handed him a new passport and residence permit (*propiska*) for Moscow.[54]

Nikolai was the first of the brothers to come home. As soon as he had written to Khrushchev, he let the others know they were in a position to make
similar applications.[55] Yet life in Norilsk after Stalin's death appears to have
been more complicated for Andrei than life in Kazakhstan was for Nikolai,
who enjoyed a comparatively idyllic stay. There were several strikes and uprisings throughout the gulag during the summer of 1953. One of the most intense of these took place in Norilsk. As Anne Applebaum has shown, the
events at Norilsk were led by many who had already been imprisoned for serious opposition activity in western Ukraine and the Baltic.[56] Lev Netto, the
older brother of Igor, was among those who played a significant role in these
events.

Netto's parents (both Estonians) had been supporters of the revolution. In
1917, they moved to Moscow from the Baltic to work with the Bolsheviks.
The father, Aleksandr, had been a member of the famed Latvian Riflemen, who
served the young government with great zeal during the civil war. Loyalty to
the revolution did not extend to loyalty for Stalin, but Aleksandr Netto did
manage to survive the purge era. The mother, Iulia, nee Tamm, worked in the
Ministry of Foreign Affairs until 1925, when Lev was born.[57] She had been a
supporter of Trotsky, for whom she continued to harbor good thoughts well
after the war. Although they saw themselves as loyal citizens of the USSR,
both parents embraced their Estonian nationality. While the Moscow-born
Igor was usually listed on Spartak's books as "Russian," he, too, was well
aware of his Baltic heritage.

Lev, a Komsomol member, was drafted in 1943 and parachuted into Nazi-
occupied Estonia, where he was taken prisoner and sent to a camp outside
Frankfurt. Eventually he suffered the common fate of returning Soviet POWs
and was arrested in 1948. While in the Krasnodar transit camp, he became a
member of the underground Democratic Party of Russia. He was then sent to
the camp at Norilsk, where he took part in the uprising.[58] While there, he
came to know Andrei Starostin. In 2004, Lev gave an oral history to the Russian organization Memorial, which has preserved the testimony of many victims of the gulag. The older Netto implied that Andrei was well aware of the
events at Norilsk and had indicated, in indirect ways, sympathy for the strikers. After his release in 1956, Lev Netto maintained his critical stance toward
the regime even as he became a party member in 1963. He revived his acquaintance with Andrei Starostin when they met at Igor's wedding in 1960.
Thereafter, Lev Netto came to the conclusion that he and Andrei were "like-

minded" (*edinomyshlenniki*). They shared, according to Lev, some of the same dissatisfactions with the regime, particularly on matters pertaining to sportsmen. Further, Lev believed Andrei was a "true democrat" who had kept many of his real views to himself.[59]

Lev Netto's testimony raises a number of questions. It suggests that Andrei, who kept the company of many intellectuals and cultural figures, was more sympathetic to the political and cultural thrust of the Thaw than he acknowledged in any of his writings or other official acts. He played the role of solid Soviet citizen and served in important capacities in the soccer hierarchy, including chief of the national team setup. We also know Andrei was a "party man" of another type. It was no secret that he was not averse to the pleasures of, what Nikolai often described as Moscow's bohemians. Perhaps the solidity of his Soviet citizenship was less than complete. One cannot be entirely certain of the Netto brothers' closeness, however. Lev had left for the front when Igor was thirteen. They did not see each other again until Igor was twenty-six and the star and captain of both Spartak and the national team. Lev indicates their contacts usually occurred at larger family functions, and there is not a molecule of anything about Lev's experiences in the several editions of Igor's memoir, all published during the Soviet period. Nevertheless, it cannot have been entirely easy for one of the leaders of the USSR's national team to play with uncomplicated emotions knowing his older brother was in a concentration camp. Which side, one may well ask, was he on? Perhaps the answer is both.

Spartak did come under the protection of the highest levels of the party after 1953, but the club continued to bear many of the scars of Stalinism. Its founders had spent twelve years in the camps. The father of its leading scorer (Simonian) had been jailed to force his son to transfer to Dinamo Tblisi. Another star (Sal'nikov) had been blackmailed into leaving the team, and, as just noted, there was the matter of the captain's brother, away in the camps. There can be no doubt that these facts, even as the club came to be favored by those in power, affected its internal atmosphere. Simonian has said the political difficulties of several team leaders were a continuing, if not dominant, subject of discussion within the club.[60]

Among the team's supporters, however, only some of these facts were widely known. The trope of the underdog continued to be a part of Spartak ideology, not only for team officials, players, and coaches but for their fans as well. At the time, word of the wounds inflicted on club insiders barely seeped into official discourse. Not even the great keeper of Spartak spirit, the hugely successful journalist Lev Filatov, could express it openly, despite the fact that his own father had been in the camps. Instead, Spartak the victim, the team of the jailed, became a classic hidden transcript. Even if civilians were back in control of the structures of force, it was still easy for fans to invoke their own version of history (their own memories) and make Dinamo and TsSKA what they could no longer be said to be—the villains of the soccer drama.

## The Boys Are Back in Town

The more than one million prisoners of the gulag who had been amnestied soon after Stalin's death did not find a hearty welcome when they returned home. Nearly all of them were criminals whose renewed presence in society led to much disorder and insecurity.[61] Such was not the case with the several thousand privileged returnees who came back in 1954.[62] Most of them returned to their houses and took up careers similar to those they had left. The Starostins' mother had been allowed to stay in their downtown apartment on Spiridonova Street after their arrest. Their sisters, however, were not allowed to leave the capital. By bizarre contrast, Andrei's wife, Olga, had been sent outside the city in 1942 but returned in 1946 during an amnesty.[63]

The fact that Nikolai showed up for a game at Dinamo Stadium soon after his reunion with his immediate family suggests that he came back to Moscow sometime after May 1954. The first to greet him was his old protégé, Vladimir Stepanov. That same day, he made a new friend when Vsevolod Bobrov introduced himself. Everyone was interested in Nikolai's future plans, and he soon met with N. N. Romanov, who asked what he wanted to do. Romanov suggested that Nikolai help Valentin Granatkin, the old Lokomotiv goalie who led what was now called the Football Federation, but Starostin refused the post. He feared his views on football would not always mesh with those of the men in charge. Nikolai instead wished to return to Spartak. He did not seek to replace Kuzin, who had served eight years in his post as head of the Spartak Society. Starostin wanted instead to devote his energies to his old team and so was once again named boss (*nachal'nik*) of the Spartak Moscow football club.[64]

Perhaps the Znamenskii brothers had been right after all, that Nikolai did want to devote all his energies to football. Nevertheless, Kuzin, whose office was one floor above Starostin's, often visited the great patriarch for advice concerning other sports, and advice was always freely given. It would appear that Starostin was not entirely comfortable with the idea of working for a state institution. He must have understood that his experience as a networker and wheeler-dealer was better suited to operating outside the official structures of power. He also must have understood that in this new environment he could best maintain his former independence by working for an organization that enjoyed a measure of autonomy. The Spartak soccer team now had to operate at a profit in order to support the activities of the larger sport society. It was best to do this in a space that received less surveillance and scrutiny than did the state or party systems. In doing so, Starostin came to develop a reputation for "correctness" that contrasted with his more flamboyant prewar public persona. It may well be that his exile had taught him some harsh lessons.[65]

Andrei, whose grasp of specific dates was no better than his brother's, appears to have come back home during September 1954. Aleksandr and Petr left no memoirs, but it is likely their return took place at the same time. Andrei entered the capital through the Yaroslavl train station along with a mass

**7.1** Nikolai Starostin and Sal'nikov with someone's new Volga. A. Soskin, *Sergei Sal'nikov.*

of bedraggled returnees. He was met by his old friend Mikhail Ianshin and their mutual buddies, the theater director Arnold Arnold and the dramatist Isidor Shtok. As they drove off in Ianshin's tiny Pobeda, they asked Andrei whether they should get tickets for the upcoming match with the powerful Hungarian national team that had recently lost in a colossal upset to the West Germans in the 1954 World Cup final. A few days later, Andrei made a triumphant return to Dinamo Stadium's north stand. He was greeted on his arrival by two old pals from the Presnia, Pavel Kanunnikov and Ivan Artem'ev. Scores surrounded him, and the questions flew back and forth for the next few hours.[66]

Shortly thereafter he was received at the party's Central Committee and asked the same questions about his future that had been posed to Nikolai. Andrei eventually began working with Spartak, but he soon developed a career as a sportswriter, novelist, and memoirist. He had ample training from his many friends in the literary world. Additionally, he became involved with the Football Federation. Aleksandr started out as the manager of a sporting goods factory and then did a stint in the auto industry, where he was able to help obtain cars for Spartak players and coaches. Petr, who had already engaged in design and construction while in the camps, embarked on a successful career as an engineer. All were rehabilitated. All had their party membership restored. None drew anti-Soviet conclusions from their experience. Nikolai recalled the hearing at which the charges (including the criminal ones) from the 1943 sentencing document were dismissed.[67] The Soviet system might have jailed him, but it had cleared him as well. If, like Andrei, the other brothers harbored impure thoughts for a Communist, they kept such sentiments to themselves. It would be ten years before Andrei discussed the matter publicly in his first book, *Bol'shoi futbol* (1964): "By the wise and de-cisive policies of our party, the Soviet government corrected the mistake, re-habilitating innocent people who suffered, making sure a repeat could not happen."[68] Millions now learned what been had been common knowledge for thousands of Spartak fans. By that time, the nation had experienced its share of political convulsions, and such statements were scarcely earthshak-ing.

The Starostins were not the only football figures to come back to the capi-tal. Mikhail Iakushin had returned to the helm of Dinamo Moscow. Now free of Beria's threatening interference, he was able to construct a new team that proved to be every bit the equal of his old sides. His brightest star was goalie Lev Iashin, who had been with the club since 1950 but blossomed under Iakushin's tutelage. Iashin went on to become, in the eyes of many, the great-est goaltender of the twentieth century, competing at the highest level until 1970. His immense talents compensated for whatever defensive weaknesses Dinamo might still have exhibited.[69] Iakushin proved that he could play the nationality game as well, inviting the Azeri striker Alekper Mamedov, who joined Vladimir Ilyin and the irrepressible Sal'nikov, with whom Iakushin could never get truly comfortable.[70] In his end-of-season report, Iakushin ad-mitted Sal'nikov was technically gifted and a hard worker, highly cultured but at the same time politically unreliable. "This is seen in his imitation of all foreign culture and disregard for all Soviet culture."[71] In their one season to-gether, the straight-laced Iakushin got only two goals from Sal'nikov. Perhaps if they had sat down with each other and listened to some jazz, things might have gone better, but even without great output from the mighty Salo, Dinamo was now a full contender for the title.

Spartak had emerged from its internal exile, but Dinamo had not gone away. The two great clubs revived their rivalry. Only in 1960, with the triumph of an energetic and innovative Torpedo team, did anyone else break the stran-glehold of the Soviet "Old Firm." Of the eight championships between 1952 and 1959, each team won four. Their equality reflected the delicately balanced equilibrium that had evolved between the supporters and opponents of the Stalin legacy. Before 1956, the complex array of forces on either side of this imprecise divide had engaged in a careful minuet. Even after Khrushchev laid down the gauntlet with his attack on the cult of personality, the campaign to de-Stalinize the USSR was never completed. It has been said, far too often, that sport follows the "golden rule": he who has the gold makes the rules. Had the so-called good Khrushchev and his supporters in society won the day, one could well imagine there would have been further competitive advantages for civilian teams. Following this logic, the sporting representatives of the struc-tures of force would have received less.

Instead, the balance between Dinamo and Spartak expressed the competing and often opposing concerns facing Khrushchev and the new leadership in the world at large. The evolution of the cold war meant that the regime continued to confront enemies foreign and domestic. At the same time, it was necessary to maintain law and order in a swiftly modernizing, increasingly urban society. A strong military and an effective police force were still needed. In the domain of sport, East-West competition led to a greater emphasis on the Olympic Games, where success could be measured in quantities of medals. The sport system that was formed under Stalin during the 1930s adapted easily and successfully to the broad demands imposed on it by the diplomatic and political needs of the state. In sports that lacked a broad domestic following Dinamo athletes proved far more successful than those of Spartak. The vast majority of Soviet Olympians came from the police and army.

The Starostins did not think big-time sport should be about fulfilling medal quotas. Although the Spartak Sport Society did not ignore the so-called minor events with their limited audiences, Nikolai always believed the most entertaining and profitable sport of all was football. The game paid the bills, in large measure because the Red and White was the USSR's most popular soccer team. At the same time, it can hardly be said that Dinamo, the White and Blue, lacked support. With a winning record and compelling stars, Lavrenti's Old Boys also pulled a large following. Fans came to see them for the most normal of reasons. They were good. Sharing the same stadium before 1956, the two teams drew roughly similar crowds, with those of Spartak only slightly larger. While we lack complete attendance information for this period, the numbers of spectators at matches in the early Khrushchev period were only minimally smaller than the chaotic mobs of the immediate postwar years.

By the middle of the 1956 season, the space available to watch football in person increased exponentially with the construction of the 103,000-place Lenin Stadium in Luzhniki Park. In the second half of the decade, this mammoth arena was often filled when Spartak played there. Dinamo played most of its games in what was now its own ground, although each season both matches with Spartak were played at Luzhniki. Additionally, any Dinamo game that showed signs of being a large draw could be shifted to Lenin Stadium. Still, overall attendance for Spartak games was greater than that for Dinamo's. This fact alone proved an important advantage, which allowed Spartak to compete against an organization that continued to receive extensive state support. At the same time, one must be careful not to interpret the greater number of tickets sold to Spartak matches as a simple sign of the team's widely imputed but empirically unproven greater popularity. Ironically, Spartak's access to Luzhniki would come back to haunt it when the overall popularity of soccer declined. At the time, many in the organization urged Nikolai Starostin to follow the British model and construct a football-only stadium for Spartak's exclusive use. Starostin always refused, and to this day Spartak remains a team without its own ground.

After two consecutive titles, the 1954 season proved difficult for Spartak. Netto, Simonian, and Nikolai Dementiev each missed a third of the twenty-four-game season because of injuries. The offensive burden fell to the thirty-

**7.2** Simonian and Netto casually lead Spartak out for warmups. *Fotoagentstvo Sportekspress.*

nine-year-old Dementiev, who managed just seven goals in sixteen games. After the defeat in Tblisi, the two great rivals met on May Day in the traditional opening of the Moscow season. Simonian was sluggish. The team appeared unprepared physically, and the Spartak players quit after going down 2–0, which proved to be the final score. Once more showing its pro-Spartak bias, *Sovetskii sport* headlined its game account "The Fans Are Disappointed," paying much more attention to Spartak's weaknesses than Dinamo's strengths. Sitting in third after a 2–1 loss to a reconstituted TsSKA, Spartak prepared to meet Dinamo Tblisi at home on June 7 for the first time since the tragic events of April. It dominated the visitors, winning 5–0. Spartak then went on a streak that soon put it in first place, but consecutive losses in August to a weak Trudovye Rezervy Leningrad and to its cross-town rivals sent the team down to second, where it finished the season four points behind Dinamo Moscow.[72]

Lev Filatov, Spartak's greatest fan, bemoaned the team's decline. Simonian's play had fallen off, and Sokolov's relations with his players had deteriorated badly. Soon, however, Filatov would have cause to be singing their praises again. As the season came to an end, the team was preparing for a trip into the heart of capitalist football, where it would meet the Belgian leaders Anderlecht and Standard Liege and the powerful English clubs Arsenal and Wolverhampton Wanderers. Before Spartak's departure, Dinamo welcomed Arsenal to Moscow for a return of the famed match in the fog won by Dinamo at the end of its 1945 tour. This time Dinamo easily handled an Arsenal side that was still finding its form and conditioning. Arsenal had arrived with a large press delegation as well as the entire leadership of the Football Association. There was no hiding the 5–0 result, a fact that made Spartak's trip to London all the more important.[73]

Before that confrontation, there was the trip to Belgium. Upon their arrival in Brussels, the Spartak coaches eschewed a walking tour of museums, fearing the old trick of tiring out the opponent, long favored by the Soviets. Instead, the team's leaders accepted an invitation to a variety show that, to the great dismay of the players' minders and the greater delight of the players, featured strippers. The team was reluctantly ushered out of the theater by the head of the delegation. Their testosterone levels no doubt raised by the previous evening's spectacle, the Spartak players went out and delivered a 7–0 mauling to Anderlecht, one of Europe's stronger sides. The beleaguered Simonian, once again healthy, had a hat trick. Four nights later, with Arsenal's manager, Tommy Whitaker, in attendance, Standard Liege was dispatched 5–2. Simonian had another hat trick. His last goal came with assists from Netto and the guesting Bashashkin.[74]

Then it was on to London for the hugely anticipated matchup with Arsenal, a clash that was heightened by rising cold war tensions. The contrast with the harmony and goodwill of Dinamo's 1945 tour could not have been more stark. Arsenal player Arthur Shaw, who did not play in the game, later said, "The game generated a huge amount of excitement. . . . I don't remember anything quite like it. . . . It was more than just a football game, there was a lot of political prestige attached to it. You couldn't get a ticket for love or money." Sixty-six thousand fans crammed into every corner of Arsenal's tiny North London stadium.[75] To even the advantage of the home field, Arsenal had agreed to let Nikolai Latyshev work the game. He'd also worked the famous 1945 Dinamo match with Arsenal amid much controversy, which he would not escape this day either.

Arsenal attacked from the first minute with three quick shots on goal. The Gunners coaching staff, which had been in Brussels, had identified the great threat of Simonian, who was closely marked. Arsenal went up in the thirty-sixth minute on a goal from Jimmy Logie. Spartak began to counterattack, winning seven corners before halftime. With two minutes before the intermission, Tatushin shot from distance, and Paramonov, playing in midfield, put in the rebound. In the second half, Simonian, Tatushin, and Paramonov began to link up on the right side, with Simonian scoring on a header in the seventieth. Spartak then held on for an intense twenty minutes. Just before the final whistle, Logie appeared to have scored again, but Latyshev ruled him offside.

**7.3** Spartak in London to play Arsenal, 1954. *Spartak Moskva: Offitsial'naia istoriia.*

This produced a tirade from Logie. Proving that Soviet team officials did not have a monopoly on stupidity, Logie was dismissed from Arsenal's playing staff for ungentlemanly conduct and never appeared for them again. A 2–2 tie would have been a creditable result, but according to Arsenal team historian Dan Brennan, "the general consensus . . . was that the better team had won."[76]

A full week later, Spartak took on Wolverhampton, champions of the previous season and at the time a much stronger side than Arsenal. Wolves dismantled Spartak 4–0. Excuses were made that the Spartak players had spent all their energies, mental and physical, in London. Their own lack of knowledge of the English game had led them to concentrate on the team with the greater historical reputation, Arsenal, whereas Wolves were then the better side. Despite the drubbing, Netto had caught the eye of English observers. Later, others in Europe were similarly impressed, prompting quickly rebuffed inquiries about purchasing Spartak's captain. In total, Spartak had played fourteen international matches in 1954, acquitting itself well.[77]

As the teams' annual reports reveal, Dinamo and Spartak had been close in other ways during the just-concluded season. Dinamo ranks included five party members (led by Beskov) and eight Komsomol members. The numbers for Spartak were four in the party, two candidate members (including Simonian), and eight in the Komsomol. The educational level of the players on the two teams was also roughly the same, Dinamo averaging 9.1 years of schooling, Spartak 8.9. If there were no overt political or educational distinctions, nationality, predictably, was a different matter. There were seven non-

Russians (including the Estonian Netto listed as Russian) on Spartak's roster. Of Dinamo's thirty-one men, all were Russian except for two Ukrainians, an Azeri, and one Jew. There were also differences in the ongoing practice of ideological-political education. Dinamo took the process seriously. Team excursions included visits to the police museum. By contrast, the Spartak *politruk* never got past the first four chapters of the *Short Course* history of the party. Even more ridiculous, according to Paramonov, the players read the same four chapters every year. Their excursions differed from those of Dinamo as well. Spartak players took repeated trips to Moscow's leading theaters in the company of their families. Showing a more friendly and less militarized team atmosphere, Spartak coaches visited the players and families in their homes, following Dangulov's practice.[78]

It is entirely possible that Dangulov made all the home visits. Sokolov's continuing boorish behavior showed none of the effects of Russian hospitality and home cooking. He was finally dismissed as head coach after the 1954 season and required to take a course on interpersonal relations at the Institute of Physical Culture. The training may have helped. Sokolov continued to coach elsewhere until 1970. He ended his career leading the national team of Chad but was never again part of the Spartak organization. Dangulov left to coach Spartak Erevan for two years before retiring from the game. Nikolai Starostin, again involved with the team, got to pick the new coach. The great patriarch named Nikolai Gulyaev (1915–2000), a Spartak veteran from 1936 to 1946 who had learned the coaching trade leading Zenit Kaliningrad for five seasons.[79]

Starostin's attempt to pry Sergei Sal'nikov away from Dinamo and return Salo to his rightful home proved his most daunting organizational task. Although there is no documentary record of this second struggle over Sal'nikov, several secondary accounts suggest Dinamo fought the transfer with great intensity. Ultimately Spartak prevailed, something that would never have happened under Stalin. In return, Sal'nikov had to forfeit his "Honored Master of Sport" title and the perks that went with it. He was also not permitted to play for Spartak until mid-May.[80] Back in the more supportive and relaxed atmosphere of Spartak, the fun-loving Sal'nikov appeared in nineteen league games, scoring twelve goals, output that was sorely needed given Simonian's absence from injury for much of the season.[81] Spartak did manage to contest the title more closely in 1955, finishing in second—a single point behind Dinamo.

As in 1954, the international calendar proved the highlight of the season. Two of the great teams of capitalist football came to Moscow during the summer. The mighty Italian power AC Milan visited in early July, while Wolves showed up for a return match on August seventh. Soviet authorities were always very shrewd in scheduling such meetings, which they took very seriously. In 2007 Simonian told Russian television these matches were

friendlies, but at that time they were evaluated and measured as if today they were matches of the Champions' League or the UEFA Cup. Interest was huge.

> The prestige attached to these appearances and their results were intensely evaluated. Both Soviet players and our opponents approached these games with great responsibility.[82]

In midsummer, squads from the West were still in preseason training and lacked conditioning and cohesion. Soviet teams, whose seasons began in March and ended in November, were in midseason form. Games in late fall had similar if less marked advantages. The Football Federation never scheduled such confrontations in the spring, when Soviet clubs were just starting their seasons and Western clubs were finding their peak form. When Soviet clubs later began to take part in the various European cup competitions, they did well in the fall stages of what were then knockout tournaments, but very few made it past the spring renewal of such competitions. World and European championships, which took place in late spring and early summer, posed similar problems for the Soviet national team.

When Milan came to Moscow, it fell 3–0 to Spartak, with forward Nikolai Parshin (b. 1929) scoring a hat trick before a crowd of sixty thousand. The result proved a big surprise in Europe, allowing the victors to believe they were among Europe's elite teams. The Italians' coach offered to purchase Netto and Sal'nikov for what would have been record sums.[83] A month later, Spartak took its revenge on Wolverhampton, also by a 3–0 score. The next day Nikolai Starostin reported in *Sovetskii sport* that Spartak had planned to impose its style on Wolves, playing speedily while keeping the ball on the ground and using the flanks. As Wolverhampton's manager, Joe Gardner, noted, his team lacked the conditioning to keep pace with Spartak. Wolves had just begun their training, a fact duly noted by Filatov in his match account. Spartak's guests, he noted, were capable of playing better than they did that day.[84]

The highlight of Soviet international play came later that month when the national team took on the recently crowned world champions from West Germany. The Soviet *sbornaia* had been resurrected in 1954 under the leadership of the well-respected Gavril Kachalin.[85] A conscious decision was made to build the side around one club—in this case the two-time champion Spartak, which contributed eleven squad members, of whom six to eight usually played. At the time, German POWs were still in the USSR, and the two nations did not have diplomatic relations. The Soviets' East German allies, correctly fearing that the match was a prelude to the restoration of contacts with West Germany, protested the plan.[86] The initiative had come from the Soviet side. In May 1955, representatives of Spartak had presented an invitation to the German embassy in Paris, which transmitted the request to the German Football Federation. At much the same time the German chancellor, Konrad Adenauer, was invited to Moscow. He accepted on July 11.

A sizable delegation of West German fans, bearing hard currency, attended the match. Hundreds of thousands of ticket requests flooded into the Dinamo Stadium box office.[87] Eight Spartak members—Ogonkov, Maslenkin, Netto, Tatushin, Isaev, Parshin, Sal'nikov, and Ilyin—were named to the starting

**7.4** Sal'nikov heads one against West Germany in 1955. Fotoagentstvo Sportekspress.

side. Iashin was in goal. Spartak's representatives comprised the entire front line. Gulyaev was named to the coaching staff.[88] The Germans had been the surprise winners of the 1954 World Cup. They had defeated the Mighty Magyars of Hungary in the rain-soaked miracle final at Bern when Hungary's great star, Ferenc Puskas, played with a severe ankle injury. The Germans had not done particularly well in subsequent friendlies. Their longtime coach, Sepp Herberger, was rebuilding the team and chose only a few of the heroes of Bern to play in Moscow.[89]

The Germans were up 2–1 well into the second half, when the Soviets began a storm that yielded two goals within four minutes. Maslenkin equalized in the sixty-ninth minute, and Ilyin, not for the last time, tallied the winner in the seventy-third. Parshin had put in the first Soviet goal. All three scorers were from Spartak. Herberger later remarked on the Soviets' speed and intimidating endurance, the result of a strong emphasis on conditioning. While this match has retained an important place in the history of the Soviet game, German accounts, not surprisingly, devote little attention to what was only a preseason friendly.[90] Indeed, one could well argue that a 1–1 draw a month later in Budapest against Hungary, with a healthy Puskas, was an even more impressive result. Perhaps more important, the Germans had been welcomed in lavish style, and their players and coaches had behaved respectfully and correctly. The German press drew the connection between sport and politics, referring to the team as "Adenauer's icebreakers."[91]

There could be no doubt that despite the blemish of their second place in the league, Spartak had done well. Vladimir Moshkarkin (1914–1994), head of the national team administration, praised Spartak lavishly in an end-of-season wrap-up. He singled out Paramonov, Netto, Tatushin, and Sal'nikov for special mention and lauded Ogonkov for retraining as a central defender, filling the gap left by the departed Bashashkin. Filatov was more measured in his assessment. It was good, he noted, that the team had become even more offensive-minded over the course of the season. He, too, singled out Netto's multiple talents but criticized Ilyin and Tatushin for not developing their games beyond a few specialized skills. The attacking approach left them open for counterattacks that exposed their defensive line and goalie, two continuing weak spots. Finally, Filatov chided Starostin, who, in his first season back at the helm, had not required Ilyin and Tatushin to expand their games. As things turned out, Filatov need not have worried. Starostin and Gulyaev were already at work on improvements that would soon bring Spartak greater glory.[92]

### For the Nation, for Spartak: The Great Year 1956

Between Stalin's death and the end of 1955, Nikita Khrushchev had been busy consolidating his power and eliminating his enemies. Virtually half of the provincial party secretaries were dismissed during this period. Khrushchev's chief rival, Malenkov, was replaced as prime minister in February 1955.[93] That Khrushchev accomplished all this without killing millions may have been his greatest gift to the party and the nation, but further progress proved to be a problem. The notion of de-Stalinization as a social-political process with an elaborated program had not yet been formed, and thousands of arch-Stalinists remained in place. Indeed, overt criticism of Stalin had been muted in public discourse before 1956 for fear of upsetting the population. Khrushchev, however, sensed changes in society that had gone well beyond the specifics of the crimes he would soon ascribe to Stalin. Millions of returnees, many of them criminal, disordered daily life, and thousands, perhaps millions, of citizens lost their fear of speaking out. The system inherited from the past, a system already in crisis, was in now danger of losing its legitimacy.

It cannot be said that the attack on Stalin in Khrushchev's Secret Speech to the Twentieth Party Congress in February 1956 went to the heart of the problem. Ascribing the tragedies of the previous twenty-five years to the historical accident of the leader's cult of personality was decidedly non-Marxist, and the failure to probe beyond the issue of Stalin's management style explains the weaknesses and uncertainties of the de-Stalinization process thereafter. "The criticism always stopped at the threshold of intrasystematic analysis. Therein lies the key to the enigmatic instability, to the fits and starts of the whole history of the struggle against the cult of personality."[94] Nevertheless, the immediate reaction to the speech was intense and helped the previously fearful talk openly not only to the authorities but to each other.

If the content of Khrushchev's message was potentially destabilizing, the method of its delivery was equally problematic. The text of the speech had been delivered to party cells around the nation for subsequent discussion. Fearing they would disillusion some while encouraging others, the new leadership sought to limit the speech's impact, but word soon spread far and wide inside and outside the nation's borders. As word spread, a global discussion began about the future of the Soviet project, a discussion that went well past the cult of personality. Foreigners now knew more of what was happening inside the USSR. At the same time, more and more Soviet citizens were traveling abroad, listening to foreign broadcasts, and receiving smuggled books and records. Futbolisty were among the most visible of the postwar tourists, particularly those of Spartak, who traveled far and wide between 1953 and 1956. Although the low educational level of most players did not make them well suited to assimilating the political lessons of contact with the West such comparatively cultured individuals as Netto, Simonian, and Sal'nikov, not to mention the Starostins, cannot have been immune to what they saw on their journeys. It is likely they shared their impressions with their actor, writer, and musician friends, who, if not oppositional figures, were surely touched in various ways by the Thaw. We do not know if someone like Sal'nikov brought back jazz records for Leonid Utesov or if Nikolai brought back more dresses for his wife, but it would not be surprising to learn that they did.

Obtaining the forbidden fruit of Western goods posed another danger for the regime. From the earliest days of Soviet sports travel, athletes had speculated in goods and currency. In order to realize profits from the great privilege of foreign travel, they were forced on their return to deal with the second economy, the black or gray markets, to dispose of their purchases. Spartak players and those who traveled with them were no better or worse than any others.[95] The party-state, in pursuit of the cold war aim of winning friends throughout the world, needed athletes to journey far and wide. To be sure, their activities were less directly threatening than the words of the many intellectuals and students who had been emboldened by Khrushchev's attack on Stalin. Nevertheless, the players' exposure to the outside world and their misdeeds while in it were unsettling to a state that wished to control their behavior.

Over the course of 1956, the serial publication in *Novy Mir* of Vladimir Dudintsev's novel *Not by Bread Alone* proved to be a politically powerful cultural event that further spurred the outpouring of public opinion. Thinking people who had been awakened by the Secret Speech now used the furor created by Dudintsev's work to raise all manner of other questions about Soviet life. The theme of the novel, opposition by entrenched bureaucrats to an innovative engineer, resonated with those professionals and other educated citizens for whom the value of individualism and the concerns of private life moved to center stage in the spirit of the Thaw. Public meetings were held in institutions all over the USSR to discuss the implications of Dudintsev's work. In scenes that evoked the postwar excitement of match day at Dinamo Stadium, people lined up for hours and squeezed into the sites of these gatherings, sometimes listening through open windows while standing in the streets. In the process of these literary discussions, other fundamental questions were inevitably raised.[96] The party's iconoclasm had unleashed popular anger and raised troubling questions. The public's activity came in the form of spontaneous outpourings from below, little of which was either overtly anti-Soviet or procapitalist. Much of the effort was instead made in the hope of reviving what many thought to be the Leninist project. Khrushchev put it in much the same way, but now society was shedding the passivity long ascribed to it by foreign experts on the USSR.

Khrushchev's actions removed much of the people's fear of reprisal. If the Thaw had been a trickle before 1956, it now became (to squeeze the metaphor a bit) the onrushing torrent of a melting glacier sweeping across the borders of the USSR into Eastern Europe. Soon the expectations of a looser grip inside the Soviet Union led to unrest in Poland and later Hungary. The international events of the summer and fall threatened Khrushchev's "liberal" Communism and emboldened those of his internal enemies who wished a return to the harsher methods of the not-so-old days.[97]

Before things came to a head in Eastern Europe, large numbers of Soviet students had engaged in the kinds of antisocial acts previously perpetrated only by marginal young rebels. What had been done without a cause now became politicized, although not in a traditional sense. Hooliganism in parks, youth clubs, and movie theaters suggested to the authorities that things were spinning out of control.[98] They also feared that those adults who had been given apartments would now retreat into private life, individualism, and selfishness. In this context, the young and famous athlete who had just been rewarded with his own personal dwelling became a tricky figure for those charged with using sport for didactic purposes.

Spartak's leadership found itself in a difficult position. Through the largesse of the party, the team had been given scores of apartments. In return, Starostin continued to make a thousand tickets available to Mossovet for important games. By giving outstanding players their own domiciles, Spartak and to a lesser extent other Moscow clubs turned out to be encouraging individualistic attitudes and acts that undermined the authority of both the party and the club's leadership. To be sure, these hastily erected Khrushchev-era apartment buildings were less than palatial, but they had their own kitchens and bathrooms, not to mention doors with locks.[99] Despite this, these apartments were not simply private spaces. They had been provided by the state, which also produced the furniture that went into them. Additionally, there were rules concerning how apartments could be decorated and committees that enforced those rules. Given the still-constrained consumer options during the fifties, choices were limited. Those who could travel abroad were often able to acquire more stylish Western items, and these exceptions were largely tolerated. Footballers had advantages in obtaining such foreign goods. Nevertheless, I have not come across a case of an athlete's being disciplined for violating the regulations on decoration or getting evicted from his apartment for bad behavior (which is not to say bad behavior did not occur).[100]

The other great oasis of privacy available to a limited number of Soviet citizens was the personal automobile.[101] This privilege of athletic success came later than did the apartment, but the car became another important element in the recruiting and retention of star athletes. Like apartments, autos were nearly always given through state agencies, which also provided facilities for fueling them and, to a much lesser extent, repairing them. In the case of Spartak, Aleksandr Starostin had spent some time administering a car factory and had been helpful with providing vehicles for the club's players, but Spartak's advantages in the allocation of housing were not as clear in the case of automobiles.

Players on all teams had always been big celebrities, but until the housing boom, the majority of them still lived in kommunalki.[102] With the continuing growth of spectator sport and the associated larger media coverage (including television), successful athletes became more visible as they acquired greater privacy. Fame and a high moral level did not always go hand in hand, however. Young and largely uncultured, many soccer players became arrogant and antisocial, convinced that their gifts entitled them to all manner of privileges. Instances of bad behavior were numerous and could occur in restaurants, taxis, planes, and locker rooms and on the playing field. Netto and Sal'nikov, two men hardly devoid of culture but possessed of big personalities, came in for severe criticism along these lines. As already noted, Netto had been drunk on a plane during the 1950 tour of Norway. Sal'nikov often behaved boorishly on the field. So, for that matter, did Netto, the team captain. In Netto's case, we have no way of knowing whether any of his actions were motivated by his brother's legal situation or simply by his generally prickly personality. Did Sal'nikov, now back with Spartak, still bear a grudge after having been forced to join Dinamo? At a meeting of the All-Union Council of Coaches late in 1956, Netto was taken to task for his boorish behavior toward referees and opponents during the matches against West Germany and Hungary. Nikolai Starostin was chided for paying insufficient attention to the "personal" actions of his stars.[103] As far as the sporting bureaucracy was concerned, the actions of the players, especially on the international stage, did indeed have political consequences.

Some worried officials may even have feared the players were reading *Not by Bread Alone* instead of the *Short Course* during their political education classes. This is, of course, an exaggeration, but a British Communist, who lived in Moscow for many years in the latter part of the Thaw and was a member of the Spartak Sport Society, suggests that even footballers were affected by the changing society of which they were so visible a part. These reactions did not always take the form of traditional political activity. On their own, the vast majority of players were largely apolitical, but the spirit of the times had an impact on the authority of coaches and on the ability of the sporting societies to micromanage their athletes' lives and careers. If Dinamo men were spending time in police museums, what about Spartak players who were hanging out with theater people—Andrei Starostin's Moscow bohemians? If

the lads were friends with actors, surely they must have become close with ac-
tresses as well. Did the players, as Simonian had said earlier, "make use of the
possibilities of the situation"? Andrei Starostin's wife, Olga, was in the theater,
as was his best friend. We can safely say that Spartak's internal atmosphere,
fostered by the Starostins, fit the looser, less militarized zeitgeist of the fifties.
The same foreign observer noted:

> Dinamo was very disciplined. If you liked to drink, you didn't go and play for
> Dinamo. The army team was the same, but Spartak was the team . . . you could
> have a good drink afterwards, have a smoke (most of them smoked). The foot-
> ball of Dinamo and TsSKA tended to be rather stereotyped, very boring to
> watch. . . . [By contrast] Spartak did allow for individual flair.[104]

Nikolai Starostin noted much the same thing before an All-Union congress of
coaches and team officials.[105]

In 1990, the lawyer Boris Nazarov sounded the same note in discussing
Spartak's performance on the playing field: "I like how they play. They play
for your pleasure. . . . Their style remains the same [as in the fifties]—improvisation, working the ball around, the beautiful and the unexpected."[106]
Claims that the Red and White was more romantic, improvisational, and
pleasurable to watch may well have reflected the influence of Spartak ideology. Still, these post hoc statements illustrate the indirect impact of the Thaw
on the football world. If a team that practiced relaxed training, creative play,
and respectful treatment of its players could be a consistent winner, the harsh
discipline and invasions of privacy that had characterized high Stalinism
were no longer required for sporting success or even production triumphs in
the new era.[107] At the same time, the success of more humane methods in
the soccer world demonstrated to both state and society the possibilities for
liberalization in other spheres. Spartak simultaneously expressed and constituted the contested values of the post-Stalin period. Here it is best to understand this not entirely direct relationship between soccer and the cultural
trends of the Thaw as a dialogical one with neither discourse determining the
other. To paraphrase Bourdieu, the bodies of Spartak players expressed what
their minds (and the minds of their supporters) could not.[108] The fans knew
what was happening in the world of football without having to utter, much
less write down, a single word.

Around the end of the 1956 football season, however, Khrushchev and his
allies reimposed a measure of control on expression. The heady days of the
winter and spring were now tempered by the limitations of a de-Stalinization
process carried out by former Stalinists who could revert to type when they
feared being soft on capitalism. Herein lay the limits of the reform process.
The state might listen, but it did not always obey. As Lewin has written, "The
inability of the regime to accept society's increasing political differentiation,
its fear and denial of independent opinions (a basic right in a modern, civilized society) demonstrates the inferiority of the system, which had found

**7.5** The young Eduard Strel'tsov. A. Vartanian, *Eduard Strel'tsov, nasil'nik ili zhertva.*

ways of tolerating more than one opinion but generally of a rather conservative nature."[109]

As that process of reform unfolded in the years between the Secret Speech and Khrushchev's ouster, Spartak strangely came to play the role of a canary in the coal mine. To be sure, the ebb and flow of the Thaw and the inconsistent success of Spartak did not track perfectly with each other. Nor are there contemporary written sources available for ascribing deeper significance to such trends. Nevertheless, the excitement of 1956 did flow over onto the pitch. As Vartanian has noted, greater openness to the West meant not only more jazz and rock music, not only more candid literature and better films, but also more games against strong Western opponents.[110] For the club's supporters, success on the field fueled their optimism about life in general. "You have to remember football and its style was a reflection of the political, economic, social situation in the country. The camps were opening in about 1956 and people were coming back. There was a lot of controversy. There was a wonderful sense of excitement."[111]

After finishing a close second in 1955 and experiencing success on the international stage, the Starostins and Gulyaev approached the new season with optimism. They brought in only one new player, left wing Ivan Mozer (b. 1933), from Spartak Minsk. Their primary aim was to get off to a good start (after having lost the title at the beginning for the previous two years) and avoid injury. Simonian and Netto had been the leading absentees the year before, but fortune now smiled on Spartak. Its stars and role players all stayed healthy. Gulyaev used only fourteen field players the entire season.[112] The result would be another championship amid a flood of goals. Four consecutive victories and an away tie with Dinamo Kiev provided the beginning that established the necessary cushion over Dinamo Moscow, Spartak's nearest pursuers. The streak came to an end, however, against a dynamic young Torpedo team led by the forwards Valentin Ivanov and Eduard Strel'tsov, a phenom who had featured in Torpedo's starting side the previous season when he was seventeen. Applying pressure throughout the field and never letting its opponents get their short passing game going, Torpedo won 2–0 before sixty thousand spectators at Dinamo Stadium.[113] Spartak, however, would lose only two more games the entire season. Both revivals of the rivalry against Dinamo ended in 1–1 draws. The season was marked by an offensive explosion of sixty-eight goals in twenty-two games. Simonian led the team with sixteen. Isaev scored fourteen times, while the newcomer Ivan Mozer, who shared the left-wing position with Ilyin, had eleven goals in just fifteen matches.[114]

Spartak claimed the title in the next-to-last game of the season with a 4–3 victory over Dinamo Kiev. Ilyin, Sal'nikov, Simonian, and Isaev scored. Writing in *Sovetskii sport*, the retired Dinamo great Konstantin Beskov saluted his old rivals: "It is no accident there are so many spectators at your games. Your play gives them much pleasure."[115] One hundred thousand showed up a week later to celebrate the championship with a 3–0 victory over TsDSA. Such enormous gates were possible because Lenin Stadium had opened up in the very same tumultuous year. It became the site of most subsequent Spartak home games. The sheer size of the crowds, indicating the number of tickets that could be sold, produced the kind of revenue that allowed Spartak to compete at the highest level.

The suppression of the Hungarian revolution was taking place as the soccer season was ending, but these events appear to have had no impact on Spartak's continuing role as the base of the Soviet national team, which went to Melbourne for the 1956 Olympic Games. It was understood that Olympic codes of amateurism meant this was a second-tier tournament, dominated by the phony amateurs of the Communist bloc, but memories of the embarrassment of 1952 meant the regime attached great importance to victory. Eleven Spartak men traveled to Australia. Eight played in the final, in which revenge was taken out on a Yugoslav team that was no longer a hated opponent now that peace had been made with Tito.[116] The great Hungarian team, which had defeated the USSR in Budapest on September 23 and could have contended for the gold, imploded after the crushing of the uprising and did not take part.[117]

**7.6** *Left to right:* Strel'tsov, Simonian, Bashashkin, and Netto greet fans on their return to Moscow after winning the gold medal at the 1956 Olympic Games. Fotoagentstvo Sport-ekspress.

After getting by the United German team and Indonesia in the preliminary round, the Soviets held on against Bulgaria for a 2–1 overtime semifinal victory on a goal by Boris Tatushin. Iashin had starred in goal, and old Spartak teammate Bashashkin featured in all these earlier matches along with Strel'tsov, who took over Simonian's center forward position. In the final, however, Kachalin favored experience over youth, and Strel'tsov sat. On a rainy afternoon on the last day of the games, Boris Tatushin sent in a cross from the right flank in the forty-eighth minute. Anatoly Isaev knew the ball would be headed toward Tatushin's favored destination, the near post. Isaev beat the Yugoslav keeper to the ball and headed it on a high arc toward the center of the goal. It appeared Isaev's shot would open the scoring, but flying in from the left wing, Anatoly Ilyin poached the goal by heading into an open net. It would not be the last such dramatic goal of Ilyin's career, and he dined out on the story for the rest of his life, causing no small amount of resentment from Isaev. An examination of the footage, however, does not support Isaev's claim that the goal should have been his. The Yugoslav goalie did not leave the goal mouth entirely empty, and Ilyin's effort was well justified.[118] Regardless of hurt feelings, the winning move had been made by three Spartak men.[119] Simonian's emotions were different. He had played only in the final while Strel'tsov had been in the lineup in every other match of the tournament, scoring two goals. According to what was then Olympic procedure, only those who played in the final could get a gold medal. Simonian repeatedly attempted to convince Strel'tsov to take his medal, but Strel'tsov refused, believing he would have other chances for international glory.

Back in Moscow, the Starostins raised a friendly toast to the champions. Their political rehabilitation was now matched by their rehabilitation in sport. The team they had founded and built, whose success had sent them to the camps, had now reflected great glory on the Soviet motherland. To be sure, the Olympic tournament was not the height of international soccer success, but the triumph did represent national footballing redemption after the disappointment of Helsinki. The winter and summer games of 1956 marked the beginning of the USSR's domination of what became a surrogate for the cold war. Olympic sport would turn out to be one of the few areas of life (along with ballet and space travel) in which the USSR could claim superiority over its capitalist rivals. While the Spartak Sport Society may not have not been a leader in producing medal winners for the sports machine, it had delivered in the one event that mattered most to the Starostins and their fellow male citizens. It made for a classic Soviet-style happy ending. Soon the former camp inmates would be guests at great Kremlin receptions, meeting with fellow celebrities, dining on fine food, and raising glasses to the champions as Khrushchev boasted of victory. The next year, Netto was given the Order of Lenin and Simonian the Order of the Red Banner, while Gulyaev and Ilyin each received the Badge of Honor.[120] Life for Spartak had definitely improved.

# 8

# Good-bye, Golden Age, 1957–1964

By the end of 1956, a still-divided party leadership began to understand the limits of its willingness to entertain the demands and dangers of the reform process. Articulate complaints from intellectuals and students, occasionally violent worker unrest, and trouble in Eastern Europe were all threatening the ultimate stability of the system. Such arch-Stalinists as Vyacheslav Molotov and Lazar Kaganovich were still in positions to undermine Khrushchev's political power. Old rival Georgii Malenkov, while no longer prime minister, remained in the party. As a result of Khrushchev's decentralizing policies, thousands of functionaries had already been required to leave the comforts of the capital to serve in the new local economic councils or in ministries that had been relocated near the activities they controlled. By these reforms alone, Khrushchev had stepped on thousands of sensitive toes, and the people attached to those toes included several at the highest levels of power.

Disturbed by the pace and consequences of de-Stalinization, Kaganovich, Molotov, Malenkov, and his successor, Nikolai Bulganin, moved to oust Khrushchev in June 1957. Against the odds, Khrushchev, with the crucial assistance of the great war hero Marshal Georgii Zhukov, was able to mobilize support in the larger Central Committee, which ultimately overruled the Presidium (formerly the Politbiuro) after prolonged debate. By October, Zhukov, who posed his own political threat to Khrushchev, was also removed. Having defeated what he called the "Antiparty Group," Khrushchev was thereafter able to rule as the unopposed head of both the party and the state, creating in the process his own, less fearsome cult of personality. Crucially, his victory did not involve arresting or executing the losers in the power struggle. They were instead demoted to lesser but not entirely inconsequential posts far from the capital. When Khrushchev was later removed from the political scene, many of them returned to Moscow to live out their lives in comfortable irrelevance.

With the archconservatives eliminated, the political dynamic changed for those people who wished to see the moral and economic qualities of their lives improve. Now, instead of operating in a sea of shifting alliances, all the contending elements were, in one way or another, fighting for Khrushchev's ear. Unfortunately, that ear, and the brain attached to it, proved to be a moving target. The mercurial, newly powerful leader was divided in his own mind about how to balance the often-conflicting goals of progress and order. Poorly conceived experiments would later turn out to be quick fixes with disastrous long-term consequences. The Virgin Lands campaign, which had been launched with such fanfare and had achieved quick success, was a case in point. The same could be said for the creation of the councils of local economy and other plans to decentralize the economy.

The further course of reform posed difficult conflicts. Improving the workers' standard of living often clashed with larger state requirements, especially those of national defense, which continued to suck resources from the long-suffering consumer sector. Modernization may have fanned the hope of catching up with the West, but the dislocations created by the urbanization it engendered undermined law and order, requiring the continued maintenance of a large repressive apparatus. On the cultural front, the uneducated Khrushchev craved the respect of the intelligentsia, but he often reacted crudely in dealing with the consequences of the Thaw. His refusal to let the great poet Boris Pasternak journey to Sweden in 1958 to claim his Nobel Prize alienated intellectuals and artists of all political stripes. Four years later, his profane reaction to the display of modern art at the Moscow Manege Show provoked the same response among artists and their many patrons. While different in their behavior and outlook from creative intellectuals, professional people, who had become more numerous and capable under the impact of economic progress, came to resent meddling in the fields for which they had been required to spend years educating themselves. Khrushchev's utter unpredictability and inconsistency undermined the limited sense of security they had been able to build for themselves.

Simply put, Khrushchev's accrual of political power did not remove all obstacles to de-Stalinization. Rather, it rearranged them. From the outset, the process had been limited by the fact that it was carried out by former Stalinists who could revert to type when they feared being branded soft on capitalism. Indeed, one of those obstacles was Khrushchev himself. Neither the Secret Speech nor the removal of the Antiparty Group resolved the uncertainties and contradictions of the reform process. Trained in Stalinist methods of using power, Khrushchev was not always comfortable with the consequences of his own populism. Nevertheless, in the aftermath of consolidating power, Khrushchev had a run of success. The first artificial satellite, Sputnik, was launched in October 1957. The 1958 harvest was good. The economy grew, and Soviet international prestige was high. Yet this did not mean the fundamental contradictions of modernization had been solved, and by 1960 things began to unravel. Economic growth, which had been extremely high, began to slow down. The agricultural sector, in which so much thought and capital had been invested, failed to feed the nation. Eventually even grain had to be imported. With shortages came higher prices that were not met by equivalent raises in wages, leading to labor unrest. In May 1962 workers protesting price rises at the north Caucasus town of Novocherkassk occupied large parts of the city and were fired on by police and soldiers; more than twenty were killed. In foreign policy, the self-inflicted Cuban Missile Crisis eroded trust in the Soviet government both internationally and domestically. By 1963, the system seemed to have come off the rails, and Khrushchev's frantic attempts to fix matters served only to unsettle his colleagues and the public.

These contradictions and ambiguities altered the power relations in the world of professional football. By the late fifties and early sixties soccer had become considerably larger. Bigger venues had been constructed in the capitals, and scores of provincial cities got sizable arenas as well. Media coverage became more intense. *Sovetskii sport* became a daily, and beginning in 1960 a weekly supplement, *Futbol,* was devoted to the sport. Televisions were becoming broadly available, and games were a part of the viewing diet, increasing the visibility and celebrity of those connected with the sport. Initially, only matches from the capital were shown, and in the process the Moscow teams developed new national, as opposed to local, followings. There were now more teams, more players, and more fans, and the game had become much more various in all of its aspects. By the beginning of the sixties new elements had risen to challenge the dominance of the Dinamo-Spartak "Old Firm."

The changes in soccer were part of a larger shift in the cultural values of Soviet sport itself. As athletes came to participate more visibly in the diplomatic processes that were part of the cold war, sportsmen and sportswomen had to be more than heroic role models for passive citizens. Even if the players themselves were not well educated, many of their new followers were. Under the impact of the Thaw, the new sports stars were asked not only to sign on to the causes of the state but also to reveal through interviews and autobiographies the inner spiritual qualities that had made their success possible.

In the summer of 1957, the young men who played for Spartak and the young men (and women) who watched them were touched by one more popular culture event that harked back to the heady days of the previous summer. Although the cultural atmosphere had tightened in the wake of the Hungarian revolt, the authorities decided to go ahead with plans to hold a World Youth Festival in Moscow. Whatever the rationale, the leadership appears to have poorly understood the impact of thousands of foreigners, even if they were Communists and fellow travelers, crawling the streets and corridors of Moscow with their strong passions for jazz, rock, and the sex and fun that so often went with them. They were literally dancing in the capital's streets, and as Bourdieu has shown, through dance, along with sex and sport, the body can express what the mind cannot.[1] If any more concrete proof were needed that a good time was had by many, nine months later a flood of multihued babies were born in Moscow. The festival's impact on Soviet youth, already troubled and uncertain about their own lives, lasted for years, fanning the antisocial attitudes and subcultures of the most alienated segments of the young. All sorts of alien musical forms, especially those that impelled the body to move, flooded in through the cracks in the borders.[2]

We have no way of knowing if the young men who played for Spartak fathered any children in their tours abroad, but we do know that jazz and later rock had piqued the interest of many team members.[3] Not all of them were culturally equipped to comprehend everything they saw (and purchased) on their many foreign trips, but there can be no doubt that men like Sal'nikov, Simonian, and Netto had a strong interest in the outside world. This did not make them supporters of a capitalist way of life or even overtly anti-Soviet, but surely it made them less accepting of official views on all manner of questions. All three had suffered from the inhumanities of arbitrary authority before 1953; none of them wanted to go back to the bad old days. With the new Soviet openness, their lives and those of their colleagues had changed immensely for the better.

## Further Chapters of the Moscow Derby

After the victory at Melbourne, the eleven Spartak Olympians spent nineteen very jolly days on a steamer back to Vladivostok with the rest of the Soviet team. The entire group then began a train journey across Siberia to the capital during which large crowds met them at important stops. The entire party got back to Moscow only in early January 1957, just in time for the start of winter training. Within a month ten Spartak team members were called to the national team as it began work for the USSR's first ever World Cup qualifiers. The men returned to their home club just before the start of the league season in April.

A long summer break in the league schedule to accommodate the qualifying matches meant that no stars were actually forced to miss games, but, with such a large contingent on the national team, Spartak suffered considerably. Its bench remained thin, and fatigue proved a problem. In 1957 it finished third behind the champion, Dinamo Moscow. Simonian managed to appear in eighteen out of twenty-two matches, scoring just twelve goals. Ogon'kov and Tatushin made large contributions, as did Netto, Sal'nikov, and Maslenkin. Most important, Spartak stabilized its situation at goalie. The Lithuanian Vlados Tuckus (1932–1988) had grown too fond of Russian vodka and had repeatedly broken training. The giant Valentin Ivakin (b. 1930), who had been riding the bench at TsSKA, was permitted by the sports committee to transfer to Spartak, settling into the position roughly halfway through the season.[4]

Preparation for the 1958 season began far from the usual southern resort towns of Sochi and Sukhumi. The team trained instead in Indonesia, while Netto, Ogon'kov, and Simonian worked with the national team in China, reuniting only on the eve of the season, which, in order to accommodate the

World Cup, began in late March. Despite ninety-degree days and torrential rainstorms, the change seemed to work wonders, and 1958 witnessed Spartak's return to the top. By the time of the break in May and June, it was undefeated and in first place, but the hiatus brought the team bad news. On the eve of the national team's departure for the final stage of the World Cup in Sweden, Torpedo's Eduard Strel'tsov, who had become a huge star by this point, was arrested and accused of raping the daughter of an army colonel while he, along with Tatushin and Ogon'kov, was out for an evening of rest and relaxation near the team's suburban training camp. In the words of one British observer, Strel'tsov had become "big-headed and full of himself."[5]

To this day, the case has been shrouded in mystery, and after the collapse of the USSR the publication of exposés on the affair became a cottage industry. Strel'tsov was known to be a serious drinker with a difficult personality. Some later claimed Strel'tsov had refused a move to Dinamo and was therefore punished. Others have suggested he was watched carefully for any sign of a slipup after profanely refusing to marry the daughter of the minister of culture, Ekaterina Furtseva. At one point the victim actually retracted her accusation. Ultimately, however, Strel'tsov spent six years in prison, returning to the game only in 1964, fatter and balder but still highly effective, rejoining Torpedo and later the national team.[6] He died at the age of fifty-four, a universally beloved figure about whose full footballing greatness fans could only guess.

Torpedo officials had long feared that Tatushin and Ogon'kov were trying to convince Strel'tsov to transfer to Spartak. Neither man was a model Young Pioneer. Both had previously been reprimanded and warned for drinking, but neither of them was charged with a crime in the rape incident after their accusers chose not to press charges. Neither went to prison, but both were disqualified for three years. Tatushin served his time away from the game and revived his career in 1961, returning to the Spartak lineup for one year before ending his run in Kishinev. Ogon'kov's story ended sadly. One of the greatest outside defenders in the history of Soviet soccer suffered a severely injured kidney in his first reserve match after his return and was forced to retire from the game.[7]

With the resumption of league play in early July, Spartak faced its two toughest traditional local derbies in consecutive matches before huge crowds at Lenin Stadium. With Simonian scoring on a pass from Mozer, Dinamo Moscow fell 1–0. Eleven days later, the army club, now called TsSK MO (Central Sports Club of the Ministry of Defense), lost 2–0, with the Simonian-Mozer combination striking again. It may have seemed clear sailing to the title at this point, but in typical Spartak fashion the next game was a 0–1 defeat to a weaker Lokomotiv team before a hundred thousand deeply annoyed spectators. The next bump in the road took place on August 15 against Dinamo Kiev in Moscow. Spartak appeared to have won 3–2 on a Simonian goal with twelve seconds left in regular time, but soon after the referee returned the ball to the center circle, he ended the match. Dinamo Kiev immediately protested that nine seconds remained, and its protest was granted. The result was annulled. There was to be a replay but only if the result would have an impact on the standings. Once again Spartak found itself in a replay drama. Netto and Nikolai Dementiev took to the pages of *Komsomol'skaia Pravda* to challenge the granting of the protest but to no avail.[8]

There were other difficult moments that fall. Two weeks after the Dinamo Kiev game, goalie Valentin Ivakin was arrested in a highly inebriated state outside Moscow's Kazan railroad station. He had entered a taxi, singing loudly and cursing royally. The driver demanded that he exit the cab, which Ivakin refused to do, screaming instead, "Step on the gas." A policeman was enlisted to help the driver physically eject the very large Ivakin from the taxi. According to *Sovetskii sport*, "It has been said by many that all policemen root for Dinamo," but Ivakin was let off on the spot with a twenty-five-ruble fine. Lacking a decent replacement, Spartak did not punish him.

When the season ended on October 2, Spartak trailed Dinamo Moscow by a single point. The dreaded replay against Dinamo Kiev still had to be played; it could be scheduled for Moscow only on November eighth. The competition for the cup intervened. Spartak easily dispatched Dinamo Kiev 4–0 at Kiev in the quarterfinal. A violent and ill-tempered semifinal against Dinamo Moscow took place almost three weeks later and saw Spartak squeeze out a 2–1 victory. By contrast, the cup final with a Strel'tsov-less Torpedo was won in gentlemanly fashion, with Simonian getting the winning goal after numerous missed opportunities and great goaltending from both sides.[9] Six days later, Spartak would again have the opportunity to go for the double.

While Spartak had been busy expending energy winning the cup, Dinamo Kiev was preparing for the replay with the assistance of Mikhail Iakushin. Dinamo Moscow had everything to gain from its Kievan colleagues' victory, and so Iakushin journeyed to the Ukrainian capital to help out. A bit later, a scrimmage was organized between the two Dinamo teams. In subsequent historical accounts of these events, pro-Spartak writers have made much of the advantages possessed by the national Dinamo Sport Society, but most coaches would argue that, barring injury and exhaustion, the kind of competition Spartak had just won was much better preparation for the replay than a single scrimmage.[10]

On a cold day in early November, Lenin Stadium was filled with the usual hundred thousand. A loss would have given the championship to Dinamo Moscow, which had already finished its schedule with thirty-one points. A tie would have required a one-match playoff between the two Moscow clubs. Only victory served Spartak's ends. With fourteen minutes to go, Spartak was trailing 2–1 when Ilyin tied the score. Sitting in the stands with Nikolai Starostin was the head of the football federation, Valentin Granatkin, who informed Starostin that the playoff would take place in four days, on the twelfth. Granatkin, a former star goalie for Lokomotiv, had no particular ax to grind. He had often worked in harmony with Starostin, who nevertheless objected that his team would be exhausted so soon after the replay. Granatkin refused to budge, but with six minutes to play, Sal'nikov sent Spartak in front with a header. Before the match ended and without accepting congratulations, Starostin got up to leave, turned to Granatkin, and said, "The twelfth will be fine."[11]

Spartak had won its third double, the first since the war. Gulyaev became the first man to play for and coach the winner of a league-cup double. Inside and outside the team, however, there was an understanding that the season's close result and the diminution of some players' skills meant this latest edition of Spartak was not as fast or strong as the 1956 team. In a sign of changing generations, Ilyin took over the team scoring lead from Simonian, who had ten goals to Ilyin's twenty. For all the glory, the massive extension of the season would lead to Spartak's eventual downfall, leaving little time for the team to restore itself for the next campaign. In 1959 several players would be past their prime; Simonian was now thirty-three and Sal'nikov thirty-four. The Golden Age of Spartak was winding down.

## Entering the International Arena

Having joined the Olympic movement in 1952, the Soviets decided in 1957 to participate in that other great global sporting megaevent, the soccer World Cup, scheduled to take place the next summer. This competition was entirely professional, and participation was a recognition that Soviet players were fully compensated for their work. In the wake of the 1952 Helsinki debacle, the national team had been reconstituted and based on Spartak, but by 1957, when qualifying matches against Poland, Israel, and Finland were held, the Spartak presence at this highest level had been considerably reduced.

There was an ultimately incorrect sense among Soviet soccer professionals that Spartak had become stale and predictable. It was said that foreign teams had figured out its style. At a gathering of coaches and officials in June 1957, Spartak was criticized for its continuing reliance on the short pass. Nikolai Starostin accepted these views. At a meeting of the football section, he acknowledged that the team's performance in the 1957 season had gone downhill but did not mention the slow start caused by the length of the previous year's Olympic schedule. Rather, Starostin admitted that his coaches gave a great deal more creative freedom to their players than did those on other teams. What worked in the domestic league, he noted, might not have been as useful on the international level.[12] Over the course of the next year, as the USSR qualified for the final round in Sweden, the Spartak presence on the national team diminished further. As we have seen, Tatushin and Ogon'kov were dismissed for their part in the Strel'tsov scandal. Whereas eleven Spartak players had participated at the 1956 Olympics, by the time of the World Cup finals only Sal'nikov, Simonian, Netto, and Ilyin were in the traveling party. There does not appear to have been any political basis to the choices made by Gavril Kachalin, who was still in charge. Rather, the policy of basing the side on a single club was abandoned, and players came from several clubs instead.

The Soviet national team had suffered a severe blow with the arrest of Strel'tsov, who had taken over Simonian's role at center forward. As things turned out, however, the performance in Sweden was by no means inadequate. The Soviets wound up in an extremely strong preliminary group with Austria, England, and the eventual champion, Brazil. A victory over Austria, a draw with England, and a 0–2 defeat to a brilliant Brazil team led by the young Pele got Kachalin's team into a playoff with England, which it won 1–0 on a goal by Ilyin. It then drew the host country, Sweden, in the quarterfinals.

Having survived the extra game against England, the Soviets were tired. Kachalin faced the question of going with his aging starters one more time or bringing on some of the younger players. He decided to play his veterans, asking them for yet another effort. In the locker room before the game he explained that a victory by a minimal score was all he could ask of them. At this point, a man, described by Simonian as "one of the leaders of the [accompanying political] delegation," reproached Kachalin. "What minimal score? Remember we destroyed the Swedes at [the battle of] Poltava. You are obligated to destroy them today." Playing in its capital in front of it home supporters, Sweden dispatched the Soviets 2–0. The night before the match there had been the usual dancing fans and construction late into the night at the Soviets' hotel. Ultimately Sweden lost in the final to Brazil, proving that the Soviet defeat to the great team of Dida, Pele, and Garrincha was no embarrassment. The Soviets had lost 0–2, while the Swedes were dismissed 5–2 in a historic game. Simonian had thought the players' performance satisfactory, but despite their effort, the team was sent home immediately after the defeat and was denounced by the leaders of the sports committee, who, according to Simonian, "preferred to dole out punishments and break heads. This is what had happened after the Helsinki Olympiad. Although time brought change and the country overcame the consequences of the cult of personality in all spheres of life, the administrative approach to sport remained the same."[13]

The result of the first Soviet participation in the World Cup did reveal a certain tactical stagnation among the various clubs, Spartak included. The Brazilians, aside from their technical virtuosity, had played what seemed a new formation, the 4-2-4, which allowed them to use their passing and technique to control the ball for long stretches before finding one of their powerful strikers. With four men in the back, they relied on a zonal approach to defending but could change instantaneously to 2-4-4 to involve the outside fullbacks in attack. The Brazilians had also prepared seriously in developing their team psychologically and physically, but it took the world a while to understand that these elements were not just natural talent but equally important parts of their greatness.[14] Most important, the Brazilian innovations touched off an ongoing debate within Soviet soccer (as elsewhere) on the remaining benefits of the W formation. A post-World Cup gathering of Soviet specialists called for the study of Brazil's approach, but as the debate evolved, a wide variety of other methods were suggested by all manner of specialists in the press and at official gatherings.[15]

In the wake of the mixed result of 1958, Andrei Starostin was put in charge of the national team, and the burden of finding a new style fell largely on him.[16] In this role, he refused, he said, to act like a "Slavophile" when it came to soccer methods. Spartak had always been open to Western trends, and Andrei now urged Soviet clubs to experiment with a variety of new formations. Ironically, for the rest of the 1958 season, Spartak stuck to what Andrei called its "calligraphic style" of play. Others dismissed the players as insufficiently physical, calling their game "a vegetarian diet." Yet the team had actually benefited in a way from the aging of its players, who were not called away to the national team in particularly large numbers. They did, as I have noted, win everything in 1958, but the next year would prove to be another matter.

Andrei Starostin's task was further complicated by taking over the job in the wake of the Strel'tsov affair. Thirty years after the event, Andrei viewed the drama as "a series of unfortunate events." "Imagine," he wrote, "what it would have been like with our national team in Stockholm if Iashin had led our defense, Netto [injured] our midfield and Strel'tsov our attack."[17] It is not possible to determine whether the Starostins and others in the soccer world had thought at the time that Strel'tsov was guilty. More recent research places the blame on Khrushchev, who was seen to be doing the bidding of powerful members of his leadership by using the great star's arrest as an excuse to banish un-Soviet behaviors from the sports scene.[18] Regardless, it is clear that the explanation offered at the aforementioned meeting of football professionals had to be taken seriously. "Huge insufficiencies in the educational work of the clubs and in the national side led to a radical change in the team on the eve of its departure [for Sweden]."[19]

In just two years, Spartak had gone from dominant contributor to the victory in 1956 to a minor role at the Soviets' first World Cup. After that, the presence of its players on the national team continued to diminish. While new Spartak men came along to play for the *sbornaia* in subsequent tournaments, only Netto made the transition during the age of Khrushchev.[20] Three major competitions took place between 1960 and 1964. A pattern seemed to be set with a poor showing in the 1962 World Cup and good results in the new European championship. These included a first place in the inaugural 1960 competition in France and an eminently respectable defeat in the 1964 final to powerful Spain in Madrid.[21] This last match led to the bizarre dismissal of coach Kontantin Beskov by an outraged Khrushchev. Second place might have been a good result, but a loss to Franco's Fascist Spain was deemed politically unacceptable. This irrational interference in the sporting process would prove to be one of Khrushchev's last acts.[22] Toward the end, he was wildly searching for some new formula to pull the nation out of the crisis into which he had led it. By October 1964 he had left the scene. By now, however, the star-crossed record of the USSR national team had become a part of the overall history of Soviet football and less a part of the story of Spartak.

## Navigating the Change of Generations

For Spartak, the bottom fell out during the 1959 season as the side Dangulov had trained and assembled and Gulyaev had later coached grew old.
Nikolai Starostin was then faced with one of his greatest professional challenges. He had not put together the team of the Golden Age. While he was
widely credited with running Spartak well and adapting to the conditions of
post-Stalinist life, the teams of the fifties were not truly his.[23] It would take
him three more years to get them back to the top. In the very broadest sense,
Spartak had earlier benefited indirectly from the relaxed conditions of the
Thaw as the club expanded both its fan base and its talent pool. Now the situation facing Starostin was different.

Much of the club's decline and subsequent resurrection can be traced to
professional concerns within the football world itself. Soccer had won more,
if far from complete, autonomy from official interference. The leading clubs
had become more numerous. Other competitors for the championship
emerged. For the first time in the history of Soviet soccer, neither Spartak, Dinamo, nor TsSKA won. Instead, Torpedo took the gold in 1960. The next season, Dinamo Kiev won championship honors for the first of what would be
numerous times. This was the first time a team outside Moscow had triumphed, and its win demonstrated the growth of provincial soccer. The contending forces in the football world became more various and harder to
micromanage. In keeping with the continuing modernizing process, soccer
had spread from its Slavic core to the other regions of the USSR.

One marker of this development was the desire of rapidly developing
provincial towns to have powerful representatives in the football league structure. Over the course of the fifties and continuing into the sixties, large arenas
were constructed in the growing cities of the USSR's periphery. In order to
support this trend, the top flight of the soccer league was expanded from
twelve to twenty-two teams. Among the cities that now got first-division football were Kuibishev, Donetsk, Alma-Ata, Baku, Riga, and Vilnius. The season
was then divided into two stages, with eleven teams in each of two preliminary groups. After ten games, the top three teams in each group took part in a
final stage for the top spots. Those who did not make the cut played each other
for seventh through twelfth places. This approach lasted from 1960 to 1962.
The preliminary rounds often featured colossal mismatches that drew few
fans in the established cities. The final rounds involving the losers in the preliminary stage sold even fewer tickets.

The entire process was political. In large measure it was an attempt to accommodate various national groups. In equal measure, it was conceived with
no regard for the realities of the market for sporting spectacles. Historically,
smaller or local teams throughout the world have been included in top-flight
football through knockout-style cup competitions open to almost everyone.
Soccer had been, of all things in the USSR, a profitable enterprise that produced funding for other sports. The new approach, by lowering attendance,

threatened that role. If not on the order of the Virgin Lands campaign, the expansion of the league (first suggested in 1938 by Beria) proved to be a failure that confused everyone and did not work. In 1963, the Soviets returned to the global standard of a single league, now with twenty teams.[24] The entire failed experiment was emblematic of the many hastily and poorly conceived reforms of Khrushchev's last years. In this particular case, the expansion of the first division was a soccer correlate of earlier decentralization schemes that had also produced, to be kind, mixed results.

Having just won the double in 1958, it was shocking for Nikolai Starostin, Gulyaev, and other Spartak officials to experience a precipitous decline in 1959. Twelve games into the season, Spartak found itself occupying eleventh place in a twelve-team league. Drawn by the impressive performance of the 1958 team, huge crowds attended these debacles. There was no hiding the rot. One hundred and six thousand witnessed a 0–2 loss to Dinamo Moscow. A week later, 110,000 watched Spartak lose to Zenit Leningrad at the second city's giant Kirov Stadium. In early August, however, Spartak managed to turn the situation around with a 3–1 defeat of Dinamo Moscow. With its well-honed sense of drama, it then went undefeated the rest of the way to come in sixth, as its chief rival won the title.[25] Consistent with the stereotypes the teams had developed over the years, commentators contrasted Dinamo's steady play with Spartak's historically maddening inconsistency.

It had become clear early in the season that the core of the great team had aged. Simonian was in and out of the lineup, managing just ten appearances and a single goal. Paramonov played in only five games all season. Sal'nikov's productivity fell drastically. In July Nikolai Starostin and Gulyaev took the highly unusual step of explaining the obvious to the readers of *Sovetskii sport.* They admitted the time for a change of generations had come. Players were either in their early thirties and losing their skills or in their early twenties and yet to acquire them. The only significant new additions had been the defenders Anatoly Krutikov (b. 1933), who had come over from TsSKA, and Aleksei Korneev (b. 1939), a product of Spartak's own football school. In keeping with Starostin's analysis, their greatest contributions would come in the future. The results of this shortage of young legs were clearly visible on the field. With the slowing of the attack, the midfield had to involve itself more often on offense, leaving gaps in the back. Valentin Ivakin, now the regular goalie and no Iashin, was not always up to the difficult task posed by a weaker defensive presence. In contrast to Andrei's search for a new approach for the national team, Nikolai admitted to tactical stagnation and a failure to adopt the latest methods then emerging in the rest of the world.[26] Left unsaid was the fact that the same accusation could be made of nearly every other Soviet club.

There was one other troubling tendency in league play this season. As the W formation lived out its last days in the USSR, coaches were loath to impose entirely new tactical approaches on their players, especially if those players were not particularly gifted. The world had been amazed by the Brazilians, but others inside and outside the USSR had learned negative lessons from the previous summer's World Cup. The result was a marked rise in physical—in other words, dirty—play, much of which went unpunished. Termed *atletizm,* the approach replaced speed and technique with strength. This trend further hurt Spartak with its physically smaller squad. Speed has always been the best tactic to avoid rough play, but with the passing of time, speed ebbs. In 1959, Spartak's older forwards found themselves literally getting squeezed. In truth, this shift toward defensive play was a global phenomenon, perfected with maximum cynicism in Italy. At the time, this search for new methods went on all over the world. The result was a steady drift toward negative play as the sport began the shift away from scoring goals to preventing them.[27]

It is important to remember that the causes of Spartak's decline at the end of the 1950s were grounded in the inescapable logic of sport itself, especially big-time professional sport. In this case, the team's great run ended with no one being sent to prison. There was no grand government or party intervention either to save or harm Spartak. No massive political scores were settled through football. The events surrounding Spartak's decline can be seen as normal parts of the sporting life. Without being naive, it can be said that Soviet football had succeeded in carving out relatively greater working room for the professionals who ran it. Of course, nowhere in the world did football ever succeed in freeing itself of the constraints of its surrounding environment. In this sense, Soviet football was no different. The domestic and international environments had changed, and so had the game in the USSR. Interference did not disappear, but the diminished control by the regime derived from four sources: (1) the irrationality of the authorities in their conflicting attempts to control the game; (2) the continuing ability of the fans to draw their own meanings from what they saw on the field; (3) the geographic expansion of the game; and (4) the very unpredictability of the sport itself. When all was said and done, the ball did continue to be round.

The off-season after 1959 brought great change for Spartak. Gulyaev was let go. Simonian and Paramonov retired. Seven others left the team for various reasons, and Nikolai Starostin began the club's renovation by naming the thirty-four-year-old Simonian head coach. With no experience at this level and younger than many of his veterans, Simonian seemed a risk. Starostin, however, understood Simonian's intelligence and humanity—qualities the great patriarch liked to see in himself. Although results did not come quickly, the choice would prove inspired. Eleven newcomers were brought in. The offense needed the most assistance, and Iuri Sevidov and Valerii Reingol'd found places on the forward line. The seventeen-year-old Muscovite Sevidov (b. 1942) joined up in late May after two uneventful seasons in Kishinev. He took over Simonian's center forward position and scored eleven goals in twenty-two games. Reingol'd (b. 1942), another Muscovite, provided much-needed speed at right wing after Tatushin's disqualification.[28]

As a young coach who had just been put in charge of men with whom he had long been close friends, Simonian might have been tempted to dispense with the veteran core that had failed so badly the previous year. He wisely chose otherwise, though he realized that dealing with Sal'nikov and Netto, never an easy job for anyone, would surely tax his patience. He moved to salvage what he could of his existing lineup. Anatoly Maslenkin (1930–1988), a fixture in the defense since 1953, transformed himself into a midfielder to make room for Krutikov and Korneev. Ivakin, Isaev, and Ilyin were also kept on.[29]

As noted, the 1960 season was contested on a new basis, but the campaign began with a twist. With all the difficulties it faced and with all the changes it needed to put in place, it can only be described as bizarre that Spartak would have "chosen" to hold its preseason training not in one of the familiar southern Soviet sites but in what was then the footballistically challenged People's Republic of China. At the time relations between the two powers of world Communism, which had recently been friendly, were rapidly deteriorating. The last thing a team in crisis might be expected to do was to go to a place where it would not be particularly welcome to prepare for a season that would surely be the most challenging in its history.

Spartak was required to play a total of five exhibition games before large audiences across the length and breadth of China. Imagine the state of Chinese transportation at this time. Understand that, for all the grandeur of Chinese cuisine, Russian athletes had never shown much culinary adaptability. Realize that two of the five games actually were draws, and one can well imagine the political leadership's unhappiness with Spartak. The team can hardly have been certain why it had been sent there for a month on what seemed a fool's errand. Perhaps Starostin had agreed to train in China because the team's preseason training before 1958 had taken place in Indonesia with no ill effects.

Despite several injuries and a multimatch disqualification for the ever-unpredictable Sal'nikov, the season proper began well enough with three wins against weak opponents, but losses to Dinamo Kiev and TsSKA in Moscow before the usual large crowds stopped any enthusiasm in its tracks.[30] A June home defeat to the minnow Neftianik Baku in front of one hundred thousand further confirmed the fears. Ultimately Spartak failed to qualify for the next round, finishing fourth one point behind TsSKA. Now it was no longer in a position to contest the title. This was obviously an enormously difficult start to Simonian's coaching career, and the public proved unforgiving. Both he and his wife received hugely profane personal abuse from fans at games and on the streets.

In late August, the second stage began—a ten-game league to determine seventh to twelfth place. Now a curious thing happened for true believers in Spartak ideology. Yet from the point of view of normal sporting logic it was not curious at all. In any spectator sport a competition among also-rans with little at stake leads to a decline in fan interest, and this is exactly what happened during this stage of the season. Instead of the mammoth audiences that witnessed the defeats of the first round, roughly twenty-one thousand took in each of the second-stage games. A match with a no doubt equally disappointed Dinamo Tblisi attracted only twenty thousand to Lenin Stadium. Perhaps even more embarrassing, two games were actually transferred back to the much smaller Dinamo Stadium.[31]

No student of the global game, unaware of the local specifics, would have been surprised by such figures. Yet one of the enduring myths that always floated around Spartak concerned the constant loyalty of their fans. So undying was their support, according to Filatov, Simonian, Merzhanov, Vartanian, and the Starostins, that supporters kept coming even in hard times. Such had been the case after the war, and it turned out to be true at difficult times in the future.[32] It would appear, however, that in 1960 poor play could dull the loyalty of even the most ardent Spartak fans. They did not, of course, disappear. For once, the spectators merely stayed away from the stadium. As had been the case before the war, there was still a general impression that Moscow fans divided 50 percent for Spartak and 50 percent for everyone else. If before 1941 that 50 percent had been almost entirely working class, now it was said that one half of all the layers of society rooted for the so-called people's team. Interestingly enough, much the same thing had been said during the Argentine soccer boom of the 1930s about the most popular club, Boca Juniors. "Boca," writes David Goldblatt, "could now claim to be the team of the masses, the team of the people, the 50 per cent plus one, as they described their support."[33] As had long been the case with Spartak, we again see—for all the differences in setting—the image of a broadly inclusive, sociologically vague "us" arrayed against a variety of enemies.

As Boca came to be rivaled within Buenos Aires by River Plate, Independiente, and San Lorenzo (each with a different fan base), so did Spartak later find itself contending with other opponents every bit as adept and well supported as Dinamo and TsSKA. Coached by Viktor Maslov and led by Valentin Ivanov, Torpedo survived the loss of Strel'tsov. Supported by the increasingly sizable resources of the giant ZIL auto factory, it took the 1960 title as Spartak finished seventh. The increasingly complex segmentation of the Soviet economy meant that new sources of wealth, in this case a growing Soviet auto industry, could produce competing resources to support high-quality football. As we have seen, for the first time none of the three powers that had long dominated the Soviet game had triumphed. On the surface, the results in 1960 seemed for Spartak to be even worse than those in 1959, but in truth the foundations for eventual success had been put in place.

In preparing for the next season, Spartak bid good-bye to Sergei Sal'nikov, who finally retired. Simonian brought in thirteen new players, three of whom would have an enormous impact. The most important new star was Galimzian Khusainov (b. 1937), a Tatar who had already played four seasons for Kryl'ya Sovetov Kuibyshev. His presence was a sign of the expansion of soccer's reach as Spartak, as well as the other top teams, was now able to recruit talent from all over the USSR. Television in particular had done much to spread the popularity of the game. Khusainov fit in immediately at left wing and replaced Simonian as Spartak's top goal scorer with fourteen in twenty-eight games. Khusainov was joined by the Muscovite Gennadii Logofet (b. 1942), a multitalented defender, and the center back Valerii Dikarev (1939–2001), who came from Baku.[34] Dikarev found kindred spirits in Sevidov and

Khusainov, both of whom, in the Spartak tradition, were lovers of jazz. All of them lived near one another and collected records from the wide variety of legal, semilegal, and illegal sources that had emerged with the so-called second economy.[35]

The process of renewal began to advance in 1961. Dikarev and Krutikov joined with Logofet to provide a revived defense, while Khusainov, Sevidov, and Reingol'd gave new life and creativity to the attack. The transition to the 4-2-4, which had sputtered the previous season, now took hold. Spartak finished the first round in third place and thus was able to continue.[36] After a poor start in the final stage, including a bad loss to Dinamo Moscow, it won seven of eight and trailed Dinamo Kiev by a mere two points. All its remaining games were in Moscow, and all were against weak opponents. Things looked good, but in typical fashion, Spartak failed to win any of its last four matches, finishing third behind Torpedo and the eventual champion, Dinamo Kiev. Bronze medals for third place were the first trophies for Spartak since 1958. It was a significant step forward. The large crowds were back, but early in the season Starostin and Simonian had been called on the carpet by their sponsors and threatened with dismissal. They asked for and were given a few months to improve the situation. The players, especially Netto and Khusainov, responded, and the boss and his coach were again solid in their positions, though the episode had reminded them that they were not invulnerable.[37]

### The Starostin Method (Postwar)

During the NEP years of partial capitalism, Nikolai Starostin had run Spartak's predecessors as small businesses, using the commercial methods of his prerevolutionary education. During the purge years, he demonstrated a considerable but obviously not infallible ability to navigate the corridors of political power at the apex of a system in which the coin of the realm was considerably different. He did this to defend the interests of the team he had helped create, provide for his own enrichment, and expand his standing and prestige in the larger society. At the time, his way of running Spartak had led to complaints about bourgeois methods, and he had paid dearly. How then did Starostin and his brothers operate after their return? What lessons, if any, did they learn? Were bourgeois methods, once anathema, acceptable during the Khrushchev era, and what larger conclusions can we draw about the general operating environment for popular culture under the Thaw?

In 2002, Aleksandr Vainshtein described Starostin as "the first president of a club in the complete Western sense of the term."[38] At the same time, Vladimir Maslachenko, a Spartak goalie who went on to become a successful television commentator, characterized the club as a "kind of private enterprise."[39] For Nikita Simonian, Starostin was a "Soviet businessman."[40] Were they saying, in the light of Communism's collapse, what could not have been directly uttered earlier? Upon his return, Starostin had refused to take over control of the entire Spartak Sport Society with all of its unprofitable sports, preferring instead to run the highly visible football club. From the thirties, his greatest interest and strength had been the production of big spectacles that sold thousands of tickets, and it appears his showmanship did not diminish in this new era.

In an overlooked 1986 memoir, Starostin complained that in Soviet society it was not considered acceptable to talk about financial matters, but such concerns, he argued, had a great impact on the success of a soccer team. Moreover, he reminded his readers that the Spartak football club, after covering its considerable expenses, during the 1980s had contributed 250,000 additional rubles a year to the general activities of the larger national sport society. "The financial question is not a neutral matter," wrote Starostin. "It is far more pleasant to count one's profits than to mask one's insufficiencies."[41] The team's greatest source of funds continued to be ticket sales. The construction of Lenin Stadium, in particular, had made it possible to accommodate more spectators than ever before, and Spartak did its job in attracting them to the new arena. While television advertised the game, it was not in itself a source of income.

Compared with the expenses of massive state enterprises, the sums involved in running a soccer team were small. Operating Spartak was not high finance, but the model was important. When other teams needed funds, they simply asked their various sponsors. Of course, all teams sold tickets, but Spartak clearly sold more, and one can make an educated guess that self-generated funds played a larger role in the operation of Spartak than was the case with other clubs. We do not know the minutiae of how this was achieved. The various wings of the Spartak Society produced numerous, highly opaque annual budgets. These documents tell us that football took up a large part of the organization's spending but do not show that football had actually generated much of that funding.

Starostin understood the general laws of big-time sport. To generate money, he had to put a good product on the field, but he also had to give his supporters reasons for coming back time after time when, perhaps, the going was not so good. To accomplish this in the USSR, money was simply not enough. The mere possession of cash could not get you what you might need. Under capitalism, money often could purchase talent, but even in the West finding good players has always been a complicated process. Rubles could provide better salaries, but wages were always just one part of the combination of privileges and rewards that could attract good players. Many elements comprising the player packages simply could not be bought. There were always long waiting lists for apartments and cars. If money was required, Starostin was able to find and use it. In one of many cases, he learned that the young Gennadi Logofet was going to sign with TSKA, whereupon Starostin immediately called Logofet, demanded to know the salary being offered, and promptly doubled it.[42]

If one could not simply buy players, neither could one buy an audience in the USSR. There was no advertising industry that could generate enthusiasm and create what today we call a brand. Even in capitalist countries, loyalty to teams had been based on a wide variety of factors, most notably community, which involved much more than money. In the fifties, the economy of favors (*blat*) and the black and gray markets had not yet emerged as powerfully as they would later, but Starostin understood that to swim in these waters he would need to intervene politically and culturally as well as economically. Fortunately, his talents extended well beyond keeping the books straight. Money, especially that generated by a version of market forces, could provide a measure of the independence Starostin had always sought, but to defend that independence one needed to operate on other fronts.

When Simonian worked with Starostin, Nikolai spent most of his time on those other fronts. Aside from salaries, apartments, and cars, there were questions about furniture, child care, and a range of other "daily life" (*bytovye*) questions. There were long waiting lists for all these things, and one needed contacts as well as cash to obtain them. Starostin took care of these problems for his players so that they and the coaches could devote their time to sport. On most other Soviet teams, these tasks fell to the coaches. In some cases, it was Starostin's own authority that got him an audience with those who could provide these services. In other cases, it was that of his team. At Mossovet, the gorkom, and a host of trade union organizations, "the door" said Simonian, "was always open to him." He exercised enormous authority within these organizations and more often than not received what he requested.[43] At times, however, apartment hunting could create its own complications. When Valerii Dikarev joined the team, he and his wife were given a big new apartment on highly desirable Kutuzovskii Prospekt. For a soccer player, this was quite an unusual address. Unfortunately, the couple soon divorced, and Dikarev's wife got the apartment. Starostin had to go back to his sponsors for yet another place for Dikarev, this time in the less fashionable Cheremushki district.[44]

The provision of such rare desirables was an unavoidable part of the talent-recruitment process. Player transfers were regulated by constantly changing rules that were selectively enforced. To be sure, Spartak did a good job of developing much of its own talent, but Starostin was not averse to using his contacts to bring in players from all over the country. Most often these were younger players who wanted to move to the big city. Their smaller clubs did not stand in their way. No money was supposed to change hands, nor were players exchanged. On the other hand, prying a star from another first-division club was frowned upon and often not allowed by the authorities. In this ongoing fight for the best players, Starostin was far from omnipotent. He won his fair share of transfer requests, but it cannot be said he was successful in all ventures.

Many of the activities in which Starostin engaged, whether he was signing players or finding apartments and cars, took place in the gray zones of Soviet life. The rules governing the acquisition of these items were either unclear, were constantly changing, or simply did not exist. Thus the possibilities for mischief and corruption in nearly everything Starostin did were almost inescapable. Given the flamboyance of his prewar career and the trouble it may well have caused him, it is interesting that over more than forty years of running the team after his return, he was not bedeviled by the kinds of accusations and rumors that had emerged in the thirties. Rather, he went to his grave with a public reputation for correctness, integrity, honesty, and even a certain asceticism. His competitors may not all have shared this view, but it does contrast dramatically with the earlier image of the man wearing a fur coat as he steps out of a Packard limousine. Soviet soccer may not have been as corrupt as it was in Italy, Brazil, or parts of Africa and Asia. Still, it was not the kind of world one could leave without being somewhat besmirched. The post-1955 Nikolai Starostin does seem to have done just that.[45]

Had his long and difficult exile changed Starostin, as it did so many others? As we have seen, it was not clear that he was guilty of the charges listed in his 1943 sentencing document. If he was, however, he now appeared determined not to make the same mistake twice, avoiding anything that could be seen as illegal. Yet running a soccer team in the Soviet Union was hardly a profession for saints. How did he handle the contradiction? A possibly apocryphal story from a slightly later period (sometime between 1969 and 1971) encapsulates the trickiness of Starostin's position and the fine line he drew to avoid new trouble. It was related to me by Evgenii Lovchev, one of Spartak's greatest stars and captain of the team during the troubled seventies. A great admirer of his former boss, he was nonetheless fully prepared to believe that Starostin might have done something less than noble during the war for which he had paid severely and that he was determined to make sure never happened again.

Throughout the history of Soviet soccer, teams had operated what were called "black cash boxes" (chernye kassy). Money came into them from various sources—local "millionaires," party bosses, perhaps organized crime. Sometimes fans even took up collections. The money could be used for all manner of purposes.[46] One of the long-standing methods of adding to this fund was the organization of midweek exhibition games against smaller regional teams a few hours' drive from the capital. The game was advertised. Tickets were sold. Local officials were paid to look the other way, as several thousand fans would show up to see one of the nation's great teams. In the case of Spartak, these matches were used to supplement the players' salaries. At the end of one particular game the players were told they would receive eighty rubles each for their efforts. As Lovchev tells it, Anzor Kavazashvili (b. 1940), a goalie from Georgia who spent three seasons with the team, then complained loudly, "Nikolai Petrovich, what's the deal? At Dinamo Kiev each player gets two hundred rubles for matches like this and we get only eighty?" There was then a pregnant silence. Starostin asked, "Anzor, have you spent time in prison [vy sideli]? Well, I have [ia sidel]."[47]

The absurdities and contradictions of postwar Soviet life are on full display in this story, one worthy of Gogol. Starostin and his team had just engaged in an act that was technically illegal. At the same time, the holding of such matches had rarely, if ever, been prosecuted. It was classically Soviet—or perhaps better Russian—to declare something illegal but never actually enforce the law. In the aftermath of the game, Starostin, perhaps fearing legal consequences, sought to mitigate his actions by proclaiming his determination to make less than others would have made in the same circumstances. By taking less money, Starostin appeared to be trying to render a dubious act more palatable to himself as well as to any possible agents of the state. One could well ask why, if playing such a match was a crime, taking eighty rubles rather than two hundred for the day's work would change the situation and somehow keep one out of jail. Adding to the general absurdity, the act in which the Spartak football team had just engaged was perfectly legal almost anywhere else in the world. Barnstorming had always been one of spectator sport's grand traditions, a chance for the great to meet the small, and it had long been part of the Soviet soccer scene as well.

It is best to see Nikolai Starostin's post-Stalin management style as yet another adaptation to the operating conditions of the broader economic and political systems rather than as a conscious attempt to impose a particular business model on the team. Under Khrushchev, the USSR was still very much a socialist economy with minimal private property. If there were elements of the capitalist in the Spartak approach, they were not extensive. Paying attention to financial concerns was not necessarily unique among Soviet institutions. The team's profitability was unusual, but profitability by itself could not guarantee success. Starostin also relied heavily on the exchange of favors. He continued to distribute highly desirable tickets to those in the Moscow government who could help the team. The value of those tickets in turn depended on the continuing popularity of the club whose image Starostin and his brothers had helped create.

In this task, essentially a cultural one, Nikolai was aided greatly by Andrei. Both men, through their writings, interviews, and other interventions, laid the basis for the controversial notion that Spartak was the team of democracy. In 1990, at the height of glasnost, Nikolai told *Sovetskii sport* that "democracy and collegiality" had long been the basis of Spartak's success.[48] Always sensitive to the tenor of the times, was he simply speaking democrat rather than Bolshevik, or was he sincere? In 2002, Nikita Simonian described Spartak as a "symbol for freedom-loving people."[49] Only at the very end of the Soviet period was the word "democracy" linked in any official publication with Spartak. The term itself is highly problematic in the Soviet context. It took on a wide range of meanings, few of which were consistent with Western notions of liberal democracy. For those in Spartak the word seems to have involved the conflation of a broad notion of democracy with the traditions of the Russian intelligentsia. Here Lovchev's words can be seen as typical: "Spartak was a 'democratic system.' . . . It was the influence of the Starostins. Spartak always had the intelligentsia behind them, that is, the creative intelligentsia. We had meetings with the Maly Teatr and all kinds of artists would show up at Tarasovka."[50]

Andrei's ties with this segment of intellectual life dated back to the twenties, but it is important to realize that he was broadly catholic in his friendships, which ranged from subtle critics to ardent defenders of the regime, from Iuri Olesha to Aleksandr Fadeev.[51] According to Lev Netto, Andrei was a "true democrat" who hid his real feelings, but the younger Starostin was careful never to engage in any activity that could have fit the description (not used in the fifties) of dissident. Nikolai, similarly, never took up the cudgel for any open critic of the Soviet state. According to Vainshtein, "Personally, I don't think, although he knew all the negative aspects of the system, he was in his deepest soul a dissident or a free-thinking person."[52] At the same time, that narrow layer of rarefied intellectuals who would go on to form the heart of the dissident movement after Khrushchev's ouster did not include many serious sports fans.[53] Rather, those intellectuals who gravitated toward Spartak were often middle-brow purveyors of popular culture, including writers, actors, and musicians.

The fact that intellectuals were thought to be at the forefront of the Thaw made the broad association of democracy with all "thinking people" a common theme of the era, even if that theme distorted the detailed realities of the various movements and tendencies that found expression in the new concept of public opinion. In the most general way, Spartak courted these figures, and some of them were only too happy to be courted. The associations and friendships did provide a connection with exciting, perhaps even fashionable, trends of the period. When these very general and broad elements were combined with the Starostins' status as returning exiles, it became a relatively short leap in an amorphous public consciousness to go from regarding Spartak as the people's team to thinking of it as a democratic system.

Yet these slim pieces of evidence cannot be pushed much further. Rather, what one sees in these years is a broad but still amorphous public yearning for a break with Stalinist methods that stopped well short of a call for the overthrow of the regime or a return to capitalism. The public mood resonated with the image of Spartak as the team of democracy, allowing the club to claim it represented more than simply success on the field of play. If rooting for Spartak had been a small way of saying no during the thirties, now some claimed it was a significant way of saying yes to change. As it had done in an earlier era, the team was able to generate loyalty by linking its success to larger issues, in this case imputing a connection with so-called progressive forces. It is in this sense that the remarks of Lovchev, Simonian, and even Nikolai Starostin, while perhaps naive, cannot be dismissed entirely.

If, as I have suggested here, seeing Spartak as a champion of democracy is a stretch, one can nevertheless find small elements of the democratic or perhaps simply the paternalistic in the way Nikolai Starostin ran the football side of the operation. The internal atmosphere at Spartak was comparatively relaxed. Players were not subject to military discipline. Nearly all the coaches hired by Starostin treated their men respectfully and solicited their opinions. Starostin himself was extensively involved in settling conflicts. He believed deeply in compromise. Publicly, the team's playing style continued to be freer, more improvisatory, and less physical or robotic—the approach Spartak fans had come to love and expect. Finally, before each match, once the coaches had laid out the game plan, Starostin would address the players, not with orders or threats but with stories, jokes, life lessons, and other motivational devices in order to prepare them mentally.[54]

Starostin always made it clear, however, that he and he alone was the boss. For all the apparent modernity of his role as team president, there was something, according to Vainshtein, of the "archaic" in Spartak's structure.[55] Nikolai Ozerov described Starostin as the center and soul of the Spartak organization, an "awe-inspiring [*groznaia*] figure who was loved and feared."[56] There does not appear to have been much formalized power sharing within the organization, nor were duties clearly delineated. If Starostin was the boss, he was a decent and respectful boss who did not always have to have his way.[57] If he could give orders, Starostin still preferred to persuade. In the eyes of the public these practices made Spartak more humane than the teams of the structures of force. Yet few if any of these were institutionalized elements of a democratic organization.

## The Failure of Reform and the Return (Once More) of Spartak

The hopes for a socialist renewal within the context of the system began to wane toward the end of the fifties and beginning of the sixties. The momentum of the process had clearly been lost as the economy slowed down, and the agricultural sector, in particular, failed to respond to Khrushchev's numerous attempts to fix it. Resistance to his reforms intensified within the hierarchy. In response, Khrushchev mounted a renewed attack on the Stalinist legacy at the Twenty-second Party Congress in October 1961. The crimes of the era were described in even greater detail, and Stalin's personal responsibility for the deaths of millions was vigorously asserted. Soon thereafter, the dictator's body was removed from the Lenin Mausoleum. The names of towns honoring him were changed. Monuments were removed, and the ubiquitous portraits were taken down.

On the surface, this seemed a victory for Khrushchev, but it masked the fact that several of his supporters had been removed from the party Presidium. His position weakened and his programs increasingly incoherent, he was consistently embattled politically and personally until his removal in 1964. Beyond the world of Kremlin politics, there was an erosion of living standards. Food prices rose, shortages increased, and wages failed to keep up. The improvements of the fifties had created rising expectations among virtually all elements of the Soviet social structure. While Khrushchev continued to play the populist card, traveling back and forth across the country in support of his programs, few outside the central institutions of power were ready to rally to his cause. By the end his departure had been long expected. The response of the public was indifference.

The deep structural changes that had taken place since the death of Stalin had transformed society in profound ways, but those very developments turned out to have had only a cosmetic impact on the methods of governance. A revised version of the old command economy had enjoyed considerable success in the fifties, but failure to carry the reform process further eventually had led to a slowdown. The failure of Khrushchev's frantic attempts to correct the slide emboldened those in the party and government who did not seek change but rather sought to protect their positions. His plan to impose a version of term limits on political figures, forced through at the 1961 congress, further undermined his support within the party. On the surface, this reform seemed designed to increase the state's responsiveness to society, lessening the power of bureaucrats and increasing the role of volunteers. Had it succeeded, the social change of the last decade might in turn have had an impact on the political system, but instead it threatened the existing cadres and hastened Khrushchev's political demise. The idea of dividing the party into industrial and agricultural sectors similarly threatened the position of thousands of functionaries, especially those forced to move from Moscow to the provinces.

By the end of the Khrushchev era, it was clear that the relationship between the Soviet state and society was still in the process of renegotiation that had begun in the postwar years. Over time, however, the borders between the regime and the public were becoming blurred. Moshe Lewin has described the emergence in these years of social forces and groups that undermined the distinction between state and society and that under the right circumstances had the potential to take on some aspects of what he called "civil society." Lewin's concept of civil society assumed the existence since the midsixties of independent elements that had the capacity on their own to influence state policy. In other authoritarian states—Franco's Spain, for example—relatively independent groups even before 1975 were able to carve out areas of activity and organization that enabled the political system to make a largely successful transition to a constitutional democracy. Although the post-Soviet outcome has not been the same as that of Spain, this does not mean that similar attitudes did not exist in the USSR.[58]

Can we see in Spartak and its fans an independent element of the kind essential to the development of civil society? Here we are hampered by the absence of social scientific data linking either occupation or political attitudes to fan support. Indeed, concrete research of the sort advocated by Bourdieu is hard to find anywhere. Worldwide, virtually all the descriptions of certain clubs as "student," "worker," "Catholic," or the people's team are constructed from journalistic and other cultural discourses produced by highly involved observers.[59] When censorship has limited the ways teams have been publicly described, followers of the sport have argued about the justice of such terms in cafes and bars, on the streets, at the stadium and in kitchens. Thus, if imputing social and cultural meanings to certain teams is a tricky enterprise even in open societies, it is still more difficult when talking about the Soviet experience. On the other hand, Spartak's associations and its self-presentation do suggest a tenuous link to the members of a potential civil society, at least to those who loved football.

But just how independent was Spartak? The club had emerged during the 1920s from a specific locality. It had later navigated the treacherous search for sponsors, survived, and prospered. Its support had come from an organization, Promkooperatsiia, whose activities were poorly understood. If Dinamo was the police, TsSKA the army, and Torpedo the auto industry, Spartak appeared to represent no one. In the post-Stalin period, sponsorship from the Moscow party similarly was tied to no particular interest group. It seemed, not entirely correctly, that Spartak was not the creation of any higher authority, and this apparent independence had allowed it to claim the broader mantle of the people's team. Something quite similar could be said about the Starostins, most notably Nikolai, whose independence before the war had been most threatening to his professional and political enemies. It was important that in 1954 he chose to come back as president of the club he had founded. As he made clear in his conversation with N. N. Romanov, he had his own views and did not think he could work well with the sports committee or some other state organization.[60] Leading Spartak allowed him to make his own decisions, at least as much as anyone in Soviet society could. His independence was far from absolute but sufficient for him to create a small world of his own in Spartak.

After 1953, it became possible to pursue such a course, despite the enormous obstacles that still existed. These views and practices, when combined with success on the field, permitted a process of identity formation for the team's new supporters similar to that which had taken place in the thirties. Now, however, the choices were being made not primarily by workers but by a number of different groups. Intellectuals and other professionals could safely assert a measure of independence by supporting Spartak—another small way of saying no. The writers Iuri Trifonov and Lev Kassil', the entertainer Leonid Utesov, the actor Mikhail Ianshin, and even the lawyer Boris Nazarov were all men whose professional work was always subject to control. They could, however, reclaim some part of themselves by identifying with Spartak. If football has been a sport in which people tell themselves stories about themselves, then support for Spartak became a means by which fans could imagine themselves as more free than they actually were. Invoking the ideological construct of Spartak spirit, they became convinced of the greater beauty and honesty of their team's play.[61] In compensating for the inadequacies of their actual lives, sport, as it has done everywhere, permitted Spartak fans of all sorts a constrained measure of utopian hope about the future and about their own ability to influence that future.

## Reaping the Harvest

For Spartak, the 1962 season permitted the continuation of a hope that had become increasingly difficult to maintain in the larger society. If the club's fortunes had previously tracked well with the oscillating success of the reform process, now its practices went against the grain. As football had become bigger, the laws of the sporting process had assumed more importance, creating a measure of insulation from the political. The ability of central authorities to control the game diminished as a wide variety of regional groups and deeper social processes impinged upon the sport. In this changed context, Nikolai Starostin found even greater room to maneuver as a professional organizer of sporting activity. He now set about the task of reviving Spartak.[62]

Along with several other Soviet clubs, Spartak had completed the transition to the 4-2-4 formation by 1962. Simonian demonstrated great ability in making the adjustment, defining each player's role with precision. Perhaps not surprisingly, the younger players—most notably Sevidov and Logofet—had the least difficulty in adapting to the new approach. Nevertheless, the team stumbled out of the gate. With Netto, Khusainov, and Maslenkin away on duty at the World Cup in Chile, it barely succeeded in making the final round of twelve.[63] Inconsistency in goal had hurt them, and in the intermission between the first and second stages, Starostin, amid great controversy, succeeded in prying the national team reserve goalie, the aforementioned Vladimir Maslachenko, away from Lokomotiv. He proved to be the missing link, and Spartak closed the season with a twelve-game unbeaten streak to take the championship on the last day of the season.

Leading Dinamo Moscow by a single point and Dinamo Tblisi by two, Spartak met the previous year's champion, Dinamo Kiev, in Kiev on November 18. That morning in their hotel the players learned that Dinamo Moscow had lost, and as they were changing for the match, Simonian entered the dressing room to inform them that Dinamo Tblisi had also been defeated. The new champions celebrated and then went out and won 2–0.[64] Sevidov had emerged as the team's offensive leader with support from Khusainov. Netto continued his high level of play, while Valerii Dikarev and Vladimir Krutikov emerged, along with Logofet, as stars on defense.[65] The change of generations was now complete. Writing in *Sovestkii sport,* Lev Filatov described it as their most difficult championship ever.[66] If the great teams of the fifties had borne the mark of others, the 1962 side was very much Starostin's own creation. He had named the coach, collected the players, and created an internal atmosphere within the club that enabled them to succeed. Later his center forward, Iuri Sevidov, would remark that this particular team had given him his greatest satisfaction. Starostin's career had been firmly reestablished. The long troubled journey that had begun with his arrest in 1942 was now over.

However, this success could not be maintained. A second-place finish to Dinamo Moscow the next year was followed by a slide to eighth in 1964. Although there had been a rash of injuries, there was no clear explanation for the streak of twelve matches without a win that drove the team down to the middle of the table, where it finally settled as attendance dropped. Most of the players who had performed so well in previous years were still around, but in typical Spartak fashion the team had taken another slide, demoralizing its fans. In another sign of changing times, Dinamo Tblisi won the title it had so long coveted and deserved. Spartak, however, had entered a new period of crisis. It faced an uncertain future when Khrushchev was ousted in October 1964, one month before the end of the football season. He was replaced by Leonid Brezhnev, who would bring a more predictable and considerably less dynamic approach to his task.

The end of the Khrushchev period marks the end of Spartak's history of high drama. The narrative arc of the Starostins' story closes as, after the requisite trials and tribulations, they returned to the place of honor they had carved out for themselves before the war. They had triumphed, and Spartak's Golden Age attested to that great victory. By the late fifties and early sixties, the Kremlin's direct involvement in domestic football had diminished. The party's approach to the game became more supervisory and less interfering. For the state, choosing sides became increasingly complicated with so many more clubs now part of the sporting picture. It was no longer clear to those in authority that the fortunes of one team were more important than those of another, as the needs of provincial sides and those in the republics also had to be taken into consideration.

Rather than curry favor with patrons at the highest levels of power, club bosses took on the kinds of organizational tasks that were normal for men in their positions all over the world. The word "normal" needs to be qualified in the Soviet context, however, since the USSR was still hardly a normal place. The daily drudgery of bureaucracy and corruption, while far from exceptional throughout the soccer world, continued to have a particular character in the USSR. Complicated rules selectively enforced created opportunities for the sort of corruption that later became endemic under Brezhnev, but for all its corrosive effect, corruption was easier to accept than the arrests, forced replays, blackmail, and intimidation of earlier decades.

By 1959 Starostin had come to operate in a minefield, a task at which he proved to be adept if not always successful. Winning became more difficult. Throughout this travail, it was also difficult to maintain the image of the people's team. The notion of Spartak as victim faded for many, and the rivalry with Dinamo could no longer replicate the old us-versus-them intensity. Newly powerful opponents had appeared by 1960—Torpedo and Dinamo Kiev, to name just two. While matches with these clubs proved compelling sporting events, the new rivals could not mobilize the hatred elicited by Dinamo Moscow, whose own ability to maintain its position at the top of the league standings had diminished along with that of Spartak.

The audience continued to change as well. As the capital grew into a more cosmopolitan place, both blue- and white-collar Muscovites found there was more competition for their time and money. Football, once "our only spectacle," was now but one of many attractions available to the city's public. These processes in turn had a significant impact on the one concrete measure of fan interest. Attendance had been Spartak's greatest strength and source of revenue. The loyalty of its fans had been a salient element of the team's identity, but full houses now grew less common. Games against famous and powerful opponents, new or old, continued to draw sizable crowds, but when the visitors were a less successful provincial side, no more than a few thousand might show up.

In the light of these changes, the always tenuous, highly subjective construct of Spartak spirit became harder for both the team and its fans to sustain. The notion that Spartak was somehow special began to diminish, attenuating in the process the ardor of its supporters. While fans may have bought into the club's family romance, that image was grounded in the earlier period of the Starostins' history and that of the club itself. Their memoirs, including those that appeared during glasnost, had focused on the earlier years, paying scant attention to later events. They had in effect taught their readers how to fall in love with Spartak, but they had done little to persuade them to continue the romance.

It is in the nature of the history of big-time spectator sport for there to be a growing dissonance between a team's founding myth and its present reality. The communities and circumstances that have given birth to football clubs and established their identities have tended to wither over time. The myths may remain the same, but historical circumstances constantly change. Manchester United and Arsenal have come a long way from their origins as factory teams to become enormous global brands catering to the highly privileged. The fact that Aston Villa began life as a church team does not mean all of its later supporters are religious. The flagman of German football, Bayern Munich, was started before the First World War by Jewish shop owners. It turns out that fans choose selectively from their clubs' histories to justify their loyalty. Such was the case with Spartak.

# 9

# Uncertainly Ever After, 1964–1991

Life under Leonid Brezhnev and his immediate successors (1964–1985) was profoundly different for Spartak. The great dramas of triumph, tragedy, and resurrection were now over. The high politics of the Kremlin were replaced by the local politics of ensuring support from the Moscow authorities. The Brezhnev years did not turn out to be particularly kind to Spartak, but the club's difficulties were not the result of decisions from above. In the sixties and most of the seventies, Spartak's record was one of mediocrity interrupted by the occasional unexpected success that kept the family romance alive. The Golden Age was now over, to be replaced by the less glamorous tasks of simply keeping the team afloat. By 1978, however, Nikolai Starostin finally succeeded in returning his club to the elite of Soviet soccer, where it stayed until the end of Soviet power. This triumph came at a price, as Starostin had to adopt methods and practices that clashed with the club's traditions and his own oft-stated principles.

It is clear from the dates of these ups and downs on the field that the shifting sands at the top of the party and state had ceased to determine Spartak's fate. There was no Brezhnev line on football that clashed with Khrushchev's. Consequently, the historical meaning and importance of Spartak changed. With each epoch of Soviet history, the Starostins had adapted to new circumstances, reflecting changes that emanated from the center. This did not mean the team followed orders from the top. As we have seen, even under Stalin there was a constant process of negotiation through which the Starostins carved out a measure of independence while the state came to understand the limits of its power when it came to football. Now Spartak found itself operating in an environment determined neither by the Central Committee nor by the secret police but instead by deeper social and economic trends over which the party had, at best, only partial control. Soccer had become a highly visible form of popular culture firmly imbedded in a swiftly evolving society whose always-tenuous connections with the political elites were again in transition.

Up to this point, the Soviet leadership's interest in the fate of the game has left a record that enables us to plot the links between Spartak and the larger historical context for each period of Soviet history. Turning to the USSR's last decades, we confront a marked shortage of archival materials and the absence of an agreed-upon master narrative. Our study of Spartak in these last Soviet years will thus reveal less about decisions from above than about deeper trends in society. The changing nature of Soviet society forced Starostin to rethink his approach yet again, and the steps he took to keep Spartak alive shed light on the direction in which the nation itself was moving.

## Change amid Stagnation

The earliest watchword of the new regime had been "stability of cadres." Khrushchev's attempts to remake the party had threatened the privileges and comforts of officialdom. The new leadership moved quickly to reverse those reforms that had decentralized power and threatened the privileges of the elite. Officials at all levels were given lifetime tenure, allowing them to grow old in their positions while cutting off upward mobility for an entire younger generation. With little incentive to work effectively or to innovate, those at the top of the state and party structures became lazy and dishonest. Without irony, Brezhnev called this situation "mature socialism." Conservative by nature, the new party leader was highly cautious. Additionally, he was burdened early in his tenure by the need to maintain collective leadership with such powerful figures as Alexei Kosygin, Andrei Gromyko, Mikhail Suslov, Yuri Andropov, and Dmitri Ustinov. Despite the able Kosygin's ultimately thwarted plans for economic reform as well as other ongoing discussions about revising old practices, there were few grand reform projects over the next eighteen years. Care was taken to avoid upsetting the public with unrealistic goals and promises.

Instead, a perverse social contract emerged in which workers, still the largest social class, were rewarded for their political acquiescence with improved living standards and a wide array of social benefits. In the words of the German scholar Christian Noack, the "new policy . . . tried to secure the Soviet citizens' loyalty to the regime by expanding consumption and by distributing far-reaching social benefits. Wages were raised, working time was reduced, and the regime refrained from harsh measures to secure social discipline. The state subsidized a better supply of food, housing, and, to a degree, consumption goods."[1] At the same time, little was done to reduce the enormous privileges of a party elite that became corrupt and later senile.[2] Although freezing the bureaucracy in place and buying off the working class were but two of many causes of the stagnation that doomed the system, one could argue that such stability was very much welcome after the terror of

Stalin and the erratic enthusiasms of Khrushchev. Even so-called progressives hailed the new leadership, having come to the conclusion that measured and reasoned change could prove more effective than Khrushchev's unpredictability.

The slowing of the reform process seemed to be mirrored on another front. Open criticism of the system was no longer tolerated. If the Thaw did not definitively come to end in 1964, it soon became clear that party conservatives had become uncomfortable with the earlier efflorescence of public opinion and free artistic expression. The result was increased repression. The 1965 arrest and subsequent trial of the writers Andrei Siniavskii and Yuli Daniel signaled a crackdown on criticism that intimidated a broad range of intellectuals and forced them to choose between silence and outright opposition. A tiny brave minority took the dangerous path of dissidence. Their demonstrations, petitions and writings circulated surreptitiously, and their small numbers guaranteed their ideas and demands would have no immediate impact on the policies of the state. Highly visible in the West but much less so at home, they were subject to arrest, exile, confinement to psychiatric wards, and dismissal from their jobs.

The dissidents' initial hope that Communism could be reformed from within vanished in 1968 with the crushing of the Czechoslovak attempt to create "socialism with a human face." Thereafter, many followed the lead of Andrei Sakharov and directed their energies toward securing basic human rights. Some took up nationalist causes, while still others like, Aleksandr Solzhenytsin, embraced religion along with Russia's historical traditions. Although the repressions were targeted at a small group of critics and stopped far short of Stalinist terror, the optimism of the Thaw had given way to pessimism and, at least initially, acceptance, particularly among those professionals and intellectuals who felt they had too much to lose by following the dissidents and defying the regime.[3]

By the late sixties, however, those who worked within the system found safe ways to work for change.[4] Composed of "broad layers of officials, political opinion makers and the party apparatus," these groups, while not open dissidents, sought to agitate for reform.[5] Operating in the blurred boundary between the regime and society, they were harbingers of the kind of civil society described in the previous chapter. Over time, many of them succeeded in being taken seriously. Outside experts and specialists were consulted on a broad range of issues. By their willingness to provide a critical voice, these figures, especially social scientists, exhibited a degree of personal independence (an essential element of any civil society) while maintaining some ability to influence state policy. Although their efforts did not have a decisive impact at the time, many of them (most notably Georgi Arbatov, Stanislav Shatalin, Aleksandr Yakovlev, Abel Aganbenian, and Tatyana Zaslavskaia) emerged as important figures during perestroika.

Outside the level of high politics, where it appeared little had changed, Soviet society was very much in flux during these years. Change was most clearly manifest in the towns. Old cities grew, and new ones, like the auto center Togliatti, were created from nothing. More and more Soviets were urban dwellers. In 1959, half the citizens of the USSR lived in towns. By the end of Brezhnev's time in office, between 65 and 75 percent of the population was urban.[6] Perhaps more important, half the population had been born in cities, producing a very different sort of urban scene. The peasant presence in the towns ebbed while the numbers of professionals continued to grow. There was also a similar expansion in the ranks of lower-status white-collar workers who performed both service and administrative tasks.[7]

All these groups, workers included, had increasingly complicated demands, tastes, and expectations that were not so easily fulfilled by an unresponsive political structure and an inefficient economic system. They sought more freedom and higher living standards—better housing, an improved diet, and more consumer goods. Despite progress on all these fronts, demand eventually outstripped the command model's ability to respond to the population's needs. The social contract began to unravel. The productionist system that measured success in gross figures for the output of basic industries was not able to make the transition to a consumer society. In the process, the "second" economy of the black market and *blat* emerged to fill the gap, eroding the line between the legal and the illegal.

Despite its fundamental weaknesses, the economy did continue to grow until the midseventies. There were more and more factories, mines, and construction sites dotting the landscape of the growing cities. As the industrial network expanded to the far ends of the Soviet Union and as older regions saw increased population and economic activity, their residents came to require not just work but the amenities of modern urban life, including leisure.[8] When they weren't working or drinking, young male members of the workforce came to play and watch soccer. Football, virtually everywhere the sport of the cities, followed the factory.[9]

### Football amid Stagnation

All around the world soccer developed in tandem with industry and commerce. Accordingly, the game was one of many markers of an increasing modernity. In Britain, the sport was the child of the middle classes, only later being adopted by the country's workers. In the USSR what we could term middle-class elements of society were drawn to soccer only after the game had caught on among the proletariat. As towns became industrial centers with larger populations, both the workers and the various white-collar elements who had joined them required not just housing and feeding but a whole range of entertainments. Millions had watched the spectacle of professional football on television. Now the citizens of these cities came to demand their own teams, and local authorities, eager to raise the prestige of their regions, were only too happy to oblige.[10]

The growth was enormous. In 1950, there had been only 33 clubs formally enrolled in the football league structure. By 1968, there were 267 teams at all levels.[11] Sport societies organized clubs that were then integrated into the national league system. A third division, with teams assigned to numerous geographic zones, stretched the entire length and breadth of the union. Stadiums were constructed. Among many new venues, Republican Stadium, seating a hundred thousand, opened in Kiev during 1965, and Erevan's Razdan Stadium, with seventy-five thousand seats, was completed in 1971. Alma-Ata, Baku, Tashkent, Voroshilovgrad, Minsk, Dnepropetrovsk, Donetsk, and dozens of other cities built slightly smaller venues. Fans from all social groups came to watch, and soon the most successful of these newer clubs were seeking entry to the highest levels of the sport. This expansion was abetted by improvements in transportation and communication, another product of development that had made the spread of sport possible everywhere. For the larger first and second divisions to function, teams had to move great distances in a timely manner. By the midsixties a flight from Moscow to Tashkent, to name just one example, was no longer a daunting prospect. The mass media expanded and became more efficient. For lovers of the game who wanted to know the scores, television, radio, and an increasingly effective and nimble sports press provided quick information. With more teams in more cities, there were more games to be played, watched, and reported on. The entire edifice of Soviet football became bigger and more complicated.

The league structures expanded to accommodate these new teams, making life more difficult for those in the capital. Moscow's domination of the game ended. According to Timothy Colton, there had been a similar drop in Moscow's authority within the party and in the larger society.[12] Now there were more suitors for the best talents, as provincial clubs came to outbid the teams in the center.[13] The state sports committee could adjudicate disputes and discipline rule violators, but with the profusion of clubs it became politically impossible to play favorites as had been done in the past. The regime's earlier support for the structures of force was no longer acceptable in the face of newly emergent and powerful regional interests.[14] With literally scores of teams, many club managers sought to circumvent the normal sporting processes for advancement to the game's higher levels. Instead of winning in the lower divisions and gaining promotion, powerful local leaders, called "patrons" (*metsenaty*), sought to use political influence and pressure to advance the cause of their teams.

With the improved capacity of television to beam games from all the major Soviet cities, not just the capital, there was greater competition for the comparatively limited airtime devoted to soccer. The same struggle for space was played out in the press, most notably *Sovetskii sport.* No longer could the most famous Moscow teams control the league's proceedings or even its most public images. Netto and Iashin publicly expressed fears that Moscow's decline would have an adverse impact on the national team's performance.[15] These developments also troubled Nikolai Starostin. Writing in *Izvestiia* in 1966, he expressed discomfort with the consequences of the enormous growth in the number of teams wishing to make it to the top flight of the game by means fair or foul:

> Adherents of tradition see in this an inadmissible violation of the sporting principle. According to the rules regulating the league championship, the way to move into the strongest group is through victories [the sporting principle]. . . . In the interest of satisfying the massive number of requests from the localities and in order to put on activities in stadiums, it was seen as advisable to advance certain cities into groups above their ranking.[16]

His view would be adopted by the state sports committee in a 1970 resolution that concluded the massive expansion had been harmful to the interests of Soviet football.[17]

More teams meant a greater number of matches on television—once a luxury item but now widely available. Four or five matches a week were available. Midweek European cup nights might involve as many as three matches, several of which took place in foreign stadiums. The possibility of watching in the privacy of one's apartment, either with friends or alone, modified the experience of fanship. The joking, complaining, and cursing that went on in the stands were even more intense in the greater anonymity of a private space. As I can confirm from extensive "ethnographic" observation (not to mention participation), free-flowing banter and unmonitored drinking created possibilities for male bonding and safe criticism of teams, players, coaches, and the game itself. Announcers like Nikolai Ozerov and Vladimir Maslachenko eschewed political didacticism in their descriptions of domestic matches. Pre- and postgame analysis did not exist, and viewers were free to construct their own meanings from what they had just witnessed.[18]

The greater complexity of the soccer world mirrored the greater complexity of society in the last Soviet decades and in the process created a very different, far less clear set of political and cultural meanings. The anthropologist Alexei Yurchak argues that the sixties and seventies witnessed a fundamental "cultural shift" that eroded the seemingly clear dualities of the earlier epochs of Soviet history. There was a blurring of the conflict between nonconformist behavior that might once have implied resistance and the "authoritative discourse" of the state and party. "The system," he writes, "was internally mutating toward unpredictable, creative multiple forms of 'normal life' that no one anticipated."

As a particularly apt case in point, Yurchak describes a Komsomol activist and loyal Soviet citizen who was also a passionate and intelligent fan of Western rock music. Similarly, those who took part in the explosion of urban countercultures in the last Soviet decades did not so much seek to challenge the authority of the regime as to avoid it. The other duality of the official and the dissident, so visible to outsiders, did not exist for legions of young people. When the Western popular culture so many of them embraced was denounced as politically dangerous by those in authority, young people simply denied any connection between politics and their favorite activities.[19] Implicit in this approach is the emergence of a disconnect between the two parts of the state-society dichotomy. Both partners in this complicated dance had evolved and changed over the course of Soviet history, but, as happened all over the world in the sixties, dancing partners no longer touched. If a renovated regime had been renegotiating its relationship with a society in transition during Khrushchev's years in power, by the time of the late Brezhnev era that process had lost its meaning and purpose. The struggle, if it can be called that, was multidirectional and many-sided.

While none of the individuals described by Yurchak evinced an interest in sport, neither the players nor their younger fans can have been immune to these trends. Spartak in particular counted a large number of jazz lovers among its members. Like footballers all over the world, they enjoyed both Western music and soccer. They wore their hair long in the style of their contemporaries, a fact referees noted disapprovingly as a sign of independence. Globally, long hair had become a sign of a new masculinity, and the lads of Spartak were not the only Soviet football players with long hair.[20] Older men like Starostin looked on uncomprehendingly as Soviet youth, trying to be free of the demands of the state, exhibited a spirit of independence.

Like so much else, the new behaviors of those who came of age during this time emerged in response to the continuing growth of the towns. The new subcultures, along with domestic and foreign forms of mass culture, were urban phenomena. During the sixties and especially the seventies, entertainment became more extensive and multifarious. Football was no longer the people's only spectacle. Attendance eroded with the greater variety of distractions and the decline in the quality of the Soviet domestic game. Pushing seventy, Starostin found himself navigating in decidedly uncharted waters, selling a product that had become less attractive to a very different audience.[21]

The processes of acquiring talent expanded from the local to the national, as teams from everywhere recruited players from all corners of the nation. By the 1960s, Spartak had long ceased to be the only club employing many different nationalities. The procedures and controls governing player transfers, not to mention the subterfuges for avoiding those rules, became more various and arcane.[22] The structure of the league was in constant flux during these years as the sports authorities struggled to find the organizational forms most appropriate to the new circumstances. Mirroring the rest of society, corruption in soccer increased exponentially with a flood of arranged (*dogovornyi*) matches. Indirect and direct methods of influencing referees became commonplace.[23] At a 1972 meeting of players, coaches, and officials, the head of the Komsomol, S. Arutiunian, admitted to an ever-broader range of problems:

> Sports organizations cannot but be threatened by the appearance in recent years of the unhealthy situation that has begun to develop around football. Greed, the patrons, the movement of players from one team to another, violations of financial discipline, ignoring of the sporting regime [drunkenness], and an atmosphere that forgives all these sins can, unfortunately be found in many teams.[24]

Finding and maintaining sponsorship took on new forms as well. The late sixties and seventies, in particular, witnessed the emergence of the afore-mentioned patrons, who were willing to do almost anything to help their teams. When they were not engaged in all manner of illegal and improper practices, these figures interfered in their club's operations, hiring and firing on a whim and seeking to name lineups.[25] If one can accept the notion that a chastened Nikolai Starostin sought to operate in an honest and legal manner after his exile, it becomes clear that the very different world of Soviet football during these last decades posed an enormous challenge for him.

Aside from urbanization, exposure to both an actual and an imagined West had further changed Soviet life. Although the economy continued to be based on an autarkic model, it increasingly became necessary to trade with capital-ist nations in order to import a wide range of items that could not be produced in the USSR. By 1975 it even became necessary to import food. This trade was financed by windfall profits from the extensive sale of oil and gold, two com-modities the USSR had in abundance. In particular, the fortuitous rise in world oil prices after the 1973 Yom Kippur War made possible a modest im-provement in living standards without more fundamental economic reform. If the aim of the authorities had been to forestall change by importing goods, the appearance of higher-quality foreign products in Soviet shops only inten-sified the lure of the West and raised questions about why Soviet factories could not produce such things. Often, imports never even made it to the stores. In some cases, goods disappeared into the second economy. In others, salespeople held back items for favored customers. Over time, the terms of this trade worked to the disadvantage of the Soviet side. Instead of using the profits from oil to invest in globally competitive industries, the leadership purchased political acceptance by improving consumers' lives at the margins.

It was similarly difficult to remain autarkic when it came to information. Foreign shortwave broadcasts literally flooded the airwaves, providing other sources of news and culture not found in official media. Knowledge of the West also flowed in through the ever-larger numbers of foreign tourists and students. Soviet audiences were able to see a controlled program of touring Western entertainers. At the same time, growing numbers of heavily vetted Soviets were able to travel to Eastern Europe and in many cases to the West.[26] A steady stream of the USSR's best musicians, dancers, actors, and athletes toured the globe earning hard currency as well as respect for the motherland. In the process, they studied, with varying degrees of intensity, the fleshpots of capitalism and brought back all manner of trophies either to display or to sell on the black market.

Football was very much a part of this cultural interaction with the outside world. After its 1958 debut, the Soviet national team was a constant partici-pant in both the European and World Cups. It did well during the sixties, tak-ing the first European championship in 1960, coming in second in 1964, and finishing fourth at the 1966 World Cup, but by the seventies the fortunes of the sbornaia had nosedived. To fix the problem, Soviet experts intensified their collection of information on Western methods and tactics, and the press expanded its coverage of the world's leading leagues. After 1966, Soviet involvement in world football took on an added dimension. Individual clubs began to take part in the hugely popular, season-long cup tournaments organized by the Union of European Football Associations (UEFA). These were the European Cup (for league champions), the Cup-winners' Cup, and the lesser UEFA Cup for teams that came close to winning their leagues. Each year several Soviet clubs played in Europe, with many of the games televised back to Soviet viewers. When foreign teams played in the USSR, they brought hundreds, even thousands, of their fans with them, along with large media contingents.

Foreign exhibition tours had long been a part of Soviet soccer, but now Soviet teams were playing games of genuine importance against Europe's best. There had always been a predictable rallying around the national team when it played, but loyalties were fractured when Soviet clubs began to take part in these tournaments. As was true elsewhere, it was not uncommon for the supporters of one team to root for their archrivals' foreign opponents. If victory by the national team could inspire a measure of patriotism and pride, the same could not always be said at the club level. The rapid growth of the domestic game during this period had already made the ascription of political and cultural meaning to football a far more murky process. Now participation in the big international tournaments added a new dimension to the arguments among supporters, journalists, officials, coaches, and players.

The football federation took a strong interest in its teams' success, viewing these competitions as yet another examination of Soviet football. For the authorities, once a team crossed the border, it took on the added responsibility of representing the nation. Schedules were rearranged to allow clubs to prepare for matches. Transfers to participating teams were looked upon more kindly.[27] Yet for all the interest these competitions provoked, Soviet successes were few. Dinamo Kiev took the less prestigious Cup Winners' Cup twice; its clubmates from Tblisi captured it a single time. In 1975, Dinamo Kiev won the commercially contrived Super Cup, defeating that year's European champion, Bayern Munich. Spartak's involvement in these tournaments was episodic and far less glorious.

There were thoroughly objective reasons for the Soviets' less-than-impressive record. Just as it hampered the efforts of the national team, the summer schedule of the domestic league, stretching from March to December, made it difficult for Soviet clubs to survive the latter stages of the European cup tournaments. As their rivals were reaching their peak of conditioning and coordination in the spring, Soviet sides were only starting their seasons. It proved difficult to compete given this situation, and they rarely passed what came to be known as the "March barrier." Additionally, many of the bigger European clubs were beginning to employ foreign players during the sixties and seventies. This quite clearly was not an option for Soviet sides. Overall, participation in the great European cups proved to be a frustrating experience. The specifics of the USSR's geography and its diminishing but still considerable economic and political isolation combined to limit Soviet success. In contrast to the great across-the-board triumphs at the Olympic Games, the spotty record in international football served to affirm the historic Russian/Soviet sense of backwardness.[28]

By the midseventies, there was good reason for Soviet citizens to feel backward. The economy began to decline. The limited growth that had been achieved up to that point was now threatened. Life expectancy dropped. Vodka consumption increased. The excitement of catching up with capitalism evaporated as the USSR lost ground to Western economies then experiencing the first waves of a scientific-technological revolution the Soviets embraced with only limited success. Brezhnev's health went into decline, and his awkward and embarrassing public appearances were symbolic of the rest of those stable, now-aging cadres who had stayed on past their time. Corruption in all spheres of life grew unchecked, eroding what little ideological idealism remained. In the face of this demoralization, Soviet media continued to paint pictures of happiness, harmony, and progress, and the contrast between these accounts and an ever-grimmer reality became untenable. In the midst of this decay, the leadership in 1979 took the disastrous step of massive military interference in Afghanistan, undermining relations with the West and sending young men off to die in the tens of thousands.

Brezhnev's life finally ended in 1982, and Suslov passed on with him. The able new head of the party, Yuri Andropov, a former KGB chief, was sensitive to the problems he had inherited. In his short time in office, he forcefully sought to combat corruption and improve economic performance. Yet his death early in 1984 brought this brief and problematic attempt at change to an end. Andropov was succeeded by Brezhnev's close comrade Konstantin Chernenko, who stood in opposition to the progressive tendencies in the party and society that had emerged over the previous eighteen years. His death in 1985 brought an end to stability at the top with the coming to power of a new generation in the person of Mikhail Gorbachev. Twenty years younger than most of his immediate colleagues, this new leader quickly realized that the political system had failed to reform itself in ways that could have enabled it to manage the changes experienced by the larger society. Here was the recipe for disaster he would spend the next six years desperately trying to avoid.

### Stagnation amid Stagnation

Nikolai Starostin had long demonstrated the ability to adapt to new circumstances. When the great team of the Golden Age eroded and collapsed in 1959, Starostin proved he was able to assemble a new group and return to the top by 1962. He achieved this not simply by stroking friends in high places but by performing the tasks of team managers all over the world, finding good players and coaches and creating an environment that enabled them to flourish. During this period, sponsorship of the team passed from Mossovet to the trade union sports system, a change that weakened Spartak's financial situation. In addition, a new power had appeared in Soviet soccer. Using all the resources of the Ukrainian Ministry of Interior, Dinamo Kiev emerged as the strongest, if not the most popular, of all Soviet clubs, a position it maintained until the collapse of the USSR. Faced with a range of new circumstances during the seventies, Starostin was not able to sustain the earlier success, and the team again found itself in a crisis that lasted until the end of the decade. Another championship in 1969 was followed by yet another return to the depths, leading ultimately to relegation in 1976, just as the larger economy was slowing down.

Before the 1965 season, Starostin had been assigned to other duties in the national Spartak organization. The task of finding apartments and dealing with all the other matters of daily life now fell to Simonian, who spent less time with the players and felt his authority with them erode. On September 18, Simonian came to understand the tragic consequences of his loss of control. At the wheel of his new Ford, a drunk Yuri Sevidov ran over and killed the eminent chemist Dmitri Ryabchikov, a corresponding member of the Academy of Sciences. The man's colleagues demanded justice, and Spartak made no attempt to defend Sevidov, who spent a year and a half in prison. He did not play organized soccer for the next five years, returning in 1970 to Kairat, where he was coached by his father, Aleksandr. Under pressure from Moscow party bosses for failing to educate his players, Simonian accepted responsibility for the incident and submitted his resignation. With the oft-injured Netto playing in only four games, a dispirited team finished the season in eighth place.[29] Nikolai Gulyaev replaced Simonian the next year, which ended with Spartak in a slightly less unsatisfactory fourth place.

Throughout this period of mediocrity, Spartak was still able to mobilize itself for big occasions. As is so often the case in football, the cup competition provided a chance to make up for poor play in the league. In the 1965 final, the team defeated Dinamo Minsk in a replay, with Khusainov scoring the winning goal on passes from Logofet and Reingol'd. The dramatic victory was in the best tradition of Spartak romanticism, allowing the faithful to continue believing in their team's possibilities.[30] Others were less impressed. Summarizing the 1966 season, Boris Arkadiev criticized "the most popular team in Moscow" for its inability to mobilize itself for every game. He remarked that the players seemed to lack unity, showing weak discipline on the field. Arkadiev attributed these problems to weaknesses in talent acquisition. Players now came from all over the country, not just Moscow, as in the old days, "and this in a city in which practically every young boy dreams of playing for Spartak."[31]

The downward trajectory of the club's fortunes was reversed in 1967. Netto had finally retired, and Nikolai Starostin returned to his old duties. After a brief experiment with Sergei Sal'nikov as coach, Simonian was brought back. Together again, they began the process of renewing Spartak, releasing several veterans and giving more time to the younger players. In 1968, the team came

**9.1** The nattily dressed Evgenii Lovchev with Nikolai Starostin. I. Goranskii, *Evgenii Lovchev.*

in second to Dinamo Kiev, which had taken the title for the third consecutive year.[32] Hope had been revived among the Spartak faithful, but Starostin and Simonian did not stand pat. They replaced the fading Maslachenko in goal with the Georgian Anzor Kavazashvili, who had come over from Torpedo, but the most important addition was a player who came to embody all the ineffable elements of Spartak spirit.

Evgenii Lovchev (b. 1949) had grown up in the semirural village of Kriukovo (now the industrial suburb of Zelenograd) on the outskirts of Moscow. Plucked from the Burevestnik club, which had been the base of the Soviet youth squad (players under seventeen), he was recommended to Simonian by the Spartak team doctor. A versatile defender who could also attack with skill, Lovchev immediately slotted in at left fullback, where he replaced Anatoly Krutikov, who had been forced to retire after suffering a torn Achilles tendon. Lovchev made an immediate and sensational impact and soon was called up to the national team, but his importance extended beyond the field of play. He exhibited that rarest of qualities among Soviet citizens; he boldly thought and spoke at the same time. Intelligent, independent, and voluble, Lovchev saw himself (and still sees himself) as an acolyte of Nikolai Starostin and a fighter for the real and imagined ideals Spartak stood for. A great interviewee, Lovchev found a willing audience among Soviet sportswriters and through them the fans.[33] Others were less positive, calling him a troublemaker who divided the team into cliques. Throughout this most difficult of periods in the team's history, he stood out as a constant example of skill and effort. When Spartak finished eleventh one season, Lovchev was actually voted player of the year, an honor that usually goes to those on winning teams.

By 1969, Simonian had found a good combination of the old and young, whom he organized into an effective variety of formations. Motivation, especially with the talkative Lovchev on the field, was no longer a problem. The players remained healthy, allowing Simonian to start the same lineup for practically every game. Spartak won its subgroup in the first half of the season, but the first sign of great possibilities came on August 23. It defeated Dinamo Kiev 2–1 in Moscow before a hundred thousand, with Logofet scoring the winning goal on a rebound off a Khusainov shot. The players returned to Kiev on October 30 tied with their opponent for first. On a rainy and snowy night with a slippery field, Nikolai Osianin (b. 1941), a Russian striker from Tartaria, received a pass thirty-five meters from the goal. He then wove through four defenders before chipping the ball over the onrushing Kiev keeper. It was the only goal of the game, sending a hundred thousand cold and shivering Kievans home disappointed.[34]

With two games to go, Spartak was ahead by two points. Through an oddity of the schedule, both matches were against TsSKA. If Spartak could win the first meeting, Dinamo Kiev could not catch them, but panic set in when the result was a 1–1 tie. The season came down to a frigid November day with only twenty-one thousand braving the elements to watch Spartak win 1–0 on a goal by Osianin.[35] Dinamo Kiev's run of three consecutive titles had been ended. Spartak once again was champion. In the wake of victory, Nikolai Starostin wrote:

> Only the most incorrigible romantics believed that the Spartak team that won silver in 1968 could turn it into gold. Spartak's victory proves that the decisive word has been and always will be "team." [It played for] the ideals which inspire it, for the relationships that cement it together and for the players in whom the team's leadership believed—[it was done] for the honorable mission of the defense of our sporting colors and, most of all, *for our principles.*[36]

Here one might ask just what principles Starostin had in mind. Match fixing had become an enormous problem by this time. Arranged games usually took the form of ties that allowed both teams to gather points while giving less than a complete effort. As had been the case in several East European countries (most notably Romania), several teams cooperated with one another. The primary aim was the avoidance of relegation. The resulting string of dull matches drove fans away from the stadiums and threatened the prized international success of Soviet soccer. As rampant as these fixed games were, no case was ever proved. Players, coaches, and officials kept silent despite the repeated efforts of journalists and sports committee officials. To this day, it is virtually impossible to get veterans of the game to talk openly on this subject.

Spartak fans, of course, believed their team never engaged in the practice, and Starostin had denounced match fixing in a number of venues.[37] Nevertheless, it appears more than likely that the last match of the 1969 season was rigged.

In September of 2000, I asked Gennadi Logofet whether he had ever engaged in a fixed game. He replied, "Just once." It was the victory over TsSKA on the final day of the 1969 season. Aksel Vartanian has confirmed similar rumors about this event. TsSKA was locked into fourth place. The result was of no importance to them. On the other hand, according to Logofet, TsSKA needed to find apartments for several of its players, and Spartak actually had better connections than the army when it came to Moscow housing. In return for four apartments, TsSKA agreed to throw the match.[38] As things turned out, Dinamo Kiev lost its final game, making the Spartak-TsSKA result moot. One could argue that ultimately no harm was done, but the episode is less than inspiring. Logofet said they knew they would win when they took the field. The players and coaches were aware of the fix. Perhaps Nikolai Starostin did not know what went on, but the price of victory—four apartments—makes this improbable. Housing was his specialty. He was known to roam construction sites to learn which apartments had been set aside for distribution by Mossovet.[39] Only he could have come up with what TsSKA was demanding.

Was this one rigged match an isolated instance? One cannot really know the answer to this question, but even as cynical an observer as the sportswriter Arkadii Galinskii believed that Spartak, along with Dinamo Moscow, was a relatively honest team. By contrast, Dinamo Kiev, especially later on, became notorious for arranging ties in its away matches. Spartak may also have engaged in these less-than-honorable methods, but it appears that its participation in fixed games was far less frequent than its opponents'. Still, this and many other dubious practices were so widespread that it is hard to believe Spartak and Starostin in particular could have stood entirely on principle and survived. The Soviet Union during the Brezhnev period was not, after all, a good place for idealists. Nor can it be said that soccer throughout the world was itself in great shape in these years. Negative play and massive corruption combined with the rise of hooliganism to threaten the very existence of the sport. In this sense, what was happening in the USSR was but one manifestation of a worldwide phenomenon.[40]

As had been the case after 1962, Spartak was not able to stay at the top after the championship of 1969. A steady slide down the standings led to a calamitous eleventh-place finish in 1972. Having lost the support of the players and feeling pressure from the trade union hierarchy, Simonian resigned. Proving he had not lost his touch, the next season he took over Ararat in the Armenian capital of Erevan. Although he had not grown up in Armenia proper, Simonian's work with his new team was something of a homecoming that found immediate rewards on the field. With little history of success, Ararat won the double in 1973. Back at Spartak, the always-faithful Gulyaev stepped in again. Igor Netto, having coached all over the world since his retirement, was his assistant. They restored order and even won a silver medal in 1974, but they found themselves falling back down to tenth in 1975. The second-place finish of the previous year had led the football federation to make Spartak the base of the Olympic team, tearing several players away from the club for numerous matches.[41]

The early seventies were especially inauspicious both for Spartak and for Moscow football in general. The provincial teams, with their fine disregard for the rules, had become so dominant that in many seasons no Moscow club finished in the top three.[42] Dinamo Kiev went from strength to strength, especially after Valerii Lobanovskii took over the coaching reins in 1974. In a 1970 resolution, the state sports committee had taken measures to combat a range of problems. Announcing the limitation of the first division (*vyshaia liga*) to sixteen teams, the committee decried both the growth in the number of clubs and the violations of the sporting principle that had led so often to undeserved promotions and thwarted relegations. There were simply not enough high-quality players available to staff so many sides. The result was the deterioration of domestic league play and the consequent failure to prepare players and teams for international competition. In order to stem the epidemic of dubious ties, the sports authorities in 1973 introduced the use of postmatch penalty kicks after every tied match. At the time, this was seen as an irrational step and was soon abandoned. Later, of course, the resort to penalties became standard global practice.[43]

These reforms could well have been seen as favoring Spartak. Both Starostin brothers had long championed the sporting principle in matters of relegation and promotion, and both had been publicly alarmed by the large numbers of drawn matches. The first and subsequent proposals to cut down on ties had been championed by those highly visible Spartak fans Lev Filatov and Konstantin Esenin, who had directly lobbied the sports committee.[44] In supporting these measures, the football authorities believed they were trying to act as honest brokers to protect the game's remaining shreds of integrity, but in the provinces some saw these steps as ways for the center to reassert its authority. Others claimed to detect shades of Russian nationalism. The Ukrainians in particular felt they were being penalized for their success.

In the fall of 1975, following Spartak's slide to tenth place, the trade union sports leadership decided fundamental change was required. Gulyaev was dismissed, and Nikolai Starostin, now seventy-seven, was assigned to less important duties running Spartak teams in the local Moscow league. Ivan Varlamov replaced him. The new coach was Anatoly Krutikov, assisted by Galimzian Khusainov. Both former stars had been coaching Spartak Nal'chik, with no great distinction. The move, ordered by the trade union sports leadership, was an enormous blow to Nikolai Starostin. At the time, many probably thought that the old man had lost his touch; no one, not even Starostin himself, could have known he would live another twenty-one years and retain his mental faculties to the very end. At the time, Vladimir Maslachenko suggested that brother Andrei should take over Spartak as a figurehead. Nikolai immediately dismissed the idea. Confirming earlier accounts of Andrei's playboy image, he told Maslachenko, "Andrei is a dramatist. He drinks, goes to horse races, and hangs out with gypsies. I worship only one god—football."[45] Lovchev led a delegation of players to demand the club's founder be retained. Instead they were told, "At the end of the season, you will thank us."[46]

By the end of the season, however, gratitude was the last thing players and their fans would be feeling. It had been forty years since the first season of professional football in the USSR, and in yet another experiment designed to bring the Soviet game closer to European practice, the schedule was divided into spring and fall seasons (as had been done in 1936). Each campaign lasted fifteen games. The spring turned out to be a grand series of friendlies. Nothing concerning medals, bonuses, or relegation was decided. Those important matters would be determined only on the basis of the fall results, which proved disastrous for Spartak. It finished the spring season in fourteenth place among sixteen teams. Attendance declined dramatically as Krutikov shuffled a total of twenty-six players in and out of the lineup. Logofet had retired, in no small measure because of his dislike for the new coach. Nikolai Osianin was injured. None of the new players performed well. As the club's internal environment deteriorated, Krutikov refused to take any counsel from Starostin, instead isolating him from the team. Oleg Romantsev (b. 1954), a defender who had been recruited from Avtomobilist Krasnoiarsk, played just a few games before he went back home, unable to abide the poisoned atmosphere.[47] To make matters worse, Dinamo Moscow, whose performances had also dropped off dramatically in recent years, won the spring title.

The fall season, which would decide the question of relegation, proved to be even worse. Krutikov continued changing his lineup while failing to explain his choices. The short schedule created the unusual situation of nine teams having virtually the same number of points. Any of them could have been sent down. Things got so bad for Spartak that sympathetic referees were awarding the club undeserved penalty kicks, which they often failed to convert. On October 22 they were in a position to guarantee their place at the top level with a win over Chernomorets Odessa. Only a thousand fans showed up at Lenin Stadium to watch them lose 0–1. Their fate was now in the hands of others. According to Nikolai Starostin, press accounts published fifteen possible scenarios for the season's last two weeks, only one of which involved Spartak's relegation. This was, however, the one variant that did in fact occur. All five of the other teams threatened with relegation won their games. Many of the results raised doubts. Four of the five matches in question ended with the suspicious score of 1–0. In each case the losers were locked into their place in the standings.[48] Spartak ultimately wound up in the drop zone in the fifteenth spot, just ahead of last-place Dinamo Minsk. It had thirteen points, one behind Ararat, Dnepr, Zarya, Shakhter, and Kryl'ya Sovetov. So tight was the race that one more victory would have put Spartak in eighth place.

Writing after the collapse of the USSR, Lovchev went so far as to accuse that year's champion, Torpedo, of selling its last game to fourteenth-place Ararat.[49] This being the Soviet Union, there was no shortage of conspiracy theories, and it may well have been that years of resentment toward Spartak and the Starostins had lubricated their slide to the second division. Yet, if there was such a plot, it appears not to have come from the top of the state sporting structure. Instead, midtable clubs joined together in pursuit of the "Romanian model." On November 15, *Pravda* noted obliquely, "There were some matches that raise questions about the level of educational work among several teams." The same day Konstantin Beskov, a lifetime Dinamovets, rose to the defense of Spartak in *Komsomol'skaia Pravda*. "There was a striking and strange predestination to the concluding matches of the fall season. With surprising ease, outsiders playing against stronger opponents received exactly as many points as they needed to stay in the top league." Ten days later, the presidium of the football federation met. Top officials defended the "sporting character" of the season, but Andrei Starostin was not convinced. "There were mistakes that took place in the organization of the fall season. At the end there was a series of games that were conducted in an unsporting manner. . . . The presidium should take an interest in the materials presented to it by the trade union sports organization and other groups as well." Indeed, there had been a flood of letters and complaints directed by individuals and groups to the state sports committee, the party Central Committee, and a wide variety of newspapers. The expression of doubts in leading national publications about the season's results, along with the decision to convene the football federation, clearly indicates that the central authorities were not pleased by the corruption in the Soviet game. Yet doing something about it raised other difficulties and problems.[50]

With the season over, the question facing the leaders of Soviet soccer was by no means simple. Would Spartak actually be relegated? In defense of his favorite club, the head of the Moscow party committee, Viktor Grishin (1914–1992), sent a letter to the Central Committee accusing other teams of fixing games and threatening Spartak players. He promised to present proof but never delivered. Some in positions of authority raised the possibility of enlarging the first division to eighteen teams, one of which would have been Spartak. This had been done numerous times in the past, especially at the lower levels. In 1967 Zenit Leningrad had retained its place at the top when the league was artificially expanded in honor of the fiftieth anniversary of the revolution. Such steps, however, violated the sporting principle the sports committee had affirmed in 1970. In this first important test of their policy, the authorities refused to budge.[51] The Moscow party and trade union leadership turned to the Starostins for advice, but the brothers argued against accepting any artificial measures. Their position may have been one of principle, but they were also prisoners of their own rhetoric. Having loudly and publicly demanded that the sporting principle apply to others, they had little choice when the ax fell on Spartak.

When it became clear the team was going down, Moscow political leaders sought other favors. On December 9, N. N. Ryashentsev, the president of the All-Union Soviet of Trade Union Voluntary Sport Societies, wrote to S. P.

Pavlov, president of the Committee on Physical Culture and Sport. Ryashent-sev asked that Spartak be allowed to pay its players at the monthly base rate of 250 rubles given to each player in the first division rather than the 150 earned by those at the lower level.[52] Two weeks later Pavlov received a similar appeal from V. F. Promyslov, president of the executive committee of Mossovet.[53] Such requests were common from teams facing relegation. In nearly every case, they were denied.[54] In a measure of Spartak's history and authority, it was granted an exception, enabling it to retain the players it wished to keep on while recruiting additions from outside.[55]

Once a powerful club is relegated, its leaders face difficult and tricky choices. Some teams, like Nottingham Forest, never see the light of the top flight again. Others, like Fiorentina of Florence, have come back fairly quickly after being sent down. Quite simply, it is a classic moment of sporting truth. Just as Spartak faced irrelevance and even extinction in Stalin's last years, it was now confronted with similar dangers in an utterly different historical context. The team could have muddled through with half measures, but instead, those concerned with the great club's welfare took great risks in the hope of reviving the Red and White.

### Resurrection Yet Again

The leaders of Mossovet, the party gorkom, and the trade unions quickly realized that in replacing the grand old man they had made a grave error. Grishin took charge of matters. Krutikov was dismissed, and Andrei and Niko-lai were brought back in to discuss the club's future. When Grishin asked them who should now coach Spartak, Andrei put forward the name of Konstantin Beskov, a man who had served Dinamo Moscow as player and coach for more than thirty years. It seemed strange that Andrei should support someone who was seen to embody Dinamo's tradition of harsh discipline and control, but the two men had worked together for two years (1963 and 1964) on the national team. Both had been unceremoniously fired by Khrushchev for having been so incompetent as to lose by a single goal to Spain in the final of the 1964 European championship, held that year in Madrid. Dismissed as Dinamo Moscow coach in 1972, Beskov was working in an administrative capacity in the Dinamo Sport Society's Russian branch, receiving the salary of a colonel. At the moment, Nikolai had his doubts about working with someone who seemed to stand for everything he had fought against in his career. Still, it was not as if he had ever agreed with everything Andrei had said about soccer. They had been arguing about the game since the old days back in the Presnia, but it was a measure of their desperation that Nikolai agreed to approach Beskov about the job.[56]

There were, however, two problems with the plan. Dinamo would not necessarily let Beskov go to a rival, and Beskov himself did not want the job. At this point, Grishin brought his influence to bear on the minister of the interior, who not only consented to let Beskov go but, acting as Beskov's superior officer, ordered him to take the job. As someone who respected authority, Beskov accepted the order, but he later told his wife, "They have given me away."[57] He did, however, have the good judgment to ask that Nikolai Starostin return as the team's boss. Beskov knew Starostin's gifts as an organizer and sought a situation that would allow him to concentrate on football and avoid paperwork. Nikolai agreed to take on Beskov, although he had only once employed a coach (Sokolov) who bullied his players. The announcement of the appointment was met with shock, primarily from Spartak supporters who saw the move as a betrayal of Spartak spirit. In his final memoir, Starostin tactfully described their relationship as "not unproblematic." Elsewhere, he said things with Beskov were "always complicated." They argued often but would patch things up for the greater good of the team. For all his discomfort with Beskov's personality, Starostin was in accord with his coach's attacking style of play. The emphasis on short passing, improvisation, and attack was, he thought, in keeping with the club's traditions. Clearly, it was not a situation that could last forever, but for twelve seasons the two men did restore Spartak to its former glory. The fans may have had their doubts, but these too were assuaged by winning.

Beskov's strengths compensated for those areas of the game in which Starostin was weak. The most important of these was the evaluation of talent. Soccer is a game that requires stars. Championships are not won simply with well-organized collections of journeymen. Even so machinelike a team as Dinamo Kiev would have achieved much less had it not had the dynamic Oleg Blokhin as its star striker. In the case of Spartak, its ups and downs over the years in the standings correspond directly to the presence or absence of familiar names in the lineup. In the club's bad periods the problem of choosing the right personnel had bedeviled Starostin. His network of contacts throughout the country enabled him to bring in players from far and wide, but they did not always turn out to be particularly useful. Beskov knew what he wanted in a player and was able to see that talent where others did not. To be able to make stars out of those discarded by other teams may be a coach's greatest gift. Here Beskov had few peers. His primary task was to remake the roster, particularly the attack.

His first move was to let several players go before the 1977 season, which would be played in the second division. Then, Beskov took on forward Vladimir Pavlenko (1955–2000), who had been with Dinamo Moscow since 1972. Pavlenko's game had fallen off the previous two seasons, and Dinamo was willing to let him go. He found a comfort zone at the lower level and scored fourteen goals, a result he could not repeat the next year when the team was back in the first division.[58] Beskov's other additions further demonstrated his ability to find talent in unusual places. The Latvian midfielder Sergei Shavlo (b. 1956) had been languishing at second-division Daugava Riga but found steady work at Spartak. Oleg Romantsev was persuaded to come back after his unpleasant experience the previous season. Twenty-nine-year-old striker Georgii Iartsev (b. 1948) had played eleven seasons in the depths of

**9.2** Konstantin Beskov instructs Vagiz Khidiatulin. Fotoagentstvo Sportekspress.

the third division. Beskov discovered him in January 1977 at the annual Moscow indoor tournament for all Spartak teams. He would lead the team with seventeen goals.

The most important new player was Iurii Gavrilov (b. 1953), who had been unable to get many games at Dinamo Moscow, playing as an out-and-out striker. Beskov was able to convince Dinamo to release Gavrilov and converted him to a play-maker role, slightly withdrawn behind the forwards. Gavrilov proved to be a gifted and original passer, very much in the Spartak mold. At the same time, he did not lose his scoring touch. Gavrilov joined the team at the end of June and immediately developed a great understanding with Iartsev. In making these acquisitions, Beskov explained to Starostin that he was seeking to build a team that would not simply return to the first division but could eventually win a championship. Shavlo, Romanstev, Iartsev, and Gavrilov all went on to become vital parts of the club's subsequent success.[59] The young Tartar defender Vagiz Khidiatulin (b. 1959) also became a fixture in the 1977 season. He would stay with Spartak until he was drafted in 1981 and forced to play for TsSKA, only to return in 1986.[60]

Spartak's season of second-division football did not begin auspiciously. There were two kinds of Soviet coaches—*trener-demokrat* (players' coach) and *trener-diktator* (tough coach). Virtually every previous Spartak coach had been in the democrat category. Beskov most definitely was not. Conflicts with

**9.3** Iuri Gavrilov. *Spartak Moskva: Offitsial'naia istoriia.*

the players cropped up immediately. Not surprisingly, Lovchev was a lightning rod. Beskov brooked no disobedience and believed he was correct about everything. Lovchev, one of Starostin's favorites, often complained to the boss. He called Beskov a "dictator who terrorized his players." Beskov at one point refused to play Lovchev, and Starostin had to intervene on his favorite player's behalf. Whether out of paternalism or a truly democratic spirit, personal favorites had proved to be one of Starostin's weaknesses as a manager. Even Simonian had found the boss's difficulty in releasing players a problem.[61] Beskov permitted no sentimentality when it came to personnel issues. For him, it was always better to let someone go before rather than after he had outlived his usefulness.

It turned out the second division had a number of strong teams who mobilized their best efforts when going against Spartak. Away games filled provincial stadiums with excited fans who sought to will their heroes to victory. It took a while to realize that only a top effort could guarantee wins. At the halfway point in the season, Beskov's team was in fifth place, but the addition of Gavrilov helped turn things around.[62] With his new teammate's service, Iartsev went on a scoring spree. Lovchev was able to compromise with Beskov, and the team stormed through the rest of the schedule, clinching the title and a return to the big time.

The 1977 season thus entered the realm of Spartak lore. One part of that legend has centered on the fans' continuing loyalty. The 1977 season proved to be a test of that commitment. Globally, attendance for relegated teams drops off substantially after they are sent down, and the number of spectators at early season games in Lenin Stadium averaged about fifteen thousand, indicating fan skepticism and disappointment. By June, as the team's play improved, so too did attendance. In late August, Lenin Stadium was closed for remodeling prior to the Moscow Olympics. The much smaller Lokomotiv Stadium was then used, and the first two games there attracted full houses of forty thousand, reflecting the building excitement about the team's likely promotion.

Much has since been made of these last facts. Some accounts claim that all the remaining matches were sellouts, but in fact attendance dropped off to much the same levels as in the early season. Clearly the devotion of Spartak fans was not unlimited. In earlier years poor play had also led to more empty seats. Moreover, the late seventies were a time of decreased attendance throughout all of Soviet soccer. The theme of half-empty stands was a constant in the press. Given the general malaise, Spartak's total attendance of 367,300, an average of 19,330 for nineteen home games, was far from disgraceful. More important, while playing at a lower level, Spartak outdrew the four other Moscow teams that played in the first division. Torpedo, TsSKA, and Lokomotiv were not huge gate attractions during the seventies. A fourth-place Dinamo team (the only other Moscow side for which we have complete information) drew approximately 263,000 for seventeen games at its own stadium, an average of 15,470 per game.[63] If the numbers for Spartak are not quite the stuff of legend, it is safe to say that it was still the most popular of the capital's clubs.

While Spartak had been away in the second division, things at the top of Soviet soccer had gotten completely out of hand. The epidemic of ties reached absurd proportions. Lobanovskii had pushed the so-called away model of winning at home and tying on the road to new heights. Of thirty games played by his Dinamo Kiev team in 1977, fifteen were draws. Even more bizarre, three other clubs, following his lead, had seventeen ties. Still more midtable teams followed the Romanian variant and agreed to ties in order to stay in the top flight. The sports committee, which had abandoned penalty kicks after two seasons, came up with a new idea to rid the game of noncombative football. It instituted a limit of eight ties. Anything beyond that number meant that neither team received a point. Some protested that this approach was excessively bureaucratic. Instead, they proposed a solution of three points for a win and one for a tie. As in the case of post-match penalty kicks, this Soviet innovation, which was eventually adopted throughout the world, found no powerful adherents at the time.

During the 1978 season it seemed the sports committee's approach actually had a positive impact. Dinamo Kiev, which finished second, had nine ties; champion Dinamo Tbilisi had eight. True to its principles, Spartak played only five draws. In its first season back at the top, it came in a more-than-commendable fifth.[64] On the surface it appeared the reform to reduce ties had worked, but now the miscreants instead adapted to the new situation by agreeing among themselves not to tie but to split the two games they would play against each other each year.[65] League play in 1978 did not begin well. Spartak stumbled at the start with two losses, and Lovchev continued his war with Beskov. The defeats convinced the Spartak captain that the club was headed right back down to the second division. Soon thereafter, he applied for a transfer to Dinamo Moscow (initially denied) and never played for Spartak again. He would later say, "I did not leave Spartak. I left Beskov." Starostin had proved unable to patch things up between his successful coach and his favorite player. Lovchev was not a simple character and may have worn out his welcome. The moment cannot have been easy for Starostin, a reminder that his authority within the club might well be slipping.[66]

The loss of Lovchev was balanced by the arrival of two newcomers who would, if anything, play even bigger roles in the club's history. In May the young Tartar goalkeeper Rinat Dasaev (b. 1957) came from Astrakhan to assume a position he would not relinquish until 1988, when he transferred to the Spanish club Sevilla. Discovered by one of Beskov's former assistants, he would go on to become one of the greatest of all Soviet goalies, ranked only behind the immortal Iashin. In his last Soviet season, Dasaev was voted the best goalie in the world.[67]

The other major addition played only seven games in 1978 but then went on to establish himself as the longest-serving and most beloved of all Spartakovtsy. A native Muscovite, Fiodr Cherenkov (b. 1959) was a product of Spartak's school. Navigating between midfield and forward, he played with an originality and eccentricity that endeared him to the public. Cherenkov was an enigmatic and fragile personality whose capacity for unexpected improvisation fit the Spartak image of the player as romantic artist. A true original, he was the embodiment of what many of Spartak's male Moscow supporters liked to believe about themselves. Lacking great speed but quick on his feet, small of stature but possessed of great guile, Cherenkov seemed to practice a new kind of masculinity, that of the urban trickster. By the time his Spartak career was over, he was the leading point producer (goal plus pass) in the team's history.[68] Perhaps even more important for the Starostins, Beskov had not found him. Cherenkov was, instead, *nash Fedya,* one of their own.

The collecting of this group of stars had taken all of two years. For all his arrogance, belligerence, and capriciousness, Beskov had worked wonders. The result was a championship in 1979. Starostin may have made a deal with the

**9.4** Fiodr Cherenkov. *Spartak Moskva: Offitsial'naia istoriia.*

devil, but this time the devil delivered. Cherenkov fit in well with Gavrilov
and Shavlo in a highly creative midfield. Throughout much of the season,
Spartak closely trailed Dinamo Kiev until the decisive match of the season on
September 28, when it won 2–0 at Kiev. Lobanovskii's team faded to third,
while Spartak clinched the title on the last day of the season, pulling out a
3–2 victory at Rostov.

Two years removed from oblivion, the team was back on top. Official affirmation of the club's place in the Soviet football galaxy came quickly. Spartak
became the base of the national team, and Beskov was put in charge. For Spartak fans, living at a time of eroding hope about the state of the nation, the
championship fed the withered strands of their highly tattered optimism. This
did not mean that they rallied to the party or affirmed their devotion to a
bright and shining future. Instead, Spartak's success made them more easily
convinced that the stories they had been telling themselves about themselves
might still be true. Compensatory as they may have been, the emotions generated by Spartak's triumph signified neither political acquiescence nor opposition but rather some small private pleasure that one part of life seemed to
be going right when so much else was going wrong.

The Spartak–Dinamo Kiev rivalry dominated Soviet soccer until the collapse of the USSR. With the exception of one year, Spartak was always among

the top three, taking the championship in 1987 and 1989. Dinamo Kiev won the title in 1980, 1981, 1985, 1986, and 1990. Of the two teams, Lobanovskii's was clearly the stronger, but Spartak's role as a constant contender permitted a fractured revival of the earlier cultural and political stereotypes ascribed to the two great national sport societies. By the 1980s, however, Spartak was no longer a victim of tyranny, and Dinamo did not use the powers of the secret police to oppress its rivals. Still, Lobanovskii's hyperrational approach was a perfect foil for the ideologues of Spartak spirit. They scorned the cynicism of the away model and scoffed at their rival's style of play. Dinamo Kiev's controlled approach on the field featured precise and constant movement to guarantee extended periods of possession. These moments would then be punctuated by long passes over a drawn-in defense to swift attackers like the great Blokhin. Lobanovskii placed his greatest emphasis on the elimination of mistakes through well-rehearsed combinations. Backed by the financial and political might of the Ukrainian Ministry of Interior, Dinamo Kiev practiced a form of the "total football" then popularized by Holland but without the charm or spontaneity of the Dutch.[69]

Beskov may have been a *trener-diktator,* much like Lobanovskii, but his playing style was altogether different. He combined the speed and movement of his old Dinamo teams with the short passing and creativity of the Spartak tradition. If Dinamo Kiev was deemed rational and scientific, Spartak, once again, was said to be romantic and artistic. Dinamo might win, but Spartak would entertain. If Lobanovskii sent his men onto the field to execute, Beskov sent his out to create. Unorthodox players like Gavrilov and Cherenkov would never have been able to play for Dinamo Kiev, and when Lobanovskii was in charge of the national team, they were rarely called. This clash of styles fed into the old duality of us and them, but now each side felt it was the noble us and its opponent the evil them.[70] It is hard to find either Spartak or Dinamo Kiev occupying the kind of higher moral ground claimed by Starostin during the Stalin period. Each team had its influential adherents and powerful backers. Each drew support from ordinary folk. Perhaps those Muscovites who favored reform had a preference for Spartak, but refusenik Jews from Kiev could just as easily support their home side and claim Spartak was the team of the big shots. At the same time, Dinamo Kiev's popularity did not extend to the entire Ukraine. Residents of Odessa expressed their independence by adopting Spartak as their "second team" after Chernomorets.[71] Even the attendance figures available for the years 1980–1982 do not give a clear picture of which team was more popular.

As we have seen, this was a period of reduced attendance throughout Soviet soccer, and it is likely the decline was felt more acutely in Moscow than in Kiev, where the home side was a consistent winner. The lack of local competition explains Dinamo's larger home attendance. Spartak had to share Moscow with four other first-division teams. Moving beyond the clubs' home cities, the figures for road games provide a sense of which was the more popular throughout the rest of the USSR. Spartak drew a somewhat greater num-

**Table 9.1** Estimated attendance for Dinamo Kiev and Spartak: 1980–1982

| Year | Team | Home | Away |
|------|------|------|------|
| 1980 | Dinamo K | 441,500 | 475,000 |
|      | Spartak  | 392,000 | 622,000 |
| 1981 | Dinamo K | 641,478 | 462,550 |
|      | Spartak  | 395,620 | 573,807 |
| 1982 | Dinamo K | 445,364 | 461,000 |
|      | Spartak  | 284,750 | 455,450 |

*Source: Izvestiia,* November 25, 1980; November 11, 1981; and November 30, 1982.

ber of spectators to its away matches. It is clear that Dinamo Kiev was also a great attraction. Both teams were constantly on television. Their stars were celebrities. Despite the disdain of Spartak supporters, there were clearly many thousands of Soviet citizens who admired Dinamo Kiev and wished to see it play in person. Spartak-Dinamo Kiev was not Spartak-Dinamo Moscow redux.

### Renovation, Globalization, and Professionalization

Two important events occurred in the Soviet Union during 1985. On March 10, a week after the soccer season began, Konstantin Chernenko died and was replaced by Mikhail Gorbachev. Soon after the football season ended in November, Konstantin Beskov reached the decision that he was sick and tired of finishing behind Dinamo Kiev. In their separate spheres, both Gorbachev and Beskov came to the conclusion that something had to be done. Both initiated processes that brought short-term success but eventual disaster. It is not hard to understand why Gorbachev felt he had to act. By this time the ills of the system were manifest.[72] Beskov, however, was another matter. Gorbachev sought to enlist society in the process of reform. He was willing to relinquish the powers of the center in order to activate the kind of critical thinking that would provide political support for change. Beskov, in contrast, sought greater control over personnel matters in order to remake what most sports observers thought was already a very fine team.

The healthy frenzy of rethinking in the early years of perestroika was propelled by the policy of open discussion and criticism known as glasnost. The nascent civil society of the Brezhnev period was now called upon to play a role in demanding change.[73] Soccer was not untouched by the ferment, but it cannot be said that the sport and its practitioners were in the forefront of reform. The last years of Soviet football were marked by a failed attempt to restructure the game, an effort that was an old-fashioned a power struggle utterly at odds with the democratizing spirit of the time.

Lobanovskii led the campaign to take control of the top Soviet divisions away from the established football federation, run since 1979 by the career sports bureaucrat Vyacheslav Koloskov (b. 1941). After teaming with Viktor Ponedel'nik, a former great international turned journalist, Lobanovskii succeeded in gaining extensive support from fellow professionals who claimed they wanted to eliminate apparatchiki from the game. Lobanovskii and his supporters employed much democratic, antibureaucratic rhetoric, but after a career of rigid personal control over his own domain, the Dinamo Kiev manager was an unconvincing apostle for change. By 1990 he had been outmaneuvered by Koloskov, and the attempt to have football people run football had failed.[74] Revealingly, Nikolai Starostin, who had also invoked an ambiguous notion of democracy, remained aloof from this battle, no doubt mistrusting his rival. If Lobanovskii were to be in charge of Soviet soccer while still running a team, the Spartak boss envisioned the absurd situation of a coach giving orders to federation officials when the normal order of things had always been the opposite. Starostin had long favored professionalism. In 1990, he told *Sovetskii sport,* "The example of foreign teams has finally convinced us that in order to catch up to professional teams we must be professionals. Professionalism is a psychology about one's responsibility toward one's work." Nevertheless, he thought the attempt to overthrow Koloskov and the federation was "premature."[75]

During perestroika, state support for football shrank dramatically as various efforts were launched to make the elite teams free-standing, self-financing entities. Enterprises and firms all over the USSR faced this same challenge. For soccer this often took the form of an open professionalism that had been denied but had long been practiced. Players were now to sign contracts for several years, and they were to be paid for what they actually did. One aspect of that professionalism involved greater contact with foreign teams, a process that after 1987 led to the sale of scores of Soviet players to capitalist clubs in order to raise the funds Soviet clubs needed to stay in business. It should not be surprising that the Starostins had little difficulty functioning in the new situation. Spartak had long been operating along the lines of a profit-making football club. Rather than drain its sponsors of funds, it had been able to generate surpluses that were given over to sports that had small audiences and did not produce revenue.

Thus Spartak adopted the new methods with little fanfare. Starostin did not claim he was making the changes in the name of renewing the Soviet project, nor did he openly jump on the Gorbachev bandwagon. More likely, he felt the bandwagon had come to him. If team bosses had to work hard and hustle to keep afloat, Starostin had long been doing just that. Clubs now had to face the scary prospect of surviving on their own. As it turned out, the other side of being forced to sink or swim was autonomy, or, to use another word, independence—a condition that had never especially troubled the Starostins. Clearly, Nikolai was comfortable with the larger trends of the last years of Soviet power. The new priority given to financial questions and profit making played to his strength, and in publishing his highly candid and revealing memoir in 1989, he embraced that other hallmark of the era—glasnost. Two championships in Soviet soccer's final six seasons made it clear that Spartak was able to prosper in the changed environment.

The 1985 league season ended with Spartak just two points behind Dinamo

Kiev. It seemed like a good result, but before the next season Beskov unceremoniously released Shavlo and Gavrilov. The public was shocked. Lev Filatov and Igor Netto denounced the move in print, as did the prominent pro-Spartak sportswriters Leonid Trakhtenberg and Ilya Baru.[76] Gavrilov in particular had been seen by the fans as an authentic Spartak man whose creativity was true to the club's traditions. Both men had appeared in twenty-six of that season's thirty-four games. Gavrilov was named to the annual list of the top thirty-three players, but Beskov had been publicly dissatisfied with both men after an early-season string of six consecutive draws. "Several players," he told the press, "have lost their sense of responsibility." Things did improve after Beskov's outburst, but a 0–2 defeat at Kiev required Spartak to win when Dinamo came to Moscow in October. Forty-two thousand witnesses at Lenin Stadium saw the team lose 1–2, relinquishing any chance of the gold medal. Shavlo was then twenty-nine, Gavrilov thirty-two. Beskov wanted the team to get younger.

As Simonian noted, Starostin had difficulty letting players go, especially those who seemed to embody the team's spirit. It could scarcely be said that either Gavrilov or Shavlo had played poorly, but it is the harsh reality of high-performance sport that athletes age and their skills erode. This fact no doubt saddened Starostin, but Beskov was no sentimentalist. He was not interested in the possibility that keeping an older man around could have a positive moral and psychological impact on the club and its supporters. Starostin acceded to Beskov's wishes, but he must have felt that some part of the Spartak spirit had been lost in the process. It might not have seemed so at the moment, but the two men would now be locked in a struggle for control of the team.

Beskov continued the search for new talent in 1986, using twenty-seven players in all. None of his new additions paid immediate dividends, and the team finished third. The club's leadership and its supporters pressured Beskov to improve, and his 1987 additions proved much more successful. Aleksandr Mostovoi (b. 1968), another product of Moscow football, found a place at midfield, as did Valerii Shmarov (b. 1965), who came from Fakel Voronezh. Beskov's third newcomer proved more controversial. Viktor Posul'ko (b. 1961) had been involved in the illegal sale of three cars during his stay at Chernomorets Odessa. He was also accused of selling games and exhibiting a bad attitude toward coaches and teammates. The football federation turned down his request, but Beskov brought as much pressure to bear as he could, and the deal finally went through. Beskov's rigidity could bend to accommodate a player's dubious moral character if he demonstrated the requisite skills on the field.

Spartak led the league throughout the season and was in position to clinch the title two weeks from the end in Erevan against Ararat. Instead, it lost 2–3, and the title had to wait a week. The situation did, however, seem promising. Last-place Guriya Lanchkhutia came into Moscow to play indoors in Olimpiskii Stadium before a full house of thirty-five thousand ready to celebrate. Despite dominating possession, Spartak was unable to score until Cherenkov finally poked one home in the eighty-fourth minute.[77] Beskov soaked up the admiration of the faithful and dined out on his victory in the off-season. Most likely, it was around this time that he developed the conviction that he and not Starostin should be in charge of the people's team. Nikolai Ozerov, a firm Starostin ally, would later accuse Beskov of engineering "a palace coup."[78] A year after what may have been his biggest triumph, the coach who had given Spartak its most consistent run of excellence was gone.

Beskov came into the 1988 season ever more convinced of his correctness in all things related to football, but his political situation inside the club had changed. Andrei Starostin had died the previous fall. As Beskov's widow would later note, Andrei had been a buffer between the coach and the nachal'nik.[79] Early in the season, Beskov became involved in a series of harsh disputes with his veteran players. He had continued to rule by fear and intimidation, but such methods were becoming less effective during perestroika. The athlete-coach relationship was evolving, and the discourses of democracy then circulating made the players less willing to accept orders unquestioningly. Starostin was forced once again to intervene. If he did not intentionally champion a liberal democratic approach, his methods of the previous fifty plus years had led him to take the players' side. Over the course of the season, the conflicts festered, and the team played inconsistently. Finally in August Beskov submitted his resignation. Soon thereafter, the Moscow City Soviet of Trade Unions organized a meeting attended by the club president Iuri Shaliapin (b. 1932) and thirteen players, eleven of whom voted to accept the coach's resignation. At the time, the matter was smoothed over, and it was decided the question would be revisited after the season. Beskov had also agreed not to penalize the players who had voted against him.[80] Characteristically, the great coach did not keep his word. Instead he benched several men and unfairly gave others bad grades for their performances. Despite all the rancor, the team still had a chance to finish as a medal winner, but a loss and two ties against weak opposition condemned it to fourth place. It was the first time in Beskov's tenure that Spartak did not finish in the top three.

Before he left on a December vacation, Beskov told Starostin he wanted to get rid of seven players. Starostin demurred, fearing the lack of adequate replacements, but Beskov countered, saying he had transfer applications from twenty-two players who wished to come over to Spartak. All these documents had been signed without Starostin's knowledge, and he refused to accept Beskov's plans. Beskov returned to Moscow in the middle of the month. On December 22 he learned that the Moscow City Soviet of Trade Union Sports Organizations had voted to confirm the "Spartak leadership's" decision to fire its coach. By all accounts, this process was not handled well. Neither the coaches nor the players attended the meeting. Starostin was not there either, although his presence permeated the event. Unsubstantiated and irrelevant stories were thrown about. Workers at Tarasovka testified that Beskov was continually drunk and spent all his time in the team's bathhouse (*banya*). No one rose to his defense, nor was there anyone present who might have defended him. Beskov never got to face his accusers. Even so strong a Starostin adherent as Aleksandr Vainshtein has said the matter was handled in a thoroughly Soviet manner.[81]

Starostin later wrote that he saw his coach's August resignation as a maneuver, an attempt to demand more control as the price for staying on. Beskov countered, claiming Starostin was not taking care of his administrative duties. He argued that Tarasovka had deteriorated, and the players' daily needs were not being addressed. He also refused to accept responsibility for the season's poor result, blaming the players instead.[82] It had taken twelve years for the fundamental tensions in the Starostin-Beskov relationship to explode. These two figures, historically central to Soviet football, had never been friends, but their work together had yielded splendid results. Lev Filatov, no enemy of Starostin, wrote in *Izvestiia* that "Beskov did too much for Spartak for it to end with an ugly and trivial conflict." Fans who had grown up on Beskov's splendid Spartak mourned his passing, even as they recognized Starostin's right to name his coach. Beskov's boorish behavior had clearly touched off the final conflict, but Starostin had handled the matter without grace or honor. In truth their talents had complemented each other. Filatov noted that Beskov understood football much better than Starostin did, but Starostin understood that "big-time football is more than just a game . . . he had a much broader view of things than [did] the coach."[83]

Where would Spartak now go, and what methods would it use to get there? At the end of the season, Dasaev was sold to Sevilla. Before that Khidiatulin had transferred to Toulouse of the French league. The prospects were not promising, but the entire organization had the unifying goal of proving it could win without Beskov. Influenced by the democratic ethos of the historical moment, the team's leadership asked the players to choose from among several possibilities for coach. Three were former Spartak greats. Oleg Romantsev was coaching Spartak Ordzhonikidze. The other two, veterans of the club, were Lovchev and Netto. Romantsev was chosen in a process that was portrayed as genuine and democratic. The vote was not close. Lovchev was seen as too unpredictable, Netto too difficult. Two lesser-known candidates were rejected as being "non-Spartak" people.

According to the well-informed Russian journalist Igor Rabiner, the process had the trappings but not the substance of democracy. It appears that Nikolai Starostin had been grooming Romantsev as a future coach from the moment of the defender's retirement. The boss had put Romantsev in charge of Spartak's "daughter" club, Krasnaia Presnia, which played in the third division. After a successful run, he took over Spartak Ordzhonikidze. Lovchev later told Rabiner that Starostin had approached him to run for the position, but Lovchev, whose personal relationship with Romantsev was strained, quickly understood that his candidacy was a mere formality.[84]

When he came in, Romantsev asked the players to choose a coach's soviet. The new council proposed a lessening of the physical demands in preseason

**9.5** Oleg Romantsev. Fotoagentstvo Sportekspress.

training in order to avoid the midseason fatigue that had led to previous declines in the level of performance. On the field, Romantsev hewed close to Beskov's methods but administered them in a respectful and humane manner. Some pillars of Soviet football found the idea of electing a coach to be absurd. One great former star, Eduard Malofeev (b. 1942), at that time coach of Dinamo Minsk, suggested such a course might work in many different sorts of organizations but not in a soccer team. Fiodr Cherenkov responded by defending Spartak's methods. Romantsev's candidacy had great support, he said, and Romantsev himself was "decent and democratic."[85]

Spartak began the 1989 season with an undefeated run of twelve games, highlighted by a 4–1 away defeat of Dinamo Kiev before a hundred thousand. The streak was ended by a strong Dnepr team, but Spartak bounced back to take a commanding lead. On August 27, the Dnepr players flew into Moscow from a commercial tour of the United States a mere five hours before their game with Spartak. It is not clear whether they thought their cause so hopeless that there was no point in booking an earlier flight. More likely, during late perestroika Dnepr's need for foreign currency was so great that it considered the domestic league a secondary priority.[86] The team lost 2–1. It seemed Spartak would now run away with the title, but in classic fashion it underestimated weak opponents. Dnepr and Dinamo Kiev closed the gap.

The season's decisive moment came in the penultimate week. Dinamo Kiev had slipped to third and had lost a chance for the gold medal. Dnepr trailed Spartak in the standings by two points. On October 23, Dinamo Kiev came into Lenin Stadium, where sixty thousand of the faithful had braved the elements

**9.6** Valerii Shmarov has just scored the championship clinching goal against Dinamo Kiev in 1989. Fotoagentstvo Sportekspress.

of a typical Moscow fall evening. Only a win would clinch the title for Spartak, but things went badly at the beginning. Dinamo's star striker, Oleg Protasov, put his team ahead in the third minute. Evgenii Kuznetsov equalized in the fifty-second. The match went into injury time with the score tied, but in the ninety-second minute, Spartak was awarded a free kick twenty-two meters straight out. Valerii Shmarov approached the ball. He was not Spartak's usual specialist, but he somehow convinced his teammates to let him try. He would later reveal that he had been practicing just such a kick from just such a spot for half the season. He bent the ball over the wall and into the upper right corner of the net as the stadium exploded. It was a beautiful play at a moment of the greatest tension. The championship was Spartak's. A crazed Shmarov ran madly toward the sideline trailed by his ecstatic comrades. He embraced Romantsev, who a minute later was flying through the air, propelled by his players in the ritual of victory. It was more high drama out of Spartak central casting. With the arrogance that had made so many despise and envy Spartak, Igor Netto summarized the season: "It has become boring at the stadium. Aside from Spartak, the majority of teams play in a [rough], physical manner."

The 1989 season turned out to be the last year the USSR's top flight had a full complement of teams. In a sign of the exploding nationalist sentiments that had emerged so powerfully in late perestroika, the Georgians and Lithuanians announced they would no longer take part in the Soviet league. With so much else crumbling around them, Spartak's unexpected title seemed to reaffirm all the myths, legends, and images that comprised Spartak ideology. Winning had never been enough for its fans. For them, Spartak had to win beautifully and dramatically, preferably against the odds. It had, once again, done just that. For the human rights lawyer Boris Nazarov, the triumph of 1989 rekindled all the emotions he had first experienced in 1937 on the east end of Dinamo Stadium when Spartak defeated the mighty Basques. The nation may have been falling apart, but he could still believe the hoary beast of Spartak spirit was alive and well.[87]

The action on the field had been complemented by innovation off it. On March 10, 1989, Spartak announced it had become a fully open, self-supporting football team, consistent with the requirements and principles of *khozraschet* (self-financing). It was not the first team to make this step (Dnepr had taken the lead), but after fifty-four years of operation, the words now used to describe the club accurately captured the nature of its operations. Iuri Shaliapin told the weekly *Futbol-khokkei,* "It must be said that a feeling of responsibility on material matters has existed here for a long time. Life has taught us this."[88] The same candor could now become the norm not just in soccer but in all of Soviet sport, as the International Olympic Committee finally welcomed the participation of full-time, well-compensated athletes, ending decades of its own hypocrisy. The fig leaf of the state amateur was removed to reveal a fully rampant professionalism as the new norm of global sport.

Even in the last days of Soviet power, as the economy ground to a halt and fans stopped coming to the stadium in large numbers, Spartak was able to turn a profit. According to Shaliapin, it cost 1,200,000 rubles a year to run the team and another 300,000 to keep up Tarasovka. As an international brand, Spartak was able to attract considerable sponsorship and advertising from foreign and domestic firms, an estimated 1,200,000 rubles. Ticket sales amounted to 700,000 rubles, and 100,000 was earned by renting club facilities to organizations for various health-related events. The profit from this activity was said to be 960,000 rubles, but none of this even included the team's main revenue streams—the sale of players and foreign tours.[89]

The devolution of the USSR in 1990 and 1991 had a predictable impact on soccer. Standing on lines for food took precedence over going to games, and, it must be added, there was no food (or drink) at the games. Attendance was minimal, although it still was possible for the right attraction to bring the fans out. Players on all teams were leaving for any foreign opportunity they could find. In late 1989 and early 1990, Cherenkov went to the second-division French club Red Star Paris. The next year, Shmarov moved to Karlsruhe in Germany, and Mostovoi signed in midseason with the Portuguese giant Benfica. A score of lesser players found work in Finland, Sweden, Korea, and Austria. The beleaguered but still energetic Romantsev was constantly revamping his lineup. Thirty-four men appeared for Spartak in 1990, thirty the next year. They came in fifth in 1990 and a close second to TsSKA in the final season of Soviet football. The last Spartak home game of the Soviet era was a 2–1 victory over Metallurg Zaparozh'e in front of a mere thousand spectators on October 27, 1991.[90]

The All-Union league, with its teams all over the vast nation, its variety of playing styles, and its many different ethnicities, disappeared as the national republics went their own ways. Each new nation formed its own, significantly weaker championship. After the collapse, politics, as it always had been (and had to be), took precedence over football. Initially, Georgians, Lithuanians, Ukrainians, Armenians, Belarussians, and most of the others felt pride in having leagues of their own. Only much later would all come to realize that in the sporting sense something quite substantial had been lost. There was no other national league in the world quite like the Soviet league. It had helped knit together a far-flung land and produced a brand of football not since seen in the former Soviet space.

### Spartak, the Ruble, and the Stadium

The link between a team and its supporters is given tangible form by that highly organized and often hallowed space the stadium. The term "ground," often used in Britain, perhaps best expresses the emotive force of this connection. For a football club and its supporters, the place where they play is that piece of land carved out of the surrounding cityscape. It is a site of continuing reunions with friends bonded by shared passions and obsessions, a scene of pleasant and comforting rituals, small and large, sacred and profane. In a ground that belongs to a club, the supporters can feel, quite incorrectly in any legal sense, that they are in a space that belongs to them, but for all the claims of Spartak fans about the club's special character, the team never had a stadium of its own. Dinamo had its place in Petrovsky Park. Lokomotiv's ground was in Cherkizovo. Torpedo had a small twenty-thousand-seater on Vostochnaia Street. Even TsSKA, which played nearly all its games at either Dinamo or Luzhniki, had an old ten-thousand-place ground on Peschanaia Street. After it opened in 1956, Lenin Stadium, the national arena, was the site of most of Spartak's home games, but every other Moscow side hosted matches there as well. Over the course of the next thirty-six years, Spartak played in all of Moscow's venues, forcing its fans to check the game site carefully. The team also played early- and late-season matches in enclosed arenas. These included its own indoor training facility and that of TSKA, as well as the enclosed thirty-five-thousand-seat Olimpiskii Stadium, built in 1980.

Did this nomadic existence weaken loyalty to the club? Certainly the lack of a consistent stadium attenuated the ties of neighborhood and community that had been so important in Spartak's prehistory (1900–1935), but it had been decades since the club was based in the Krasnaia Presnia region. Moscow had developed in ways that weakened the distinctions among neighborhoods.

Table 9.2 Comparative average attendance for Spartak and Dinamo in years of Spartak success

| Year | Place | Spartak | Place | Dinamo |
|------|-------|---------|-------|--------|
| 1969 | 1 | 40,188 | 4 | 29,838 |
| 1979 | 1 | 31,058 | 5 | 8,605* |
| 1989 | 1 | 33,616 | 8 | 14,142 |

*Home games at Torpedo Stadium, capacity 20,000

Comparative average attendance for Spartak and Dinamo in years of Spartak failure

| Year | Place | Spartak | Place | Dinamo |
|------|-------|---------|-------|--------|
| 1965 | 8 | 25,562 | 5 | 31,062 |
| 1975 | 10 | 26,466 | 3 | 23,556 |
| 1985 | 2 | 22,747 | 14 | 7,884 |

Source: Eduard Nisenboim, *Spartak Moskva: Offitsial'naia Istoriia* (Moscow, 2002); I. S. Dobronravov, *Na bessrochnoi sluzhbe futbola* (Moscow, 1999).

It therefore cannot be said that Dinamo "represented" north Moscow in the same way that Tottenham Hotspur and Arsenal authentically still represent north London. In this sense, Spartak probably did not lose that much by not having a ground of its own. If anything, the fact of having no permanent site may have allowed it to be seen as the team of all Moscow. In 2004, a group of architects and urban planners from Germany's famed Bauhaus School studied the siting of Moscow's arenas and proposed for Spartak the fictional slogan "the city is our stadium."[91]

Stadium or no stadium, Starostin and Simonian, among many at Spartak, always stressed the exceptional loyalty of their followers regardless of the results on the field. The club's leadership was also fond of pointing out its popularity in comparison with the other Moscow clubs, most notably Dinamo. The boasting could well be seen as yet another example of Spartak ideology, but one can verify or refute the claims by examining attendance figures. A sampling of average gates for the sixties, seventies, and eighties (choosing successful as well as unsuccessful seasons) reveals that the claims were not entirely arrogant bragging.

During the last three Soviet decades, overall soccer attendance steadily declined. This fall-off was not restricted to the USSR but was a worldwide phenomenon. Spartak was not immune to the game's general malaise. If the drop in attendance during the seventies and eighties was not precipitous in Spartak's case, it was still unmistakable. Furthermore, as we have seen, Spartak was not failure-proof. Bad play on the field was indeed punished at the turnstile. The fans may have been loyal, but they were not blind. While much has been made of the strong attendance at Spartak's games during 1977 when the team was in the second division, the fact is that it drew fewer people than it had in 1975 when it finished tenth in the top flight. The numbers also show that while Dinamo was clearly less popular than Spartak, its following was still substantial, and it remained so until the eighties, when the team fell into

crisis. The record, then, does not contradict the broad claims of Spartak loy-
alists about the solidity of their support, but it does indicate some basis for
tempering their enthusiasm. Spartak did not defy gravity. While losers may
continue to draw good audiences in provincial markets where the team is one
of few entertainments, this is rarely the case in large cities with several teams,
not to mention concert halls, movie theaters, and nightclubs. The Moscow
soccer market, as well as the entertainment market, proved to be highly elas-
tic and inconsistent.

Ticket sales provided much but not all of Spartak's revenue. The prices of
those tickets (one to three rubles) were by no means high. Sponsorship provided the support that the gate did not or could not. By the midsixties,
Promkooperatsiia and the Moscow party had turned over responsibility to the
Moscow trade union sports system. A broad range of workers, many of them
in white-collar positions and service industries, then came under the wing of
the Spartak Sport Society, but union funding proved less generous than that
of the party, not to mention the army or police. When attendance declined in
the early seventies, Spartak had to scramble to fill the gap. In 1973, Aeroflot,
the Soviet airline, came to the club's aid. By the 1977 season, Viktor Grishin
became sufficiently concerned about the great club's fate for the party again to
increase its involvement with Spartak. Starostin had to scramble for support
from a variety of sources. Thus Spartak was once more associated with no
clear and dominant patron, a situation that reinforced the enduring but de-
ceptive image of independence.

In order to grow revenues, Starostin greatly expanded the practices of barnstorming and midweek friendlies that went back to the twenties. As discussed
in the previous chapter, the primary purpose of these games was to increase
the money available to the players. Provincial clubs were offering much higher
salaries than the Moscow teams, and touring was one way Starostin could
compete. Here he was trading on the somewhat withered Spartak brand. The
Red and White might have known better days, but to folks in a small town
who had seen the players only on television, their presence was a grand hol-
iday(*prazdnik*). Once Spartak got back to the top, these events became even
bigger and more lucrative attractions. The number of these matches varied
from year to year, ranging from as few as five to as many as twenty, and did
not include preseason games, which were more clearly justified in terms of
preparing the team.

By 1985, in the less restrictive environment of perestroika, Spartak played
more than twenty friendlies a year. After going professional in 1989, the club
even took the experimental step of forming a commercial touring team composed of reserves and marginal first-team players. The real Spartak could play
in Lenin Stadium one day, and the next night someone called Spartak might
appear hundreds of miles away. The practice was, however, discontinued after
one season.[92] It must, of course, be emphasized that the playing of midseason
commercial friendlies was in no way limited to Spartak. The sports committee sought to control and limit the practice, but it was widespread. Nor was

the pursuit of financial gain limited to the domestic arena. Foreign tours also presented an opportunity for both the teams and their players to enrich themselves.

Those who filled the stadiums and purchased the tickets did not consume the spectacles in an orderly and healthy manner. Especially during the seventies, Soviet soccer fans, in the best tradition of internationalism, adopted many of the pathologies then common throughout the world. Violence had always been part of Soviet football but never in epidemic proportions. While Spartak supporters had been involved in such acts, it was not clear they were any more rowdy than the fans of other teams. That changed during the seventies. When hooliganism began to appear inside and outside Soviet stadiums, many of Spartak's younger supporters appear to have been at the cutting edge, transforming themselves into a new type of fan called *fanaty,* perhaps best translated in contemporary football parlance as "ultras." Their emergence was one sign of the problems that had enveloped the entire world of soccer. Those problems were in turn part of the global revolution among youth. As early as the 1969 season, young men with long hair, dressed in jeans and accompanied by girlfriends, were showing up at Spartak matches, chanting and singing their own original contributions to Spartak spirit.[93]

Hooliganism, drunkenness, and disorder became even more common, eroding attendance every bit as much as colorless play and endless ties. It was not until 1970, however, that accounts of violence inside and outside the stadium became common in the press. Disorderly "lovers of football" were surely a part of the Soviet sporting crowd from the twenties on, but the problem apparently did not trouble the authorities until decades later. Large numbers of loud and drunken fans at a jam-packed Lenin Stadium were said to have been ejected from the Spartak–Dinamo Kiev match on April 18, 1970. The police displayed a mountain of vodka bottles taken from fans when both Torpedo Moscow and Torpedo Kutaisi played Spartak. *Sovetskii sport* did not mention many episodes of this sort involving fans of other clubs, but this alone should not be taken as proof that Spartak fans were drunker than others.[94]

By 1972, fan rowdiness took a new form among the teenagers and young men who rooted for Spartak and stood together at the ends of Lenin Stadium. They had grown frustrated by the team's poor performance and sought to find a way to contribute to an improvement in Spartak's fortunes. These young supporters had also seen that the participation of Soviet teams in the European club tournaments revealed the clear superiority of foreign football. They had been especially impressed by the televised final of that year's Cup Winners' Cup involving Glasgow Rangers and Dinamo Moscow. With the Rangers ahead by two goals, Dinamo produced a storm of energy toward the end of the match that brought it back to within one, whereupon the Scottish supporters invaded the field, causing the match to be temporarily suspended for several minutes. When play resumed, Dinamo had lost its momentum, and the Rangers went on to triumph 3–2.[95] This was truly a way, thought the fanaty, to influence the outcome on the field of play.

The next spring, about forty young men gathered at one end of Lenin Stadium. They had joined twenty thousand others for the first game of the Moscow season as Spartak took on Ararat. They were wearing red and white scarves and waving Spartak banners. These items had not been purchased in the Spartak team store, which did not exist at the time, nor were they sold anyplace else in the city. These new ultras had produced their gear on their own. In time, this practice spread. As the USSR opened up to the rest of the world, Soviet hooligans were able to study the "English model."[96] Forty grew to hundreds and then thousands, who stood in one or another unpopulated section, chanting, singing, and cheering. They do not appear to have been especially drunk or violent at this point, but their sheer exuberance and spontaneity attracted the attention of both the police and volunteer militias (*druzhiny*) who were charged with maintaining calm in the stands. The sometimes brutal treatment from overzealous guardians of order pushed these exuberant fans into less benign activities. Over the next twenty years, the first groups of *fanaty* were joined by masses of disaffected youths who traveled in packs to away matches, engaged in fights, threatened bystanders, and destroyed property.[97]

Such behavior had the potential to end in tragedy and did so for Spartak supporters. On October 20, 1982, the team was playing Haarlem of the Netherlands in the first leg of an early-round UEFA Cup match on a frigid fall evening that brought the season's first snow. Only ten thousand of the faithful showed up, many of them teenagers and young men. The hardy group was confined to a few sideline sections that fed into one narrow exit tunnel leading to an ice-covered stairway. Despite dominating the contest, Spartak had managed to push through only one goal, an unconvincing margin before the return leg in Holland. With a few minutes to go, a group of fans headed for the exits, moving slowly through the only open tunnel. This restriction on crowd flow was a deliberate policy designed to slow the rush of fans into the metro. With twenty seconds left in the match, Sergei Shvetsov (b. 1960), a striker from Georgia, scored a vital second goal. Those leaving heard the roar of the crowd, immediately reversed direction and headed back to the stands. Within seconds they ran into the stream of other fans leaving the arena. The result was carnage. Many slipped on the icy stairway and were trampled. Others were crushed between the two masses of humanity. Police and soldiers began to carry the bodies of the dead out onto the small Lenin Stadium parking lot. It would be a half hour until the first ambulance appeared.

The next day *Vechernaia Moskva* was the only newspaper to hint at the enormity of what had occurred. "Yesterday, at Luzhniki, after the end of the football match, an unfortunate event occurred. There were casualties among the spectators."[98] In the aftermath, the police were quick to blame the dead for their own fate. The fanatic behavior of the young men and boys who died was said to explain the chaos. The link to hooliganism was all too clear. It was an argument that sought to deflect the blame from the stadium administration whose sloth and disregard for safety had created the conditions for the disaster. Ultimately, the police official in charge that night was sentenced to a year and a half in jail. At the time, the death toll was given as sixty-six. Seven years later in the full light of glasnost, *Sovetskii sport* ran an exposé on the tragedy. According to a group of parents of the dead, the actual loss of life numbered 340.[99] If the figure is close to being correct, the toll dwarfed the two great European stadium disasters of the 1980s—the Heysel tragedy of 1985 that took thirty-nine lives and the Hillsborough crush in 1989 that killed ninety-six.[100]

Ultimately, Hillsborough produced reforms on a global scale that changed the spectator experience forever. The standing terraces, which were never part of Soviet stadiums, were replaced in much of the world by seats. Police methods were changed. By contrast, no reforms of any sort took place in the USSR in the aftermath of the tragedy at Luzhniki. Instead, the matter was systematically covered up, and Spartak fanaty continued to provoke trouble especially at away matches. On September 19, 1987, after Spartak defeated Dinamo Kiev 1–0 in Kiev, a group of several hundred Spartak fans was attacked in the railroad station as they prepared to go home. A pitched battle ensued with massive damage and many injuries but luckily no loss of life. The next year there were similar disorders when Spartak came to Vilnius. In 1989 more than five thousand guardians of order were mobilized for Spartak's annual appearance in Kiev. When Dinamo Kiev came to Moscow for the season-deciding match, there were fights, and six metro cars were severely damaged.[101]

On September 24, 1990, I sat in a car with the veteran Soviet sportswriter Gennadi Larchikov as he drove me to see Spartak play Rotor Volgograd at Luzhniki. "Spartak," he told me, "is the team of intellectuals and hooligans." Iuri Shaliapin, the club's president, told the weekly *Futbol-Khokkei* much the same thing. The team, he said, had "two categories of fans." First, there were the young fanaty who were "noisy and aggressive" but did not really know either football or the club's history. The second category was composed of "people from various professions who had been supporters for decades and were genuinely knowledgeable about the game."[102] This bifurcated fan base raises an interesting question. Did the working class and professional supporters of Spartak share anything else beyond their love of the team? Before the war, a significant portion of the largely proletarian soccer audience had used Spartak to establish distance from the state and the elites who ran it. After the war, members of elite social groups joined the football public and supported Spartak. Workers and intellectuals appear to have been drawn to the people's team for similar reasons, but it is not clear how much they shared once the game was over.

## Spartak and the World

Spartak's contact with football outside the borders of the USSR took three forms—participation on the national team, games in European Cup tournaments, and foreign commercial tours. Of the three, the club's relationship with the sbornaia was the most fraught. As was true throughout the world, the na-

tional team was supposed to be a symbol of patriotism and loyalty. In the Soviet Union, it was controlled directly by the state sports committee, whose
interests often clashed with those of the clubs just as they did in capitalist
countries. In a system as centralized as the USSR, however, the national team's
needs were given the highest priority, and the clubs were in no position to resist such demands. There were, of course, complaints when players away on
international duty missed league games, but those burdens were shared by
many teams.

Starostin had been involved with international select teams as early as the
twenties. When they called, he and his team were always willing participants.
There was never any question of a Spartak player's demonstrating independence by refusing a call-up to the nation's first team. Not even the feisty
Lovchev ever balked at playing for so dictatorial a figure as Lobanovskii. Instead, the arguments were the normal ones surrounding national teams. When
Spartak stars were not picked, there was annoyance, but the choices were dic-
tated by the tastes and loyalties of the coach in charge rather than by the array
of political power inside the Kremlin. All those who led the Soviet national
team were loyal citizens. Even after Khrushchev's folly in dismissing Beskov
and Andrei Starostin for placing second at the 1964 European championship,
the post went to the man most likely to produce results.

Spartak's dominance of the international setup during the fifties may have
reflected the party's reassertion of authority over the secret police, but the
team's role diminished when the stars of the Golden Age began to retire. By
the time Khrushchev had left the political stage, only Khusainov was a constant on the national team that achieved its best result ever—fourth place at
the 1966 World Cup. Lovchev was capped in his first year (1969) and remained a fixture throughout the seventies, when results were considerably
less glorious. Over the course of both decades, Logofet was the only other
Spartak man to be called with some frequency.[103] Starting with Dinamo Kiev's
great success in 1975, it was decided that Lobanovskii's side should be the
base of the national team and that he should be coach. In order to maintain the
integrity of what had been a successful system, Lobanovskii quite rationally
limited his choices from other clubs. His machine had little or no room for
artists whose improvisations would disrupt the system, but this seemingly
sensible approach ultimately failed. League games, international duty, and
European Cup ties exhausted the players. Poor results at the 1976 Olympics
and at that year's European championship led to Lobanovskii's dismissal. He
was replaced by Simonian, who failed to get the team into the 1978 World
Cup. The job then went to Beskov after he had won the 1979 league championship. He named a host of Spartak players to the side. Beskov also led the
Olympic team in 1980 at the Moscow Games. That squad included Dasaev,
Khidiatulin, Romantsev, Shavlo, Gavrilov, and Cherenkov—an impressive
array of Spartak talent that managed to lose 0–1 to the German Democratic Republic in the semifinal.[104]

That failure prompted a return to a Dinamo Kiev–dominated lineup, with

Dasaev and Gavrilov thereafter the only steady representatives from Spartak. Beskov got this squad to the final stage of the 1982 World Cup in Spain, where despite some good performances, it failed to advance to the later rounds. He was relieved of his duties, and for the rest of the Soviet period, Dasaev was the only Spartak player to play a constant role with the sbornaia. From 1986 on, Lobanovskii was back in charge with predictable results for Spartak. Khidiatulin and Sergei Rodionov joined Dasaev a number of times, but the player whose star-crossed relationship with the national team most riled Spartak fans was that of their beloved Fiodr Cherenkov.

On the eve of both the 1986 and 1990 World Cups nash Fedya was on the squad, and both times he was dropped at the last minute by Lobanovskii, who had little patience with Cherenkov's unpredictability on and off the field. His fate encapsulated the contrasts between Spartak and Dinamo Kiev. Cherenkov was the most popular player on Beskov's team. He was the player of the year in 1983 and 1989. The darling of the Moscow public, Fedya was a local boy with whom the residents of the capital could identify. His spontaneity and creativity were qualities they admired. He seemed to embody the humanism and democracy that flowered during the last Soviet decade. When he was not given a place on the national team, the fans were reminded of all that the larger system had denied them. Cherenkov's special popularity and thwarted dreams reflected their own frustrations, but this was yet another case of Spartak supporters telling themselves stories about themselves. For Cherenkov truly did not fit in. Spartak fans were not entirely fair in criticizing Lobanovskii's soccer system as the perfect expression of the declining command-administrative economic system with its excessive planning and false rationality.[105]

Compared with the great triumphs of Dinamo Kiev, Spartak's record in the European cups proved yet another arena of frustration relieved by the occasional and unexpected miracle. The team made its debut in the 1966–1967 Cup Winners' Cup, exiting quickly from the competition. Its first appearance in the 1970–1971 Champions' Cup was similarly brief. During the seventies, it took part in the UEFA Cup three times and the Cup Winners' Cup once. It was only with the eras of Beskov and Romantsev, starting in 1980 and continuing until Nikolai Starostin's death in 1996, that Spartak became a constant participant in one or another of the tournaments. In 1981, Beskov took the team to the quarterfinals of the Champions' Cup, where they went out to Real Madrid, tying 0–0 in a match played at Tblisi and losing 0–2 in the Spanish capital. They made it to the quarterfinals of the 1983–1984 UEFA Cup, dispatching a powerful Aston Villa club along the way on a last-minute away goal by Cherenkov. The rest of their record under Beskov was less impressive, consisting of early exits in the UEFA Cup.[106]

Spartak's greatest European triumph actually came under Romantsev at a time when the club was undergoing all the difficulties through which Russian football passed in the final phase of perestroika. The lineup had been in constant turmoil as players continually left to pursue their careers in whatever

European league would have them. Attendance was in free fall throughout the league. Thus the team began the 1990–1991 Champions' Cup with few expectations. After dispatching Sparta Prague, Spartak drew Napoli, which at the time featured no less a figure than Diego Armando Maradonna. A 0–0 draw in Italy set the stage for a dramatic return leg. The great Argentine Pibe de Oro was then going through one of his periodic stretches of debauchery and irresponsibility. Missing the team plane after a night of revelry, he flew into Moscow a day late on his private jet, behavior for which he was benched in the first half. Eighty-six thousand showed up at Lenin Stadium on a cold seventh of November to witness a scoreless tie. The match then went to penalty kicks, won by Spartak 5–3.[107]

The resumption of the competition in the spring of 1991 held an even greater challenge for Spartak when it drew Real Madrid. The last time it had met Real, the first leg had been held in Tblisi, but with the Georgians' withdrawal from the Soviet league, that option was off the table. On March 3, eighty-one thousand braved a temperature of minus three degrees centigrade to watch the last great international contest of the Soviet era. Real, coached by its legendary star Alfredo di Stefano, was in the midst of a crisis both in the boardroom and on the field. The team had come into Moscow occupying fifth place in La Liga. Given the difficult weather conditions and the famously poor quality of the Lenin Stadium playing surface, di Stefano elected to play for a draw, benching his prolific Mexican striker, Hugo Sanchez, and the great Romanian midfielder, Gheorghe Hagi. Despite Spartak's domination of play, Di Stefano got his result. Both Soviet and Spanish journalists expected little trouble for Real when the scene shifted to Madrid at the Bernabeu on March 20. The result, however, was a shocking 3–1 victory for Spartak, with Dmitri Radchenko (b. 1970) scoring two goals. The Spanish fans applauded Spartak off the field, and a few days later, di Stefano resigned.[108] Their foe in the semifinal was Olympique Marseilles, owned by the controversial French businessman and Socialist Party politician Bernard Tapie. In the midst of the excitement, Spartak wound up selling the television rights for the game to not one but two French companies.[109] By then, however, its luck had run out, and it was easily eliminated.

The great run had, however, provided grist for the mills of the true believers in Spartak spirit. As had happened so often in the past, victory had come when it was least anticipated. Spartak had managed to defeat the club with more European championships than any other at a time when its own fortunes seemed to be waning along with those of the rest of Soviet soccer. The triumph over Real went down in history along with the win over the Basques in 1937, the 1939 replay against Dinamo Tblisi, the 1946 cup final, the replay victory over Dinamo Kiev in 1958, and Shmarov's miracle goal to clinch the title in 1989. The legend of the inspired underdog lived on, made all the more vivid by the fact that Real Madrid, Franco's favorite team, had always played much the same political role in the Spanish game as Dinamo had in the USSR.

The European cups were an important source of hard currency, divided among the team, the federation, and the government. Spartak then supplemented this source of *valiuta* with the time-honored practice of commercial tours to capitalist countries. No hole in the league calendar, large or small, went unused when there was money to be made abroad by both the team and its players. Such opportunities were not available to all Soviet clubs. Spartak and the various Dinamo sides were the only Soviet teams with significant name recognition outside the country. Once the Soviet season ended in November, Spartak would begin its journeys. Starting in the late sixties, Spartak played in Italy, usually against second-tier opposition before small crowds. By the seventies, August tournaments on the eve of the Spanish season had become an annual event for Spartak. Regular tours of France took place in February. A six-game December trip through Morocco in 1977 must have been a delightful reward for Spartak's promotion back to the top flight.[110] Over the course of the last decades of Soviet power, the team played in Japan, Mexico, Zaire, Guinea, the United Kingdom, Brazil, West Germany, Argentina, and the United States. The Spanish tournaments involved exhibition games with Barcelona, Real Madrid, and Atletico Madrid. A February 1987 trip to Argentina produced draws with Boca Juniors and River Plate, but most of Spartak's opponents elsewhere were not drawn from the great sides of world football.

While the club received sizable fees for these appearances, the players were busy acquiring so-called *defitsitnye* items to sell on their return home. In 1937, the Starostins had shopped extensively in the stores of Paris. The practice of Soviet tourists' buying and selling had long predated that trip and continued right up to 1991. Lovchev, Logofet, and Galinskii have all stressed that the purchase and resale of foreign items constituted a significant and vital supplement to the players' salaries. Logofet has described one particularly lucrative tour of Lebanon, Jordan, and Syria. The club winked at speculation in order for Spartak to compete with the heavily subsidized provincial sides. Beyond this, the chance to leave the country and see the world proved to be an effective recruiting tool. Like all other Soviet delegations, Spartak surely had its minders on these trips, but Logofet has suggested that when abroad, Spartak players were given more freedom than their Dinamo counterparts, who were subject to military discipline. Customs agents at Sheremetevo Airport, employed by the Ministry of Interior and likely fans of Dinamo, enforced the regulations selectively. Returning Spartak traveling parties usually had no problems, but when it suited the purposes of the authorities or some difficult customs agent, players entering and leaving the country were detained. Punishments for these so-called crimes often took the form of disqualifications, and it was common for those caught to lose their right to travel.[111]

These practices were by no means unique to Spartak. Foreign travel was the greatest privilege any Soviet citizen could enjoy, and shopping was always a big part of such journeys. Things could, however, get complicated upon returning home. To realize a benefit from their business dealings, players often had to sell what they had hunted and gathered not at secondhand stores but on the black market. In the process, they came in contact with organized crime figures whose interest in soccer might have been more than casual. Match fixing was thought to extend beyond agreements among coaches to include illegal gambling—the so-called black *totalizator* run by various groups of gangsters. With the second economy encompassing an ever-increasing range of consumer goods and services, many athletes of all sorts found themselves in touch with criminal and semi-criminal activity. The ensuing corruption, so endemic in the last Soviet decades, corroded respect for what passed for the law and fostered the deep cynicism that pervaded all levels of society. It would be naive to think that Spartak's players and coaches were untouched by this most basic fact of Soviet life. The Starostins' "entrepreneurialism" had pervaded the club, and after the collapse of the USSR Aleksandr Vainshtein felt comfortable calling Nikolai a "socialist businessman."[112] Iuri Shaliapin was no doubt right that a respect for material matters had long been one reason for the club's success.

### After the Fall

In the turbulent early post-Soviet years, a new twenty-team Russian league was established after a struggle that predictably left those who had been in power still in power. This structure was a far cry from the Soviet league. It included many weak and struggling teams in midsize towns with small stadiums. As he had done so often, Starostin adapted well to the new/old capitalism that deranged so much of the population. Consistent with the neoclassical economic shock therapy of this period, the state had gotten out of the sports business and the clubs were on their own. Starostin's independence and his profit-making orientation, honed under Communism, served him well in the very different business climate after the collapse. In this sense, as Russia became just another capitalist country, Spartak became just another pretty good football team, not all that different from scores of others throughout the world. In 1994, in a move that had troubled Starostin, Romantsev had used the players' support to force out the fiscally challenged Shaliapin and replace him as team president, although the team was in a relatively good financial state. It had survived Russia's rocky transition to a bare-knuckle brand of capitalism and dominated post-Soviet football in Russia into the next century, but in the process Spartak's internal atmosphere had deteriorated. Early in 1996, Nikolai Ozerov would complain in an open letter to *Izvestiia* that Romantsev had grown arrogant and "tactless" in his dealings with journalists, officials, and veterans of the club.[113]

Nevertheless, Romantsev succeeded in keeping the team afloat despite the constant turnover of personnel. In 1992, the first year of Russian football, Spartak thrived. It played thirty-two league games and lost just once. As players left to play in the West, Spartak used its old network to recruit replacements from all over the former Soviet Union. Just as Russian stars were drawn by the higher pay and better competition of the big European leagues, players in the new republics' smaller and poorer competitions were attracted to Russia. Many of them then found that a season or two, especially if spent with Spartak, could be a stepping-stone to the European big time. Between the breakup of the Soviet Union and the beginning of the new millennium Spartak won the league title in every year except 1995.[114]

As the perennial leader of Russian football, Spartak was also able to gain international visibility, prestige, and no small amount of hard cash as constant participants in the hugely successful Champions' League organized by UEFA. Spartak had thus far failed to advance beyond the group stages, but Starostin's disappointment at the third-place finish in the 1995 league season was greatly soothed by the team's success in the fall of 1995. With the advantage of a weak draw, Spartak won all its Champions' League preliminary games and moved on to the quarterfinals, which were to resume on March 6, 1996. As he met the new year, Nikolai Starostin must have been looking forward to that moment, but like Stalin in 1953, he did not live to learn the final result. He died on February 17, 1996, at the age of 98. Unlike Stalin, Starostin surely would have cared about the outcome of the match, and he would have been greatly disappointed. Before the resumption of play in the spring, Spartak sold a raft of its best players to European clubs, and it was eliminated by Nantes of the French league.[115]

Without Starostin, Spartak became something quite different. His presence had helped create the aura that fed Spartak ideology. His public rectitude and humane reputation, whether or not fully justified, allowed the club's older supporters to continue believing in the moral superiority of their cause. The brothers' exile, survival, and successful return had served for decades as a small model of hope for a nation that had undergone great suffering. As victims of Stalinist repression, the Starostins and their team sought to portray themselves as parts of the healthier side of the Soviet legacy, but by the time of Nikolai's passing and Romantsev's inheritance of the reins, that legacy had become attenuated. After 1991, Spartak could no longer claim to be a site of resistance against the tyranny of a powerful state. Its fans no longer saw themselves as victims. Instead, Spartak, as Russia's strongest team, took on the mantle of the nation and attracted the support of Russian nationalists. Many of these elements were violent right-wing groups, including skinheads and others who flaunted the same growing racism that had swept European soccer crowds in the 1990s and continues up to the present day. Many of these groups became heavily involved in an expanding hooliganism that was all too similar to trends in the rest of the world.[116]

In the post-Soviet moment organized crime became even more involved with football than it had been previously. Corruption was widespread, and few clubs were untouched. Rumors continuously circulated about Spartak's secret admirers in the underworld. There were stories of various *gruppirovki* buying the team matches without the knowledge of anyone at the club. As Simonian did note, Spartak had always numbered many shady characters among its fans. Yet the role of gangsters in the sport, especially when it came to match fixing, has been difficult to verify, and few journalists, not to mention policemen, have been willing or brave enough to try.[117] On the other side of the law, the new Russian president, Boris Yeltsin, also embraced Spartak. He attended big matches and was present at its celebrations. In the sharply contested elections of 1996, Yeltsin had the support of the players and team officials in his battle with the remnants of the Communist Party. The market, after all, had been good to Spartak.

As a reward for his success at the club level, Romantsev was made coach of the national team in preparation for the 1996 European championship, but Russia fared poorly at that competition and again at the World Cup in 1998. Things did not improve in the next cycle, and by 2002, Romanstev was gone in more ways than one. The pressures of his multiple duties at Spartak and the unsuccessful run with the sbornaia drastically changed Romantsev, who descended into alcoholism and paranoia. His judgment deteriorated, and he was removed.[118] The club was then challenged domestically by TsSKA, Lokomotiv, and Zenit, all of which had been taken over by different groups of wealthy businessmen. Spartak began a slide down the league table. Coaches came and went, and a variety of scandals wracked the club. Yet for all the withering of the team's image and despite the great changes in the world of post-Soviet soccer, Spartak's history had not been fully forgotten. During one particularly dispiriting run of failure, a group of fans unfurled a large banner with Nikolai Starostin's portrait on it. It was inscribed with the words "He sees all."

# Conclusion

When the Soviet Union died, it took with it a thousand great jokes. For whatever reasons, post-Soviet humor seems to have suffered a serious irony deficiency. One of the few good lines to emerge from the years after the collapse is the answer to the question "What was Communism?" Communism, it turns out, was the "shortest historical transition from capitalism to capitalism." Much the same could be said for Spartak. What started as MKS in 1922 soon became an enterprise and is today a fully professional football club. In between, however, the team assumed a variety of forms. While the defenders of Adam Smith might argue that neither the pre- nor post-Soviet economic system represents capitalism at its finest, there can be no disagreement that the USSR was a nation always in transition. One does not have to believe in modernization theory to accept the notion that the Soviet embrace of the modern world was never comfortable or complete. Similarly, football clubs all over the world have changed over the course of the last two centuries. These teams were institutions born in an early capitalism that came to full maturity in the late twentieth century. Here Spartak was no exception. It continually adapted to circumstances from 1900 until 1991 and even after. The club's ongoing evolution thus demonstrates the constancy of deep and continuing social change over the entire course of Soviet history.

During the years it has taken to write this book, my views on Spartak and specifically the Starostins have also changed. I began this project as a fan whose avocation was soccer. I finish it as a scholar whose vocation is history. I got to meet Nikolai Starostin in 1990 when I was working on a study of Soviet spectator sports. In that interview I treated him as a useful source. I had not yet read his final memoir, and my knowledge of the Soviet game was then still rudimentary. Needless to say, as a Spartak fan I was more than a trifle starstruck, and my two hours with the great patriarch did little to diminish my positive view. Over the course of our time together this ninety-two-year-old man spoke openly and interestingly about his life and his team and got only one minor detail wrong. If I had known then what I know now, however, I would have asked a very different set of far less comfortable questions.

I cannot say the realities of the research process have led me to abandon my positive view of the man and his club, but my understanding of their history is now a great deal more complicated. If Starostin can no longer be seen as an unalloyed hero, he does remain a very impressive figure with strengths and weaknesses. His self-revelations, as is always the case, are highly selective, and there are large chunks of his personality that remain a mystery. As the firstborn of six children, he had leadership thrust upon him, especially after his father's early death in 1920. Even the family name evoked his position of seniority. The Russian word for the oldest male in a family or other group is, after all, *starosta*. Perhaps, this status can explain the firm sense of entitlement and self-importance he exhibited all his life.

The ambiguities of Starostin's psyche were replicated in the contradictions of Spartak's history. The club could not escape the universal realities of elite professional soccer. Those very ambiguities in turn undermine many old certainties about the Soviet experience. Spectator sports may cater to the masses, but they are never run by their customers. Fans may be offered all manner of reasons to support a team, but those teams are always controlled by elites, regardless of the political and economic system. The powerful in any society have historically dominated big-time sport, and soccer, the most popular of sports, has always provided a space in which that power was both displayed and contested. At the game's highest levels, the expression "political football" always was and continues to be a classic tautology. Throughout its history, Spartak encouraged its branding as the people's team and developed the image of the romantic underdog and exploited victim. Yet the methods of projecting and defending that image evolved constantly. The Starostins had to navigate at the highest levels of the Soviet political system in order for their club to prosper. To that purpose, the public image of the team of outsiders was always foregrounded. At the same time, Spartak evoked a diffuse and imprecise populism that masked its support from powerful institutions. This contradiction was simply unavoidable if the Starostins were to attain their goal of running a successful, visible, and profitable attraction that would make them famous and, by Soviet standards, rich.

Over time, fans from a broad variety of social groups came to use Spartak as a vehicle for a muted form of resistance that never rose to the level of outright opposition. The extent, degree, and forms of that resistance varied enormously. There were even those who fully embraced both the regime and Spartak, just as there were those in opposition who rooted for Dinamo and TsSKA. No less loyal Communists than Konstantin Chernenko and Egor Ligachev also loved the Red and White.[1] If legions of Spartak supporters harbored resentments toward the elites of Soviet society, those grievances never led to a longing for a "return" of capitalism. This was even more true after World War II, when many of those elites came to support Spartak. The state-society dichotomy that seemed to drive the Spartak-Dinamo rivalry during the thirties changed to reveal a vastly more multidirectional set of tensions and discontents.

The reasons for rooting for Spartak became more various, just as there were many more ways for citizens of the USSR to be Soviet. The stark choices posed during the Stalin era were but a part of the entire Soviet experience. The ambiguities of Spartak's constantly evolving relationship with the regime can truly be said to reflect (rather than distort) all the complexities of life in the USSR from its beginning to its collapse. One could suggest that in continually changing their business model the Starostins were cynical chameleons, but here they were responding to the demands of a political system that was also constantly in flux.

If soccer turned out to be a slippery tool in the hands of the authorities, it is similarly slippery in the hands of scholars. If Spartak is that small piece of history that tells us big truths about Soviet history, the answers are far from clear-cut. The views of the fans turn out to be the hardest piece of the puzzle to locate and identify given their highly subjective nature. We know what the team's leaders thought and did, but learning the emotions and attitudes of the sporting public has been a much harder process given the limitations of official Soviet discourse. We have good information on how many spectators took the trouble to attend, and we also know what circumstances made them want to do so. Yet there is precious little direct contemporary testimony about why Soviet citizens supported one or another club.

The problem may lie with the subjectivity of the game itself. What was the role of play within an ideology that centered on labor? If culture had to be didactic and entertainment was supposed to be instrumental, a game that crazily denied players the use of a fundamental part of their bodies can hardly have been all that useful to a regime that sought wide-ranging control. The workers whose brawny arms guided the engines of Soviet industry could not always use those arms when it came to their favorite game—football. Olympic sport could be graphed and quantified in parallel and perpendicular ways that gave the appearance of rationality. Long columns of medal counts were a press staple. On the other hand, the football, as the great German coach Sepp Herberger famously noted, was always round.

Beginning in the late nineteenth century and well into the twentieth, play and leisure were embraced by the political right in order to justify social hierarchy. In *Homo Ludens,* his classic text of 1938, Johan Huizinga, a moderate conservative, argued that play, the product of leisure, was the engine of culture creation and culture was the engine of history.[2] Materialists and others on the left—who, like the Soviets, privileged production in their analyses—bobbled the ball. Only a few radical voices, mainly the football-loving but physically disabled Antonio Gramsci, understood the centrality of the ludic in particular and of popular culture in general. Yet at the turn of the new millennium, the lessons of the founding father of Italian Communism have been well learned. These days, historians of the Right and the Left are practically all culturalists of one sort or another. Sport matters, and fun is serious business. To his credit, Nikolai Starostin understood this from his first days on the streets of the Presnia district. He was born before there was a Soviet Union and died after it ceased to exist. He gave pleasure to millions through his creation and endured great pain for having done so. Spartak proved to be a site on which all the contradictory elements of Soviet life were played out. Like its founder, it outlived the USSR. As we continue to engage in the collective endeavor of learning the historical lessons of the now-complete Communist period, this small but enduring piece of history tells us much about what it meant to have lived in the USSR and been Soviet.

# Appendix 1

## Team Records, 1922–1991

| MOST GAMES (LEAGUE) | | MOST SEASONS PLAYED | |
|---|---|---|---|
| Fiodr Cherenkov | 398 | Igor Netto | 18 |
| Igor Netto | 368 | Gennadii Logofet | 15 |
| Gennadii Logofet | 349 | Fiodr Cherenkov | 15 |
| Galimzian Khusainov | 347 | Sergei Rodionov | 15 |
| Rinat Dasaev | 335 | Anatoly Ilyin | 14 |

| MOST GOALS (ALL COMPETITIONS) | | GAMES AS CAPTAIN | |
|---|---|---|---|
| Nikita Simonian | 160 | Rinat Dasaev | 213 |
| Sergei Rodionov | 152 | Oleg Romantsev | 187 |
| Galimzian Khusainov | 129 | Igor Netto | 175 |
| Fiodr Cherenkov | 121 | Vasili Sokolov | 163 |
| Iuri Gavrilov | 115 | Galimzian Khusainov | 133 |

| ASSISTS (ALL COMPETITIONS) | | CLEAN SHEETS (ALL COMPETITIONS) | |
|---|---|---|---|
| Fiodr Cherenkov | 136 | Rinat Dasaev | 185 |
| Iuri Gavrilov | 91 | Stanislav Cherchesov | 96 |
| Galimzian Khusainov | 76 | Vladimir Maslachenko | 89 |
| Nikita Simonian | 66 | Aleksandr Prokhorov | 69 |
| Sergei Rodionov | 57 | Anzor Kavazashvili | 45 |

*Source:* Eduard Nisenboim, *Spartak Moskva: Offitsial'naia istoria, 1922–2002* (Moscow, 2002).

# Appendix 2

## Annual Results

| | |
|---|---|
| 1922 | Champions, Class B |
| 1923 | Champion |
| 1924 | Champion |
| 1925 | Champion |
| 1926 | Third place |
| 1927 | Champion, fall season |
| 1928 | Third place |
| 1929 | Second place |
| 1930 | Eighth place, fall season |
| 1931 | Seventh place |
| 1932, 1933 | No competition |
| 1934 | Champion, spring; fourth place, fall |
| 1935 | Second place |

SOVIET LEAGUE

| | |
|---|---|
| 1936 | Third place, spring; champion, fall |
| 1937 | Second place |
| 1938 | Champion; cup winner |
| 1939 | Champion; cup winner |
| 1940 | Third place |
| 1941 | Season not completed |

MOSCOW LEAGUE

| | |
|---|---|
| 1942 | Champion, fall; Moscow Cup winner |
| 1943 | Third place |
| 1944 | Third place |

SOVIET LEAGUE

| | |
|---|---|
| 1945 | Tenth place |
| 1946 | Third place; cup winner |
| 1947 | Eighth place; cup winner |
| 1948 | Third place |
| 1949 | Third place |
| 1950 | Fifth place; cup winner |
| 1951 | Sixth place |
| 1952 | Champion |
| 1953 | Champion |
| 1954 | Second place |
| 1955 | Second place |
| 1956 | Champion |
| 1957 | Third place |
| 1958 | Champion; cup winner |
| 1959 | Sixth place |
| 1960 | Seventh place |
| 1961 | Third place |

| 1962 | Champion | 1978 | Fifth place |
| 1963 | Third place; cup winner | 1979 | Champion |
| 1964 | Eighth place | 1980 | Second place |
| 1965 | Eighth place; cup winner | 1981 | Second place |
| 1966 | Fourth place | 1982 | Third place |
| 1967 | Seventh place | 1983 | Second place |
| 1968 | Second place | 1984 | Second place |
| 1969 | Champion | 1985 | Second place |
| 1970 | Third place | 1986 | Third place |
| 1971 | Sixth place; cup winner | 1987 | Champion; winner of Federation Cup |
| 1972 | Eleventh place | | |
| 1973 | Fourth place | 1988 | Fourth place |
| 1974 | Second place | 1989 | Champion |
| 1975 | Tenth place | 1990 | Fifth place |
| 1976 | Fourteenth place (relegated) | 1991 | Second place |
| 1977 | First place, second division | | |

# Appendix 3

## Edelman's Spartak Hall of Fame

*Goalies:* Rinat Dasaev, Anatoly Akimov, Vladimir Maslachenko

*Defenders:* Aleksandr Starostin, Vasili Sokolov, Evgenii Lovchev, Gennadii Logofet, Anatoly Krutikov, Mikhail Ogon'kov, Oleg Romantsev

*Midfielders:* Igor Netto, Andrei Starostin, Iuri Gavrilov, Petr Isakov, Ivan Artemev, Petr Artemev

*Attackers:* Nikita Simonian, Fiodr Cherenkov, Sergei Sal'nikov, Nikolai Dementiev, Aleksei Paramonov, Anatoly Ilyin, Pavel Kannunikov, Vladimir Stepanov, Galimzian Khusainov, Nikolai Starostin

*Coaches:* Konstantin Kvashnin, Konstantin Beskov, Nikita Simonian, Abram Dangulov

# Abbreviations

# Notes

## Introduction

1. For a discussion of the role of Soviet subjectivity in the construction of the self, see Jochen Hellbeck, *Revolution on My Mind: Writing a Diary under Stalin* (Cambridge, MA, 2006), pp. 1–14 and 347–64. On the public and private, see Lewis Siegelbaum, ed., *Borders of Socialism: Private Spheres of Soviet Russia* (New York, 2006), pp. 1–21.

2. Simon Kuper, *Football against the Enemy* (London, 1994), p. 46. The anthropologist in question is the Armenian scholar Levon Abramian, whose work has centered on festival in antiquity. See Abramian, *Pervobytnyi prazdnik i mifologiia* (Erevan, Armenia, 1983), pp. 11–14.

3. Kuper, p. 40. The "Soviet scholar" in question is quoted by Kuper but is not named.

4. On the question of resistance and its discontents, see Michael David-Fox, Peter Holquist, and Marshall Poe, eds. *The Resistance Debate in Russian and Soviet History,* Kritika Historical Studies 1 (Bloomington, IN, 2003). On violent protest, see Vladimir Kozlov, *Mass Uprisings in the USSR: Protest and Rebellion in the Post-Stalin Years* (Armonk, NY, 2002), pp. 3–21 and 311–14.

5. Anthony King, *The End of the Terraces: The Transformation of English Football in the 1990's* (London, 1998), pp. 16–24. Clifford Geertz, "Deep Play," *Daedalus* (Winter, 1972):26.

6. On soccer and identity, see, among many possibilities, Anthony King, "New Directors, Customers and Fans: The Transformation of English Football in the 1990's," *Sociology of Sport Journal,* no. 14 (1997): 236. On the close connections between teams and communities during the origins of soccer, see Tony Mason, *Association Football and British Society, 1863–1914* (Brighton, UK, 1981); Bill Murray, *Football: A History of the World Game* (Aldershot, UK, 1994), pp. 1–50; Murray, *The Old Firm, Sectarianism, Sport and Society in Scotland* (Edinburgh, 1984), pp. 4–25. Christiane Eisenberg, "Football in Germany: Beginnings, 1900–1914," *International Journal of the History of Sport* 8, no. 2 (1991):205–20; Heiner Gillmeister, "The Fate of Little Franz and Big Franz: The Foundation of Bayern Munich FC," *Soccer and Society* 1, no. 2 (Summer 2000): 80–106; Rogan Taylor, *Football and Its Fans: Supporters and Their Relations with the Game, 1885–1985* (Leicester, UK, 1992), pp. 3–13; Charles Korr, *West Ham United: The Making of a Football Club* (Urbana, IL, 1986), pp. 1–17; Pierre Lanfranchi, "Bologna: The Team That Shook the World," *International Journal of the History of Sport* 8, no. 3 (December 1991): 336–46; Chris Bethell and David Sullivan, *Millwall Football Club, 1885–1939* (Stroud, UK, 1999), pp. 5–8; John Foote, *Calcio: A History of Italian Football* (London, 2006), pp. 1–41; Joe McGinniss, *The Miracle of Castel di Sangro* (New York, 1999); Phil Ball, *White Storm: 100 Years of Real Madrid* (Edinburgh, 2002), pp. 59–72; Jimmy Burns, *Barca: A People's Passion* (London, 1999), pp. 70–96.

7. *Sovetskii sport* (hereafter SS), 3/8/59.

8. Pierre Bourdieu, "Program for a Sociology of Sport," *Sociology of Sport Journal,* no. 5 (1988): 160. See also Bourdieu, *The Logic of Practice* (Stanford, 1990), p. 160, and *Distinction: A Social Critique of the Judgment of Taste* (Cambridge, MA, 1984), p. 214. On Bourdieu, see Susan Brownell, *Training the Body for China: Sports in the Moral Order of the People's Republic* (Chicago, 1995), p. 11.

9. On body culture, see Thomas Laqueur and Catherine Gallagher, eds., *The Making of the Modern Body: Sexuality and Society in the Nineteenth Century* (Berkeley, 1987); Henning Eichberg, *Body Cultures: Essays on Sport, Space and Identity* (London, 1998); Mike Featherstone and Bryan Turner, eds., *The Body: Social Process and Cultural Theory* (London, 1991).

10. R. W. Connell, *Masculinities: Knowledge, Power and Social Change* (Berkeley, 1995). Arjun Appadurai, *Modernity at Large: Cultural Dimensions of Globalization* (St. Paul, 1995), p. 93.

11. Eric Dunning, "Sport as a Male Preserve: Notes on the Social Sources of Masculinity and Its Transformations," in *Women, Sport and Culture,* ed. Susan Birell and Cheryl Cole (Urbana, IL, 1994), pp. 163–79; Eduardo Archetti, *Masculinities: Football, Polo and the Tango in Argentina* (Oxford, 1999), pp. 161–89; John Hoberman, *Sport and Political Ideology* (Austin, 1984), p. 11; Elliot Gorn and Warren Goldstein, *A Brief History of American Sport* (New York, 1993).

12. On the competing models of sport as well as a discussion of the most useful theoretical approaches to understanding modern sport, including Bourdieu, Foucault, Gramsci, and Stuart Hall, see Richard Gruneau, "The Critique of Sport in Modernity," in *The Sports Process: A Comparative and Developmental Approach,* ed. Eric Dunning, Joseph Maguire, and Robert Pearton (Urbana, IL, 1993), pp. 85–105.

13. Among many works on Soviet popular culture, see Richard Stites, *Russian Popular Culture: Entertainment and Society since 1900* (Cambridge, UK, 1992); Karen Petrone, *Life Has Become More Joyous, Comrades: Celebrations in the Time of Stalin* (Bloomington, IN, 2000), pp. 24, 31–34; Frederick Starr, *Red and Hot: The Fate of Jazz in the Soviet Union* (Oxford, 1984); Denise Youngblood, *Movies for the Masses: Popular Cinema and Soviet Society in the 1920's* (Cambridge, 1992); Anne Gorsuch and Diane Koenker, eds., *Turizm: The Russian and East European Tourist under Capitalism and Socialism* (Ithaca, 2006); Alexei Yurchak, *Everything Was Forever, Until It Was No More: The Last Soviet Generation* (Princeton, 2006).

14. James Scott, *Domination and the Arts of Resistance: Hidden Transcripts* (New Haven, 1990), p. 120. On the ambiguity of the everyday, see Alf Ludtke ed. *The History of Everyday Life: Reconstructing Historical Experiences and Ways of Life* (Princeton, 1995), p. 12.

## Chapter 1. Spartak's Roots

1. Cited in Bill Murray, *The World's Game: A History of Soccer* (Urbana, IL, 1996), pp. 29–30.

2. Boris Chesnokov, "Sport v staroi Moskve," *Fizkul'tura i sport,* no. 9 (1947), cited in Louise McReynolds, *Russia at Play: Leisure Activities at the End of the Tsarist Era* (Ithaca, 2003), p. 95.

3. On soccer in the United Kingdom, see among many possibilities Mason, *Association Football;* Richard Holt, *Sport and the British: A Modern History* (Oxford, 1989).

4. A. S. Perel', *Otechestvennomu futbolu 60 let* (Moscow, 1958), p. 16.

5. Rossiiskii Futbol'nyi Soiuz, *Sto let rossiiskomu futbolu, 1897–1997* (hereafter Sto let) (Moscow, 1997), p. 23; Peter Frykholm, "Soccer and Social Identity in Pre-Revolutionary Moscow," *Journal of Sports History* 24, no. 2 (Summer 1997): 144; McReynolds, pp. 76–112.

6. Richard Holt, cited in Frykholm, p. 144.

7. Victor Peppard, "The Beginnings of Russian Soccer," *Stadion* 8–9 (1982–83): 159.

8. Allen Guttmann, *Ritual to Record: The Nature of Modern Sports* (New York, 1978), pp. 1–55.

9. Leopold Haimson, *Russia's Revolutionary Experience, 1905–1917, Two Essays* (New York, 2005), pp. 31–32; Robert Johnson, *Peasant and Proletarian: The Working Class of Moscow at the End of the Nineteenth Century* (New Brunswick, NJ, 1979).

10. Joseph Bradley, *Muzhik and Muscovite: Urbanization in Late Imperial Russia* (Berkeley, 1985); Robert Thurston, *Liberal City, Conservative State, Moscow and Russia's Urban Crisis, 1906–1914* (Oxford, 1987); Diane Koenker, *Moscow Workers and the 1917 Revolution* (Princeton, 1981); Laura Engelstein, *Moscow, 1905: Working-Class Organization and Political Conflict* (Stanford, 1982); Victoria Bonnell, *Roots of Rebellion: Workers' Politics and Organizations in St. Petersburg and Moscow, 1900–1914* (Berkeley, 1983).

11. Steven A. Smith, *Red Petrograd: Revolution in the Factories, 1917–18* (Cambridge, UK, 1983); David Mandel, *The Petrograd Workers and the Fall of the Regime: From the February*

*Revolution to the July Days, 1917* (London, 1983), and *The Petrograd Workers and the Soviet Seizure of Power: From the July Days, 1917 to July, 1918* (London, 1984); Heather Hogan, *Forging Revolution: Metal Workers, Managers and the State in St. Petersburg, 1890–1914* (Bloomington, IN, 1993); William Rosenberg and Diane Koenker, *Strikes and Revolution in Russia, 1917* (Princeton, 1989); Mark Steinberg, *Moral Communities: The Culture of Class Relations in the Russian Printing Industry, 1867–1907* (Berkeley, 1992); Alexander Rabinowitch, *The Bolsheviks Come to Power: The Revolution of 1917 in Petrograd* (New York, 1976); Gerald Suhr, *1905 in St. Petersburg: Labor, Society and Revolution* (Stanford, 1989).

12. See William J. Baker, *Sports in the Western World* (Totowa, NJ, 1982); Tony Mason, *Passion of the People? Football in South America* (London, 1995); Tony Mason, Christiane Eisenberg, Pierre Lanfranchi, and Alfred Wahl, *100 Years of Football: The FIFA Centennial Book* (London, 2004), pp. 36–57.

13. V. A. Pirogov, *Futbol, Khronika Sobytia, Fakty* (Moscow, 1995), pp. 3 and 9.

14. Ian Pickup, "French Football from Its Origins to Euro 84," in *France and the World Cup: The National Impact of a World Sporting Event,* ed. Hugh Dauncey and Geoff Hare (London, 1999), pp. 22–40.

15. James Riordan, *Sport in Soviet Society: Development of Sport and Physical Education in Russia and the USSR* (Cambridge, UK, 1977), p. 10.

16. Peppard, p. 159; Riordan, pp. 13 and 18.

17. On the early Olympic movement see Allen Guttmann, *The Olympics: A History of the Modern Games* (Urbana, IL, 1992); John MacAloon, *This Great Symbol: Pierre de Coubertin and the Origins of the Modern Olympic Games* (Chicago, 1984).

18. Peppard, p. 155; Riordan, p. 22; Sto Let, p. 12; McReynolds, p. 102; Pirogov, p. 3.

19. Sto let, p. 28; L. P. Pribylovskii, *Trenery bol'shogo futbola* (Moscow, 1980), p. 8; Riordan, p. 22; Pirogov, p. 4; L. G. Lebedev, ed., *Rossiskii Futbol za 100 let: Entsiklopedicheskii spravochnik* (hereafter ERF) (Moscow, 1997), p. 20; V. Tarasov and S. Tikhonov, *Futbol: Istoriko-sportivnyi ocherk* (Tblisi, 1948).

20. Pirogov, pp. 5–6; Riordan, p. 22; Iu. I. Korshak, *Staryi, staryi futbol* (Moscow, 1980), p. 8. Mikhail Romm, *Ia Boleiu za Spartak: Sport, puteshestvia, voskhozhdenia* (Alma-Ata, Kazakhstan, 1965); Andrei Starostin, *Bol'shoi futbol* (Moscow, 1964), p. 16; Pirogov, pp. 15–19.

21. Peppard, pp. 156–57; Sto let, p. 19; Riordan, p. 19. Mikhail Sushkov, *Futbol'nyi teatr* (Moscow, n.d.), p. 52.

22. See Barbara Engel, *Between the Fields and the City: Women, Work and Family in Russia, 1861–1914* (Cambridge, UK, 1994); Caroline Brooke, *Moscow: A Cultural History* (Oxford, 2006), pp. 63–65.

23. Andrei Starostin, *Flagman futbola* (Moscow, 1988), p. 15.

24. Sir Stanley Matthews, *The Way It Was: My Autobiography* (London, 2000), p. 9.

25. Daniel Brower, "Labor Violence in Russia in the Late Nineteenth Century," *Slavic Review* 41, no. 3 (Fall 1982): 419, 423; Frykholm, p. 143; Sto let, p. 26; Sushkov, p. 22; Nikolai Starostin, *Zvezdy Sovetskogo futbola* (Moscow, 1967), p. 88.

26. SS, 10/25/57; Pavel Vasilievich Batyrev, "Pobeda novoi taktiki," in *Stranitsa iz proshlogo* (Moscow, 1951), pp. 7–10.

27. SS, 10/23/57; Frykholm, pp. 145–46; Romm, p. 16; Sushkov, pp. 26–27; Sto let, p. 25.

28. Leonid Gorianov, *Kolumby moskovskogo futbola* (Moscow, 1983), p. 28; Pirogov, p. 6; Sto let, p. 23; Romm, p. 17; SS, 9/11/57.

29. Konstantin Esenin, *Moskovskii futbol* (Moscow, 1974), pp. 14 and 74; Sushkov, p. 16; Gorianov, *Kolumby,* p. 29.

30. Romm, p. 21; Sto let, p. 23; Gorianov, *Kolumby,* p. 30; Chesnokov, "Sport v staroi Moskve," p. 23.

31. Sto let, p. 20; Sushkov, p. 16; Pirogov, p. 7; Gorianov, *Kolumby,* p. 30; Esenin, p. 15; Blair Ruble, *Second Metropolis: Pragmatic Pluralism in Gilded Age Chicago, Silver Age Moscow and Meiji Osaka* (Cambridge, UK, 2001), p. 272.

32. Sushkov, p. 17; Esenin, p. 16; Gorianov, *Kolumby,* p. 31.

33. Romm, p. 19; Sushkov, pp. 18 and 22; McReynolds, p. 93.

34. McReynolds, p. 106; Pirogov, pp. 10–14; Romm, p. 15; Korshak, pp. 105–11; SS, 4/13/54 and 5/1/58.

35. Esenin, pp. 16 and 20; Pirogov, p. 7; Sto let, p. 25; Romm, pp. 21 and 25; ERF, p. 158; SS, 9/21/57.

36. Sto let, p. 17; Andrei Starostin, *Bol'shoi,* p. 14; Pirogov, pp. 10–11 and 19–23; Nikolai Starostin, *Moi futbol'nye gody* (Moscow, 1986), p. 9; Sushkov, pp. 29–30; Frykholm, 144–45.

37. Andrei Starostin, *Povest' o futbole* (Moscow, 1973), p. 15; Nikolai Starostin, *Futbol skvoz' gody* (Moscow, 1989), p. 15; Bonnell, p. 40; Sto let, p. 49.

38. Sto let, p. 49; Nikolai Starostin, *Zvezdy,* p. 131; Sushkov, p. 49; Andrei Starostin, *Vstrechi na futbol'nom orbite* (Moscow, 1978), pp. 30–31; Richard Stites, *Russian Popular Culture: Entertainment and Society since 1900* (Cambridge, UK, 1992), pp. 18–19; Sushkov, pp. 48 and 53.

39. Sushkov, p. 53.

40. Pirogov, p. 8.

41. Bonnell, p. 37.

42. Sto let, pp. 44–45; Andrei Starostin, *Bol'shoi,* p. 15; Andrew Davies, *Leisure, Gender and Poverty: Working-Class Culture in Salford and Manchester, 1900–1930* (Buckingham, UK, 1992), pp. 38–39.

43. Frykholm, p. 147; Peppard, p. 152.

44. ERF, p. 696.

45. Gorianov, *Kolumby,* p. 27.

46. Ibid., pp. 33–34.

47. ERF, p. 696; Gorianov, *Kolumby,* p. 35.

48. ZKS had been the champion in 1914. Gorianov, *Kolumby,* pp. 35–39; McReynolds, p. 105; ERF, pp. 393 and 696. *Izvestiia* (hereafter Izv), 10/14/40.

49. Andrei Starostin, *Povest',* p. 54.

50. Ruble, p. 272; Bradley, p. 4.

51. Bonnell, p. 21.

52. Bradley, pp. 4 and 64.

53. Ruble, p. 265.

54. William Chase, *Workers, Society and the Soviet State: Labor and Life in Moscow, 1918–1929* (Urbana, IL, 1987), p. 180.

55. Bradley, p. 196.

56. Koenker, p. 16.

57. Kenneth Strauss, *Factory and Community in Stalin's Russia: The Making of an Industrial Working Class* (Pittsburgh, 1997), p. 33.

58. Engelstein, p. 45; Koenker, p. 20.

59. Eduard Nisenboim and V. Rasinksii, *Ot MKS do Spartaka* (Moscow, 2000), p. 3; Timothy Colton, *Moscow: Governing the Socialist Metropolis* (Cambridge, MA, 1995), p. 47.

60. Bradley, pp. 87–88.

61. Bradley, p. 139; Koenker, p. 20; Ruble, p. 271; Colton, p. 48.

62. Bradley, p. 215.

63. Engelstein, p. 49.

64. Koenker, p. 146; Colton, p. 65; Engelstein, p. 216.

65. Engelstein, pp. 215–16; Koenker, p. 54.

66. Koenker, p. 16; Ruble, p. 263.

67. Andrei Starostin, *Bol'shoi,* p. 6.

68. Andrei Starostin, *Povest',* pp. 4–6; *Bol'shoi,* p. 21; Nikolai Starostin, *Futbol,* p. 15.

69. Andrei Starostin, *Povest',* p. 8; Nikolai Starostin, *Futbol,* p. 11.

70. Nikolai Starostin, *Futbol,* p. 12; McReynolds, p. 83.

71. On liminality see Victor Turner, *From Ritual to Theater: The Human Seriousness of Play* (New York, 1982), pp. 20–59.

72. Andrei Starostin, *Flagman,* p. 7; *Bol'shoi,* p. 25.

73. Nikolai Starostin, *Zvezdy,* p. 140.

74. Andrei Starostin, *Bol'shoi,* p. 27,

75. Andrei Starostin, *Vstrechi* pp. 14–19.

76. Gorianov, *Ozhivshie legendy* (Moscow, 1969), p. 129.

77. Anatoly Akimov, *Zapiski vratar'ia* (Moscow, 1968), p. 66–68.

78. Gorianov, *Legendy,* pp. 135–36; ERF, p. 177; Andrei Starostin, *Povest',* pp. 54 and 107–8; Nisenboim and Rasinskii, p. 98; Frykholm, p. 147.

79. Akimov, p. 6. Andrei Starostin, *Bol'shoi,* p. 33.

80. Gorianov, *Legendy,* pp. 140–41 and 156.

81. Gorianov, *Legendy,* pp. 132, 158, 160, and 162; *Kolumby,* p. 54.

82. Frykholm, p. 150; Andrei Starostin, *Povest',* p. 14.

83. Andrei Starostin, *Povest',* p. 54.

84. Andrei Starostin, *Bol'shoi,* p. 25.

85. Andrei Starostin, *Povest'*, pp. 12–19.

86. Andrei Starostin, *Povest'*, p. 19.

87. Nikolai Starostin, *Gody*, p. 10; Andrei Starostin, *Povest'*, p. 58.

88. Andrei Starostin, *Povest'*, p. 8; Nikolai Starostin, *Futbol*, pp. 7–11. Christine Worobec, "Masculinity in Late-Imperial Russian Society," in *Russian Masculinities in History and Culture*, ed. Barbara Clements et al. (New York, 2002), p. 82.

89. Brower, pp. 425–27.

90. Nikolai Starostin, *Futbol*, pp. 8–10.

91. Ibid., pp. 8–10, 17; Romm, p. 72.

92. Andrei Starostin, *Povest'*, pp. 46–48; Nikolai Starostin, *Zvezdy*, pp. 131–35.

93. Andrei Starostin, *Povest'*, pp. 56–57; *Bol'shoi*, pp. 21–24.

94. Andrei Starostin, *Povest'*, pp. 61–62.

95. Andrei Starostin, *Bol'shoi*, p. 24.

96. Gorianov, *Kolumby*, p. 128; Andrei Starostin, *Flagman*, p. 24.

97. Gosudarstvennyi Arkhiv Rossiiskoi Federatsii (hereafter GARF), f. 7583, o. 60, d. 4105, ll. 2–5, and f. 7576, o. 13, d. 77, l. 77b.

98. *Okt'iabr na krasnoi presne, vospominania k X godovshchine* (Moscow, 1927).

99. Koenker, p. 213.

100. Romm, p. 11; ERF, p. 447.

101. S. A. Smith, "Masculinity in Transition: Peasant Migrants to Late-Imperial St. Petersburg," in Clements et al., p. 108 (emphasis added).

## Chapter 2.  Before There Was Spartak, 1917–1935

1. Sto let, p. 51; Esenin, 29; Baruch Hazan, *Olympic Sports and Propaganda Games* (New Brunswick, 1982), p. 20.

2. Sto let, p. 51; Pribylovskii, pp. 10 and 23; Pirogov, p. 26; Riordan, p. 69; Esenin, p. 19; Gorianov, *Legendy*, 163–65.

3. Andrei Starostin, *Bol'shoi*, p. 41; Gorianov, *Legendy*, p. 164.

4. Pirogov, p. 9; Romm, p. 72.

5. Sto let, p. 50.

6. Andrei Starostin, *Povest'*, p. 87.

7. Gorianov, *Kolumby*, p. 62; Nikolai Starostin, *Zvezdy*, p. 4; ERF, pp. 158 and 170; Eduard Nisenboim, *Spartak Moskva: Offitsial'naia istoriia* (hereafter SOI) (Moscow, 2002), pp. 790–91.

8. Sto let, pp. 50–51; Esenin, pp. 75–78.

9. Andrei Starostin, *Bol'shoi*, p. 41.

10. Gorianov, *Legendy*, p. 164.

11. Eric Naiman, *Sex in Public: The Incarnation of Early Soviet Ideology* (Princeton, 1999), p. 6; Anne Gorsuch, *Youth in Revolutionary Russia: Enthusiasts, Bohemians, Delinquents* (Bloomington, IN, 2000), p. 24.

12. Gorsuch, p. 9.

13. Stites, pp. 37–40.

14. Anatoly Lunacharsky, *Mysli o sporte* (Moscow, 1930).

15. Gorsuch, p. 116.

16. Frederick Starr, *Red and Hot: The Fate of Jazz in the Soviet Union* (Oxford, 1984), p. 58.

17. Gorsuch, p. 116–17; Starr, p. 58; Stites, p. 52; Alan Ball, *Russia's Last Capitalists: The Nepmen, 1921–1929* (Berkeley, 1997), p. 17.

18. Gorsuch, pp. 116–17; Stites, p. 49; Natalia Lebina, *Posednevnaia zhizn' Sovetskogo goroda: Normy i anomalii* (St. Petersburg, 1999), p. 254.

19. Starr, p. 60; Stites, p. 47.

20. Youngblood, pp. 14, 21, 25–28; Stites, pp. 56, 60, 63; Gorsuch, p. 65; Lebina, pp. 245–47.

21. Andrei Starostin, *Povest'*, p. 68; *Vstrechi*, p. 51.

22. Andrei Starostin, *Flagman*, p. 35.

23. Andrei Starostin, *Povest'*, p. 70.

24. Andrei Starostin, *Vstrechi*, p. 50.

25. Ibid., pp. 31–41.

26. McReynolds, pp. 90–92; Andrei Starostin, *Vstrechi*, pp. 44 and 59.

27. Chase, pp. 157–64; Lewis Siegelbaum, *Soviet State and Society between Revolutions, 1918–1929* (Cambridge, UK, 1992), p. 104; Gorsuch, pp. 38–40; A. I. Vdovin and V. Z. Drobizhev, *Rost rabochego klassa SSSR, 1917–1940 gg.* (Moscow, 1976), pp. 87 and 115.

28. Konstantin Beskov, "Moia zhizn' v futbole," *Futbol,* no. 4 (1991), p. 4.

29. SOI, p. 12.

30. Siegelbaum, pp. 12–13.

31. Nikolai Starostin, *Gody,* p. 10.

32. Gorianov, *Kolumby,* p. 62; Nisenboim and Rasinskii, pp. 5–6; Nikolai Starostin, *Futbol,* pp. 17, 21, and 22; Andrei Starostin, *Vstrechi,* p. 114.

33. Andrei Starostin, *Bol'shoi,* p. 44; Nikolai Starostin, *Futbol,* p. 16; Gorianov, *Legendy,* p. 169; *Kolumby,* p. 91.

34. SOI, p. 10.

35. Gorianov, *Legendy,* p. 167; Andrei Starostin, *Bol'shoi,* p. 44; *Povest',* pp. 72–75; Gorianov, *Legendy,* p. 170; SOI, p. 11.

36. SOI, p. 11.

37. Nikolai Starostin, *Futbol,* p. 17; SOI, p. 12.

38. SOI, p. 14.

39. Nikolai Starostin, *Zvezdy,* p. 7.

40. Gorianaov, *Kolumby,* p. 94; SS, 11/14/50; Sto let, pp. 52–53; Esenin, p. 36; Pirogov, p. 27; Pribylovskii, p. 5.

41. Esenin, p. 38; Andrei Starostin, *Bol'shoi,* p. 72.

42. Nikolai Starostin, *Gody* p. 10; *Futbol;* SOI, p. 17.

43. *Vechernaia Moskva* (hereafter VM), 3/27/29.

44. Mason, *Association Football,* pp. 83–123.

45. V. Vinokurov and O. Kucherenko, *Dinamo Moskva '67* (Moscow, 1968), p. 11; SOI, pp. 14–22.

46. Sushkov, p. 107.

47. SOI, p. 15.

48. SS, 2/13/70.

49. Sto let, p. 54; Pirogov, p. 28; *My iz Dinamo* (Moscow, 1968), p. 5.

50. Esenin, p. 104; *Krasnyi Sport* (hereafter KS), 5/1/36; Vinokurov, p. 8; *My iz Dinamo* p. 6.

51. Gorianov, *Kolumby,* p. 104; *My iz Dinamo,* p. 8.

52. Esenin, p. 105.

53. Nikolai Starostin, *Zvezdy,* p. 8. I. S. Dobronravov, *Na bessrochnoi sluzhbe futbolu* (hereafter DE) (Moscow, 2000), pp. 142–43.

54. Esenin, p. 105; Nisenboim and Rasinskii, p. 18; Nikolai Starostin, *Futbol,* p. 22.

55. Gorianov, *Legendy,* pp. 179–80; *Kolumby,* p. 100.

56. Nikolai Starostin, *Zvezdy,* pp. 8 and 11; *Gody,* p. 11.

57. Esenin, p. 106; Gorianov, *Legendy,* p. 179; *Kolumby,* p. 100.

58. SOI, p. 790.

59. See Moshe Lewin, *The Making of Soviet Society: Essays in the History of Interwar Russia* (New York, 1985); Ronald Suny, *The Soviet Experiment: Russia, the USSR and the Successor States* (Oxford, 1998), p. 217.

60. Sto let, p. 54.

61. Ibid., p. 56.

62. SOI, pp. 20–22.

63. Andrei Starostin, *Bol'shoi,* p. 91; *Football in the USSR* (Moscow, 1958), p. 6.

64. Andrei Starostin, *Bol'shoi,* p. 98; Nikolai Starostin, *Futbol,* p. 22.

65. Nikolai Starostin, *Futbol,* p. 21.

66. Nisenboim and Rasinskii, p. 33; Nikolai Starostin, *Futbol,* p. 22; SOI, p. 21.

67. SOI, p. 790.

68. Anatoly Akimov, *Zapiski Vratar'ia* (Moscow, 1968), pp. 4 and 7; Andrei Starostin, *Bol'shoi,* p. 32.

69. SOI, p. 16; Andrei Starostin, *Flagman,* p. 30; Sto let, p. 62.

70. Pirogov, pp. 25–26; Esenin, pp. 36–38; SOI, p. 16.

71. Esenin, pp. 36–38 and 107.

72. SOI, p. 21; KS, 11/23/24; Pirogov, p. 27.

73. Aleksandr Vainshtein, interview with the author, Moscow, December 8, 1999.

74. Chase, p. 171.

75. Vainshtein, interview; Nikolai Starostin, *Zvezdy,* p. 91.

76. Andrei Starostin, *Vstrechi,* pp. 85 and 91.

77. SOI, p. 23.

78. Nisenboim and Rasinskii, p. 94; Sto let, p. 66.

79. Nisenboim and Rasinskii, p. 35.

80. Ronald Suny, ed., *The Structure of Soviet History* (Oxford, 2003), pp. 220–21.

81. Sto let, p. 69.

82. SS, 3/26/46. Rossiiskii Gosudarstvennyi Arkhiv Sotsial'no-Politicheskoi Istorii (hereafter RGASPI), f. 17, o. 113, d. 238, l. 4 and f. 17, o. 3, 652, l. 5.

83. KS, 9/25/27.

84. SOI, p. 29.

85. Colton, 214.

86. Sheila Fitzpatrick, "The Bolshevik Invention of Class: Marxist Theory and the Making of 'Class Consciousness' in Soviet Society," in Suny, *Structure*, pp. 164–77.

87. VM, 3/2/29, 3/13/29, 10/1/29.

88. VM, 8/6/ 29.

89. VM, 8/9/29.

90. *Fizkul'tura i sport*, 5/12/28, 6/30/28; *Pravda*, 6/19/28

91. VM, 9/9/29; Sto let, p. 57.

92. Mikhail Iakushin, *Vechnaia taina futbola* (Moscow, 1988), p. 17.

93. SOI, p. 34; Sushkov, p. 115.

94. Esenin, p. 18. Igor Goranskii, *Kak vozrozhdali Spartak* (Moscow, 2008), p. 4.

95. Nikolai Starostin, interview with the author, Moscow, September 25, 1990.

96. SOI, p. 39.

97. Nikolai Starostin, interview.

98. Nikolai Starostin, *Futbol*, p. 25

99. SS, 2/13/70. Andrei Starostin, *Bol'shoi*, p. 165.

100. SS, 2/22/58 and 2/13/70.

101. Andrei Starostin, *Flagman*, pp. 72–73.

102. Starr, p. 107.

103. Sheila Fitzpatrick, "Petitions, Patronage and Blat: Reflections on their Importance in the Stalinist System" (paper presented at conference on the Stalin years, University of California, Riverside, April 19, 1998), p. 9.

104. Alena Ledeneva, *Russia's Economy of Favors: Blat Networking and Informal Exchange* (Cambridge, UK, 1998).

105. Andrei Starostin, *Bol'shoi*, pp. 122–23.

106. GARF, f. 7576, op. 2, d. 160, l. 1.

107. Barbara J. Keys, *Globalizing Sport: National Rivalry and the International Community in the 1930's* (Cambridge, MA, 2006), p. 159.

108. Of seventeen players, five were from Spartak, seven were from Dinamo, and five were from other teams. GARF, f. 7576, o. 1, d. 205, l. 2.

109. GARF, f. 7575, o. 1, d. 209, l. 8.

110. Iakushin, p. 30.

111. Sto let, p. 82; Andrei Starostin, *Povest'*, p. 136; Iakushin, p. 31; Pirogov, p. 54.

112. GARF, f. 7576, o. 2, d. 160, ll. 1–51.

113. SOI, pp. 42–43.

## Chapter 3.  The Battle Is Joined, 1936–1937

1. http://www.sport-express.ru/art.shtml?71816 (accessed 9/20/03).

2. See Nicholas Timasheff, *The Great Retreat: The Growth and Decline of Communism in Russia* (New York, 1946).

3. See Lewis Siegelbaum, *Stakhanovism and the Politics of Productivity in the USSR, 1935–1941* (Cambridge, UK, 1988).

4. Karen Petrone, *Life Has Become More Joyous, Comrades: Celebrations in the Time of Stalin* (Bloomington, IN, 2000), pp. 14–15.

5. See J. Arch Getty and Oleg Naumov, *The Road to Terror: Stalin and the Self-Destruction of the Bolsheviks, 1932–1939* (New Haven, 1999).

6. Getty and Naumov; Sarah Davies, *Popular Opinion in Stalin's Russia: Terror, Propaganda and Dissent, 1934–1941* (Cambridge, UK, 1997); Sheila Fitzpatrick, *Everyday Stalinism, Ordinary Life in Extraordinary Times: Soviet Russia in the 1930's* (Oxford, 1999).

7. See Robert Conquest, *The Great Terror: Stalin's Purge of the Thirties* (Harmondsworth, UK, 1971); J. Arch Getty, *Origins of the Great Purges: The Soviet Communist Party Reconsidered* (Cambridge, UK, 1985).

8. Iakushin, pp. 48–49.

9. Sushkov, p. 165.

10. Robert Edelman, *Serious Fun: A History of Spectator Sports in the USSR* (Oxford, 1993), p. 50.

11. RGASPI, f. 17, o. 3, d. 974, l. 11.

12. Izv, 12/23/35; Andrei Starostin, *Flagman*, p. 73.

13. Iakushin, p. 49.

14. Iakushin, p. 50; Andrei Starostin, *Bol'shoi*, p. 154.

15. Andrei Starostin, *Povest'*, p. 138; *Flagman*, pp. 73–75; *Bol'shoi*, pp. 151–61; Romm, pp. 90–92; Sto let, pp. 83–86; Merzhanov, pp. 7–10; Akimov, p. 25; Pribylovskii, p. 34; Iakushin, pp. 52–54; Pirogov, p. 55.

16. *International Herald Tribune*, 1/2/36.

17. Iakushin, pp. 53–54; Andrei Starostin, *Bol'shoi*, pp. 160–61; *Sportexpress*, 3/19/01.

18. RGASPI, f. 17, o. 3, d. 976, l. 68; http://www.sport-express.ru/art?77457 (accessed 11/17/03); RGASPI, f. 17, o. 114, d. 606, l. 116; Keys, *Globalizing Sport*, pp. 170–72.

19. Izv, 1/3/36; Nikolai Starostin, *Zvezdy*, p. 59.

20. Petrone, pp. 106–8.

21. Keys, "The Dictatorship of Sport" PhD diss., Harvard University, 2001), p. 226.

22. Nikolai Starostin, *Futbol*, p. 59; Nikolai Starostin, interview.

23. GARF, f. 7576, o. 1, d. 275, ll. 33–34, cited in Keys, "Dictatorship of Sport," pp. 226–29 (translation by Keys).

24. Keys, "Dictatorship of Sport," p. 228; Keys, *Globalizing Sport*, p. 174.

25. Nikolai Starostin, *Futbol*, p. 72.

26. Izv, 3/21/40.

27. Tony Mason, personal electronic communication to author, July 29, 2003.

28. http://www.sport-express.ru/art.shtml?76446 (accessed 10/24/03).

29. http://www.sport-express.ru/art.shtml?74887 (accessed 9/29/03).

30. SOI, pp. 46–50; GARF, f. 7576, o. 13, d. 14, l. 16.

31. *Sportexpress*, 3/5/01 and 3/12/01; GARF, f. 7576, o. 13, d. 39, ll. 8–9.

32. Nikolai Starostin, *Futbol*, p. 39; KS, 7/ 23/37 and 7/25/37. With his characteristic weakness on dates, Starostin said the announcement in newspapers came August 21, 1937.

33. *Sportexpress*, 4/9/01.

34. "Spartak na pole istorii," NTV television network, 2001.

35. Fitzpatrick, *Everyday Stalinism*, p. 42; Strauss, p. 37.

36. James Scott, *Domination and the Arts of Resistance: Hidden Transcripts* (New Haven, 1990), p. 120; Peeter Tulviste and James Wertsch, "Official and Unofficial Histories: The Case of Estonia," *Journal of Narrative and Life History* 4, no. 4 (1995): 311–29.

37. Yuri Oleshchuk, "Mistika Spartaka," *Sportekspress zhurnal*, no. 1 (1999): 10. All three Oleshchuk quotes are from the same page. See also Andrei Starostin, *Bol'shoi*, p. 45.

38. The Russian word *bit'* has the literal meaning of beat with one's fists or an object not to defeat, in a game.

39. Boris Lavrentlvich Nazarov, interview with author, Moscow, October 6, 1990.

40. Aksel' Vartanian, interview with the author, Moscow, December 6, 1999.

41. Vainshtein, interview; Lev Filatov, "Teatr Andreia Starostina: Vospominania kumira," *Fizkul'tura i sport*, no. 5 (1995): 31–32.

42. Yuri Oleshcuk, "Fanaty Vremen Bobrova," *Sportekspress zhurnal*, no. 10 (1999): 86.

43. http://www.sport-express.ru/art.shtml?77458 (accessed 11/17/03).

44. KS, 11/1/36; Akimov, pp. 59–62.

45. Vartanian, interview, 1999.

46. KS, 5/9/37.

47. Izv, 5/6/40; KS, 4/15/37, 9/3/38, 6/12/39, 7/2/40.

48. Aksel' Vartanian, "Draki pri sotsializme," *Sportexpress futbol*, no. 27 (1999): 32–35; GARF, f. 7576, o. 13, d. 108, ll. 63–69, 77, 79 (reports on "chaotic" matches).

49. See Davies; Fitzpatrick, *Everyday Stalinism;* Lebina; Gabor Rittersporn, *Stalinist Simplifications and Soviet Complications: Social Tensions and Political Conflicts in the USSR, 1933–1953* (Chur, Switz., 1991); Elena Osokina, *Our Daily Bread: Socialist Distribution and the Art of Survival in Stalin's Russia, 1927–1941* (Armonk, NY, 2001); Lynne Viola, *Peasant Rebels under Stalin: Collectivization and the Culture of Peasant Resistance* (Oxford, 1996); David-Fox et al., *The Resistance Debate*, pp. 69–102.

50. Fitzpatrick, *Everyday Stalinism*, pp. 42–50.

51. Nick Hornby, *Fever Pitch* (London, 1992), p. 20.

52. Vartanian, interview, 1999.

53. http://www.sport-express.ru/art/shtml?102517 (accessed 4/24/05).

54. Donald Filtzer, *Soviet Workers and Stalinist Industrialization: The Formation of Modern Soviet Production Relations, 1929–1941* (London, 1986), pp. 1, 8, and 255.

55. Simon Kuper, *Ajax, the Dutch and the War* (London, 2003), pp. 135 and 160.

56. Clifford Geertz, "Deep Play: The Balinese Cock Fight," in *The Interpretation of Cultures* (New York, 1973), p. 434.

57. Eduardo Galeano, *Football in Sun and Shadow* (London, 1997), p. 6.

58. Eric Dunning, *Sport Matters: Sociological Studies of Sport, Violence and Civilization* (London, 1999), pp. 3–4.

59. James Van Geldern, *Bolshevik Festivals, 1917–1920* (Berkeley, 1993).

60. Edelman, *Serious Fun*, pp. 37–44.

61. Petrone p. 25.

62. Ibid., pp. 40–45.

63. Ibid., p. 39.

64. "Spartak na pole istorii."

65. Nikolai Starostin, *Futbol*, pp. 29–32. Rossiiskii Gosudarstvennyi Arkhiv Kinematografii (hereafter RGAK), reel no. 1-30605-1; http://www.sport-express.ru/art.shtml?104119 (accessed 5/27/05).

66. For definitions of body culture and their attachment to particular models of sport, see Brownell, p. 11.

67. Gruneau, "Critique of Sport," pp. 85–105.

68. *Fotoal'bom spartakiada* (Moscow, 1929).

69. On sacred and profane rituals, see Victor Turner, ed., *Celebration: Studies in Festivity and Ritual* (Washington, DC, 1982); Turner, *From Ritual to Theater.*

70. http://www.sport-express.ru/art.shtml?77458 (accessed 11/17/03).

71. V. Vinokurov and O. Kucherenko, *Dinamo Moskva* (Moscow, 1973); *Vsesoiuznoe fizkul'turno-sportivnoe ordena Lenina obshchetvo Dinamo* (Moscow, 1956).

72. Christel Lane, *The Rites of Rulers: Ritual in Industrial Society-The Soviet Case* (Cambridge, UK, 1981).

73. Nikolai Starostin, *Futbol*, pp. 29–34; RGAK, reel no. 1-30605-1.

74. On urban masculinity in the 1930s, see Thomas Schrand, "Socialism in One Gender: Masculine Values in the Stalinist Revolution," in Clements et al., pp. 194–209.

75. Dunning, "Sport as a Male Preserve," p. 167. Gruneau and Whitson, *Hockey Night in Canada: Sport, Identities and Cultural Politics* (Toronto, 1993), p. 192.

76. Vartanian, "Draki"; N. Arutunian and N. Naumenko, "Ispoved belo-golubogo fanata," *Sport dlia vsekh*, no. 16 (1998): 2. On the distinction between rough and respectable manhood see Stephen Meyer, "Work, Play and Power: Masculine Culture on the Automotive Shop Floor, 1930–1960," in *Boys and Their Toys?: Masculinity, Technology and Class in America*, ed. Roger Horowitz (New York, 2001).

77. Khavin, p. 7; Riordan, *Sport*, pp. 320–22; Romm, p. 11; Merzhanov, p. 4.

78. Nikolai Starostin, *Futbol*, p. 32.

79. Phil Ball, *White Storm: 100 Years of Real Madrid* (Edinburgh, 2002), pp. 33–34.

80. Phil Ball, *Morbo* (London, 2001), pp. 70–93; Sto let, p. 87. For a comprehensive account of the Basque tour of the USSR see Mathieu Boivin-Chouinard, "Le Soccer Comme Arme Antifascite: Une Histoire Politique, Culturelle et Sociale de la Tournee de L'Equipe Nationale Basque en URSS Pendant la Guerre Civile Espanol," unpublished master's essay. University of Quebec at Montreal, December, 2008.

81. Ball, *White Storm*, p. 83.

82. RGASPI, f. 17, o. 162, d. 21, l. 57; KS, 5/7/37, 6/11/37, and 6/13/37.

83. Andrei Starostin, *Bol'shoi*, p. 170; *Vstrechi*, p. 153; KS, 5/7/37, 6/11/37, and 6/13/37; Nikolai Starostin, *Futbol*, p. 33; *Spartak na pole istorii.*

84. KS, 6/29/37; http://www.sport-express.ru/art.shtml?81639 (accessed 2/14/04); Pribylovskii, p. 36.

85. http://www.sport-express.ru/art.shtml?82595 (accessed 3/5/04).

86. KS, 7/1/37, 7/17/37, and 7/31/37.

87. KS, 7/1/37.

88. KS, 7/7/37. Showing less than perfect recall, Nikolai Starostin recounted the halftime score as 3–3. See Nikolai Starostin, *Futbol*, p. 34.

89. Pribylovskii, pp. 36–37; Nikolai Starostin, *Zvezdy,* p. 93; Andrei Starostin, *Povest',* pp. 147–49; *Vstrechi,* p. 138.

90. Romm, p. 104.

91. Nikolai Starostin, *Futbol,* p. 37; Andrei Starostin, *Bol'shoi,* p. 178; *Spartak na pole istorii.*

92. Akimov, p. 69; Sto let, p. 88; Andrei Starostin, *Vstrechi,* pp. 167–68.

93. Merzhanov, p. 16.

94. KS, 7/9/37; Nikolai Starostin, *Futbol,* p. 38; http://sport-express.ru/art.shtml?84414 (accessed 4/13/04).

95. Nikolai Starostin, *Futbol,* p. 39.

96. GARF, f. 7576, o. 13, d. 108, l. 4.

97. RGASPI, f. 1-m, o. 5, d. 75, l. 3; http://www.sport-express.ru/art.shtml?31706 (accessed 7/23/03). While Kosmachev did indeed work again as a referee, he worked only one game in each of the last three prewar years. Thus the question of his fate is much more ambiguous than depicted by Starostin.

98. Nikolai Starostin, *Futbol,* p. 38.

99. Grigory Fedotov, *Zapiski futbolista* (Moscow, 1952), pp. 54, 59, 63, 66, and 68.

100. Akimov, p. 83; KS, 8/3/37 and 8/9/37.

101. Vainshtein, interview.

102. Andrei Starostin, *Vstrechi,* p. 179.

103. Read, p. 100.

104. Nikolai Starostin, *Futbol,* p. 42.

105 http://www.sport-express.ru/art.shtml?85842 (accessed 5/11/04).

106. KS/7/37; Nikolai Starostin, *Futbol,* pp. 42–43. Riabokon' while being "interrogated" accused the Starostins of planning to overthrow the government during the 1937 Physical Culture Day Parade by assassinating the leadership standing on Lenin's mausoleum. If Nikolai Starostin was aware of Ryabokon''s role when he wrote his last memoir, it is not possible to detect it.

107. RGASPI, f. 1-m, o. 23, d. 1268, l. 10 (letter to Stalin), ll. 11–16 (letter to Molotov).

108. RGASPI, f. 1-m, 0. 23, d. 1268, ll. 1–2 and 9 (letter to Kosarev); Andrei Starostin, *Vstrechi,* pp. 184–86; Nikolai Starostin, *Futbol,* pp. 41–42; Nikolai Starostin interview; *Futbolkhokkei,* 5/13/90. On Yezhov see J. Arch Getty and Oleg Naumov, *Yezhov: The Rise of Stalin's "Iron Fist,"* (New Haven, 2008), p. 127.

109. Vainshtein, interview.

110. Lev Filatov, "Romb Nikolaia Petrovicha, sekta gde verkhovodili Starostiny," *Sportivnaia zhizn' Rossii,* no. 3 (1997): 2–7.

111. http://www.sport-express.ru/art.shtml?85197 (accessed 4/26/04).

## Chapter 4. On Top and Bottom, 1937–1944

1. Lev Filatov, *Obo vsem po poriadku: Reportazh o reportazhe* (Moscow, 1990), p. 58; SOI, p. 52; KS, 9/5/37 and 9/13/37.

2. KS, 10/25/37.

3. KS, 11/13/39.

4. KS, 1/17/38.

5. http://www.sport-express.r./art.shtml?95134 (accessed 11/17/04). This approach had the potential for unfairness. The point of the home-and-away schedule is that no team has a home-field advantage over the course of a season. If teams met only once during the season, it was extremely important against whom they played and where. If one took on strong opponents, it was clearly better to face them at home. One could take one's chances on the road against weaker teams. Thus the schedulemakers, who were acting at the last minute in 1938, could have stacked the deck, although there is no evidence of a conspiracy here.

6. http://www.sport-express.ru/art.shtml?92648 (accessed 9/24/04).

7. KS, 8/23/38, 8/25/38, 9/13/38, 9/15/38, 10/3/38, 11/13/39, 11/17/38, 11/19/38, and 11/23/38; SOI, pp. 56–60; http://www.sport-express.ru/art.shtml?98806 (accessed 2/4/05).

8. KS, 6/29/38 and 9/25/38.

9. KS, 6/28/38 and 11/7/39.

10. N. G. Okhotin and A. B. Roginskii, eds., *Kto rukovosil NKVD, 1934–1941* (Moscow, 1999), p. 107.

11. Getty and Naumov, p. 411.

12. Nikolai Starostin, *Futbol,* p. 56; Vartanian, interview, 1999; Pavel Aleshin, interview with the author, Moscow, December 10, 1999.

13. http://www.sport-express.ru/art.shtml?101485 (accessed 4/2/05).

14. KS, 9/10/39.

15. Nikolai Starostin, *Futbol,* p. 47; *Zvezdy,* p. 52. In classic Starostin fashion, Nikolai gets the dates of the various games wrong. In his 1989 book, he says the final took place two weeks after the semifinal and the replay a month after that. The replay took place September 30 in Moscow.

16. http://www.sport-express.ru/art.shtml?105407 (accessed 6/24/05).

17. Simon Martin, *Football and Fascism: The National Game under Mussolini* (Oxford, 2004), pp. 173–208; John Foot, *Calcio: A History of Italian Football* (London, 2006), pp. 33–36; Alex Belos, *Futebol: Soccer, the Brazilian Way of Life* (New York, 2002), p. 141; David Goldblatt, *The Ball Is Round: A Global History of Football* (London, 2006), pp. 627–31.

18. KS, 12/13/39.

19. Filatov, "Romb," p. 5.

20. KS, 10/1/39.

21. Evgenii Lovchev, interview with the author, Moscow, September 15, 2003.

22. *Spartak na pole istoriii.*

23. Esenin, p. 138.

24. Vainshtein, interview.

25. VM, 12/2/39. The old star from Krasnaia Presnia, Petr Isakov, shared Starostin's view in KS, 12/13/39.

26. RGASPI, f. 1–m, o. 5, d. 75, l. 4.

27. *Futbol-khokkei,* no. 19 (1990).

28. For a full description of the Soviet and Western literature on the Soviet working class, see Edelman, "A Small Way of Saying 'No': Moscow Working Men, Spartak Soccer and the Communist Party, 1900–1945," *American Historical Review* (November, 2002), pp. 1441–74. See also A. I. Vdovin and V. Z. Drobizhev, *Rost Rabochego klassa SSSR, 1917–1940* (Moscow, 1976), p. 87; Akademia Nauk, Institut Istorii SSSR, *Istoria Moskovskikh rabochikh, 1917–1945* (Moscow, 1983), p. 137.

29. Daniel Orlovsky, "The Hidden Class: White-Collar Workers in the 1920's," in *Making Workers Soviet,* ed. Lewis Siegelbaum and Ronald Suny (Ithaca, 1994), p. 222–48.

30. RGAK, reel nos. I-3490, I-30361, IX-3752, I-2281, I-2262, I-2435, I-2471, I-2462, I-4374, I-3507, I-4079, I-3102, I-3118, 1-30605-1, I-3221.

31. Vdovin and Drobizhev, p. 183; Strauss, p. 29.

32. S. L. Selianskii, *Izmenenia v sotsial'noi strukture sovestkogo obshchestva, 1938–1970* (Moscow, 1973), pp. 8–9.

33. Vdovin and Drobizhev, pp. 112–15; *Istoriia Moskovskikh rabochikh,* p. 183. Mason, *Association Football,* pp. 138–67.

34. Vdovin and Drobizhev, pp. 195–212; *Istoriia Moskovskikh rabochikh,* p. 352; Siegelbaum, *Stakhanovism,* pp. 42–43.

35. Nikolai Starostin, *Futbol,* p. 83.

36. KS, 7/1/36.

37. See Benedict Anderson, *Imagined Communities: Reflections on the Origin and Spread of Nationalism* (New York, 1991).

38. Iuri Oleshchuk, interview with the author, Moscow, December 12, 1999. Vainshtein took particular exception to the term "dissident," noting the number of highly placed and successful people like Ianshin, Kassil', and Shostakovich who supported Spartak, although Shostakovich was more often thought to be a fan of Zenit Leningrad.

39. KS, 5/1/36.

40. For classically hagiographic accounts of the Znamenskiis see *Sportsmeny* (Moscow, 1965), p. 65; SS, 7/8/58; A. Salutskii, *Bratiia Znamenskie* (Moscow, 1973).

41. "Bol'shye roditel'i," produced by ART Proekt Plus, shown on NTV network, 2000. Given the source of this information and its unflattering content, one must take Znamenskaia's statements seriously.

42. KS, 1/5/39 and 1/11/39.

43. RGASPI, f. 1-m, o. 23, d. 1268, ll. 18–25. Thanks to Barbara Keys for bringing this material to my attention.

44. See RGASPI, f. 1-m, o. 23, d. 1268, ll. 24–25; Vartainian, interview, 1999; Keys, "Dictatorship of Sport," pp. 251; *Spartak,* no. 5 (May 2000): 16–17.

45. Rossiiskii Gosudarstvennyi Voennyi Arkhiv (hereafter RGVA), f. 9, op. 29, d. 562, ll. 39 and 42. These documents were found in the Russian State Military Archive. A commission headed by Lev Mekhlis had been organized to oversee the tour to Bulgaria. In order to determine

whether Nikolai Starostin was politically suitable for the trip, a copy of his police file was apparently forwarded to Mekhlis. Thanks to Tim Paynich for furnishing me with these materials.

46. Ibid., l. 45.

47. Ibid., l. 50.

48. Ibid., ll. 66 and 71.

49. http://www.sport-express.ru/art.shtml?131002 (accessed 12/7/06).

50. Izv, 1/30/38 and 12/1/38.

51. RGVA, f. 9, o. 29, d. 562, ll. 73–77; James Riordan, "The Strange Story of Nikolai Starostin, Football and Lavrentii Beria," *Europe and Asia Studies,* no. 4 (1994): 689.

52. RGVA, f. 9, o. 29, d. 562, ll. 78–79.

53. Ibid., ll. 79–80.

54. Ibid., l. 81.

55. Ibid., l. 63.

56. Vainshtein, interview.

57. RGVA, f. 9, o. 29, d. 562, l. 78.

58. http://www.sport-express.ru/art.shtml?110695 (accessed 10/7/2005).

59. Nikolai Starostin, *Futbol,* pp. 63–64; http://sport-express.ru/art.shtml?131002 (accessed 12/7/06).

60. http://www.sport-express.ru/art.shtml?116243 (accessed 2/7/06).

61. http://www.sport-express.ru/art.shtml?117653 (accessed, 3/3/06).

62. Nikolai Starostin, *Futbol,* pp. 78–79; SOI, p. 55.

63. Nikolai Starostin, *Futbol,* p. 73.

64. GARF, f. 7583, o. 60, d. 4105, l. 3.

65. Ibid., l. 4.

66. This suggestion was made by Arch Getty in a personal communication after reading the documents.

67. James Heinzen, "A 'Campaign Spasm': Graft and the Limits of the 'Campaign' against Bribery after the Great Patriotic War," in *Late Stalinist Russia: Society between Reconstruction and Reinvention,* ed. Juliane Furst (London, 2006), pp. 123–37. See also Edelman, "A Small Way of Saying 'No.'"

68. So far as I can tell, Vainshtein was unaware of the existence of the documents cited here when he was interviewed. On the matter of Starostin's guilt and broader well-founded skepticism about his account, see Jonathon Wilson, *Behind the Curtain: Travels in Eastern European Football* (London, 2006), p. 284.

69. Nikolai Starostin, *Futbol,* p. 80.

70. On Aleksandr's whereabouts see Gosudarsvtennyi Arkhiv Permskoi oblasti (hereafter GAPO), f. 1366, o. 1, d. 657, l. 65. According to this document, Beria was informed of the Starostins' coaching in 1946. Thanks to Mikhail Loukianov for making this document available.

71. http://www.sport-express.ru/art.shtml?132359 (accessed 12/22/06).

72. http://www.sport-express.ru/art.shtml?135287 (accessed 3/2/07).

73. SOI, pp. 73–80.

74. Stephen Kotkin, "Coercion and Identity: Workers' Lives in Stalin's Showcase City," in Siegelbaum and Suny, p. 278.

75. For useful definitions of popular and mass culture as well as "contested terrain," see Stuart Hall, "Notes on Deconstructing the Popular," in *People's History and Socialist Theory,* ed. Raphael Samuel (London, 1981), p. 232.

76. Oleshchuk, interview.

### Chapter 5. The Golden Age of Soviet Soccer

1. Abbot Gleason, *Totalitarianism: The Inner History of the Cold War* (Oxford, 1995), p. 3. See also Anna Krylova, "The Tenacious Liberal Subject in Soviet Studies," in David-Fox, Holquist, and Poe, p. 183.

2. Alexei Kojevnikov, "Rituals of Stalinist Culture at Work: Science and the Games of Intraparty Democracy circa 1948," *Russian Review* 57 (1998): 51.

3. Stites, p. 121; Julian Graffy, "Cinema," in *Russian Cultural Studies: An Introduction,* ed. Catriona Kelly and David Shepherd (Oxford, 1998), pp. 165–91.

4. "Futbol nashogo detstva," (hereafter FND), Gosteleradio, 1984, directed by Alexei Gavrilovich.

5. Dinamo also played second-division Cardiff City, which it defeated 10–1. *Sportexpress,*

11/18/05. The first hint of an invitation had been made by the English side as early as May. There were also invitations from Bulgaria, Yugoslavia, and Rumania. RGASPI, f. 17, o. 125, d. 309, ll. 52 and 55.

6. Nikolai Starostin, *Futbol,* p. 109; Andrei Starostin, *Vstrechi,* p. 101; Iakushin, p. 87.

7. Sto let, p. 100.

8. Anthony King, *The End of the Terraces: The Transformation of English Football in the 1990's* (Leicester, UK, 1998), p. 38.

9. For two views that paint a more complex picture, see Werner Hahn, *Post-War Soviet Politics and the Defeat of Moderation* (Ithaca, 1982), p. 9; Eric Duskin, *Stalinist Reconstruction and the Confirmation of a New Elite* (New York, 2001), p. 2.

10. For a discussion of the new literature on late Stalinism, see Stephen V. Bittner, *The Many Lives of Khrushchev's Thaw: Experience and Memory in Moscow's Arbat* (Ithaca, 2008), p. 10.

11. Sheila Fitzpatrick, "Post-War Soviet Society: The 'Return to Normalcy,'" in *The Impact of World War II on the Soviet Union,* ed. Susan Linz (Totowa, NJ, 1985).

12. Elena Zubkova, *Russia after the War: Hopes, Illusions and Disappointments* (Armonk, NY, 1998) p. 22.

13. Lewin, *The Soviet Century* (New York, 2005), p. 143.

14. Zubkova, pp. 37 and 47.

15. Filtzer, *Soviet Workers,* pp. 7, 74, and 99; Duskin, p. 23.

16. Lewin, p. 143.

17. Filtzer, p. 99.

18. Vera Dunham, *In Stalin's Time: Middle-Class Values in Soviet Fiction* (Cambridge, UK, 1976), p. 17.

19. Zubkova, p. 95; Lewin, p. 143; Duskin, pp. 57 and 138.

20. On youth culture, see Juliane Furst, "The Importance of Being Stylish: Youth, Culture and Identity in Late Stalinism," in Furst, *Late Stalinist Russia,* pp. 209–32. On workers see Donald Filtzer, "Standard of Living versus Quality of Life: Struggling with the Urban Environment in Russia during the Early Years of Post-war Reconstruction," in Furst, pp. 81–102. On debates in science see Kojevnikov, "Rituals"; Ethan Pollack, *Stalin and the Soviet Science Wars* (Princeton, 2006).

21. Vartanian, interview, 1999.

22. Nikita Simonian, *Futbol, tol'ko li igra?* (Moscow, 1995), p. 42.

23. Simonian, p. 42; FND; Lev Filatov, *Naedenie s futbolom* (Moscow, 1977), p. 15.

24. Simonian, pp. 42–43; FND.

25. FND.

26. FND; Filatov, *Obo vsem,* p. 96.

27. Norbert Elias and Eric Dunning, *The Quest for Excitement: Sport and Leisure in the Civilizing Process* (Oxford, 1986), p. 43.

28. Filatov, *Naedenie,* p. 15; *Obo vsem,* pp. 27 and 61.

29. Filatov, *Obo vsem,* p. 64.

30. On rituals sacred or profane, see Victor Turner, *From Ritual to Theater.*

31. FND.

32. Merzhanov, p. 36.

33. Iakushin, p. 86; Anatoly Ilyin, *My byli pervymi* (Moscow, 1978), p. 9; Simonian, interview with the author, Moscow, December 6, 2001; Andrei Starostin, *Vstrechi,* p. 102; *Sportexpress,* 11/18/05.

34. Andrei Starostin, *Vstrechi,* p. 101; Nikolai Starostin, *Futbol,* p. 109.

35. FND; Igor Netto, *Eto futbol* (Moscow, 1974), p. 31; Filatov, *Naedenie,* p. 151; Filatov, *Obo vsem,* p. 23. Invitations from the United Kingdom had been received as early as the spring. RGASPI, f. 17, o. 125, d. 309, ll. 55 and 90–98.

36. There are conflicting stories about how Stepanov lost both legs. He may have been despondent at not having been picked for a particular game and fallen under a tram while not paying attention or after drowning his sorrows in drink. Other accounts say he lost his legs in an industrial accident in 1942. He then became a team official before being asked to coach, despite limited experience. SOI, p. 611.

37. Merzhanov, pp. 34–36; Filatov, *Obo vsem,* p. 66; SOI, p. 81; Fedotov, p. 106; Netto, pp. 30–31; RGASPI, f. 17, o. 125, d. 309, ll. 49–50.

38. These figures are based on newspaper estimates compiled in the official Spartak and Dinamo team histories. No similar work exists for TsDKA and its successor teams. An examination of inconsistently given figures in the press seems to indicate that, at least in 1945,

attendance at TsDKA's games was roughly comparable to that at Dinamo's. That situation would soon change. SOI, p. 81.

39. SOI, p. 82.
40. Filatov, *Naedenie,* pp. 77–78.
41. Aleksandr Soskin, *Sergei Sal'nikov* (Moscow, 2003), pp. 8–9.
42. VM, 5/9/46; SS, 5/21/46.
43. VM, 5/20/46.
44. SOI, pp. 85–87 and 550.
45. SS, 10/26/46.
46. SS, 10/26/46; VM, 10/21/46.
47. RGAK, reel no. 1-5354.
48. Esenin, p. 151; Filatov, *Obo vsem,* p. 66.
49. SS, 10/22/46.
50. Filatov, *Obo vsem,* p. 67; Simonian, p. 60.
51. http://www.sport-express.ru/art.shtml?168162 (accessed 10/17/08). This account comes from Vartanian, who initially heard about it from Spartak's goalie, Aleksei Leontiev. He then came across archival confirmation of the story in RGASPI, f. 17, o. 125, d. 643 (he does not give the page number) and GARF, f. 7576. While Vartanian does not offer further archival numbers, he noted that the order from N. N. Romanov was numbered 699 and was dated December 3, 1946.
52. SOI, pp. 89–90; SS, 7/15/47, 7/22/47.
53. SOI, pp. 93–96.
54. Aleksei Paramonov, interview with author, Moscow, December 11, 2001; Aleksei Paramonov, *200 Vydaiushchikhsia deiateli sovremennosti: Ot A do Ia* (Moscow, n.d.), p. 385.
55. SS, 4/24/48.
56. Andrei Starostin, *Vstrechi,* p. 83; SS, 5/25/48.
57. SOI, pp. 93–95.
58. Sto let, p. 2; Merzhanov, p. 5; SOI, pp. 93 and 567; SS, 5/25/48.
59. SS, 7/3/48, 7/27/48.
60. SS, 8/28/48.
61. Vartanian, interview, 1999; Simonian, interview; Filatov, *Obo vsem,* p. 55.
62. See, for example, *Pervenstvo SSSR po futbolu 1949* (Moscow, 1949), pp. 10 and 28.
63. Compiled from Spartak and Dinamo encyclopedias.
64. Andrei Starostin, *Vstrechi,* p. 194.
65. Nikolai Starostin, *Futbol,* pp. 87–104.
66. Andrei Sukhomlinov, *Vasilii, Syn Vozhd'ia* (Moscow, 2001), p. 152.
67. Nikolai Starostin, *Futbol,* p. 113.
68. Sukhomlinov, p. 144.
69. Nikolai Starostin, *Futbol,* p. 126.
70. Vainshtein, interview.
71. Filatov, Obo vsem, p. 74.
72. Ibid., p. 72.
73. Ibid., p. 38
74. Netto, p. 42.
75. Simonian, p. 186.
76. Filatov, *Naedenie,* p. 108; *Obo vsem,* p. 38.
77. On Spartak support among the theater crowd, see Bittner, p. 86.
78. Simonian, pp. 92 and 249.
79. Andrei Starostin, *Vstrechi,* p. 206.
80. On the array of political attitudes among writers, see Maria Zezina, "Crisis in the Union of Soviet Writers in the Early 1950's," *Europe-Asia Studies* 46, no. 4 (1994): 649–61.
81. Filatov, *Obo vsem,* pp. 69–70; Merzhanov, p. 5.
82. Simonian, p. 246.
83. In March 1948 a group of Spartak Masters of Sport took the step of writing to Stalin protesting Promkooperatsiia's unwillingness to improve the team's facilities. RGASPI, f. 17, o. 125, d. 642, ll. 28, 29, 31, 32.
84. Simonian, p. 59.
85. Vainshtein, interview.
86. Vartanian, interview, 1999.

## Chapter 6. Spartak Resurgent, 1949–1952

1. Hahn, pp. 77 and 149; Zubkova, p. 128; Duskin, p. 85.
2. Zubkova, pp. 53–54, 84, 102, 107, 128; Alec Nove, *An Economic History of the USSR* (Harmondsworth, UK, 1975), pp. 285 and 303; Geoffrey Hosking, *The First Socialist Society* (Cambridge, MA, 1985), p. 302; Duskin, pp. 85, 92, 133; Donald Filtzer, *Soviet Workers and Late Stalinism: Labour and the Restoration of the Stalinist System after World War II* (Cambridge, UK, 2002), pp. 42 and 115; Lewin, *Soviet Century,* p. 127; Julie Hessler, *A Social History of Soviet Trade: Trade Policy Retail Practices and Consumption* (Princeton, 2004), p. 297.
3. Duskin, p. 25; Lewin, *Soviet Century,* p. 132; Amy Knight, *Beria, Stalin's First Lieutenant* (Princeton, 1993), p. 141; Beria was not strictly a Georgian but a member of the small Mingrelian nationality. The arrest of several party members in this part of the Georgian Republic was seen as an expression of Stalin's lack of happiness with Beria. The majority of the doctors who attended to high party figures and were arrested were Jewish. Their arrest was seen as an anti-Semitic act. They were quickly exonerated after Stalin's death. Zubkova, pp. 109 and 130.
4. Chris Ward, *Stalin's Russia* (London, 1999), p. 225.
5. Hessler, pp. 297 and 309.
6. Duskin, p.129.
7. Zubkova, p. 148.
8. Lewin, *Soviet Century,* p. 203.
9. L. Bronshtein and Iu. Sholomnitskii, *Liubimaia igra* (Tashkent, Uzbek., 1961), p. 19.
10. The link between ideological-political education and player behavior was made clear by former Lokomotiv star and later head of Soviet football, Valentin Granatkin. Speaking at the 1952 plenum of the football section, he emphasized that a recent rash of on-field fights and off-field drunkenness was the result of a slacking off of education. GARF, f. 7576, o. 13, d. 145, l. 74.
11. Nikita Simonian, telephone interview with author, Moscow, December 17, 2001.
12. GARF, f. 7576, o. 13, d. 115, l. 2.
13. *Sportexpress,* 8/20/2001.
14. Edelman, *Serious Fun* p. 95.
15. GARF, f. 7576, o. 13, d. 115, l. 2.
16. Pribylovskii, 49–50; GARF, f. 7576, o. 13, d. 60, ll. 186–87.
17. GARF, f. 7576, o. 13, d. 67, ll. 26–29.
18. GARF, f. 7576, o. 13, d. 66, ll. 74, 86–89; d. 62, ll. 148–58; d. 60, l. 146–48; d. 60, l. 182.
19. Lewin, *Soviet Century,* p. 130.
20. Merzhanov, p. 51; SOI, p. 97.
21. Esenin, pp. 153 and 170–72; SOI, p. 97.
22. Merzhanov, p. 53; Simonian, pp. 48 and 58; ERF, p. 105; SOI, pp. 762–63; Filatov, *Naedenie,* pp. 17 and 76.
23. Simonian, interview.
24. Simonian, interview.
25. Eduardo Archetti, *Masculinities: Football, Polo and the Tango in Argentina* (Oxford, 1999), pp. 128–60; SOI, p. 557; Filatov, *Obo vsem,* pp. 74–76.
26. SOI, p. 97; Simonian, interview. On southern stereotyping, see Nikolai Starostin, *Zvezdy,* p. 55; Merzhanov, p. 42.
27. Filatov, *Obo vsem,* p. 74.
28. Simonian, interview. He made no mention of TsDKA.
29. Aleksey Paramonov, interview with author, Moscow, December 16, 2001.
30. Simonian, interview.
31. Furst, pp. 211–12.
32. Simonian, p. 45.
33. Filatov, *Obo vsem,* p. 76.
34. Merzhanov, pp. 63–67; Simonian, interview; SOI, p. 605.
35. SS, 4/27/46.
36. SOI, p. 732.
37. Simonian, pp. 50–53.
38. Ibid., pp. 58–60.
39. SOI, pp. 732 and 679.
40. Igor Netto, *Eto futbol* (Moscow, 1974), pp. 21–36.
41. Simonian, pp. 67–72; Filatov, *Naedenie,* p. 80.

42. SOI, pp. 97–101; SS, 4/6/49, 5/10/49, 5/19/49, 5/31/49, 6/4/49, 6/7/49; VM, 9/14/49.

43. VM, 9/14/49.

44. SS, 10/4/49; VM, 10/3/49; SE, p.99; I. S. Dobronravov, *Na Bessrochnoi Sluzhbe futbolu* (hereafter DE) (Moscow, 2000), p. 277; FND; Filatov, *Obo vsem,* p. 83.

45. SS, 10/20/49.

46. SS, 11/1/49; SOI, p.100.

47. DE, p. 464.

48. RGASPI, f. 17, o. 137, d. 265, ll. 141–42. See Marc Bennets, *Football Dynamo* (London, 2008), p. 4.

49. RGASPI, f. 17, o. 137, d. 265, ll. 143–47.

50. Ibid., ll. 138–41.

51. FND; Oleshchuk, "Fanaty Vremen Bobrova," *Sportekspress zhurnal,* no. 10 (1998): 84–89.

52. RGASI, f. 17, o. 137, d. 448, ll. 18–19.

53. Ibid., ll. 15–17; *Sportexpress,* 8/20/01.

54. RGASPI, f. 17, o. 137, d. 448, ll. 30–34.

55. RGASPI, f. 17, o. 137, d. 265, ll. 4–6 and 8–10.

56. The biography of Sal'nikov by a respected veteran sportswriter, Aleksandr Soskin, debunks the story of Nikolai Starostin's relationship to Sal'nikov. While it is true that Sal'nikov was raised near the training base at Tarasovka, he was born in 1925 at far-off Krasnodar. At that It is unlikely that Starostin was ever near Krasnodar at that time. It is also true that the base at Tarasovka was not built until well after 1925. Soskin, pp. 11–19.

57. RGASPI, f. 17, o. 137, d. 448, ll. 35–37.

58. Ibid.

59. Ibid., l. 60.

60. Ibid., ll. 68–70.

61. Ibid., ll. 71–73.

62. Ibid., ll. 74 and 101–8. By contrast, the more famous Bobrov's transfer from TsDKA to VVS at the same time drew no similar protests. See http://sport-express.ru/art.shtml?/80000.

63. SS, 4/15/50.

64. Simonian, p. 73.

65. Vartanian, interview, 1999; SOI, p. 102.

66. Soskin, pp. 20–23; Pavel Aleshin, telephone interview, Moscow, with author in La Jolla, CA, February 16, 2006.

67. SS, 4/20/50.

68. SOI, p. 103.

69. SS, 5/16/50, 5/20/50, 6/3/50, 6/8/50.

70. VM, 5/20/50, 6/7/50.

71. SS, 7/15/50.

72. SS, 8/15/50, 8/17/50, 9/12/50; SOI, p. 102.

73. See VM, 10/7/50; SS 10/7/50, 10/14/50, 10/19/50, 10/24/50 on the tour. See GARF, f. 7576, o. 13, d. 62, l. 154 on the drinking, as well as RGASPI, f. 17, o. 137, d. 499, l. 192.

74. SOI, p. 105.

75. SS, 11/7/50.

76. SOI, p. 108; SS, 5/8/51, 5/15/51, 6/12/51.

77. Annual Spartak team report to sports committee, GARF, f. 7576, o. 13, d. 152, ll. 7 and 21.

78. SS, 8/28/51.

79. Sergei Savin, *Sovetskaia shkola futbola* (Moscow, 1952), p. 6.

80. Sto let, p. 108; ERF, pp. 720–21; GARF, f. 7576, o. 13, d. 863, l. 45.

81. Edelman, pp. 102–10.

82. SOI, p. 640.

83. SOI, p. 116.

84. SS, 8/12/52, 9/1/52, 9/23/52; SOI, pp. 112–15; SS, 11/3/52.

85. RGASPI, f. 17, o. 137, d. 57, 1. 98.

86. Boris Khavin, *Vse o Sovetskikh Olimpitsakh* (Moscow, 1985), p. 7.

### Chapter 7. Thaw, Change, and Resurrection, 1953–1956

1. Catriona Kelly, introduction to Kelly and Shepherd, pp. 249 and 253; Vladimir Kozlov, *Mass Uprisings in the USSR: Protest and Rebellion in the Post-Stalin Years* (Armonk, NY, 2002), pp. 313–14; Lewin, *Soviet Century,* p. 169.

2. Zubkova, p. 156; Polly Jones, introduction to *The Dilemmas of De-Stalinization: Negotiating Cultural and Social Change in the Khrushchev Era,* ed. Polly Jones et al. (London, 2006), pp. 11–12.

3. Timothy Colton, *Moscow: Governing the Soviet Metropolis* (Cambridge, 1995), pp. 359–61; Lewin, *Soviet Century,* p. 180; Hosking, p. 329; Anne Applebaum, *GULAG: A History* (New York, 2003), p. 487.

4. Christopher Read, *The Making and Breaking of the Soviet System* (Basingstoke, UK, 2001), p. 147.

5. Hosking, pp. 333, 348, and 354; Lewin, *Soviet Century,* p. 183; Basile Kerblay, *Modern Soviet Society* (New York, 1983), p. 213.

6. Sto let, p. 113.

7. Archetti, *Masculinities,* p. 17. Archetti got the idea of mirrors and masks from A. I. Strauss, *Mirrors and Masks: The Search for Identity* (London, 1977), p. 9.

8. Applebaum, pp. 476–80; William Taubman, *Khrushchev: The Man and his Era* (New York, 2003), p. 246.

9. Stephen Cohen, foreword to *Khrushchev: A Political Biography,* by Roy Medvedev and Zhores Medvedev (New York, 1978), p. v.

10. Lewin, *Soviet Century,* p. 199.

11. Ibid., p. 202.

12. Hosking, pp. 336 and 361.

13. Hilary Pilkington, "The Future Is Ours: Youth Culture in Russia, 1953 to the Present," in Kelly and Shepherd, p. 370.

14. Donald Filtzer, "From Mobilized to Free Labor: De-Stalinization and the Changing Legal Status of Workers," in Jones et al., p. 156.

15. Applebaum, pp. 476–82; Lewin, *Soviet Century,* pp. 174–76.

16. Taubman, p. 242.

17. Aleksandr Pyzhikov, *Khrushchevskaia ottepel'* (Moscow, 2002), p. 261.

18. Colton, p. 376; Hosking, p. 353; Taubman, p. 267; Christine Varga-Harris, "Forging Citizenship on the Home Front: Reviving the Socialist Contract and Constructing Soviet Identity during the Thaw," in Jones et al., p. 102; Medvedev and Medvedev, p. 44.

19. Zubkova, p. 167.

20. Kozlov, p. 5.

21. Mark Banting, Catriona Kelly, and James Riordan, "Sexuality," in Kelly and Shepherd, p. 337.

22. Polly Jones, "From the Secret Speech to the Burial of Stalin: Real and Ideal Responses to De-Stalinization," in Jones et al., p. 42.

23. Hosking, p. 333; Jones, introduction, p. 9.

24. Cited in Zubkova, p. 163.

25. Zubkova, p. 156; Stites, p.124.

26. Evgenii Lovchev, interview with the author, Moscow, September 15, 2003; Simonian, interview; Andrei Starostin, *Flagman,* p. 123.

27. Jones, introduction, p. 14.

28. Iuri Aksiutin, *Khrushchevskaia "ottepel'" i obshchestvenye nastroienia v SSSR v 1953–1964 gg.* (Moscow, 2004), pp. 3–4.

29. Mikhail Prozumenshikov, *Bol'shoi Sport, Bol' shaia Politika* (Moscow, 2004), p. 70.

30. GARF, f. 7576, o. 13, d. 5, ll. 25–26.

31. GARF, f. 7576, o. 13, d. 71, l. 169.

32. Lewin, *Soviet Century,* p. 180; Hosking, p. 333.

33. Colton, p. 360; Vartanian, interview, 1999; Vainshtein, interview.

34. Arkadii Galinskii, interview with the author, Moscow, October 16, 1990.

35. Colton, p. 368.

36. Iakushin, p. 138; ERF, p. 721.

37. Vainshtein, interview; Leonid Trakhtenberg, interview with author, Moscow, October 11, 1990; Pirogov, pp. 65–66; Prozumenshikov, pp. 378–79.

38. John Foot, *Calcio, a History of Italian Football* (London, 2006), pp. 81–83; Simon Martin, *Football and Fascism: The National Game under Mussolini* (Oxford, 2004), p. 29; Paddy Agnew, *Forza Italia: A Journey in Search of Italy and Its Football* (London, 2006), p. 59.

39. Prozumenshikov, p. 364.

40. Medvedev and Medvedev, p. 19.

41. SOI, p. 605; GARF, f. 7576, o. 13, d. 5, l. 78.

42. More precisely, Bashashkin joined Spartak in May of 1953 from a team that was a rump TsDKA. Called MVO (Moskovskii Voennyi Okrug), the team was disbanded along with VVS when the Ministry of Defense decided (temporarily, as it turned out) to get out of the sports business.

43. Vartanian, interview, 2000; Prozumenshikov, pp. 67–68; Sto let, p. 110.

44. SOI, pp. 563 and 742.

45. SS, 7/16/53.

46. VM, 7/21/53 and 7/28/53; SS, 7/21/53 and 7/28/53.

47. SS, 8/29/53.

48. Vartanian, interview, 2000; SS, 4/6/54; *Sovetskii sport*'s account gives not even a hint of the events surrounding the game.

49. SOI, p. 122; VM, 10/14/53 and 10/19/53; SS, 10/15/53 and 10/20/53.

50. SOI, p. 122.

51. Simonian, p. 68.

52. Simonian, interview.

53. Because they did not write memoirs, we know little of Aleksandr and Petr's activities during this period.

54. Nikolai Starostin, *Futbol,* pp. 127–28.

55. Ibid., p. 133.

56. Applebaum, p. 487.

57. Arkhiv Memorial, f. 12, o. 20, d. 1, l. 1. Thanks to Orlando Figes for sharing this material with me.

58. See also Orlando Figes, *The Whisperers: Private Life in Stalin's Russia* (New York, 2007), p. 469.

59. Arkhiv Memorial., f. 12, o. 20, d. 2, ll. 90–92.

60. Simonian, interview; Lovchev, interview; Genaddii Logofet, interview with the author, Moscow, September 5, 2000.

61. Miriam Dobson, "Show the Bandit-Enemies No Mercy! Amnesty, Criminality and Public Response in 1953," in Jones et al., pp. 24–25.

62. Hosking, p. 332.

63. Andrei Starostin, *Flagman,* p. 105.

64. Ibid., pp. 129 and 137.

65. Lovchev, interview.

66. Andrei Starostin, *Bol'shoi,* pp. 217–23.

67. Nikolai Starostin, *Futbol,* pp. 133–36; Andrei Starostin, *Bol'shoi,* p. 217; *Flagman,* p. 98.

68. Andrei Starostin, *Bol'shoi,* p. 200.

69. DE, pp. 138–40; ERF, pp. 723–24.

70. DE, pp. 93 and 107.

71. GARF, f. 7576, o. 13, d. 72, l. 122.

72. SS, 5/4/54, 5/29/54, 6/8/54, 8/7/54, 10/10/54; SOI, pp. 124 and 659–60.

73. Dan Brennan, "Moscow Nights," *Arsenal,* November 2004, p. 72; SS, 10/7/54; Merzhanov, p. 78.

74. Merzhanov, pp. 76–77; SS, 11/11/54; SOI, p. 127; Ozerov, *Vsiu zhizniu na sinnoi ptitse* (Moscow, 1995), p. 224; SS, 10/30/54.

75. Brennan, pp. 70–73. Before it was torn down in 2006, Arsenal's stadium in the Highbury region of North London held thirty-seven thousand after it went all-seater.

76. Brennan, p. 72; Merzhanov, p. 77; SOI, p. 127; SS, 11/11/54.

77. GARF, f. 7576, o. 13, d. 72, l. 44.

78. Ibid., ll. 36–39 and 106–11; Paramonov, interview.

79. SOI, pp. 128, 605, 658, 735–36, 762; GARF, f. 7576, o. 13, d. 5, l. 78.

80. Soskin, pp. 47–49; Simonian, pp. 74–76; SOI, p. 597.

81. SOI, p. 728.

82. Letopis' Sporta, "Sovetskie kluby vkhodiat na mezdunarodnuiu arenu," Rosmediakom, 2007.

83. Merzhanov, pp. 85–86; SS, 7/12/55; SOI, p. 132.

84. SS, 8/9/55.

85. Andrei Starostin, *Flagman,* p. 103; GARF, f. 7576, o. 13, d. 111, l.1; Netto, p. 62; Prozumenshikov, pp. 67–68.

86. Sto let, p. 116.

87. Netto, p. 57.

88. Sto let, p. 110; SOI, p. 129. Simonian was injured and could not play.

89. Merzhanov, p. 88; Netto, p. 57.

90. Sto let, p. 116. See Alan Tomlinson and Christopher Young, eds., *German Football: History, Culture, Society* (London, 2006), and Ulrich Hesse-Lichtenberger, *Tor: The Story of German Football* (London, 2003).

91. E. Eggers and M. Kneifl, "'Wir sind die Eisbrecher von Adenauer gewesen': Das Fussball-Landerspeil Sowjetunion vs. BRD am August 21, 1955 in Moskau im Kontext der bundesdeutschen Aussenpolitik," *SportZeiten,* 6 Jahrgang 2006, Heft 1, pp. 111–42.

92. SS, 12/8/55, 12/12/55, 12/22/55.

93. Hosking, p. 335; Thomas Wolfe, *Governing Soviet Journalism: The Press and the Socialist Person after Stalin* (Bloomington, IN, 2005), p. 108.

94. Wolfe, p. 180; Taubman, p. 279.

95. Galinskii, interview; Logofet, interview; Edelman, *Serious Fun,* p. 179.

96. Taubman, p. 307; Zubkova, pp. 171 and 193; Medvedev and Medvedev, p. 73.

97. Denis Kozlov, "Naming the Social Evil: The Readers of *Novyi Mir* and Vladimir Dudintsev's *Not by Bread Alone,* 1956–59 and Beyond," in Jones et al., pp. 80–90.

98. Juliane Furst, "The Arrival of Spring: Changes and Continuities in Soviet Youth Culture and Policy between Stalin and Khrushchev," in Jones et al., p. 137.

99. Read, p. 160.

100. On the complexities of the Soviet apartment see Susan Reid, "The Meaning of Home: 'The Only Bit of the World You Can Have to Yourself,'" pp. 154–70, and Steven Harris, "'I Know the Secrets of My Neighbors': The Quest for Privacy in the Era of the Separate Apartment," pp. 171–90, both in Siegelbaum, *Borders of Socialism.*

101. On the Soviet automobile, see Lewis Siegelbaum, *Cars for Comrades: The Life of the Soviet Automobile* (Ithaca, 2008).

102. Iuri, Oleshchuk, "Futbol'nyi obikhod," *Sportekspress zhurnal,* no. 9 (September 2000): 102–5.

103. GARF, f. 7576, o. 13, d. 121, ll. 72–76.

104. James Riordan, interview with author, Chichester, UK, August 31, 2000.

105. GARF, f. 7576, o. 13, d. 163, l. 55.

106. Nazarov, interview.

107. Vartanian, interview, 2000.

108. Pierre Bourdieu, "A Program for the Sociology of Sport," p. 161.

109. Lewin, *Soviet Century,* p. 200.

110. Sto let, p. 115; Prozumenshikov, p. 70.

111. Riordan, interview.

112. SOI, p. 133.

113. SS, 5/5/56.

114. SOI, pp. 133–35; SS, 6/26/56 and 9/8/56.

115. SS, 10/16/56; SOI, p. 134.

116. Merzhanov, pp. 94–97.

117. Sto let, p. 113.

118. Historical film fragment seen on *Sport Planeta,* distributed by Russian Media Group, March 11, 2007, during halftime of live telecast of Dinamo-Spartak game from Moscow.

119. SOI, p. 563; Ilyin, p. 19.

120. Pirogov, p. 69.

## Chapter 8. Good-bye, Golden Age, 1957–1964

1. Bourdieu, "Program for a Sociology of Sport," p. 160.

2. Furst, "Arrival of Spring," pp. 148–49; Stites, p. 132.

3. Soskin, pp. 8–9.

4. GARF, f. 7576, o. 13, d. 121, l. 48.

5. Riordan, interview.

6. Two of the better recent accounts, each in its own way, are Aleksandr Nilin, *Strel'tsov: Chelovek bez loktei* (Moscow, 2002), and Aksel' Vartanian, *Eduard Strel'tsov, nasil'nik ili zhertva* (Moscow, 2001).

7. SOI, p. 584; see also Wilson, p. 271.

8. SS, 7/22/58; SOI, pp. 144 and 146; Netto, p. 277.

9. SS, 10/24/58, 11/2/58, 11/4/58, 11/11/58, 11/28/58.

10. DE, p. 7; Simonian, p. 91.

11. SOI, p. 146; Simonian, p. 91.

12. GARF, f. 7576, o. 13, d. 163, ll. 47–59; f. 7576, o. 13, d. 121, l. 88.

13. Simonian, p. 131.

14. Goldblatt, p. 357–95; Alex Bellos, *Futebol: Soccer the Brazilian Way* (New York, 2002).

15. Simonian, p. 122; GARF, f. 7576, o. 13, d. 11, 1. 45.

16. Andrei Starostin, *Flagman,* p. 107.

17. Ibid., pp. 110 and 111.

18. Prozumenshikov, pp. 41–48.

19. GARF, f. 7576, o. 13, d. 111, l. 38.

20. Netto, pp. 103 and 108.

21. Ibid., p. 103; Sto let, p. 127.

22. Prozumenshikov, p. 87; Andrei Starostin, *Flagman,* p. 167.

23. Yuri Sevidov, quoted on videocassette, *Nikolai Starostin—Otets Spartaka* (2002, Order of Spartak Football Club).

24. SOI, pp. 157–78.

25. SOI, pp. 151–56; SS, 8/8/57.

26. SS, 7/24/59.

27. SS, 5/19/59; Merzhanov, pp. 106–7 and 111.

28. Merzhanov, p. 113.

29. SOI, p. 157–58.

30. SS, 4/18/60 and 5/10/60.

31. SOI, p. 160.

32. Vartanian, interview, 1999.

33. Goldblatt, p. 269.

34. SOI, p. 164; Riordan, interview.

35. SOI, pp. 560, 599, and 621.

36. SS, 8/26/61.

37. SS, 8/1/61; SOI, p. 165; Merzhanov, p. 113; Simonian, p. 142.

38. *Otets Spartaka.*

39. Ibid.

40. Simonian, interview.

41. Nikolai Starostin, *Moi futbol'nye gody,* p. 13. The same figure for the same time period was also cited in *Futbol skvoz' gody,* p. 145.

42. Logofet, interview.

43. Simonian, interview; Vartanian, interview, 1999; Simonian, pp. 187–88.

44. SOI, p. 560.

45. Lovchev, interview.

46. Vartanian, interview, 2000.

47. Lovchev, interview.

48. SS, 4/28/90.

49. Simonian, interview.

50. Ibid.

51. Vartanian, interview, 2000.

52. Vainshtein, interview.

53. Liudmilla Alexeeva, *The Thaw Generation: Coming of Age in the Post-Stalin Era* (Pittsburgh, 1990).

54. Simonian, pp. 101, 140, and 190.

55. *Otets Spartaka.*

56. Ozerov, p. 64.

57. *Otets Spartaka;* Simonian, p. 192; Logofet, interview; Lovchev, interview.

58. Pamela Radcliffe, "The Revival of Associational Life under the Late Franco Regime: Neighborhood and Family Associations and the Social Origins of the Transition," in *Spain Transformed: The Franco Dictatorship, 1959–1975,* ed. Nigel Townson (London, 2007).

59. See, for example, Archetti, pp. 161–72. Archetti, an anthropologist, conducted much of his research pertaining to this question in bars and cafes.

60. Nikolai Starostin, *Futbol Skvoz' gody,* p. 137; Lovchev, interview.

61. Nazarov, interview; Arkadii Galinskii, interview with author, Moscow, October 16, 1990.

62. *Otets Spartaka.*

63. Netto, p. 139.

64. VM, 11/19/62.
65. SOI, pp. 171–73.
66. SS, 11/20/62.

## Chapter 9. Uncertainly Ever After, 1964–1991

1. Christian Noack, "Coping with the Tourist: Planned and 'Wild' Mass Tourism on the Black Sea Coast," in *Turizm: The Russian and East European Tourist under Capitalism and Socialism,* ed. Diane Koenker and Anne Gorsuch (Ithaca, 2006), p. 282.

2. William Thompson, *The Soviet Union under Brezhnev* (London, 2003), p. 88.

3. Bittner, pp. 221–29.

4. Vladimir Shlapentokh, *Soviet Intellectuals and Political Power: The Post-Stalin Era* (Princeton, 1990), p. 117.

5. Moshe Lewin, *The Gorbachev Phenomenon* (Berkeley, 1991), pp. 80–81; Thompson, p. 107. See also Georgi Arbatov, *The System: An Insider's Life in Soviet Politics* (New York, 1992).

6. Thompson, p. 86; Lewin, pp. 43–56; Boris Kagarlitsky, *The Dialectic of Change* (New York, 1990), p. 285.

7. Geoffrey Hosking, *The Awakening of the Soviet Union* (Cambridge, MA, 1990), p. 3; Irene Boutenko and Kirill Razlogov, eds., *Recent Social Trends in Russia, 1960–1995* (Montreal, 1997), p. 99.

8. L. Gordon and E. Klopov, *Man after Work: Social Problems of Daily Life and Leisure Time, Based on the Surveys of Workers' Time Budgets in Major Cities of the European Part of the USSR,* trans. John Bushnell and Kristine Bushnell (Moscow, 1975), pp. 119–35; Basile Kerblay, *Modern Soviet Society* (New York, 1983), pp. 57–62.

9. Mason, *Association Football,* pp. 69–78; Goldblatt, pp. 85–111; Murray, *The World's Game,* pp. 21–41.

10. Leonid Trakhtenberg, interview with the author, Moscow, October 11, 1990.

11. SS, 9/5/70.

12. Colton, pp. 388 and 453.

13. Igor Goranskii, *Evgenii Lovchev: Biografia v otkrovennykh besedakh* (Moscow, 2002), p. 32.

14. SS, 1/29/66.

15. Izv, 2/19/74.

16. Izv, 4/4/66.

17. SS, 9/5/70.

18. Edelman, *Serious Fun,* pp. 166–69; Kristin Roth-Ey, "Finding a Home for Television in the USSR, 1950–1970," *Slavic Review* 66, no. 2 (2007): 278–82.

19. Yurchak, pp. 125, 208, and 254.

20. www.sport-express.ru/art.shtml?146949 (accessed 9/29/07).

21. Arbatov, p. 86. The USSR's leading expert on the United States, Arbatov worked at the Central Committee during the 1960s in a section that housed numerous reformers. He mentioned that in addition to politics, soccer was one of the subjects of their informal conversations.

22. SS, 2/2/69.

23. Galinskii, interview.

24. SS, 2/2/72.

25. For a sports committee report on financial irregularities in football during 1974, see GARF, f. 7576, o. 33, d. 121, ll. 29–32.

26. Anne E. Gorsuch, "Time Travelers: Soviet Tourists in Eastern Europe," in Gorsuch and Koenker, pp. 205–26.

27. SS, 4/2/67 and 12/18/76.

28. Sto let, pp. 124–75.

29. SOI, p. 194; Simonian, p. 163.

30. SOI, p. 196.

31. SS, 12/10/66.

32. SOI, pp., 200–223.

33. Goranskii, pp. 22–24.

34. SOI, p. 227.

35. SOI, p. 229. SS, 11/12/69.

36. Sto let, p. 150 (emphasis added).

37. Goldblatt, p. 706; Wilson, p. 222; Nazarov, interview; Izv, 4/4/66; SS, 10/26/69; Nikolai Starostin, *Moi Futbol'nye Gody,* pp. 30–33.

38. Logofet, interview; Vartanian, interview, 2000; Wilson, p. 284.

39. Goranskii, pp. 31–32.

40. Goldblatt, pp. 542–605.

41. SOI, pp. 259–60 and 266.

42. Prozumenshikov, p. 383.

43. SS, 9/5/70. 11/16/73.

44. SS, 3/29/73 and 12/24/74; DE, p. 65.

45. *Otets Spartaka;* Nikolai Starostin, *Moi Futbol'nye Gody,* p. 22; SOI, p. 272.

46. Goranskii, p. 34.

47. Logofet, interview; SOI, pp. 274 and 597. According to the account of Russian journalist Igor Rabiner, Romantsev took personal umbrage at an insult from Lovchev. See Rabiner, *Kak ubivali Spartak: Sensatsionnye podrobnosti padenia velikogo kluba* (Moscow, 2006), p. 53.

48. http://www.sport-express.ru/art.shtml?152539 (accessed January 18, 2008). The scores were Dnepr-TsSKA, 1–0; Zarya-Kryl'ya Sovetov, 1–0; Shakhter-Lokomotiv, 1–0; Ararat-Torpedo, 1–0. Only Chernomroets' 2–0 win over last-place Dinamo Minsk seems to reflect the balance of strength between the two contestants.

49. Izv, 9/26/76; Nikolai Starostin, *Moi Futbol'nye Gody* p. 23; Goranskii, p. 36.

50. Vartanian has cited these events and interventions in a recent article. His use of the stenographic report for the meeting of the football federation comes from the sports committee's fond in GARF. See http://www.sport-express.ru/art.sthml?152539 (accessed January 18, 2008).

51. Prozumenshikov, p. 384; Goranskii, p. 37; Izv, 11/16/76; SS, 11/20/76 and 12/4/76.

52. GARF, f. 7576, o. 33, d. 170, l. 111.

53. Ibid., l. 114.

54. Ibid., ll. 9–12 and 77–85; d. 148, ll. 2, 25, 49, 60, 75; d. 105, ll. 76–77.

55. GARF, f. 7576, o. 33, d. 194, l. 6.

56. Nikolai Starostin, *Moi Futbol'nye Gody,* p. 23; Goranskii, p. 38; SOI, p. 280.

57. Aleksandr Nilin, *Nevozmozhnyi Beskov* (Moscow, 1989), p. 6.

58. SOI, p. 709.

59. SOI, pp. 280–86, 551, 597, 619, 625, 629, 651, 724, 749, 754, 760.

60. The practice of the army's drafting players in midcareer had long been common. The Ministry of Interior could also draft players for its internal forces but did so less often. Dinamo Kiev also did this but limited such actions to the Ukraine. See Prozumenshikov, p. 364.

61. Goranskii, pp. 38 and 43; Simonian, interview.

62. SS, 11/7/77.

63. SOI, pp. 283–84; DE, pp. 367–71. The raw data for these figures come from rough estimates by journalists. The numbers track well with the performance of home teams and the attractiveness of visitors. There is no reason to doubt their general accuracy, nor is it likely that sportswriters brought any particular bias to their estimates. Since thousands had seen the evidence with their own eyes, these numbers differ from many other Soviet statistics in their reliability.

64. SOI, p. 287; DE, p. 65; Sto let, p. 171; Nikolai Starostin, *Moi Futbol'nye Gody,* pp. 30–33; *Komsomol'skaia pravda* (hereafter KP), 9/12/78.

65. http://www.sport-express.ru/art.shtml?152539 (accessed January 18, 2008).

66. Goranskii, p. 55; Simonian, p. 157.

67. SOI, pp. 558 and 651.

68. SOI, pp. 623 and 752. *Master i miach: Chestnyi futbol Fiodora Cherenkova* (Moscow, 2000).

69. Goldblatt, pp. 588–89; Prozumenshikov, p. 371; Wilson, p. 14.

70. Nazarov, interview; Vartanian, interview, 1999.

71. Rabiner, p. 5.

72. Mikhail Gorbachev, *Memoirs: Mikhail Gorbachev* (New York, 1996), p. 171.

73. Ibid., p. 175.

74. Edelman, *Serious Fun,* pp. 231–36.

75. SS, 4/28/90.

76. Nilin, *Beskov,* p. 53.

77. SOI, pp. 362–63.

78. Ozerov, p. 269.

79. Rabiner, p. 45.

80. Nilin, *Beskov,* p. 73.

81. Sto let, p. 192; Nilin, *Beskov,* p. 70; Vainshtein, interview, 2000.

82. SS, 12/29/88 and 1/6/89; KP, 1/4/89.

83. Izv, 1/14/89.

84. Rabiner, pp. 47–53.

85. *Futbol-Khokkei,* no. 12 (1989) and no. 14 (1989); SOI, p. 377; Lovchev, interview; SS, 4/28/90.

86. SS, 8/29/89.

87. SOI, p. 378.

88. *Futbol-Khokkei,* no. 19 (1989).

89. Ibid.; Izv, 6/27/89; Nikolai Starostin, interview.

90. SOI, p. 400.

91. Bauhaus Kolleg V, *Transit Spaces* (Dessau, Ger., 2003).

92. Exhibition games, or friendlies, called *tovarishcheski matchy* (comradely matches) are detailed in the official Spartak history. These include preseason games, domestic friendlies, and international matches, abroad and in the USSR. The second category is the one I am stressing here.

93. There are entire histories of this fan movement on the Spartak website. For one example, see http://fcspartak.ru/fanats/stat/7–spartak.php3 (accessed May 21, 2004).

94. SS, 8/4/70.

95. Sto let, p. 162.

96. Goranskii, p. 48; *Fizkul'tura i sport,* no. 1 (1989) p. 7.

97. Klub Bolel'shchikov Spartaka, Unofficial Match Program, Spartak vs. Rotor, Volgograd, September 24, 1990.

98. Quoted in SS, 7/8/89.

99. Ibid.; SOI, p. 320.

100. Goldblatt, p. 543.

101. *Los Angeles Times,* 11/14/87; Gosteleradio, Pervaia programma, 1989, "Futbol'noe obozrenie," October 24, 1989; SS, 10/10/87, 11/4/88, 4/22/89; http://fcspartak.ru/fanats/stat/8–10maxach.php3 (accessed May 21, 2004).

102. *Futbol-Khokkei,* no. 19 (1989).

103. Sto let, pp. 133–41 and 159.

104. SS, 7/30/80.

105. Lovchev, Nazarov, Simonian, and Vartanian, interviews.

106. Sto let, pp. 149, 172–74, 200–205, and 226–27.

107. Ibid., p. 226; SOI, p. 390.

108. *Futbol,* no. 10 (1991); SOI, p. 402.

109. SS, 4/9/91.

110. SOI, p. 286.

111. Goranskii, p. 28; Lovchev, Logofet, and Galinskii, interviews.

112. *Otets Spartaka.*

113. Rabiner, pp. 56 and 60.

114. SOI, pp. 448–59. In 1995 the gold medal was taken by the North Ossetian team of Spartak Vladikavkaz, whose success was fueled by the illegal trade in spirit alcohol.

115. Wilson, p. 294.

116. For a chronology of major hooligan moments see http://fcspartak.ru/fanats/stat/8–10maxach.php3 (accessed May 21. 2004).

117. Edelman, "There Are No Rules on Planet Russia: Post-Soviet Spectator Sport," in *Consuming Russia: Popular Culture, Sex and Society since Gorbachev,* ed. Adele Barker (Durham, NC, 1999), pp. 217–38.

118. Wilson, p. 290.

## Conclusion

1. Wilson, p. 285. Sergei Korolev, *Kak ia stal bolet' zu Spartak* (Moscow, 2008), p. 40.

2. Johan Huizinga, *Homo Ludens: A study of the Play Element in Culture* (London, 1970), p. 3.

# Index